Nelson Series in Human Resources Management

Management of Occupational Health and Safety

Fourth Edition

HRM

NELSON SERIES IN HUMAN RESOURCES MANAGEMENT

Management of Occupational Health and Safety

FOURTH EDITION

E. KEVIN KELLOWAY
SAINT MARY'S UNIVERSITY

LORI FRANCIS
SAINT MARY'S UNIVERSITY

SERIES EDITOR:
MONICA BELCOURT
YORK UNIVERSITY

NELSON EDUCATION

NELSON EDUCATION

Management of Occupational Health and Safety
Fourth Edition

by E. Kevin Kelloway and Lori Francis

Associate Vice President, Editorial Director:
Evelyn Veitch

Editor-in-Chief, Higher Education
Anne Williams

Acquisitions Editor:
Shannon White

Marketing Manager:
Kathaleen McCormick

Developmental Editor:
Tracy Yan

Permissions Coordinator:
Mattea Kennedy

Content Production Manager:
Carrie McGregor

Copy Editor:
Kelli Howey

Proofreader:
Kelli Howey

Indexer:
Belle Wong

Production Coordinator:
Ferial Suleman

Design Director:
Ken Phipps

Interior-Design Modifications:
Katherine Strain

Cover Design:
Wil Bache

Compositor:
GEX Publishing Services

Printer:
Transcontinental

Printed and bound in Canada
5 6 7 8 13 12 11 10

For more information contact Nelson Education Ltd., 1120-Birchmount Road, Toronto, Ontario, M1K 5G4. Or you can visit our Internet site at http://www.nelson.com

Library and Archives Canada Cataloguing in Publication Data

Kelloway, E. Kevin (Edward Kevin), 1959-
Management of occupational health and safety / E. Kevin Kelloway, Lori Francis. — 4th ed.

Includes bibliographical references and index.
ISBN 978-0-17-644233-0

1. Industrial hygiene—Management—Textbooks.
2. Industrial safety—Management—Textbooks.
3. Industrial hygiene—Textbooks.
4. Industrial safety—

Textbooks. I. Francis, Lori D. (Lori Denise), 1974- II. Title.

HD7261.H44 2007 363.11
C2007-902955-8

ISBN-13: 978-0-17-644233-0
ISBN-10: 0-17-644233-2

For Debra, who continues to be the main contributor to my health and safety.

(EKK)

For Brian and Owen, who motivate my work–life balance.

(LF)

Brief Contents

About the Series *xxiii*

About the Authors *xxv*

Preface *xxvii*

Acknowledgments *xxix*

PART ONE INTRODUCTION AND OVERVIEW 1

Chapter 1 Introduction 3

Chapter 2 Legislative Framework 23

Chapter 3 Workers' Compensation 53

PART TWO HAZARDS AND AGENTS 79

Chapter 4 Physical Agents 81

Chapter 5 Chemical and Biological Agents 107

Chapter 6 Psychosocial Hazards 135

Chapter 7 Hazard Recognition and Assessment 169

PART THREE INTERVENTIONS 207

Chapter 8 Hazard Control 209

Chapter 9 Training 239

Chapter 10 Motivating Safety Behaviour at Work 273

Chapter 11 Emergency Response and Emergency Preparedness 301

Chapter 12 Accident Investigation 323

Chapter 13 Workplace Wellness: Work–Family and Worksite Health-Promotion Programs 353

Index *391*

Detailed Contents

About the Series xxiii

About the Authors xxv

Preface xxvii

Acknowledgments xxix

PART ONE INTRODUCTION AND OVERVIEW 1

Chapter 1 Introduction 3

Historical Development of Modern Occupational Health and Safety 6
- Changing Perspectives on Risk and Liability 7
- Occupational Health and Safety Notebook 1.1: Preventing Computer Vision Syndrome 8

The Importance of Health and Safety 8
- Economic Considerations 9
- Occupational Health and Safety Today 1.1: Direct and Indirect Costs of Injury 9
- Legal Considerations 10
- Occupational Health and Safety Today 1.2: The Costs of Unhealthy Behaviour 11
- Moral Considerations 11

The Stakeholders 11
- Government 11
- Employers 12
- Employees 13
- Organized Labour 13
- Occupational Health and Safety Today 1.3: A Predictable Path to Disaster at Westray 13
- Partnerships 14
- Occupational Health and Safety Today 1.4: Young Workers at Risk 14
- Health and Safety Professionals 15

The Role of Human Resources 15
- Occupational Health and Safety Notebook 1.2: Safety Professionals 16
- Safety Is a People Issue 16
- Safety Requires Legislative Compliance 17
- Safety Decreases Costs 17
- Safety Relates to Other Human Resource Functions 17

Summary 17

Key Terms 18

Weblinks 18
RPC Icons 18
Discussion Questions 20
Using the Internet 20
Exercises 20
Case 1: Production or Safety? 21
Case 2: Do We Need Health and Safety? 21
Endnotes 21

Chapter 2 Legislative Framework 23
- Occupational Health and Safety Notebook 2.1: Occupational Health and Safety Legislation in Canada 25

The Scope of OH&S Legislation 25
- Occupational Health and Safety Notebook 2.2: A New Standard for Safety 26
- Occupational Health and Safety Notebook 2.3: Canadian Government Departments Responsible for OH&S 27

Duties and Responsibilities of the Major Players 27
- Duties of Employers, Owners, and Contractors 27
- Occupational Health and Safety Notebook 2.4: Jurisdictions and OH&S Components 28
- Occupational Health and Safety Today 2.1: Nelson Education Ltd.'s Safety Philosophy 29
- Duties of Supervisors 29
- Duties of Workers 30
- Joint Health and Safety Committees 30
- Occupational Health and Safety Notebook 2.5: Legislative Requirements for Joint Health and Safety Committees 31
- Occupational Health and Safety Notebook 2.6: Joint Health and Safety Committees at a Glance 31

Work Refusals 32
- Occupational Health and Safety Today 2.2: Farm Safety 32

Stop-Work Provisions (Ontario) 33
Workplace Hazardous Materials Information System 33
- Labels 34
- Material Safety Data Sheets 36
- Training 42

Environmental Legislation 42
- Occupational Health and Safety Notebook 2.7: Federal Statutes Relevant to OH&S 43
- Occupational Health and Safety Notebook 2.8: Provincial and Territorial Statutes 44

Transportation of Dangerous Goods 45

Corporate Liability 45
Occupational Health and Safety Today 2.3
Corporate Killing: The Westray Legislation 46
Summary 46
Key Terms 47
Weblinks 47
RPC Icons 48
Discussion Questions 50
Using the Internet 50
Exercise 50
Case 1: Workplace Tragedy 51
Case 2: Work Refusal at Regional Hospital 51
Endnotes 52

Chapter 3 Workers' Compensation 53

Historical Roots 55
Workers' Compensation in Canada 55
Administration and Responsibilities 55
Occupational Health and Safety Today 3.1: Workers' Compensation Premiums (averages per $100 of payroll) 57
Occupational Health and Safety Notebook 3.1: Contact Information for the Provincial and Territorial Workers' Compensation Boards 58
Compensation Rates and Methods 59
Medical Aid and Accident Prevention 60
Social Goals of Workers' Compensation 60
Occupational Health and Safety Today 3.2: Spiralling Disability Costs 6s1
Provision for Second Injuries 61
Occupational Health and Safety Today 3.3: Return-to-Work Programs 62
Rehabilitation 62
Occupational Health and Safety Today 3.4: Workers' Compensation at Work 63
Occupational Diseases and Workplace Stress 63
Assessments 64
Occupational Health and Safety Notebook 3.2: Illustrative Industry Assessment Rates 65
Experience Rating 65
Occupational Health and Safety Notebook 3.3: Experience Rating Programs in Ontario 66
Occupational Health and Safety Today 3.5: Integrated Disability Management 67

How Organizations Can Manage Disability 67
Return to Work 69
Occupational Health and Safety Today 3.6: The Duty to Accommodate 70
Summary 70
Key Terms 71
Weblinks 71
RPC Icons 71
Discussion Questions 74
Using the Internet 75
Exercises 75
Case 1: The Employer's Duty 76
Case 2: A Stressful Job 76
Appendix 76
Calculating Injury Frequency and Severity Rates 76
Endnotes 78
PART TWO HAZARDS AND AGENTS 79
Chapter 4 Physical Agents 81
Noise 83
Types of Hearing Loss 84
Noise Exposure Standards 86
Occupational Health and Safety Notebook 4.1: Noise in the Workplace: Signs and Levels 87
Occupational Health and Safety Today 4.1: Hearing Protection for Fire Fighters 87
Noise Control 88
Occupational Health and Safety Notebook 4.2: Choosing Hearing Protectors 89
Vibration 90
Occupational Health and Safety Notebook 4.3: Hand–Arm Vibration Syndrome (HAVS) 91
Occupational Health and Safety Notebook 4.4: Controlling Vibration 91
Thermal Stress 92
Occupational Health and Safety Today 4.2: Beat the Heat 93
Occupational Health and Safety Notebook 4.5: Measuring Thermal Stress 94
Radiation 94
Ionizing Radiation 94
Nonionizing Radiation 95
Occupational Health and Safety Notebook 4.6: Effects of Nonionizing Radiation 95

Summary 96
Occupational Health and Safety Today 4.3: Is Your Cell Phone a Physical Agent? 97
Key Terms 97
Weblinks 97
RPC Icons 98
Discussion Questions 100
Using the Internet 101
Exercise 101
Case 1: Monty's Problem 101
Case 2: Expensive Jewellery 102
Appendix 102
Calculating Noise Levels 102
Shift Adjustment for Noise Exposure 104
Hearing Protection Types or Classifications 105
Endnotes 106

Chapter 5 Chemical and Biological Agents 107
Chemical Agents 109
Occupational Health and Safety Today 5.1: Deadly Fires Burning: Fire Fighters at High Risk for Occupational Cancer 110
Occupational Health and Safety Notebook 5.1: Types of Contaminants 111
Toxicology: An Overview 111
Occupational Health and Safety Today 5.2: Occupational Asthma: The Case of Snow Crab Workers 112
Respiration (Inhalation) 112
Skin Absorption 114
Occupational Health and Safety Today 5.3: Good Scents? 114
Occupational Health and Safety Notebook 5.2: Illnesses Linked to Asbestos Exposure 115
Occupational Health and Safety Notebook 5.3: Toxicity Terminology 116
Ingestion 116
Occupational Health and Safety Notebook 5.4: Classification of Toxic Substances 117
Penetration 119
Characteristics and Properties of Solvents 119
Inorganic Solvents 120
Organic Solvents 121
Biological Agents 121

Control of Exposures 124
Occupational Health and Safety Notebook 5.5: Classification of Biological Agents 125
Engineering Controls 125
Work Practices and Procedures 126
Occupational Health and Safety Today 5.4: Needlestick Injuries: A Spreading Health and Safety Concern 126
Administrative Controls 127
Personal Protective Equipment 127
Personal Hygiene Practices 127
Medical Surveillance 128
Summary 128
Key Terms 128
Weblinks 128
RPC Icons 129
Discussion Questions 131
Using the Internet 132
Exercise 132
Case 1: Mass Hysteria? 132
Case 2: Unexpected Gas 133
Endnotes 133

Chapter 6 Psychosocial Hazards 135

Stressors 138
Stressors in the Workplace 139
Stress 139
Occupational Health and Safety Notebook 6.1: Occupational Health Psychology 140
Stress Moderators 141
Strain 142
Psychological Strain 143
Occupational Health and Safety Today 6.1: Depression and Work 143
Physical Strain 144
Behavioural Strain 144
Organizational Strain 144
Managing Psychosocial Hazards 145
Primary Interventions 145
Secondary Interventions 145
Tertiary Interventions 147
Emerging Stressor: Workplace Violence 147
Consequences of Workplace Violence 149

Occupational Health and Safety Notebook 6.2: Tips for Dealing with Workplace Violence 149
Emerging Stressor: Sexual Harassment 150
Occupational Health and Safety Today 6.2: Prototypical Cases of Sexual Harassment: Not What You Expect? 151
Sexual Harassment as a Health and Safety Issue 151
Emerging Stressor: Injustice at Work 152
Creating a Fair Workplace 153
Emerging Stressor: Technology 154
Occupational Health and Safety Today 6.3: Too Much Mail? 154
Occupational Health and Safety Notebook 6.3: Technology-related Stressors 155
Summary 155
Key Terms 156
Weblinks 157
RPC Icons 157
Discussion Questions 162
Using the Internet 162
Exercises 163
Case 1: A Stressful Job 164
Case 2: Violence on the Job 165
Case 3: Technology at Work 165
Case 4: The New Leader 165
Endnotes 166

Chapter 7 Hazard Recognition and Assessment 169
Terminology 170
Types of Injuries 172
Overt Injuries 172
Occupational Health and Safety Notebook 7.1: An Iceberg Model of Health and Safety Costs 172
Overexertion Injuries 174
Occupational Health and Safety Notebook 7.2: Twelve Rules for Proper Lifting 174
Repetitive-Strain Injuries 176
Occupational Health and Safety Notebook 7.3: Recognizing RSI: Risk Factors and Symptoms 177
Awkward Working Positions 178
Occupational Health and Safety Today 7.1: Artistic Occupations at Risk 178
Hazard Identification 179
Ergonomic Factors 179
Human Factors 179

Occupational Health and Safety Today 7.2: Safety Policy at Saskferco: "First We Walk the Walk" 180
Occupational Health and Safety Notebook 7.4: Interaction of Factors 181
Situational Factors 182
Environmental Factors 182
Choosing a Hazard Identification Program 183
Source of Request 183
Nature of Hazards 183
Cost 183
Use of Safety Experts 183
Components of the Hazard Identification Program 184
Analysis of the Plant, Tasks, and Jobs 184
Reports and Audits 185
Hazard Analysis 186
Risk Assessment 186
Occupational Health and Safety Notebook 7.5: Job Safety Analysis 186
Follow-up 189
Summary 189
Key Terms 190
Weblinks 190
RPC Icons 191
Discussion Questions 193
Using the Internet 194
Exercise 194
Case 1: Industrial Hazard Assessment 194
Case 2: Danger in the Grocery Store 195
Appendix 195
Fault Tree Analysis 196
Lifting Calculations Using the NIOSH Method 200
Endnotes 204

PART THREE INTERVENTIONS 207

Chapter 8 Hazard Control 209

Administrative Control 210
Safety Awareness 211
Occupational Health and Safety Today 8.1: Young Worker Awareness Program 212
Awards and Incentives 212
Housekeeping 213

Occupational Health and Safety Notebook 8.1: Preventing Slips and Falls through Housekeeping 214
Preventive Maintenance 214
Occupational Health and Safety Notebook 8.2: Administrative Controls for Struck-by-Object Injuries 214
Occupational Health and Safety Today 8.2: Tragedy on the Farm 220
Engineering Control 220
Design of Hand Tools 220
Substitution 221
Occupational Health and Safety Notebook 8.3: Controlling RSI through Workspace Design 222
Workstation Design 223
Process Modification 226
Isolation or Segregation 226
Purchasing 226
Machine Guarding 227
Occupational Health and Safety Today 8.3: Death in a Bakery 229
Contact Control 229
Postcontact Control 230
Source–Path–Human 230
Monitoring/Auditing 231
Record Keeping 232
Summary 232
Key Terms 232
Weblinks 232
RPC Icons 233
Discussion Questions 235
Using the Internet 236
Exercise 236
Case: Hazard Control 236
Endnotes 236

Chapter 9 Training 239

The Role of Occupational Health and Safety Training 241
Occupational Health and Safety Today 9.1: The LifeQuilt 241
Occupational Health and Safety Today 9.2: The Vital Role of Health and Safety Training Following the "Westray" Legislation 242
Health and Safety Training Programs 243
Needs Analysis 243
Organizational Analysis 244

Job/Task Analysis 246
Person Analysis 246
Training Design and Delivery 247
Occupational Health and Safety Notebook 9.1: An Example of Training Objectives for a Health and Safety Course 248
Occupational Health and Safety Notebook 9.2: How to Select a Good Training Provider 250
Occupational Health and Safety Notebook 9.3: Learning Theory and Training Delivery 251
Occupational Health and Safety Today 9.3: Online WHMIS Courses 253
Training Evaluation 254
Occupational Health and Safety Notebook 9.4: Underreporting of Injury and Illness: A Question of Record Keeping? 257
Occupational Health and Safety Today 9.4: Safety Training Receiving Increased Attention in Accident Prevention and Investigation 258
Common Safety Training Initiatives 259
Safety Orientation 259
First Aid 259
WHMIS Training 260
Summary 260
Key Terms 261
Weblinks 261
RPC Icons 262
Discussion Questions 267
Using the Internet 267
Exercises 268
Case 1: The New HR Manager at A1 Manufacturing 269
Case 2: A Young Worker's Quandary 269
Endnotes 269

Chapter 10 Motivating Safety Behaviour at Work 273
Safety Behaviour 275
Occupational Health and Safety Notebook 10.1: Elements of a Behaviour-based Safety Program 276
Motivating Safety Behaviour 278
Reinforcement Theory 278
Occupational Health and Safety Notebook 10.2: A Risky Side of Behaviour-based Safety Programs? 280
Goal Setting 281
Increasing Opportunity for Safety Behaviour 282

Occupational Health and Safety Today 10.1: Safety Leadership at Canadian Pacific Railway: "Fundamental Social Responsibility" 285
Bringing It All Together: Organizational Health and Safety Programs 286
Program Objectives 286
Policy 287
Occupational Health and Safety Notebook 10.3: The 5*22 Program 287
Occupational Health and Safety Today 10.2: Setting a Goal for Safety: "Nobody Gets Hurt" at Imperial Oil 288
Accountability 289
Occupational Health and Safety Notebook 10.4: Health and Safety Policy Checklist 289
Auditing the Program 290
Summary 291
Key Terms 291
Weblinks 291
RPC Icons 292
Discussion Questions 295
Using the Internet 295
Exercises 296
Case 1: Noncompliance with Safety Standards 297
Case 2: Safety in the Bakery 297
Case 3: Working to Change Safety 297
Endnotes 298

Chapter 11 Emergency Response and Emergency Preparedness 301

Introduction 302
Occupational Health and Safety Notebook 11.1: Emergency Measures Organizations 303
Emergency Preparedness 304
Occupational Health and Safety Today 11.1: Norwalk Outbreak at Mount Allison 305
Precontact 306
Occupational Health and Safety Notebook 11.2: Futureproofing 307
Occupational Health and Safety Today 11.2: Pandemic Planning 307
Occupational Health and Safety Notebook 11.3: Evacuation Plans 308

Contact 309
Occupational Health and Safety Notebook 11.4: Emergency Operations Centres (EOCs) 310
Occupational Health and Safety Notebook 11.5: Rescues 313
Occupational Health and Safety Notebook 11.6: Chemical Spills 313
Occupational Health and Safety Notebook 11.7: Legislated First-Aid Requirements 314
Postcontact 314
Getting Back to Normal 315
Occupational Health and Safety Notebook 11.8: Business Continuity Planning 316
Summary 316
Key Terms 316
Weblinks 317
RPC Icons 317
Discussion Questions 319
Using the Internet 319
Exercises 319
Case: Biological Terrorism 320
Endnotes 320

Chapter 12 Accident Investigation 323
Rationale for Accident Investigation 324
Critical Factors in the Investigative Process 325
Timing 325
Severity 325
Occupational Health and Safety Today 12.1: What to Investigate 326
Legal Requirements 326
Types of Information Collected 326
Human Factors 327
Occupational Health and Safety Notebook 12.1: The Eyewitness 327
Situational Factors 328
Environmental Factors 328
Who Investigates? 328
Investigative Methods 329
Observations or Walkthroughs 329
Occupational Health and Safety Notebook 12.2: Analysis of an Accident 329
Interviews 330

Reenactments 330
Occupational Health and Safety Notebook 12.3: Cognitive Interviewing 331
Investigative Tools 332
Accident/Incident Reports 332
Accident Analysis 343
Domino Theory 343
Occupational Health and Safety Today 12.2: Hazardous Occurrence Investigation in the Canadian Forces 343
The Swiss Cheese Model 345
Normal Accidents 345
The Psychology of Accidents: Cognitive Failures 345
Summary 346
Key Terms 346
Weblinks 346
RPC Icons 346
Discussion Questions 349
Using the Internet 349
Exercise 349
Case 1: Accident Investigation 349
Case 2: Office Accident 350
Endnotes 350

Chapter 13 Workplace Wellness: Work–Family and Worksite Health-Promotion Programs 353

Work–Family Conflict: Family-Friendly Policies in the Workplace 356
Occupational Health and Safety Today 13.1: Work–Life Balance: Some Canadian Statistics 357
Causes of Work–Family Conflict 358
Outcomes of Work–Family Conflict 358
Family-Friendly Policies 359
Flexible Work Arrangements 359
Personal Leave Systems 360
Family-Care Benefits 361
Family-Friendly Policies: An Evaluation 361
Occupational Health and Safety Notebook 13.1: Reducing Work–Life Conflict: Strategies for Organizations 363
Health-Promotion Programs 364
Employee Assistance Plans 364
Occupational Health and Safety Notebook 13.2: Building a Business Case for Wellness 365
Stress Management Programs 365

Effectiveness of Stress Management Training 367
Worksite Health Promotion: A Focus on Lifestyle Changes 367
Occupational Health and Safety Today 13.2: Healthy Organizations: Wellness and Work–Family Programming at Canadian Companies 371
Developing a Successful Worksite Health-Promotion Program 372
Issues with EAPs and WHP Programs 373
Unintended Consequences of WHP Programs 373
Overall Evaluation 374
Occupational Health and Safety Notebook 13.3: Using Evaluation to Build a Business Case for Health-Promotion and Family-Friendly Programs 375
Summary 376
Key Terms 376
Weblinks 376
RPC Icons 377
Discussion Questions 381
Using the Internet 382
Exercises 383
Case 1: Mandatory Aerobics 385
Case 2: Evaluating the Benefits of WHPs 385
Case 3: Job Sharing in a Telecommunications Firm 385
Endnotes 386

Index 391

About the Series

The management of human resources has become the most important source of innovation, competitive advantage, and productivity, more so than any other resources. More than ever, human resources management (HRM) professionals need the knowledge and skills to design HRM policies and practices that not only meet legal requirements but also are effective in supporting organizational strategy. Increasingly, these professionals turn to published research and books on best practices for assistance in the development of effective HR strategies. The books in the *Nelson Series in Human Resources Management* are the best source in Canada for reliable, valid, and current knowledge about practices in HRM.

The texts in this series include

- *Managing Performance through Training and Development*
- *Management of Occupational Health and Safety*
- *Recruitment and Selection in Canada*
- *Strategic Compensation in Canada*
- *Strategic Human Resources Planning*
- *An Introduction to the Canadian Labour Market*
- *Research, Measurement, and Evaluation of Human Resources*
- *Industrial Relations in Canada* (November 2007)
- *International Human Resources* (August 2008)

The *Nelson Series in Human Resources Management* represents a significant development in the field of HRM for many reasons. Each book in the series is the first, and now, best selling text in the functional area. Furthermore, HR professionals in Canada must work with Canadian laws, statistics, policies, and values. This series serves their needs. It is the only opportunity that students and practitioners have to access a complete set of HRM books, standardized in presentation, which enables them to access information quickly across many HRM disciplines. The books are essential sources of information that meet the requirements for the CCHRA (Canadian Council of Human Resources Associations) National Knowledge exam for the academic portion of the HR certification process. This one-stop resource will prove useful to anyone looking for solutions for the effective management of people.

The publication of this series signals that the field of human resources management has advanced to the stage where theory and applied research guide practice. The books in the series present the best and most current research in the functional areas of HRM. Research is supplemented with examples of the best practices used by Canadian companies that are leaders in HRM. Each text begins with a general model of the discipline, and then describes the implementation of effective strategies. Thus, the books serve as an introduction to the functional area for the new student of HR and as a validation source for the more experienced HRM practitioner. Cases, exercises, and endnotes provide opportunities for further discussion and analysis.

As you read and consult the books in this series, I hope you share my excitement in being involved in and knowledgeable about a profession that has such a significant impact on organizational goals, and employees' lives.

Monica Belcourt, Ph.D., CHRP
Series Editor
October 2006

About the Authors

E. Kevin Kelloway

Dr. Kelloway is a professor of management and psychology at Saint Mary's University, Halifax, Nova Scotia. He was the founding director of the CN Centre for Occupational Health and Safety and a founding principal of the Centre for Leadership Excellence. Currently, he holds the position of Senior Research Fellow at the CN Centre for Occupational Health and Safety.

Dr. Kelloway is a prolific researcher, having published more than 100 articles, book chapters, and technical reports. His research interests include occupational health psychology, leadership, the development and measurement of work attitudes and values, unionization, and the management of knowledge workers. He is coauthor of *The Union and Its Members: A Psychological Approach* (Oxford University Press), *Using Flexible Work Arrangements to Combat Job Stress* (John Wiley & Sons), and *Management of Occupational Health and Safety* (Nelson), and the author of *Using LISREL for Structural Equation Modeling: A Researcher's Guide* (SAGE Publications). With Dr. Julian Barling (Queen's University), he edited the book series *Advanced Topics in Organizational Psychology* (SAGE Publications) and has co-edited the volume *Young Workers: Varieties of Experience* (APA Books). Recent projects included co-editing the *Handbook of Work Stress* and the *Handbook of Workplace Violence* (both with SAGE Publications).

Dr. Kelloway frequently reviews for academic journals or conferences and serves on the editorial boards of the *Journal of Occupational Health Psychology*, *Work & Stress*, and the *Journal of Organizational Behavior*. As a consultant, Dr. Kelloway maintains an active practice consulting with private- and public-sector organizations on issues related to leadership, safety and safety leadership, occupational stress, performance management, and measurement of employee attitudes and performance.

Lori Francis

Lori Francis holds a Ph.D. in industrial/organizational psychology from the University of Guelph. She is currently an Associate Professor in the Department of Psychology at Saint Mary's University in Halifax, Nova Scotia. Dr. Francis has broad research interests in occupational health psychology, including work stress, workplace aggression and violence, health-related interventions in the workplace, and organizational justice. Her Ph.D. dissertation on organizational injustice as a workplace stressor was awarded the International Alliance of Human Resources Researchers best doctoral dissertation award. She is a member of the CN Centre for Occupational Health and Safety. Dr. Francis also has an extensive consulting record, having worked with government, military, and private industry.

Preface

Occupational health and safety (OH&S) has long been the preserve of safety engineers and technical experts. However, in most organizations health and safety is housed within the human resource management function for a number of reasons (see Chapter 1 of this text). The immediate implication is that human resource managers must have a solid understanding of health and safety issues, legislation, and programs. Like the previous three editions of this text, the fourth edition is intended to give the HR manager and the HR professional a basic understanding of the elements that combine to create an effective occupational health and safety program.

We think of the fourth edition as comprising three relatively distinct areas relevant to health and safety. In the first set of chapters, we set the stage by providing an overview of health and safety with specific reference to the human resource function (Chapter 1), the legislative context of health and safety in Canada (Chapter 2), and issues relating to Workers' Compensation and disability management (Chapter 3).

The next set of chapters focuses on the types of hazards in the workplace, with special reference to techniques for controlling those hazards. Chapter 4 considers physical agents such as noise, vibration, temperature, and radiation. Chapter 5 focuses on chemical and biological agents in the workplace. Chapter 6 extends the focus on hazards to include psychosocial hazards in the workplace. Chapter 7 takes a more general approach to hazard recognition and assessment. While these are arguably the most technical chapters in the book, we have tried to maintain a non-technical focus and to present the information in a way that is most useful to human resource managers.

The last set of chapters in the book speak more directly to human resource managers and outline some of the major ways in which human resource managers become actively involved in health and safety. Chapter 8 considers techniques of hazard control including fundamental processes (e.g., evacuation plans) that should be in place in all organizations. Chapter 9 focuses on training—one of the most popular, and arguably the most effective, health and safety interventions. Chapter 10 focuses on motivating safe working behaviour and considers the role of both safety culture and safety leadership in organizations. Chapter 11 presents an overview of emergency response planning, while Chapter 12 summarizes accident investigation techniques. Finally, Chapter 13 summarizes attempts to promote employee health and wellness in the workplace.

Throughout the text we have attempted to provide the reader with current examples, clear definitions of technical terms, and links to the vast amount of information found on the Web. The nature of occupational health and safety legislation in Canada, and the existence of jurisdictional differences, means that the information presented in this text will need to be supplemented with (for example) provincial or territorial standards and legislative requirements. We hope that the student will find this book useful in and of itself and will also use it as a guide to other resources.

In addition to the new material and updating, the fourth edition continues several of the features that accompanied the third edition of this book, including opening vignettes, Using the Internet, and Weblinks. This book also maintains reference to the professional capabilities that provincial and territorial human resources associations throughout Canada have agreed on for granting the designation of certified human resources professional (CHRP). Applicants for the CHRP designation must now pass two national exams based on 203 required professional capabilities. We have linked sections of the text to relevant RPCs through icons appearing in the text. These RPCs are listed by functional area on the Professional Assessment Resource Centre (PARC) website at http://www.cchra-ccarh.ca/parc//en/section_3/ss33e.asp.

This text, and others in this series, covers material that may cut across functional lines, as presented on PARC. The RPCs on PARC are not numbered, making it difficult for us to reference them. We have adopted the following system. When we reference an RPC, we designate it with a margin icon. Each RPC is numbered and is preceded by the chapter number. For example, RPC 8.2 is the second RPC presented in Chapter 8. At the end of the chapter, we list the specific RPCs that we have identified as being relevant to the text. We have also included additional information on the RPCs that is not included on PARC. This material suggests knowledge, skills, abilities, and other tasks that we think are essential to a broader understanding of the duties specified by the RPC. We hope that this linkage of our content to the RPCs will help students and practitioners in preparing for the CHRP assessments.

For instructors, this edition is accompanied by an Instructor's Manual, with test questions and PowerPoint slides that can be downloaded directly from http://www.hrm.nelson.com. These instructor's resources are also available via CD-ROM.

In addition, we provide interactive text-specific slide sets. For more information on the interactive tool, *JoinIn*™ on TurningPoint®, please contact your sales representative.

New to the fourth edition is the updated student website containing chapter quiz questions, allowing students to self test their understanding of chapter content.

Acknowledgments

For taking the time to read drafts of the major revision incorporated in the 3rd Edition, we thank the following instructors: Alan Chapelle, Malaspina University College; Julie Aitken Harris, University of Western Ontario; Linda Lauzon, Fanshawe College; Linda Piper, Canadore College; Martha Reavley, University of Windsor; and D. J. (Nick) Sunday, Cambrian College of Applied Arts & Technology. Your input continues to be evident in this fourth edition.

We would especially like to thank Catherine Fitzgerald of Okanagan University College for her comments and suggestions for exercises to include in the book.

We would like to thank our colleagues at the CN Centre for Occupational Health and Safety (Vic Catano, Arla Day, Mark Fleming, Debra Gilin, Camilla Holmvall, Steve Smith, Veronica Stinson, and Anthony Yue) here at Saint Mary's for their support and acknowledge our network of colleagues across the country who are making significant contributions to the human resource side of occupational health and safety. These include Julian Barling (Queen's University), Kate Dupré (Memorial University), Gail Hepburn (University of Lethbridge), Rick Iverson (Simon Fraser University), Catherine Loughlin (University of Toronto), Aaron Schat (McMaster University), and Nick Turner (University of Manitoba). We are also grateful for the support and guidance of Monica Belcourt (York University) and Shannon White and Tracy Yan at Nelson Education Ltd.

We also wish to thank James Montgomery who made important contributions as an author on previous editions.

E. Kevin Kelloway, Ph.D.
Professor of Management and Psychology
Senior Research Fellow, CN Centre for Occupational Health and Safety
Saint Mary's University

Lori Francis, Ph.D.
Associate Professor of Psychology
Saint Mary's University

Part One

Introduction and Overview

Chapter 1 Introduction

Chapter 2 Legislative Framework

Chapter 3 Workers' Compensation

Chapter 1

Introduction

Chapter Learning Objectives

After reading this chapter, you should be able to:

- define occupational health and safety, occupational injury, and occupational illness
- describe the financial and social costs associated with occupational injuries and illnesses
- trace the development of modern models of health and safety management
- list and describe the role of the major stakeholders in occupational health and safety
- explain the connection between human resource management and occupational health and safety
- describe the links between human resource practices and health and safety

THE IMPORTANCE OF TRAINING

It was his first day on the job at Redden Manufacturing. He was assigned to the shearing machine, which is used to cut pieces of rebar. His new supervisor was in a meeting, so coworkers showed him basically how to work the machine, and he set to work. Before the day ended, he had suffered a broken finger because of an improper hand position.

Investigation by the Nova Scotia Department of Labour resulted in five orders to the company:

1. The employee could not return to this task until he had received orientation and training.
2. The firm had to develop a safe work practice for working on the shearing machine.
3. An accident investigation had to be conducted and a copy of the report filed with the Department of Labour.
4. The shearing machine had to be inspected and brought to standard.
5. The shearing machine had to be taken out of use until the "banana" arms were repaired to manufacturer's specifications.

As this incident illustrates, occupational health and safety is an integral part of human resources management. The injury to the worker was attributed to a lack of proper orientation and training, traditional responsibilities of the human resources department. As a result of the incident, the worker was off work until his injury healed. During this time, the company incurred costs attributable to absenteeism, as well as a potential increase in Workers' Compensation premiums. Minimizing these costs while ensuring that workers return to work as soon as possible is also the responsibility of the human resources department. Finally, the provincial Department of Labour made several orders that the company had to comply with. Several of these orders dealt with repairing equipment; others dealt with providing adequate training and ensuring that safe working procedures were developed. Again, the human resource department plays these roles.

Source: "Worker in NS did not receive OH&S training before first shift." (2003, September 22). *Canadian Occupational Health and Safety News.*

Most of us go to work each day expecting to return home in more or less the same condition as when we left. However, for a distressingly high number of workers, this is not the case. Workplace accidents continue to occur, with consequences ranging from minor property damage to death. As the organizational unit most clearly responsible for the well-being of employees, it is clear that human resource management has to focus on occupational health and safety. The costs of failing in this responsibility are immense.

As shown in Figure 1.1, the number of workplace fatalities in Canada continues to increase. The most recent figures suggest that more than 1,000 workers each year die as a result of workplace accidents, and almost 340,000 suffer an injury serious enough to warrant missing time from work (frequently called a **lost-time injury;** see Table 1.1). As one might expect, workplace fatalities and injuries are concentrated by industry, with primary industries (e.g., mining, forestry) being the most dangerous. More than half of workplace fatalities are attributable to occupational diseases, with the effects of asbestos accounting for most of these deaths.[1]

lost-time injury
a workplace injury that results in the employee missing time from work

Occupational health and safety (OH&S) is the identification, evaluation, and control of hazards associated with the work environment. These hazards range from chemical, biological, and physical agents to psychosocial disorders such as stress. The goal of an organization's health and safety program

occupational health and safety (OH&S)
the identification, evaluation, and control of hazards associated with the work environment

FIGURE 1.1

Workplace Fatalities in Canada: A Ten-Year History

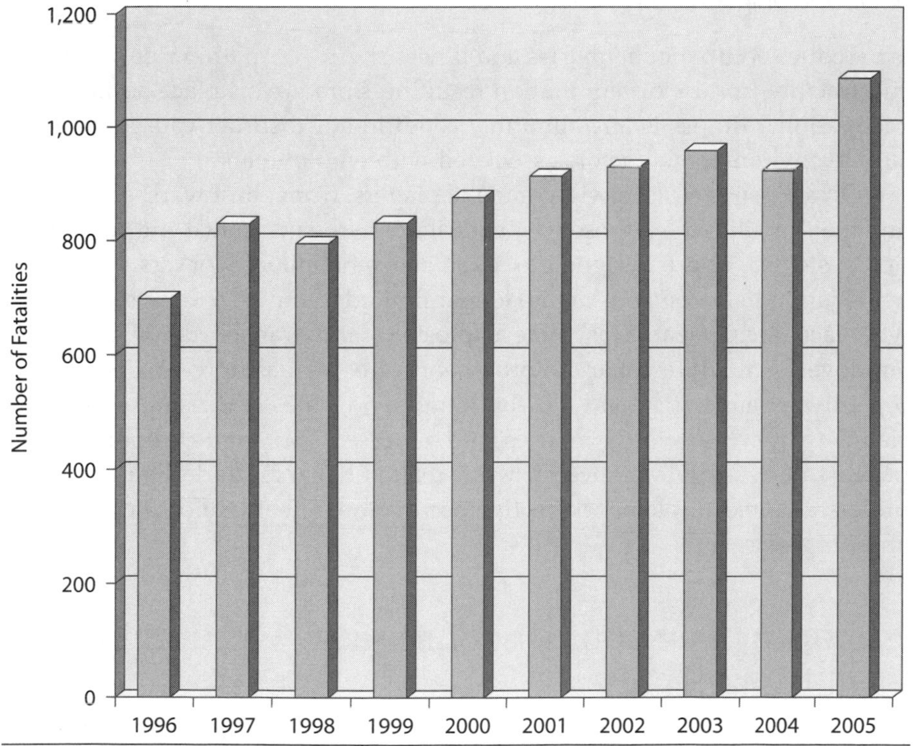

Source: Association of Workers' Compensation Boards of Canada, "National Work Injuries Statistics Program." Retrieved from http://www.awcbc.org/english/NWISP_Stats.asp#Accepted_time-loss_injuries, February 7, 2007.

TABLE 1.1

Lost-Time Injuries by Province and Territory, 2005

	NUMBER OF LOST-TIME INJURIES
Alberta	36,305
British Columbia	60,340
Manitoba	17,785
New Brunswick	4,439
Newfoundland and Labrador	4,821
Northwest Territories and Nunavut	950
Nova Scotia	8,998
Ontario	89,734
Prince Edward Island	876
Quebec	99,067
Saskatchewan	14,170
Yukon	445
CANADA	337,930

Source: Based on data available from Association of Workers' Compensation Boards of Canada, "National work injuries statistics program." Retrieved from http://www.awcbc.org/english/NWISP_Stats.asp#Accepted_time-loss_injuries, February 6, 2007.

occupational injury
any cut, fracture, sprain, or amputation resulting from a workplace accident

occupational illness
any abnormal condition or disorder caused by exposure to environmental factors associated with employment

is to reduce occupational injuries and illnesses. An **occupational injury** is any cut, fracture, sprain, or amputation resulting from a workplace accident. An **occupational illness** is any abnormal condition or disorder caused by exposure to environmental factors associated with employment.

OH&S issues affect a wide range of players, from employers, employees, and their families to all those who contribute to the insurance and compensation systems that are designed to assist and rehabilitate workers. Moreover, health and safety concerns are no longer limited to industrial-sector workers, who face such hazards as mine explosions and transportation accidents; employees in white-collar environments are increasingly anxious about repetitive-strain injury and sick-building syndrome. The rising costs associated with work-related injuries and illnesses and, more important, the public's decreasing tolerance for work-related hazards, underlie the need to understand and implement effective occupational health and safety policies and programs.

Historical Development of Modern Occupational Health and Safety

Occupational injuries and illnesses have been with us throughout history. Documented cases of work-related illnesses go back as far as ancient Egypt, when stonemasons and potters experienced respiratory problems. As societies became more technologically advanced, cases of copper-induced dermatoses (skin diseases), vomiting, and hepatic (liver) degeneration began to occur. Labourers who worked with iron and in the various alloying operations risked not only such symptoms as high fever, coughing, and headache, but also diseases like lung cancer.[2]

With the advent of the Industrial Revolution, machinists and others working in the new industries were exposed to oils used for lubrication during the cutting and removal of metal. These oils, in conjunction with poor personal hygiene practices, resulted in serious dermatoses, such as acne and skin melanomas. When the spinning and weaving industries were mechanized, the resultant dust from hemp and flax caused *byssinosis* (**brown lung**).

brown lung
a disease of the lungs caused by excessive inhalation of dust; the disease is in the pneumoconiosis family and frequently afflicts textile workers

In Canada, concern for occupational health and safety was first evident in the late nineteenth century, when Ontario passed legislation that established safety standards such as mandating guards on machines. Quebec soon followed suit, and by the early twentieth century every jurisdiction in Canada had passed factory laws that regulated heating, lighting, ventilation, hygiene, fire safety, and accident reporting. Factory inspectors were appointed in each province and territory to enforce these standards and to conduct regular inspections of workplaces.

The Royal Commission on the Relations of Capital and Labour in Canada (1889) had an important influence on the development of health and safety regulations. First, the commissioners made several recommendations about improving health and safety by establishing standards and mandating regular inspections. Second, the commissioners were the first to recommend a system for compensating victims of industrial accidents, regardless of who was at fault in the accident. Finally, the commissioners recommended that a labour bureau be created to oversee these activities.

The 1960s and 1970s were an important time for health and safety in Canada, witnessing the implementation of the Canada Labour (Standards) Code and the Canada Labour (Safety) Code. In 1974, the Ontario government formed the Royal Commission on the Health and Safety of Workers in Mines. Chaired by Dr. James Ham, this commission was the first to articulate the three principal rights of workers: the right to refuse dangerous work without penalty, the right to participate in identifying and correcting health and safety problems, and the right to know about hazards in the workplace. These three rights continue to be enshrined in current legislation and provide the basis for much of the health and safety programming in Canada. For example, in 1988, legislation was passed that established the Workplace Hazardous Materials Information System (WHMIS). Through federal and provincial cooperation, WHMIS has been established in every jurisdiction in Canada and is based on workers' fundamental right to know about potential hazards in the workplace.

Changing Perspectives on Risk and Liability

Until the early twentieth century, the dominant model of dealing with hazards in the workplace was the legal doctrine of the **assumption of risk.** In essence, the assumption of risk stated that when a worker accepted employment, he or she also accepted all the normal risks associated with that occupation. Under

assumption of risk
the belief that a worker accepted the risks of employment when he or she accepted a job

Occupational Health and Safety Notebook 1.1

Preventing Computer Vision Syndrome

Work-related health concerns are not just of historical interest. The advent of new technologies has resulted in new health and safety concerns. One of these is computer vision syndrome, which results from the glare caused by the combination of bright office lights and computer monitors. It is estimated that 70 percent of adults experience computer vision syndrome. To reduce the health concerns associated with glare, organizations can do several things:

- Reduce ambient lighting levels (most offices are more than twice as bright as they need to be).
- Place monitors so they are 90 degrees from any light source.
- Use task lighting (i.e., adjustable desk lamps).
- Ensure that monitors are functioning properly with minimal flicker and are adjusted for the comfort of the user.

Sources: Home Vision Therapy System, "Frequently asked questions." Retrieved from http://www.homevisiontherapy.com/faqs.html I, February 7, 2007; Alberta Association of Optometrists, "Are your kids at risk for computer vision syndrome?" Retrieved from http://www.optometrists.ab.ca/press/releases.htm?Step=2&PRK=4, February 7, 2007; and Canadian Centre for Occupational Health and Safety, "Eye discomfort in the office." Retrieved from http://www.ccohs.ca/oshanswers/ergonomics/office/eye_discomfort.html, February 7, 2007.

this doctrine, employers bore little or no responsibility for worker health and safety. Indeed, employers were not responsible for providing compensation to injured workers unless the accident was *solely* the fault of the employer. Given that workplace accidents rarely have only one cause, it is not surprising that cases in which workers were compensated were few.

Associated with the assumption of risk doctrine was the belief that occupational injuries were caused by worker carelessness. In its most extreme form, this notion was expressed as a belief in the accident-prone personality. The concept of **accident proneness** was a focus for research for most of the twentieth century and assumed that some individuals are inherently more likely to be involved in accidents than are others and that therefore the majority of workplace accidents are caused by a small proportion of workers. Because workers in dangerous occupations or workplaces do tend to have more accidents than others, the belief in accident proneness appears to be supported. However, this is equivalent to saying that Ontario drivers are the worst in Canada because of the high number of accidents on Highway 401. When we consider that the volume of traffic on the 401 exceeds all other highways in Canada, the higher number of accidents can be seen in perspective. It is now recognized that the concept of accident proneness has little empirical support. Modern health and safety programs have moved beyond these early beliefs to the recognition that enhancing occupational health and safety requires cooperation among multiple stakeholders. Government, employers, and employees all have a role to play in enhancing health and safety outcomes.

accident proneness
the notion that some individuals are inherently more likely than others to be involved in accidents, as a result of individual characteristics

The Importance of Health and Safety

Effective occupational health and safety programs have important and far-reaching benefits for both employers and employees. Employers, employees, and the public should care about occupational health and safety for economic, legal, and moral reasons.

Economic Considerations

The economic costs associated with work-related injury can be broken down into direct and indirect costs. The example given in Occupational Health and Safety Today 1.1 shows some of the direct and indirect costs that can result from a work-related injury. Note that the costs illustrated in this one example are repeated hourly across the country. Cost calculations for specific injuries and workplaces can be estimated using an online calculator provided by WorkSafeBC.

The costs of workplace injury are estimated to exceed $12 billion a year.[3] And the lost time attributable to injuries exceeds that of labour disruptions such as strikes or lockouts.[4] These costs are unequally distributed: in Ontario, for example, it is estimated that 2 percent of all workplaces are responsible for 10 percent of all injuries and 21 percent of all costs.[5]

For at least two reasons, direct and indirect estimates must be considered underestimates of the true costs of workplace illness and injury. First, considerable evidence shows that workplace injuries are not accurately reported. Indeed, studies have suggested that the number of reported injuries may represent only one-tenth of actual injuries.[6] Second, occupational injury statistics do not adequately capture the extent of illnesses that are caused or exacerbated by exposure to workplace conditions. Deaths that *might* be attributable to occupational illnesses are not typically accounted for in the statistical analysis of occupational fatalities.

It is clear that safety problems cost every man, woman, and child in Canada hundreds of dollars annually based on the direct and indirect costs of occupational injuries. But these figures represent costs associated with

Occupational Health and Safety Today 1.1

Direct and Indirect Costs of Injury

A construction worker falls 3 metres off an unguarded scaffold and lands on the main floor, breaking his ankle and forearm. The direct costs of the injury include that worker's lost time, the time spent in investigating the incident, and the finding/training of a replacement worker, and are estimated at $1,810. This does not include the indirect costs (including the potential increase in Workers' Compensation Board assessment and the potential fines and legal costs associated with allowing an unsafe condition in the workplace). These indirect costs can be more than 10 times the direct costs of the incident. It is important to note that these costs come right from the bottom line—every dollar in cost is a dollar lost in profit. It is estimated that this one incident (direct costs only) will take 18 days' profit from the firm. There are other costs to consider. The average cost of a Workers' Compensation claim is approximately $19,000, and these costs are paid by all employers through the assessment. There are also the costs experienced by the individual in the form of pain and suffering and the potential for long-term effects of the injury. The cost of claim was derived by inserting fictional facts and data into the WorkSafeBC Safety Calculator. The Calculator may be accessed through the following link: http://www2.worksafebc.com/sc/tours/default.htm. The actual cost of any claim may differ due to the variables such as time involved and the hourly rates used in the Calculator.

Source: For this and other cost scenarios, see the incident cost calculator at http://www.hre.gov.ab.ca/whs/smallbus/calculator/tours/default.htm. Retrieved February 7, 2007.

an injury once it has occurred. Other costs to the employer include work stoppages and strikes due to unsafe working conditions. For example, in 1987, one thousand employees at McDonnell Douglas Canada refused to work after the Ontario Ministry of Labour cited the company for hundreds of infractions of the province's Occupational Health and Safety Act. Labour disputes involving such safety issues as pollutant levels, safety equipment, and first-aid facilities result in thousands of lost days of worker production. Incalculable costs include those associated with employees who quit or refuse to work in companies because of safety or health concerns.

Another indirect cost to companies is that of negative publicity when a death, an accident, or a serious health problem becomes public. The Occidental Chemical Company in California had a public-relations nightmare to cope with when the media learned that one of its chemicals caused sterility in the workers handling the compound. However, managers who are committed to safety can turn adverse publicity into a marketing and recruitment advantage by advertising their concerns for employee safety. Employers that are *not* concerned about the health and safety of their employees affect other employers and taxpaying citizens. Workers' Compensation rates are determined by industry sector. A negligent employer forces others in the sector to pay higher rates, and these costs are significant. The 12 Workers' Compensation Boards across Canada pay out $3 billion annually. The Alberta board estimates that a totally disabled young worker with children will have received $7 million in payments by age 72. Unsafe working conditions cause insurance premiums to escalate and health expenditures to increase.

In contrast, industry estimates indicate that up to 90 percent of safety-related changes made can result in positive paybacks through the associated reduction in Workers' Compensation premiums. Programs such as the New Experimental Experience Rating (NEER) reward employers for implementing safe work practices by reducing Workers' Compensation costs based on the company's actual experience. Therefore, organizations have an economic interest in lowering the number of accidents and providing a safe working environment.

Legal Considerations

Every worker has the legal right to safe working conditions under occupational health and safety acts. The Occupational Health and Safety Act of Ontario, section 25(2)(h), requires an employer to "take every precaution reasonable in the circumstances for the protection of a worker." The legal term for this requirement is **due diligence.**

due diligence
an expected standard of conduct that requires employers to take every reasonable precaution to ensure safety

From a legal perspective, due diligence is considered a measure of prudence to be expected from, and ordinarily exercised by, a reasonable and prudent person under the particular circumstances depending on the relative facts of the special case. In other words, due diligence is a standard of conduct measured by what could be expected of a reasonable person in the same circumstances. Due diligence requires a business to foresee all unsafe conditions or acts and requires it to take precautions to prevent accidents that can

Occupational Health and Safety Today 1.2

The Costs of Unhealthy Behaviour

Although there is no doubt that substantial human and economic costs are associated with unsafe workplaces, employers also incur substantial costs attributable to individual lifestyle choices. In their effort to promote "wellness" (see Chapter 13), many employers have implemented smoking-cessation programs (often in conjunction with provincial or territorial legislation that prohibits smoking in the workplace). Substantial economic gains may be associated with such initiatives. Based on a review of research from around the world, Kelloway and Barling concluded that smokers were absent from work 43 percent more often than nonsmokers. Although such estimates do not show up in the lost-time injury figures, absenteeism associated with smoking is a real and substantial cost for employers.

Sources: Kelloway, E. K., & Barling, J. (2003). Smoking and absence from work. In M. Krausz & M. Koslowsky (Eds.), *Voluntary employee withdrawal and inattendance* (pp. 167–178). New York: Plenum; and Henningfield, J. E., Ramstrom, L. M., Husten, C., Giovino, G., Barling, J., Weber, C., Kelloway, E. K., Strecher, V. J., & Jarvis, M. J. (1994). Smoking and the workplace: Realities and solutions. *Journal of Smoking-Related Diseases, 5*, 261–270.

reasonably be anticipated.[7] Similarly, a worker is required to work in compliance with health and safety legislation. This legislation is discussed at length in Chapter 2.

Moral Considerations

Aside from legal and economic considerations, employers have a moral obligation to employees and their families to provide the safest working environment possible. Two decades of research have provided consistent evidence that management commitment to health and safety will result in higher levels of employee motivation to work safely and better organizational safety records. Similarly, workers have a moral responsibility to learn about safety and health, to follow recommended workplace practices, and to be alert and responsible. In at least one study, the perception that managers, supervisors, and coworkers were committed to health and safety was the single biggest predictor of an employee's willingness to participate in health and safety programs.[8] Clearly, the economic, human, and social costs associated with workplace injury and illness are intolerable, and both employers and employees must work together to enhance occupational health and safety.

The Stakeholders

Government

In Canada, Ontario was the first province to enact compensation legislation with the passage of the Workmen's Compensation Act in 1914. This legislation provided lost-time wages to almost every injured worker, thereby removing the right of workers to sue their employers. Following World War I, the federal and other provincial and territorial governments began to enact RPC 1.2

legislation designed to protect the worker. The two main goals of this legislation were (1) to ensure that injured workers received compensation and that employers accepted liability, and (2) to prevent accidents and illness through the establishment of safe work environments.

As a result of continued improvement to health and safety legislation, the number of workplace accidents declined. For example, despite the addition of two million workers to the Canadian workforce between 1985 and 1993, the number of accidents dropped from 554,793 to 423,184.[9]

In addition to their legislative function, governments solicit or conduct research on health and safety issues and disseminate information. Ontario, Nova Scotia, and British Columbia are world leaders in the development of chemical-exposure standards that are as strict as reasonably attainable based on hard scientific evidence. The federal government created the Canadian Centre for Occupational Health and Safety (CCOH&S) as a vital health and safety research and resource organization. CCOH&S accesses a number of databases from around the world in addition to creating and maintaining its own comprehensive database. The goal of this organization is to provide health and safety information to any worker who requests it.

One important contribution of CCOH&S has been the creation of an online information service called CCINFOWEB. This program's vast database contains information on chemicals, material safety data sheets (MSDS), toxicological effects of chemicals and biological agents, and health and safety legislation for all jurisdictions in Canada. CCOH&S also produces a wide variety of safety infograms and other publications.

Employers

Although every player has a role in occupational health and safety, that of a company's management team is the most pivotal. Managers have the means and the authority to monitor the workplace and to ensure compliance with safe practices. Moreover, organizations have the resources to hire health and safety professionals.

The employer is responsible for preparing a written occupational health and safety policy and ensuring that it is prominently displayed in the workplace. Employers are also required to

- provide and maintain equipment, materials, and protective devices
- ensure that the manner in which the work is performed is safe and that the environment is free from hazards and serious risks
- monitor their workplace and report minor, critical, disabling, and fatal injuries, as well as occupational illnesses and toxic substances (and to maintain the records of these occurrences for many years)
- establish health and safety committees with strong employee representation
- alert employees to any known or perceived risks and hazards in the workplace
- provide employees with health and safety training

Managers have to be trained in the recognition and control of unsafe work environments; they cannot monitor and control what they do not recognize as unsafe. Supervisors who participated in a study of 70 construction sites failed to recognize 44 percent of the workplace hazards and felt that another 64 percent did not fall within their jurisdiction. Further, these supervisors stated that 20 percent of the hazards were inevitable.[10] Clearly, in order to fulfill their responsibilities, managers must receive health and safety training.

Employees

Employees of an organization have a role to play in occupational health and safety both as individuals and as members of organized labour groups. As individuals, employees are required to perform their duties and tasks in a safe and responsible manner and to wear protective equipment in compliance with company and legislative regulations. They are also required to report defective equipment and other workplace hazards to the safety professional, the joint health and safety committee, or the manager. Any employees who feel that a particular activity will endanger them or others have the right to refuse to carry out the activity.

Organized Labour

Organized labour also has a role to play in ensuring the proper management of safety at work.[11] One role of organized labour is to bring emerging problems and issues in health and safety to the attention of government and employers

Occupational Health and Safety Today 1.3

A Predictable Path to Disaster at Westray

On May 9, 1992, at 5:20 a.m., the Westray coal mine in Plymouth, Nova Scotia, exploded. Despite extensive rescue efforts involving more than 170 mine rescue workers, 26 miners died in the mine. Charged with investigating the cause of the disaster, Justice Peter Richard entitled his final report *The Westray Story: A Predictable Path to Disaster*, emphasizing that the disaster that rocked the community had been entirely preventable.

Although Justice Richard documents many causes of the disaster, he particularly focuses on a management style that emphasized production over safety and showed disdain for safety concerns: Workers were not provided training in safe mining procedures; supervisors did not have the authority to correct unsafe conditions; and dangerous shortcuts were taken in the performance of mine tasks. Work procedures (e.g., the use of 12-hour shifts for miners) were also in violation of safety regulations. Despite excessive levels of gas and coal dust in the mine, unsafe procedures (e.g., the use of torches) were condoned if not encouraged. No meaningful dialogue existed on safety matters at the Westray mine–the joint health and safety committee did not function effectively. As Justice Richard notes, the operation of the mine defied every principle of safe mining.

The explosion at Westray also provides a cautionary tale for human resource managers–it illustrates what happens when management does not make safety a priority and does not promote a culture of safety.

Source: Government of Nova Scotia, *The Westray story: A predictable path to disaster*. Retrieved from http://www.gov.ns.ca/enla/pubs/westray/, February 7, 2007.

and to pressure other stakeholders to take corrective action. Organized labour and professional associations have also used the collective bargaining process to incorporate health and safety provisions in many contracts. These labour contracts attempt to formalize voluntary measures and extend legislative programs. For example, some contracts state that a union must have a full-time safety representative in all plants. Others bargain for more training on safety measures or more information on exposure to known toxic chemicals.

Partnerships

Although all stakeholders support the concept of safe working conditions, not everyone is committed to the implementation of OH&S programs. There may be several reasons for stakeholders' lack of action in this area. Employers may be more concerned with production quotas than with safety records, because the costs of production are more visible. Employers may clean up their locations just before an announced safety inspection, thus ensuring a pass. Sometimes managers do not even recognize unsafe conditions, or they feel unable to do anything about those they do identify. Similarly, employers may be unaware of the methods and instruments by which rigorous monitoring of the workplace can be achieved. This situation is compounded by the fact that health and safety is rarely mentioned in management research, composing less than 1 percent of such research.[12] As a result, managers and prospective managers receive little or no training in health and safety issues. Health and safety issues may also be addressed in an industrial relations climate that emphasizes conflict between management and the union. In such an environment, health and safety issues may be seen as another bargaining chip.[13]

Occupational Health and Safety Today 1.4

Young Workers at Risk

On November 18, 1994, Sean Kells, a husky young football player, was at work—it was his third day on the job. He was pouring a chemical from a large unmarked vat into a smaller container. A spark triggered by static electricity set off an explosion in which Sean suffered burns to 95 percent of his body, resulting in his death.

The Industrial Accident Prevention Association (IAPA) reports that young workers between the ages of 15 and 24 accounted for 3,740 lost-time injuries in Ontario in 2005. This translated into more than 50,000 lost days and costs approaching $5 million.

Young people are at particular risk in the workplace for several reasons. First, a lack of experience and training means they may not recognize hazards in the workplace. Second, they may not be aware of their right to a safe working environment and their right to refuse unsafe work; they may not want to "rock the boat." Finally, as part-time or short-term employees, they may not be offered the same level of safety training as full-time employees.

Increasing recognition of the hazards faced by young people in the workplace has resulted in efforts to make sure they know their rights and responsibilities. Programs such as the Young Worker Awareness Program are designed to integrate this training in high-school curricula.

Sources: Safe Communities Foundation, "Sean Kells' story." Retrieved from http://www.safecommunities.ca/seankells.htm, February 7, 2007; and IAPA "Lost time injury illness analysis for young workers age 15–24, 2005." Retrieved from http://www.iapa.ca/documents/2005_IA_young_workers.pdf, February 7, 2007.

Another barrier to the implementation of OH&S programs is that the general medical establishment is neither well versed nor well trained in OH&S issues and occupational medicine. For instance, the effects of some industrial diseases are not apparent for years and are complicated by factors such as the worker's lifestyle and failure to follow safety regulations such as wearing protective equipment.

One way to overcome the barriers to the implementation of OH&S programs is to form alliances among the stakeholders. The three parties—employers, employees, and unions—have the same goal: the reduction of injuries and illnesses. It is a win–win situation in bargaining. The employer, by investing in health and safety programs, gains economically through a reduction in direct and indirect costs, and it gains through an improved public image that may strengthen employee loyalty and increase marketing opportunities. Employees gain through reduced risk of work-related injuries and illnesses. Unions gain through their ability to successfully champion the health and safety interests of their clients.

The federal and most provincial and territorial governments require the establishment of joint health and safety committees (employer and worker representatives) in organizations with five or more employees; Ontario has no requirement regarding the minimum number of employees if a designated substance—such as asbestos—is present. These committees respond to accidents; monitor the workplace; notify authorities about serious hazards, critical injuries, or death; hear complaints; and make recommendations.

Health and Safety Professionals

One way to develop an effective OH&S program is to employ health and safety professionals. Employing a health and safety professional can produce returns equal to factors of two or more times the salary paid. When the Oshawa Group employed safety professionals, its accident rate declined by 30 percent over five years.[14]

Managers and human resource experts cannot be expected to develop, manage, and evaluate an OH&S program, particularly when the issues cover the spectrum from chemical hazards to workplace violence. To assist managers in the operation of an OH&S program, various types of safety and health experts may be hired or consulted. Health and safety experts can be located through their associations, the Yellow Pages, or safety associations and provincial departments. There are no legal requirements for the practice of occupational health and safety.

The Role of Human Resources

Traditional views of safety have emphasized **the three Es**. The goal was to develop *engineering* solutions to ensure safe work environments, equipment, and personal protective devices. Then, health and safety professionals were tasked with *educating* supervisors and employers in the use of the equipment. Finally, health and safety programs focused on *enforcing* existing regulations and practices. To a great extent, these approaches have been successful in

the three Es
a traditional approach to occupational health and safety that emphasized engineering, education, and enforcement

Occupational Health and Safety Notebook 1.2

Safety Professionals

Canadian registered safety professionals (CRSPs) are trained to (1) identify and appraise workplace hazards and evaluate the severity of an accident or loss, (2) develop and communicate hazard-control policies, methods, and programs, (3) devise motivational programs to integrate safety procedures into operations, and (4) measure and evaluate the effectiveness of these programs and revise them as necessary. To achieve certification, safety professionals must meet specified academic, experience, and examination requirements.

Registered occupational hygienists (ROHs) are educated in a variety of fields (with degrees in chemistry, engineering, physics, biology, or medicine) and are trained to evaluate and control workplace hazards that may lead to sickness, impaired health, significant discomfort, and inefficiency.

Registered occupational hygienist technologists (ROHTs) perform similar functions as ROHs but typically have a college diploma rather than a university degree.

Occupational physicians who enter the field of occupational medicine must do postgraduate work in such subjects as industrial toxicology, work physiology, industrial hygiene, respiratory diseases, and biostatistics.

Occupational health nurses are concerned with the prevention, recognition, and treatment of worker illness and injury and the application of nursing principles to individuals in the workplace.

creating safer workplaces. However, we now recognize that the three Es do not provide a total solution and that focusing on the people side of the workplace is likely to result in a safer workplace.

Not surprisingly, you will find that occupational health and safety is almost exclusively "managed" under the human resources function. There are several reasons for this organizational structure.

Safety Is a People Issue

Although great advances have been made through engineering solutions, it is increasingly apparent that effective safety programming depends on developing individual skills and abilities and on motivating individuals. These are the traditional concerns of human resources. Through the use of orientation and other training programs, human resource professionals develop employee knowledge and skills. Through a variety of strategies including compensation and awareness programs, human resource professionals motivate safe working.

Perhaps most important, research has increasingly identified variables such as safety leadership[15] and safety climate[16,17] as predictors of safety outcomes (e.g., incidents, accidents, injuries). These issues are discussed in Chapter 10. Traditional areas of human resource practice such as job design have also been linked to safety outcomes.[18] More broadly, management programs such as the implementation of high-performance work systems[19] or lean manufacturing[20] have implications for occupational safety. Finally, safety concerns have direct implications for outcomes such as stress and turnover,[21] traditional areas of HR concern.

Safety Requires Legislative Compliance

As we have already seen, and will discuss in detail in Chapter 2, occupational health and safety is a very well developed area of labour law. Numerous standards and requirements are imposed on employers to maintain workplace safety. Administering compliance is a natural outgrowth of the human resource function. Human resource professionals already ensure compliance with other areas of labour law (e.g., employment equity, human rights legislation) and thus are well versed in dealing with such concerns.

Safety Decreases Costs

Workers' Compensation premiums, long-term disability coverage, sick-time provisions, and health plans all add to the costs of doing business. It is the responsibility of human resources to see that such costs are minimized. This duty has assumed increasing importance in an era in which double-digit increases in benefit premiums are not uncommon. Aside from minimizing costs, human resources has a role in ensuring that the benefits an organization pays for are used most effectively to help injured workers and ensure a prompt return to health (and to work).

Safety Relates to Other Human Resource Functions

Safety is also linked to other human resource functions and needs to be considered in all areas of human resource management. Indeed, occupational health and safety is one of the outcomes of adopting a particular strategic orientation to health and safety.[22]

Safety programming in organizations frequently hinges on training initiatives, a traditional human resource function. Training is one of the most popular, and arguably one of the most effective, health and safety initiatives available[23] and is discussed in detail in Chapter 9. Research has established links between job insecurity and safety,[24] such that individuals who experience job insecurity are more likely to commit safety violations. The use of performance-based pay systems has been associated with increased injury rates, while the implementation of teams in organizations may be associated with reduced injuries.[25] Clearly, the way we manage human resources has direct implications for occupational health and safety.

Summary

This chapter has established the importance of occupational health and safety. First, the economic, legal, and moral considerations for enhancing OH&S were presented. Second, government, employers, and employees were presented as the major stakeholders involved in OH&S, and the value of partnerships among those stakeholders was emphasized. Finally, the role of health and safety professionals was described and the role of human resources in managing health and safety was briefly outlined.

Key Terms

accident proneness 8
assumption of risk 7
brown lung 7
due diligence 10
lost-time injury 5
occupational health and safety (OH&S) 5
occupational illness 6
occupational injury 6
the three Es 15

Weblinks

Business News Network, "Health and Safety News"

http://www.esourcecanada.com/bnn/healthandsafety.asp (p. 5)

Civilization.ca, "Beginnings: Craft Unions"

http://www.civilization.ca/hist/labour/labv08e.html (p. 7)

Canadian Centre for Occupational Health and Safety

http://www.ccohs.ca (p. 7)

WorkSafeBC, "Safety Calculator"

http://www.healthandsafetycentre.org/sc/calculator/default.htm (p. 9)

Workplace Safety and Insurance Board of Ontario, "New Experimental Experience Rating Program (NEER) Program Overview"

http://www.wsib.on.ca/wsib/wsibsite.nsf/public/NEER (p. 10)

Workers' Health & Safety Centre, Ontario

http://www.whsc.on.ca (p. 13)

Young Worker Awareness Program

http://www.youngworker.ca (p. 14)

RPC Icons

RPC 1.1 Ensures due diligence and strict liability requirements are met, e.g., records are kept and formal procedures established.

- relevant legislation and common law
- company policies and procedures
- industry best practices
- program and policy development
- training and development techniques
- risk analysis
- common and statutory law (e.g., employment standard: labour relations)

- worker protection (including health and safety and Workers' Compensation)
- theories and practices for protection of individuals and groups

TASK & KNOWLEDGE REQUIREMENTS

- occupational health and safety legislation (e.g., Occupational Health and Safety Act of Ontario, Workplace Safety and Insurance Act—Bill 99, Workplace Hazardous Materials Information System, transportation of dangerous goods legislation, environmental legislation, smoking in the workplace legislation, civil rights legislation)
- management techniques for OH&S programs

RPC 1.2 Ensures that security programs and policies minimize risks while considering the obligation of the employer and the rights of employees, union, and third parties.

- nature of the business and physical work environment
- relevant legislation
- industry best practices
- program and policy development
- safety and security equipment in the workplace
- risk assessment/techniques
- cost/benefit analysis

TASK & KNOWLEDGE REQUIREMENTS

- available community resources
- worker protection (including health and safety and Worker's Compensation)
- unions' role in health and safety and in employee involvement
- occupational health and safety legislation (e.g., Occupational Health and Safety Act of Ontario, Workplace Safety and Insurance Act—Bill 99, Workplace Hazardous Materials Information System, transportation of dangerous goods legislation, environmental legislation, smoking in the workplace legislation, civil rights legislation)
- emergency preparedness procedures
- management techniques for OH&S programs
- types of employee assistance and wellness programs

RPC 1.3 Establishes a joint responsibility system as required by law e.g., worker-management health & safety committees, investigations, audits, testing and training, to ensure employee safety.

- relevant occupational health and safety legislation
- inspection techniques and procedures
- hazard recognition
- principles of training and development

- program and policy development
- audit processes
- joint health and safety committee functions
- worker protection (including health and safety and Workers' Compensation)
- occupational health and safety legislation (e.g., Occupational Health and Safety Act of Ontario, Workplace Safety and Insurance Act—Bill 99, Workplace Hazardous Materials Information System, transportation of dangerous goods legislation, environmental legislation, smoking in the workplace legislation, civil rights legislation)
- management techniques for OH&S programs

Discussion Questions

1. Why have people historically been more concerned with work-related injuries than work-related illnesses?
2. How has our understanding of personal liability for accidents changed over the years?
3. On what grounds, beside humanitarian ones, should workplace hazards be controlled?
4. Who are the stakeholders in health and safety? What roles do they play?

Using the Internet

1. How do organizations treat occupational health and safety? Find the websites for major corporations in your area. Search the website for information on health and safety. Who in the organization administers health and safety programs? What kinds of programs are in place?

Exercises

1. Are the media stakeholders in health and safety? For one week, read the local newspapers and listen to the news. Make a note of the main topic of every article or item pertaining to occupational health and safety. What roles are the media playing? What OH&S issues are most likely to gain attention? Give reasons for your answers.
2. Interview a human resource manager regarding occupational health and safety. What is HR's role in the effective management of health and safety at work? What HR functions are involved in meeting the health and safety requirements?

Case 1

Production or Safety?

Atlantic Radiators Inc. manufactures automotive radiators. Demand for their products has resulted in an empty warehouse and there is an urgent need to increase production to satisfy current customers. John Roberts is an employee of Atlantic Radiators Inc. His job is to spray each radiator core with a dilute solution of hydrochloric acid and to bake the radiators in an oven. The acid acts as a flux on the solder-coated tubes and the baking process solders the radiator together.

John's supervisor has spoken to him several times about the need to speed up and not be the bottleneck in the production process. As a result, John has been taking some shortcuts, including neglecting to wear the proper eye protection. Today, he splashed some of the acid mixture in his eye and will now be off work for several days. As plant manager, you are responsible for reviewing this incident. Who is at fault here? What can be done to ensure that similar incidents will not occur in the future?

Case 2

Do We Need Health and Safety?

As the newly appointed manager of Global Insurance Company, Anuradha Das was trying to learn as much as possible about her new workplace. She was surprised to note the absence of the traditional health and safety bulletin board and asked her manager how health and safety information was communicated to employees. "Are you kidding?" he replied. "This is an office. Our employees are mostly data-entry clerks. We don't have machines or equipment—what do we need with health and safety programs?" If you were Anuradha, how would you reply?

Endnotes

1. Sharpe, A., & Hardte, J. (2006). Five deaths a day: Workplace fatalities in Canada 1993–2005. *CSLS Research Report 2006–04.* Ottawa: Centre for the Study of Living Standards.
2. Janson, H. W. (1985). *History of art* (2nd ed.). Englewood Cliffs, NJ: Prentice Hall.
3. Moro, T. (2004, July 9). Ontario hiring 200 workplace inspectors. *London Free Press.*
4. Barling, J., Kelloway, E. K., & Zacharatos, A. (2002). Occupational health and safety. In P. B. Warr (Ed.), *Psychology and work* (6th ed.). London: Penguin.
5. Moro, T. (2004, July 9). Ontario hiring 200 workplace inspectors. *London Free Press.*
6. Barling, J., Kelloway, E. K., & Zacharatos, A. (2002). Occupational health and safety. In P. B. Warr (Ed.), *Psychology and work* (6th ed.). London: Penguin.
7. Strahlendorf, P. (2000). *Occupational health and safety law study guide.* Toronto: Ryerson Polytechnic University Press.

8. Cree, T., & Kelloway, E. K. (1997). Responses to occupational hazards: Exit and participation. *Journal of Occupational Health Psychology, 2,* 304–311.
9. Statistics Canada. (1994). *Work injuries, 1991–1993*. Ottawa: Ministry of Supply and Services.
10. Abeytunga, P. K., & Hale, H. R. (1982, July). Supervisor's perception of hazards on construction sites. Paper presented at the 20th Congress of the International Association of Applied Psychology, Edinburgh, U.K.
11. Kelloway, E. K. (2003). Labor unions and safety. In J. Barling & M. Frone (Eds.), *Psychology of occupational safety*. Washington, DC: APA Books.
12. Barling, J., Kelloway, E. K., & Zacharatos, A. (2002). Occupational health and safety. In P. B. Warr (Ed.), *Psychology and work* (6th ed.). London: Penguin.
13. Kelloway, E. K. (2003). Labor unions and safety. In J. Barling & M. Frone (Eds.), *Psychology of occupational safety*. Washington, DC: APA Books.
14. Boyes, S. (1993, July/August). Doubles strategy: When human resources and occupational health and safety work in synchrony, everybody wins. *Human Resources Professional, 10(7),* 17–19.
15. Barling, J., Loughlin, C., & Kelloway, E. K. (2002). Development and test of a model linking safety-specific transformational leadership and occupational safety. *Journal of Applied Psychology, 87,* 488–496.
16. Zohar, D. (2000). A group-level model of safety climate: Testing the effect of group climate on microaccidents in manufacturing jobs. *Journal of Applied Psychology, 85,* 587–596.
17. Zohar, D. (2002). The effects of leadership dimensions, safety climate, and assigned priorities on minor injuries in work groups. *Journal of Organizational Behavior, 23,* 75–92.
18. Barling, J., Kelloway, E. K., & Iverson, R. (2003). High-quality work, job satisfaction and occupational injuries. *Journal of Applied Psychology, 88,* 276–283.
19. Zacharatos, A., Barling, J., & Iverson, R. (2005). High-performance work systems and occupational safety. *Journal of Applied Psychology, 90,* 77.
20. Mehri, D. (2006). The darker side of lean: An insider's perspective on the realities of the Toyota production system. *The Academy of Management Perspectives, 20,* 21.
21. Barling, J., Kelloway, E. K., & Iverson, R. (2003). Accidental outcomes: Attitudinal consequences of workplace injuries. *Journal of Occupational Health Psychology, 8,* 74–85.
22. Shaw, J. D., & Delery, J. E. (2003). Strategic HRM and organizational health interventions. In D. A. Hoffman & L. E. Tetrick (Eds.), *Health and safety in organizations: A multilevel perspective*. San Francisco: Jossey-Bass.
23. Burke, M. J., & Sarpy, S. A. (2003). Improving worker safety and health through interventions. In D. A. Hoffman & L. E. Tetrick (Eds.), *Health and safety in organizations: A multilevel perspective*. San Francisco: Jossey-Bass.
24. Probst, T. (2002). Layoffs and tradeoffs: Production, quality, and safety demands under the threat of job loss. *Journal of Occupational Health Psychology, 7(3),* 211–220.
25. Kaminksi, M. (2001). Unintended consequences: Organizational practices and their impact on workplace safety and productivity. *Journal of Occupational Health Psychology, 6(2),* 127–138.

Chapter 2

Legislative Framework

Chapter Learning Objectives

After reading this chapter, you should be able to

- describe the regulatory framework surrounding occupational health and safety
- outline the duties of the major players under occupational health and safety legislation
- describe the structure and role of joint health and safety committees
- list and describe the three central elements of a WHMIS program
- describe the purpose and basic provisions of the transportation of dangerous goods acts

The Right to Know

Eight workers were renovating classrooms at New Westminister Secondary School. On April 26, 2005, they removed the linoleum floor, the backing label, and the tiling. The work sent dust throughout the building, and some teachers complained to WorkSafeBC. Subsequent investigation revealed that the flooring, tiles, and backing material all contained traces of asbestos and that this information was available to the employer prior to the renovation. Because they did not know and were not informed, the workers involved in the renovation did not have the opportunity to refuse the unsafe work conditions or to acquire appropriate protective gear. In this case, the employer's failure to inform workers of their risk was deemed to be a serious violation and WorkSafeBC imposed fines.

This case illustrates one central feature of Canadian occupational health and safety legislation—the right of workers to be informed of or to know about hazards in the workplace. Other rights of workers and employers are discussed in this chapter.

Source: Workers weren't apprised of asbestos risk. (2007, January 30). *Canadian Occupational Health and Safety News.*

RPC 2.1

act
a federal, provincial, or territorial law that constitutes the basic regulatory mechanism for occupational health and safety

regulations
explain how the general intent of the act will be applied in specific circumstances

guidelines and policies
more specific rules that are not legally enforceable unless referred to in a regulation or act

standards and codes
design-related guides established by agencies such as the CSA or ANSI

Occupational health and safety is regulated under a variety of mechanisms, including acts, regulations, guidelines, standards, and codes. Moreover, each province and territory publishes its own regulations in addition to the federal regulations (see Occupational Health and Safety Notebook 2.1 for a complete list of regulations). Although this may seem confusing, the vast majority of workers and workplaces are regulated by provincial or territorial legislation. Thus, employers and employees who operate in one area typically have to be familiar with, and comply with, only one set of safety standards. The purpose of this section is to provide an overview of the regulatory framework for occupational health and safety.

An **act** is a federal, provincial, or territorial law that constitutes the basic regulatory mechanism for occupational health and safety. Each jurisdiction publishes an act that sets out the basic intent and the general rights and duties of individuals affected by the law. **Regulations** explain how the general intent of the act will be applied in specific circumstances. Typically developed by Ministry of Labour officials, regulations have the same force of law as the act. **Guidelines and policies** are more specific rules but are not legally enforceable unless referred to in a regulation or act. Finally, **standards and codes** are design-related guides. Standards are established by the Canadian Standards Association (CSA), the American National Standards Institute (ANSI), the International Labour Organization (ILO), the International Organization for Standardization (ISO), the National Institute for Occupational Safety and

Occupational Health and Safety Notebook 2.1

Occupational Health and Safety Legislation in Canada

Jurisdiction	Legislation Enforcement
Canada	Canada Labour Code, Regulations, Labour Canada
Alberta	Occupational Health and Safety Act, Department of Labour
British Columbia	Regulations under Workers' Compensation Board Compensation Act
Manitoba	Workplace Safety and Health Act, Department of Environment & Workplace Health and Safety
New Brunswick	Occupational Health and Safety Act, Occupational Health and Safety Commission
Newfoundland and Labrador	Occupational Health and Safety Act, Department of Labour
Northwest Territories and Nunavut	Northwest Safety Act, Commissioner of the Northwest Territories/Nunavut
Nova Scotia	Occupational Health and Safety Act, Department of Labour
Ontario	Occupational Health and Safety Act, Ministry of Labour
Prince Edward Island	Occupational Health and Safety Act, Department of Fisheries and Labour
Quebec	Act Respecting Occupational Health and Safety, Commission de la santé et de la sécurité du travail
Saskatchewan	Occupational Health and Safety Act, Department of Labour
Yukon	Occupational Health and Safety Act, Commissioner of the Yukon Territory, administered by the Workers' Compensation Board

Health (NIOSH), or the American Conference of Governmental Industrial Hygienists (ACGIH). Occupational health and safety regulations frequently refer to standards set by these last two agencies.

The Scope of OH&S Legislation

The scope of the OH&S legislation differs from jurisdiction to jurisdiction. The statutes and regulations that have been enacted to protect the rights of workers have also established duties that require compliance. The statutes provide the legal foundation, while the regulations enacted under the statute establish the framework within which the employer will conduct business in order to comply with the law.

Under common law, an employer is obliged to take reasonable precautions in ensuring the safety of an employee. This common-law duty is dormant in some jurisdictions, because it has been superseded by other legislation relating to Workers' Compensation. The compensation legislation either bars or limits the employer's duty by proscribing civil actions between employees and their employers in exchange for awards or pensions that may be allowed following an occupational accident or illness. All Canadian occupational health and safety legislation includes the following elements:

- an act
- powers of enforcement

- the right of workers to refuse to do unsafe work
- protection of workers from reprisals
- duties and responsibilities assigned to employers and others

Other elements, which differ among jurisdictions, include mandatory establishment of joint labour/management health and safety committees, health and safety policies, accident-prevention programs, and advisory councils on occupational health and safety.

Those responsible for the management of health and safety and Workers' Compensation should be familiar with the administrative structure as it relates to enforcement, education, and compensation in their particular jurisdiction. Multinational and transportation companies may fall under two or more jurisdictions, which increases the administrative complexities.

The general duty provision requiring employers to take every reasonable precaution to ensure employee safety is Canada-wide. In the federal jurisdiction, the duty is sufficiently broad in scope that an employer could be held liable for having failed to ensure the health and safety of an employee even if there was an absence of a specific violation to a regulatory provision. The term "ensure" is applied across Canada and is accepted to mean the strongest responsibility possible short of a guarantee.

It is important to note that labour legislation and standards relating to occupational health and safety are not static. Rather they are continually updated. Changes may be limited and specific, such as the current proposal to enact a regulation dealing with workplace violence in Nova Scotia. Or the changes can be more general, amounting to a complete overhaul of relevant legislation. For example, the Yukon published new and substantially updated occupational health and safety legislation in 2006. Human resource practitioners and safety professionals need to maintain current awareness of standards, regulations, and legislation.

Occupational Health and Safety Notebook 2.2

A New Standard for Safety

In 2006, the Canadian Standards Association published CSA Z1000-06 Occupational Health and Safety Management. The standard is based on wide consultation and described as "Canada's first consensus based approach to occupational heath and safety." The purpose of the standard is to provide organizations with a model for implementing a health and safety program. While standards do not have the force of legislation, they provide organizations with "best practices" and may provide the basis for a due diligence defence in the case of legal action.

Sources: CCOHS, "Canada's first consensus-based occupational health and safety management standard." Retrieved from http://www.ccohs.ca/headlines/text190.html, February 7, 2007; and CSA, "CSA announces new standard to help prevent Canadian workplace injuries and fatalities." Retrieved from http://www.ccohs.ca/headlines/text190.html, February 7, 2007.

Occupational Health and Safety Notebook 2.3

Canadian Government Departments Responsible for OH&S

Below are the websites for agencies across Canada that are responsible for occupational health and safety in federal, provincial, and territorial jurisdictions.

Federal	Occupational Health and Safety: Labour Program, Human Resources and Social Development Canada: http://www.hrsdc.gc.ca/en/home.shtml
Alberta	http://www.gov.ab.ca/hre/whs/
British Columbia	http://www.worksafebc.com
Manitoba	http://www.gov.mb.ca/labour/safety/
New Brunswick	http://www.whscc.nb.ca/
Newfoundland and Labrador	http://www.gov.nl.ca/gs/ohs/
Northwest Territories and Nunavut	http://www.gov.nt.ca
Nova Scotia	http://www.gov.ns.ca/enla/ohs/
Ontario	http://www.labour.gov.on.ca/english/hs/
Prince Edward Island	http://www.wcb.pe.ca
Quebec	http://www.csst.qc.ca
Saskatchewan	http://www.labour.gov.sk.ca
Yukon	http://www.wcb.yk.ca

Duties and Responsibilities of the Major Players

2.2

The statutes in most provinces and territories outline the duties and responsibilities of the major players in occupational health and safety. These include employers, owners, contractors, supervisors, and workers. Some provinces and territories also impose duties on joint health and safety committees or representatives, but the majority of jurisdictions are silent on this subject. The human resource practitioner should be well versed in labour laws and OH&S laws in order to make informed decisions about the corporation's health and safety program. The OH&S components attached to the various jurisdictions are listed in Occupational Health and Safety Notebook 2.3.

Duties of Employers, Owners, and Contractors

Employers have a primary duty to provide a safe work environment. Other duties include providing supervision, education, training, and written instructions where applicable, as well as assisting the joint health and safety committee or representative and complying with statutes and regulations. In Ontario, the employer's responsibilities are extensive and include the following:

- ensuring that equipment is provided and properly maintained
- appointing a competent supervisor

- providing information (including confidential information) in a medical emergency
- informing supervisors and workers of possible hazards
- posting the OH&S Act in the workplace
- preparing and maintaining a health and safety policy and reviewing it annually (see Occupational Health and Safety Today 2.1)

prescribed
under Ontario OH&S legislation, something to be undertaken because of legal or employer requirement, such as a rule or direction

All federal and provincial or territorial occupational health and safety acts include **prescribed** duties that may come into effect by regulation at some time. These prescribed duties may include an employer's responsibility to establish occupational health services, or a description of the written procedures that may be required.

Occupational Health and Safety Notebook 2.4

Jurisdictions and OH&S Components

Jurisdictions	Committees	Duties	Advisory Councils	Safety Policies	Accident-Prevention Programs
Canada	✔	✔		✔	
Alberta	Minister may order	✔	Report to Minister, may hear appeals, other duties as assigned	✔	
British Columbia	✔	✔		✔	✔
Manitoba	✔	✔	✔	✔	
New Brunswick	✔	✔		✔	
Newfoundland and Labrador	✔	✔		✔	
Northwest Territories/Nunavut	✔	✔		✔	✔
Nova Scotia	✔	✔	✔	Director may order a code of practice	
Ontario	Minister may order	✔	Sector-based advisory councils/ associations	✔	
Prince Edward Island	Minister may order	✔	✔	✔	
Quebec	Established by request of certified association, or Commission may order	✔	Sector-based advisory councils/ associations	Supply personal protective equipment free of charge	
Saskatchewan	✔	✔	✔	✔	
Yukon	✔			✔	

Occupational Health and Safety Today 2.1

Nelson Education Ltd.'s Safety Philosophy

Nelson Education Ltd.'s Health & Safety committee is vitally interested in the health and safety of its employees. Protection from injury or occupational disease is a major continuing objective of Nelson and we will make every effort to provide a safe, healthy working environment.

Nelson will meet and, where possible, exceed the letter and intent of all applicable legislation. Health & Safety will be managed as a priority area in Nelson with adequate resources and employee involvement in the development of programs. Objectives and standards will be established for health and safety programs, and performance will be measured. Hazards in the workplace will be identified and eliminated or controlled. Where hazards cannot be eliminated, programs will be put into place to safeguard the health and safety of the employees. Information necessary for the protection of our employees will be maintained and communicated to those affected.

Every employee must recognize and accept their own responsibility to work safely, maintain a safe workplace, and to report any and all unsafe conditions and practices immediately.

Constructors/primary contractors have responsibilities similar to those outlined for employers. In some jurisdictions, when a construction project is scheduled to commence, a constructor/primary contractor has a duty to notify the authority within a specified time. Some jurisdictions require a written "Notice of Project" to be filed outlining the approximate cost, scope, commencement date, and duration of the project.

constructor
in health and safety legislation, a constructor is a person or company who oversees the construction of a project and who is ultimately responsible for the health and safety of all workers

In Ontario, an owner or contractor is responsible for notification by way of tender when any designated substance (e.g., asbestos or UFI insulation) is likely to be encountered during a construction project. Designated substances are those substances, identified by regulation and requiring strict control, that could inflict either acute or chronic damage on a worker when ingested, inhaled, or absorbed in the body.

Duties of Supervisors

The duties assigned to supervisors are similar across Canada. "Supervisor" is broadly interpreted to refer to a person (with or without a title) who has charge of a workplace and authority over a worker. Supervisors can be union members, association members covered under a collective agreement, plant managers, general managers, lead hands, forepersons, school principals, or self-employed individuals. The criteria used in Ontario to determine whether a person would be held to be a supervisor include having the authority to promote or recommend promotion, to discipline workers, or to schedule or assign work. In addition to these criteria, in Ontario a competent supervisor is familiar with the OH&S Act and regulations and has knowledge of potential hazards, and so on, in the workplace (OH&S Act, s.1(1), 25(2)(c)). A supervisor's duties include the following:

- ensuring that workers comply with the OH&S Act and regulations
- ensuring that workers use or wear safety equipment, devices, or clothing

- advising workers of possible hazards
- providing written instructions if applicable
- taking every reasonable precaution to ensure the protection of workers

Duties of Workers

Duties of workers are included in the majority of statutes. In some jurisdictions, the responsibilities are laid out by regulation. The inclusion of workers' responsibilities and duties is relatively new in health and safety legislation. Before the late 1970s, all responsibility for workplace health and safety rested with the employer. Now, though the employer is totally responsible for paying for health and safety activities, everyone is responsible for making them work.

A worker's duties include the following:

- complying with the OH&S Act and regulations
- properly using the safety equipment and clothes provided
- reporting hazards, such as defective equipment, to the supervisor
- reporting any contraventions of the act or regulations

Workers are prohibited from making any safety device ineffective, using any hazardous equipment or machine in unsafe conditions, or engaging in rough or boisterous conduct.

Joint Health and Safety Committees

A recent addition to OH&S legislation is the creation of joint health and safety committees in the workplace. These committees are required by law in nine jurisdictions; the minister responsible has the discretionary power to require the formation of committees in the remaining four jurisdictions.

The primary function of the joint health and safety committee is to provide a nonadversarial atmosphere in which labour and management can work together to create a safer and healthier workplace. Joint committees are structured such that equal or better representation is required from workers who do not exercise managerial responsibilities. Each workplace requiring a committee must train and certify at least one management member and one worker member. Subjects taught during the training (which may run from one to three weeks) include law, general safety, hygiene, routes of entry (into the body), indoor air quality, chemical safety, certified workers' rights and duties, and joint committees. Certified members may be involved in inspections, work refusals, and bilateral work stoppage when there is an imminent hazard to a worker. They may also investigate critical accidents, attend at the beginning of hygiene testing, and respond to worker concerns.

The existence of joint health and safety committees grows out of the idea of an internal responsibility system (IRS)—the suggestion that work and safety are inexorably linked and that all parties in the workplace have a responsibility to improve health and safety.[1] A review of the literature generally supports the effectiveness of joint committees in managing health and safety.[2] In particular, the existence of joint health and safety committees leads to a reduction in the number of workplace injuries.[3] As Weil points out, the existence of a joint health and safety committee does not mean that the committee is effective.[4]

Occupational Health and Safety Notebook 2.5

Legislative Requirements for Joint Health and Safety Committees

Committees are mandatory in

Federal	Workplaces with 20 or more employees
Alberta	Workplaces that are required to establish a committee by the ministry
British Columbia	Workplaces with 20 or more employees
Manitoba	Workplaces with 20 or more employees
New Brunswick	Workplaces with 20 or more employees
Newfoundland and Labrador	Workplaces with 10 or more employees
Northwest Territories and Nunavut	As determined by the chief safety officer
Nova Scotia	Workplaces with 20 or more employees
Ontario	Workplaces with 20 or more employees
Prince Edward Island	Workplaces with 20 or more employees
Quebec	Workplaces where the union (or 10% of the workforce) requests the employer to establish a committee
Saskatchewan	Workplaces with 10 or more employees
Yukon	Workplaces with 20 or more employees

Indeed, like any other workplace group, committees may take some time before they become effective. Joint committees can improve health and safety through prevention, education, and training and by providing an ongoing forum for problem resolution.[5]

Occupational Health and Safety Notebook 2.6

Joint Health and Safety Committees at a Glance

Joint health and safety committees are made up of representatives from both management and unions or workers. They are charged with the responsibility of enhancing health and safety in the workplace.

Most health and safety legislation mandates the establishment of joint committees. For example, in Ontario the legislation requires a committee in workplaces with more than 20 employees, unless designated substances (such as asbestos) are present. The size of the committee varies with the number of employees, but the intent is to represent all areas of the workplace.

The committee has four principal functions:

1. identify potential hazards
2. evaluate these potential hazards
3. recommend corrective action
4. follow up implemented recommendations

To do so, the committee is required to meet regularly (at least every three months) and to regularly inspect the workplace. At least two members of the committee (one management and one labour) receive specialized training that meets standards established by the Workplace Safety and Insurance Board (in Ontario) and play more specialized roles as certified health and safety committee members.

Source: Ontario Ministry of Labour, "A guide for joint health and safety committees (JHSCs) and representatives in the workplace." Retrieved from http://www.gov.on.ca/LAB/english/hs/jhsc/, February 7, 2007.

Work Refusals

The right to refuse unsafe work without fear of reprisals is now available to workers in every jurisdiction in Canada. Exceptions or limitations to the right to refuse unsafe work vary across the country. In essence, a worker does not have the right to refuse unsafe work if the work is a normal condition of employment, or if the worker, by his or her refusal, places another life in jeopardy.

In Ontario, police, fire fighters, teachers, and health care workers are among those professionals who have been granted what is known as a limited right of refusal. For example, a fire fighter has the right to refuse to use unsafe equipment during an exercise. A nurse has the right to refuse to use equipment suspected to be defective until his or her concern has been investigated and resolved; however, a nurse does not have the right to refuse unsafe work if the lives of patients are placed in jeopardy as a result of the refusal. The Ontario Provincial Police had their old revolvers replaced by modern pistols after a refusal based on the defectiveness of the old units; other police services followed.

The procedure for reporting a refusal to perform unsafe work is, for the most part, consistent across jurisdictions. Once the worker has apprised the supervisor of the suspected work hazard, an investigation is conducted by the supervisor and a worker representative (union, joint health and safety committee member, or coworker).

The investigation results in either a return to work or a continued refusal. In the latter situation, a ministry inspector/officer conducts an investigation and then provides a written decision. In the meantime, a replacement worker may not be assigned the work that has been refused unless he or she has been informed about the circumstances surrounding the refusal. The refusing worker who continues to receive the regular remuneration for the job may be assigned alternative work but not sent home.

In New Brunswick and Prince Edward Island, the supervisor and joint health and safety committee can make a judgment that the refusal is not based on reasonable grounds. The employee may then refer the matter to an

Occupational Health and Safety Today 2.2

Farm Safety

As part of a new emphasis on workplace safety, the province of Ontario acted to put farms and farm safety under the provisions of the Occupational Health and Safety Act. Ontario had been one of only three provinces to exempt farming from the provisions of the act (PEI has also eliminated the farm exemption; Alberta continues the exemption). Under the new provisions farms will be required to have an occupational health and safety policy and a program to implement the policy. They will be required to conduct job hazard analysis and to develop safe work procedures. Like other workplaces, they will have a trained health and safety representative or committee (depending on size), will carry out regular inspections and training for all employees, and will conduct annual workplace audits.

Source: Keith, N., & Walsh, G. (2005). Bringing farms into the fold. *OH&S Canada, 21,* 50–51.

occupational health and safety officer, who will make the final determination. As "reasonable grounds" is not defined, it appears to leave the door open for a subjective rather than an objective decision being reached.

Stop-Work Provisions (Ontario)

In 1990, an Act to Amend the Ontario Occupational Health and Safety Act was given royal assent. The amendments are far reaching and promise profound changes in how employers will do business in Ontario. Among the most significant provisions are expanded powers for certified members of the joint health and safety committee.

The provisions for stopping work take two forms, one bilateral and the other unilateral. A certified member of a joint health and safety committee may, in the course of an inspection or investigation, have reason to believe that a dangerous circumstance exists. The certified member will ask a supervisor (and possibly a second certified member of the joint health and safety committee) to investigate. Following the investigation and possible remedial actions taken by the supervisor, if the certified members, representing both management and labour, find that the dangerous circumstance still exists, they may direct the employer to stop work. The legislation defines "dangerous circumstance" as follows:

- a provision of the act or the regulation is being contravened
- the contravention presents a danger or a hazard to a worker
- the danger or hazard is such that any delay in controlling it may seriously endanger a worker

The unilateral provision will apply in the case of an employer who has, in the opinion of a government-appointed adjudicator, taken insufficient steps to protect workers from serious risk to their health and safety. The action will be taken by a certified worker member. A second circumstance may allow the unilateral provision to apply. An employer may advise the joint health and safety committee in writing of a willingness to adopt the unilateral power of the certified worker member to stop work in dangerous circumstance; this advisory is required in Ontario.

Workplace Hazardous Materials Information System

The Workplace Hazardous Materials Information System (WHMIS) began in the United States in the early 1980s in the form of the Hazard Communication Standard. WHMIS reflects the belief that workers have the right to know about hazards that may be associated with certain chemicals used in the workplace, and, by extension, the community. In Ontario this right to know extends to citizens.

WHMIS is the brainchild of industry, labour, and government representatives committed to developing regulations that meet the right-to-know standard. In Canada, all jurisdictions were involved in creating the first Canada-wide health and safety legislation. The federal government created a model OH&S regulation that was used by the provincial and territorial governments to ensure the desired consistency in regulations. The Hazardous

Products Act defines a hazardous product and controls its use by requiring disclosure of the substance and its concentration in a manufactured product. Other federal statutes and regulations governing controlled products include the Controlled Products Regulations, the Ingredient Disclosure List, and the Hazardous Materials Review Act and related regulation.

The federal legislation, which was limited in application to federally regulated workplaces, required the provinces and territories to create enabling legislation to empower the jurisdictions. The WHMIS legislation came into force across Canada between 1988 and 1990. Workers now have a right to know about the potential hazards of any chemical they handle, including handling, storage, use, and emergency instructions.

The WHMIS legislation is based on three elements:

1. labels designed to alert the worker that the container contains a potentially hazardous product
2. material safety data sheets (MSDS) outlining a product's potentially hazardous ingredient(s) and procedures for safe handling of the product
3. employee training

Ontario added three further elements:

1. hazardous materials inventory requirement
2. physical agents (such as noise)
3. the public's right to know

Labels

That controlled substances need labelling is the most widely understood element of the WHMIS program. There are two types of WHMIS labels: workplace labels and supplier labels. Workplace labels identify the WHMIS class of the material. There are six WHMIS classes (some of which have subclasses) as follows:

- Class A—Compressed Gas
- Class B—Flammable and Combustible Material
  - Division 1: Flammable Gas
  - Division 2: Flammable Liquid
  - Division 3: Combustible Liquid
  - Division 4: Flammable Solid
  - Division 5: Flammable Aerosol
  - Division 6: Reactive Flammable Material
- Class C—Oxidizing Material
- Class D—Poisonous and Infectious Material
  - Division 1: Materials causing immediate and serious toxic effects
    - Subdivision A: Very toxic material
    - Subdivision B: Toxic material
  - Division 2: Materials causing other toxic effects
    - Subdivision A: Very toxic material
    - Subdivision B: Toxic material
  - Division 3: Biohazardous Infection Material

Class E—Corrosive Material
Class F—Dangerously Reactive Material
(See Figure 2.1 for WHMIS class symbols and subclass designations.)

FIGURE 2.1

WHMIS Class Symbols and Subclass Designations

What the symbol represents

Class A–
Compressed gas

Class D, Division 2–
Poisonous and
infectional material:
Other toxic effects

Class B–
Combustible and
flammable material

Class D, Division 3–
Poisonous and
infectional material:
Biohazardous
infectious material

Class C–Oxidizing
material

Class E–
Corrosive material

Class D, Division 1–
Poisonous and
infectious material:
Immediate and
serious toxic effects

Class F–
Dangerously
reactive material

The supplier label, the more comprehensive of the two, must be attached to the container when it is delivered to the workplace. (See Figure 2.2 for an example of a supplier label.) The supplier label must have a black-and-white border and must contain the following information (in both English and French):

1. The product identifier (Controlled Products Regulations, s.2(1)), including the brand name or code number. Information may include the chemical name, generic name, or trade name.
2. The supplier identifier (Controlled Products Regulations, s.2(1)); that is, the name of the manufacturer or supplier.
3. A statement that the material safety data sheet is to be referred to for more information.
4. Hazard symbol(s) (Controlled Products Regulations, s.11) that correspond to the class and division that allocates the product as a controlled substance.
5. Risk phrases (Controlled Products Regulations, s.2(1)) that correspond to the class and division to which the product is allocated.
6. Precautionary measures to be followed when handling or using the controlled product.
7. First-aid measures to be taken in the event of an exposure to a controlled product.

The requirement for workplace labels takes effect when the product is removed from its original container to be used or distributed. Workplace labels are also required for storage tanks or large in-house containers. The workplace label must contain a product identifier, safe-handling instructions, and the location of a material safety data sheet. (See Figure 2.3 for an example of a workplace label.)

Material Safety Data Sheets

The objective of safety data information is to identify potentially harmful ingredients in products that the worker may be handling, to present factual information about the nature of the harmful ingredients, and to provide guidance in the use and disposal of the product.

The material safety data sheet (MSDS) must contain information as set out by the Hazardous Products Act, s.11(1) and the Controlled Products Regulations, ss.12 and 13. (See Figure 2.4 for an example.) The information must be comprehensive, up to date (revisions are required every three years), and made available in the two official languages. The following nine sections form the minimum standard:

1. Product information including the name, address, and phone number of the supplier or manufacturer and the product identifier and use.
2. A hazardous ingredients list, including all controlled substances in the product and their concentrations. The list generally includes the chemical abstract number (when available); the allowable concentration limits, known as threshold limit values (TLV), set by the American Conference of Governmental Industrial Hygienists (ACGIH); the lethal-dose range tested for a specific animal population; and routes of entry.

FIGURE 2.2

Example of a Supplier Label

ISOPROPYL ALCOHOL

FLAMMABLE
HARMFUL IF INHALED
HARMFUL IF SWALLOWED
MAY CAUSE SKIN IRRITATION
MAY CAUSE EYE IRRITATION

First Aid: Obtain medical attention. Induce vomiting by sticking finger down throat. If breathing stopped, begin artificial respiration. If inhaled, remove victim to fresh air. For skin contact, wash with soap and water while removing contaminated clothing. For eye contact, flush with running water for at least 15 minutes, call physician.

Precautions: Wear chemical goggles. Wear resistant gloves. Do not take internally. Do not inhale vapour or mist. Use with enough ventilation to keep below TLV. Avoid skin or eye contact. Wash hands thoroughly after use. Keep container closed. Never use pressure to empty container. Do not reuse container for any purpose until commercially cleaned. Container must be grounded when emptied. Use explosion-proof equipment. Keep away from heat, sparks, and flame. No smoking. Do not keep near foodstuffs.

ALCOOL D'ISOPROPYLE

INFLAMMABLE
NOCIF SI INHALÉ
NOCIF SI AVALÉ
RISQUE D'IRRITATION CUTANÉE
RISQUE D'IRRITER LES YEUX

Premiers soins: Obtenir des soins médicaux. Faire vomir en enfonçant le doigt dans la gorge. En cas d'arrêt respiratoire, pratiquer la respiration artificielle. En cas d'inhalation, transporter la victime à l'air frais. En cas de contact avec la peau, laver au savon et à l'eau tout en retirant les vêtements souillés. En cas de contact avec les yeux, laver à l'eau courante pendant au moins 15 minutes. Appeler un médecin.

Mise en garde: Porter des lunettes antiproduits chimiques. Porter des gants résistants. Pour usage externe. Ne pas inhaler les vapeurs et les bruines. Utiliser avec assez de ventilation pour ne pas dépasser la QLP. Éviter tout contact avec la peau ou les yeux. Bien se laver les mains après utilisation. Garder le contenant fermé. Ne jamais utiliser de la pression pour vider le contenant. Ne pas réutiliser le contenant pour n'importe quel usage avant de l'avoir nettoyé professionnellement. Effectuer la prise de terre du contenant avant de le vider. Utiliser un equipment à l'épreuve des explosions. Tenir à l'écart des étincelles, des flammes et de la chaleur. Interdit de fumer. Ne pas garder à proximité d'aliments.

SEE MATERIAL SAFETY DATA SHEET FOR PRODUCT/ VOIR FICHE SIGNALÉTIQUE

Company X
Brampton, Ontario

FIGURE 2.3

Example of a Workplace Label

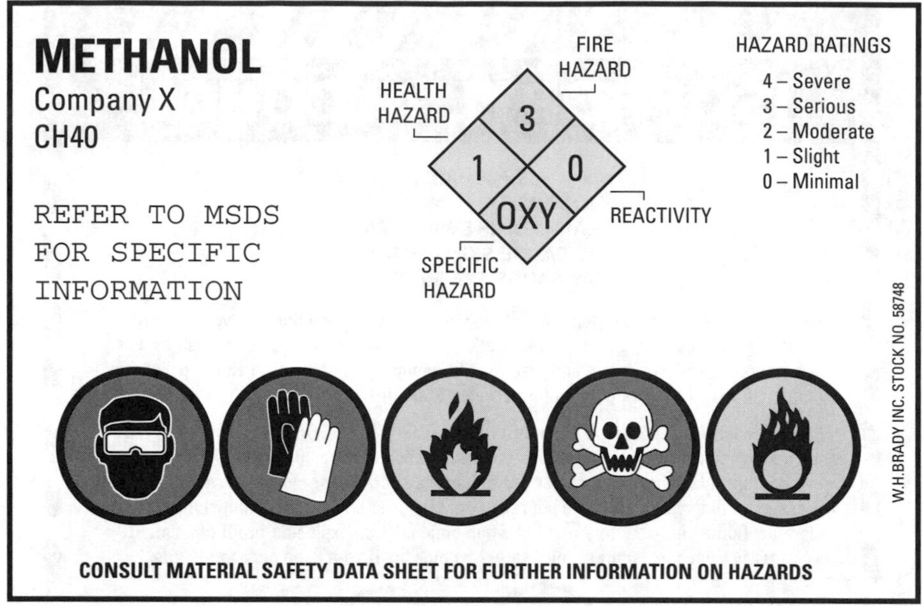

3. Physical data including information on appearance: odour, density, boiling point, corrosiveness, and so on.
4. Fire and explosion information, including data on the flammability of the hazardous ingredients.
5. Reactivity information outlining the conditions under which the material may react with other chemicals or materials. The section will also identify the hazardous products produced by decomposition in a fire situation.
6. Toxicological data including all available information on the possible health effects from chronic or acute exposure.
7. Preventive measures to be used while dealing with the product, including information on personal protective equipment, ventilation requirements, storage, handling, and waste disposal.
8. First-aid measures, providing specific recommendations for treatment for exposure to the material.
9. Preparation information, including the name of the person(s) who prepared the MSDS, a phone number for contact, and the date of issue of the MSDS.

The manufacturer or supplier must develop or cause to be developed an MSDS for each product supplied for use in the workplace. The MSDS must be transmitted to the purchaser on or before the date of sale or delivery of the product. The information on the MSDS must be current at the time of sale or delivery, and the MSDS must be dated no more than three years before the date of sale or delivery.

FIGURE 2.4

Material Safety Data Sheet

Form #CH3 **MATERIAL SAFETY DATA SHEET** name of product:

SECTION I – HAZARDOUS INGREDIENTS

Chemical Identity	Concentration	CAS Number	PIN Number	LD_{50} Species and Route	LC_{50} Species and Route

SECTION II – PREPARATION INFORMATION

Prepared by (Group, Department, Etc.)	Phone Number	Date of Preparation

SECTION III – PRODUCT INFORMATION

Product Identifier			
Manufacturer's Name		Supplier's Name	
Street Address		Street Address	
City	Province	City	Province
Postal Code	Emergency Tel. No.	Postal Code	Emergency Tel. No.
Product Use			

SECTION IV – PHYSICAL DATA

Physical State	Odour and Appearance		Odour Threshold
Specific Gravity (water = 1)	Co-efficient of Water/Oil Distribution		Vapour Pressure
Boiling Point (°C)	Freezing Point (°C)	pH	Vapour Density (Air = 1)
Evaporation Rate (BuAc = 1)		Percent Volatile (by volume)	

FIGURE 2.4

Material Safety Data Sheet (continued)

Form #CH3 **MATERIAL SAFETY DATA SHEET** name of product:

SECTION V - FIRE OR EXPLOSION HAZARD		
Conditions of Flammability		
Means of Extinction		
Explosion Data Sensitivity to Mechanical Impact	Sensitivity to Static Discharge	
Flashpoint (°C) and Method	Upper Flammable Limit %	Lower Flammable Limit %
Autoignition Temperature (°C)	Hazardous Combustion Products	

SECTION VI - REACTIVITY DATA
Stability
Incompatible Materials
Conditions of Reactivity
Hazardous Decomposition Products

SECTION VII - TOXICOLOGICAL PROPERTIES		
Route of Entry ☐ Skin Contact ☐ Skin Absorption ☐ Eye Contact ☐ Inhalation ☐ Ingestion		
Effects of Acute Exposure to Product		
Effects of Chronic Exposure to Product		
Exposure Limits	Irritancy of Product	Synergistic Products
Evidence of Carcinogenicity, Reproductive Toxicity, Teratogenicity or Mutagenicity?		Sensitization to Product

FIGURE 2.4

Material Safety Data Sheet (continued)

Form #CH3 **MATERIAL SAFETY DATA SHEET** name of product:

SECTION VIII- PREVENTIVE MEASURES	
Personal Protective Equipment	
Gloves (specify)	Respiratory (specify)
Eye (specify)	Footwear (specify)
Other Equipment (specify)	
Engineering Controls (e.g. ventilation, enclosed process, specify)	
Leak and Spill Procedure	
Waste Disposal	
Handling Procedures and Equipment	
Storage Requirements	
Special Shipping Information	
SECTION IX- FIRST AID MEASURES	
Inhalation	
Ingestion	
Eye Contact	
Skin Contact	

Additional Information	Sources Used

The requirement for supplying MSDS is twofold. Suppliers are regulated by the federal legislation under the Controlled Products Act and provincial or territorial regulations, while employers are regulated only under provincial or territorial regulations. Should an employer also be a manufacturer or produce research products not intended for sale, the responsibility for creating an MSDS becomes the employer's.

Training

Education in WHMIS is commonly defined as the process of acquiring knowledge through systematic instruction. By contrast, training is defined as bringing a person to a desired state or standard of efficiency by instruction and practice. One area that often escapes scrutiny when the inspector/officer applies a performance-based regulation is the application of the education received. A worker may know to check for labels, know where to find the MSDS, and know the employer's procedures for handling a spill; however, the same worker may not know how to read the MSDS or understand it in sufficient depth to apply it in the workplace. Training and education should include a practical process to ensure that the worker understands how to apply the knowledge acquired.

After completing a training program, the worker should understand the purpose and origin of WHMIS and be able to

- identify WHMIS hazard symbols
- read WHMIS supplier and workplace labels
- read and apply the applicable information on an MSDS

The WHMIS program must be reviewed annually or as changes occur in products or processes in the workplace.

Environmental Legislation

Environmental and occupational health and safety legislation are solidly entwined. In recognition of this fact, many companies and institutions have occupational environmental health and safety departments. The health and safety professional will be conscious of the overlap in environmental and OH&S statutes and regulations. Chemicals that can cause damage to a worker may also cause damage to the ecosystem if released into the environment. Federal and provincial or territorial statutes relating to some aspect of environmental or health and safety management are listed in Occupational Health and Safety Notebooks 2.7 and 2.8.

Occupational Health and Safety Notebook 2.7

Federal Statutes Relevant to OH&S

Canadian Environmental Protection Act, R.S.C. 1985
Hazardous Products Act, R.S.C. 1985
Canadian Charter of Rights and Freedoms, Part I of the Constitution Act 1982
Pest Control Products Act, R.S.C. 1985
Radiation Protection Act, R.S.C. 1985
Radiation Emitting Devices Act, R.S.C. 1985
Transportation of Dangerous Goods Act, 1992, S.C. as amended
Canada Labour Code, Part IV

Regulatory legislation related to environmental assessment, public health, waste disposal, buried fuel tanks, and storage or use of pesticides affects the environment, the occupational health and safety of employees, and the public. As the following scenario indicates, the practitioner is required to understand environmental and OH&S jurisdictions and the potential for overlap:

> If a release of a potentially hazardous substance occurs within a building (other than residential) it falls under the jurisdiction of the authority enforcing the health and safety legislation. If the release is outside the building, or if the potentially hazardous substance is released into the sewer, storm system, water, or air, it falls under the jurisdiction of the authority enforcing the environmental legislation. Any single occurrence might involve both authorities.

The parallels between environmental and OH&S legislation have extended to the courts. In *R. v. Bata Industries Ltd., Bata, Marchant and Weston,* Bata Industries Ltd. and three of its directors were charged with allowing a large chemical waste storage site containing many deteriorating and leaking containers to discharge known toxic industrial chemicals into the ground environment. The defendants used the defence of due diligence, arguing that the legislation was vague and imprecise and contrary to the Canadian Charter of Rights and Freedoms. The company was convicted, as were two of the directors (the third director was acquitted). The court found that the two defendants had not exercised due diligence. The court stated that although it did not expect a board of directors to make all environmental decisions, these decisions were too important to be delegated to subordinates.

Occupational Health and Safety Notebook 2.8

Provincial and Territorial Statutes

Province	Transportation	Environment	Other
Alberta	Transportation of Dangerous Goods Act, S.A. 1982	Environmental Protection and Enhancement Act, S.A. 1992	
British Columbia	Transportation of Dangerous Goods Act, S.B.C. 1985	Waste Management Act, S.B.C. 1982/Amended 1990, 1992	
Manitoba	Dangerous Goods Handling and Transportation Act, R.S.M. 1987	Environment Act, S.M. 1987–88/Waste Reduction and Prevention Act, S.M. 1989–90	
New Brunswick	Transportation of Dangerous Goods Act, S.N.B. 1988		
Newfoundland and Labrador	Dangerous Goods Transportation Act, R.S.N. 1990	Department of Environment and Lands Act, R.S.N. 1990/ Waste Material Disposal Act, R.S.N. 1990/Water Protection Act, R.S.N. 1990	
Northwest Territories and Nunavut	Transportation of Dangerous Goods Act, 1990, S.N.W.T.		
Nova Scotia	Dangerous Goods Transportation Act, R.S.N.S. 1989	Environment Act (draft)/Litter Abatement Act, S.N.S. 1989	
Ontario	Dangerous Goods Transportation Act, R.S.O. 1990	Environmental Protection Act, R.S.O. 1990 as amended/ Environmental Bill of Rights, 1993, S.O. 1993/Ontario Water Resources Act, R.S.O. 1990/Waste Management Act, R.S.O. 1992/Environmental Assessment Act	Gasoline Handling Act, S.O. 1990/Health Protection and Promotion Act, R.S.O. 1990/ Municipal Act, R.S.O. 1990/ Pesticides Act, R.S.O. 1990/Public Health Act, R.S.O. 1980/Energy Act, R.S.O. 1990
Prince Edward Island	Dangerous Goods Transportation Act, R.S.P.E.I. 1988	Environmental Protection Act, R.S.P.E.I. 1988	
Quebec		Environmental Quality Act, R.S.Q. 1990	
Saskatchewan	Dangerous Goods Transportation Act, S.S. 1984–85–86	Litter Control Act, R.S.S. 1978	
Yukon	Dangerous Goods Transportation Act, R.S.Y.T. 1986	Environment Act, S.Y. 1991	

Transportation of Dangerous Goods

The regulation of environmental hazards, occupational health and safety, and transportation of dangerous goods is not the exclusive domain of either the federal, provincial, or territorial governments. Therefore, the practitioner should be familiar with the statutes relevant to his or her particular jurisdiction. In essence, the environmental and transportation legislation seeks to supply the framework within which society can protect itself from the risk that attends the transportation of inherently dangerous materials.

The federal legislation governing the transportation of dangerous goods applies to all persons who handle, offer for transport, transport, or import any dangerous goods. The provincial or territorial legislation does not always go this far, making it sometimes impossible to determine which statutes apply. Notwithstanding some provincial or territorial limitations, dangerous goods legislation applies to carriers, shippers, and transportation intermediaries such as freight forwarders and customs brokers. Various regulations exist with respect to the identification and placarding of dangerous goods, the control of quantities, and the training and certification of workers. The regulatory wording complements the WHMIS requirements and the OH&S responsibility of employers and supervisors to educate and train workers.

In *R. v. Midland Transport Ltd.* (1991), the New Brunswick Provincial Court made the following observation about the legislation:

> The Transportation of Dangerous Goods Act and the Regulations thereunder with the act fall in the category of legislation which creates public welfare offences. Recognizing the potential dangers, it establishes safety guidelines for the handling of hazardous materials to ensure the protection of the public and the environment.

Corporate Liability

Whereas in the past directors and officers of incorporated entities were responsible solely to the corporation and shareholders, their zone of accountability now extends to the public at large. Environmental and occupational health and safety statutes have been amended to include broad responsibilities for directors and officers. The liabilities that directors and officers now face include the following:

- fines or imprisonment for corporate pollution causing or permitting the discharge of liquid industrial waste into the ground
- cleanup costs associated with a property the corporation owns, controls, or occupies
- fines for failing to comply with regulatory legislation

Canadian jurisprudence has followed the lead of the United States in extending legal responsibility to the boardroom. The executives of a company are no longer permitted to hide behind the laws of incorporation.

Occupational Health and Safety Today 2.3

Corporate Killing: The Westray Legislation

Bill C-45 deals with issues of corporate liability with respect to both fraud and occupational health and safety; the Bill was passed by Parliament in 2003 and became law in March 2004. The so-called "Westray legislation" makes company executives more accountable when workers are killed or injured on the job because of management negligence. It is named after the Westray tragedy, in which a mine explosion was attributed to corporate negligence (see Chapter 1). Ultimately, it could lead to a corporation and its management being criminally prosecuted if found negligent in providing an appropriate standard of occupational health and safety in the workplace resulting in an employee injury or death. This brings the notion of "corporate homicide" into the Canadian Criminal Code for the first time.

The act makes a company responsible for

- the actions of those who oversee day-to-day operations (e.g., supervisors and mid-level managers)
- managers (either executive or operational) who intentionally commit, or have employees commit, crimes to benefit the organization
- managers who do not take action when they become aware of offences being committed
- the actions of managers who demonstrate a criminal lack of care (i.e., criminal negligence)

Passage of the Westray legislation substantially raises the stakes for managers and corporations. In addition to introducing criminal liability into the OH&S arena, the act takes away the ability of the company to shift blame to frontline managers. That is, companies are now responsible not only for ensuring that frontline staff know the appropriate rules, regulations, and working procedures, but also that employees follow the procedures. It is no longer possible to claim that employees were derelict in their responsibility—even if true, the company is liable.

The passage of Bill C-45 was greeted with great fanfare; the first charges (relating to the death of a construction worker) were laid in 2004 but were subsequently withdrawn in 2005. To date, there have been no successful charges under the act and there is some concern that the law has no "teeth" in practice. Whenever charges can be laid under the safety legislation (provincial) or the Criminal Code (federal), the preference seems to be for safety legislation to prevail. C-45 is likely to be invoked in only the most severe, egregious, and atypical cases. As a result, many who heralded the new stricter legislation are now expressing disappointment in the actual functioning of the law.

Sources: Department of Justice Canada, "Parliament passes Bill C-45: Stronger laws affecting the criminal liability of organizations." Retrieved from http://canada.justice.gc.ca/en/ news/nr/2003/doc_31024.html, February 7, 2007; and Vu, U. (2006, June 29). "Unions decry lack of charges under 'corporate killing' law," *Canadian HR Reporter*.

Summary

The complexities associated with OH&S legislation in Canada continue to grow. This chapter has outlined the scope of this legislation and the changing climate surrounding it. In particular we focused on some of the duties of each of the major stakeholders under the legislation and the role of joint health and safety committees. The elements composing the Workplace Hazardous Materials Information System were reviewed and some consideration was given to ancillary legislation (e.g., environmental, transportation of dangerous goods).

Key Terms

act 24
constructor 29
guidelines and policies 24
prescribed 28
regulations 24
standards and codes 24

Weblinks

Canadian General Standards Board

http://www.pwgsc.gc.ca/cgsb/home/index-e.html (p. 25)

Canadian Standards Association

http://www.csa.ca (p. 25)

Standards Council of Canada

http://www.scc.ca (p. 25)

Underwriters' Laboratories of Canada

http://www.ulc.ca (p. 25)

American National Standards Institute

http://www.ansi.org (p. 25)

American Society for Testing and Materials

http://www.astm.org (p. 25)

International Organization for Standardization

http://www.iso.org/iso/en/ISOOnline.frontpage (p. 25)

Ontario Ministry of Labour, "Joint Health and Safety Committees"

http://www.labour.gov.on.ca/english/hs/ohsaguide/ohsag_4.html (p. 30)

Ontario Ministry of Labour, "The Right to Stop Work"

http://www.labour.gov.on.ca/english/hs/ohsaguide/ohsag_8.html (pp. 32, 33)

Health Canada, "Workplace Hazardous Materials Information System (WHMIS)"

http://www.hc-sc.gc.ca/hecs-sesc/whmis/ (p. 33)

RPC Icons

RPC 2.1 Provides input on matters related to the drafting and/or application of legislation or regulations related to health, safety security, and Workers' Compensation.

- legislation
- process and means of influencing legislative change
- linkages with change agents (e.g., HR Associations, interest groups, politicians, bureaucrats)
- report writing
- Common and statutory law (e.g., employment standard: labour relations)
- Worker Protection (including health and safety and Workers' Compensation)
- Theories and practices for protection of individuals and groups
- Occupational health and safety legislation (e.g., Occupational Health and Safety Act of Ontario, Workplace Safety & Insurance Act—Bill 99, Workplace Hazardous Materials Information System, Transportation of Dangerous Goods legislation, environmental legislation, smoking in the workplace legislation, civil rights legislation)

RPC 2.2 Ensures that security programs and policies minimize risks while considering the obligation of the employer and the rights of employees, union, and third parties.

- nature of the business and physical work environment
- relevant legislation
- industry best practices
- program and policy development
- safety and security equipment in the workplace
- risk assessment/techniques
- cost/benefit analysis

Task & Knowledge Requirements

- available community resources
- Worker Protection (including health and safety and Workers' Compensation)
- Unions' role in health and safety and in employee involvement
- Occupational health and safety legislation (e.g., Occupational Health and Safety Act of Ontario, Workplace Safety & Insurance Act—Bill 99, Workplace Hazardous Materials Information System, Transportation of Dangerous Goods legislation, environmental legislation, smoking in the workplace legislation, civil rights legislation)
- Emergency preparedness procedures
- Management techniques for OH&S Programs
- Types of employee assistance and wellness programs

RPC 2.3 Establishes a joint responsibility system as required by law, e.g. worker-management Health & Safety committees, investigations, audits, testing and training, to ensure employee safety.

- relevant Occupational Health and Safety legislation
- inspection techniques and procedures
- hazard recognition
- principles of training and development

Task & Knowledge Requirements

- program and policy development
- audit processes
- Joint Health and Safety Committee functions
- Worker Protection (including health and safety and Workers' Compensation)
- Occupational health and safety legislation (e.g., Occupational Health and Safety Act of Ontario, Workplace Safety & Insurance Act—Bill 99, Workplace Hazardous Materials Information System, Transportation of Dangerous Goods legislation, environmental legislation, smoking in the workplace legislation, civil rights legislation)
- Management techniques for OH&S Programs

RPC 2.4 Responds to any refusals to perform work believed to be unsafe.

- relevant Occupational Health and Safety legislation
- procedure for dealing with work refusals
- policy and program development
- conflict resolution procedures
- emergency procedures
- government inspection agencies such as the Ministry of Labour
- Common and statutory law (e.g., employment standard: labour relations
- Worker Protection (including health and safety and Workers' Compensation)
- Communication theories and techniques
- Concepts and processes of politics and conflict
- Occupational health and safety legislation (e.g., Occupational Health and Safety Act of Ontario, Workplace Safety & Insurance Act—Bill 99, Workplace Hazardous Materials Information System, Transportation of Dangerous Goods legislation, environmental legislation, smoking in the workplace legislation, civil rights legislation)
- Hazard identification and control

RPC 2.5 Implements and evaluates practices in the areas of health, safety, security, and Workers' Compensation.

- investigative techniques
- hazard recognition

- disaster recovery techniques
- relevant legislation
- resource information
- common health and safety practices
- company policies and procedures
- Worker Protection (including health and safety and Workers' Compensation)
- Theories and practices for protection of individuals and groups
- Occupational health and safety legislation (e.g., Occupational Health and Safety Act of Ontario, Workplace Safety & Insurance Act—Bill 99, Workplace Hazardous Materials Information System, Transportation of Dangerous Goods legislation, environmental legislation, smoking in the workplace legislation, civil rights legislation)
- Hazard identification and control
- Management techniques for OH&S Programs

Discussion Questions

1. What are the three fundamental workers' rights that underlie most health and safety legislation?
2. What is the difference between the responsibilities assigned to companies under occupational health and safety and those assigned under environmental legislation?
3. What three components make up WHMIS compliance?
4. Describe the structure and role of joint health and safety committees.

Using the Internet

1. What legislation applies in your jurisdiction? Find the body responsible for occupational health and safety and review the legislation. What are the major provisions and their implications for employers? for employees? for human resource managers?
2. WHMIS training is widely available online. Using a search engine and keywords such as "WHMIS online training," find a local provider of online WHMIS training.

Exercise

1. Health and safety legislation can be crafted following different approaches. One approach is to force compliance through establishing standards, conducting rigorous inspections on a regular basis, and harshly punishing failures to meet the established standards. A second approach is to facilitate self-reliance by providing the parties with the information and resources necessary to monitor and enhance

health and safety in their workplaces. What are the relative merits of these two approaches? What advantages and disadvantages accrue under each system? What is the appropriate balance between enforcement and encouragement?

Case 1

Workplace Tragedy

An auto-parts manufacturer employs 500 workers. The plant operates on three shifts, and its various lines include large punch presses, conveyors, paint-spray booths, and overhead cranes. A worker has been killed following an accident on the overhead-crane line. The worker was guiding the load hoisted by the crane when the load slipped, causing a failure of the supporting cables. The worker was killed when the falling load struck him. Although this is the most serious accident, there have been several others at the plant in the past. As plant manager, you are responsible for ensuring the safety of your employees. Outline the steps you plan to take to improve health and safety in the plant.

Case 2

Work Refusal at Regional Hospital

Regional Hospital is a 100-bed acute-care facility providing services to a mid-sized Canadian city. Recently, the hospital took advantage of a special government grant to develop and operate an HIV-treatment ward. Although the ward is now open, there is considerable disquiet among the staff. Two nurses have refused to work their assigned shift on the ward, claiming that it is their right to refuse unsafe work. Moreover, workers have been petitioning their certified representative on the Joint Health and Safety Committee to close the workplace because of the safety standard. As the HR representative for Regional Hospital, what is your planned response? How do you balance the workers' right to refuse unsafe work against the need to staff the ward?

WHMIS Regulations Consulted
Model OH&S Regulations

Alberta	Chemical Hazards Regulation
British Columbia	Workplace Hazardous Materials Information System Regulations
Manitoba	Workplace Hazardous Materials Information System Regulations
New Brunswick	Workplace Hazardous Materials Information System Regulations
Newfoundland and Labrador	Workplace Hazardous Materials Information System Regulations

Northwest Territories/Nunavut	Work Site Hazardous Materials Information System Regulations
Nova Scotia	Workplace Hazardous Materials Information System Regulations
Ontario	Workplace Hazardous Materials Information System Regulations
Prince Edward Island	Workplace Hazardous Materials Information System Regulations
Quebec	An Act to Amend the Act respecting Occupational Health and Safety
Saskatchewan	The Occupational Health and Safety Act 1993, Part IV, Workplace Hazardous Materials Information System
Yukon	Workplace Hazardous Materials Information System Regulations

Endnotes

1. Strahlendorf, P. (2007). Is your committee effective? *OH&S Canada, 23,* 24–31.
2. Kelloway, E. K. (2003). Labor unions and safety. In J. Barling & M. Frone (Eds.), *Psychology of occupational safety*. Washington, DC: APA Books.
3. Reilly, B., Paci, P., & Holl, P. (1995). Unions, safety committees, and workplace injuries. *British Journal of Industrial Relations, 33,* 275–288.
4. Weil, D. (1999). Are mandated health and safety committees substitutes for or supplements to labor unions? *Industrial and Labor Relations Review, 52,* 339–361.
5. Weil, D. (1995). Mandating safety and health committees: Lessons from the United States. *Proceedings of the 47th annual meeting of the Industrial Relations Research Association* (pp. 273–281), Madison, WI.

Chapter 3

Workers' Compensation

Chapter Learning Objectives

After reading this chapter, you should be able to

- outline the goals and methods of Workers' Compensation Boards (WCBs)
- discuss the problems associated with compensating for psychological conditions and occupational illnesses
- describe the assessment methods of WCBs
- with the use of the chapter appendix, understand the methods of calculating injury frequency and severity rates

Should Safety Be Equated with Workers' Compensation?

In any discussion of occupational health and safety the focus will soon switch to workers' compensation. As was evident in Chapter 1, Workers' Compensation Boards are the main purveyors of accident statistics, and provincial/territorial health and safety policies are frequently driven by trends in the workers' compensation data. There are good reasons for equating safety and workers' compensation. Compensation premiums are a major cost for organizations and provide an economic lever through which companies can be induced to focus on workplace safety. There are also good reasons why we should not rely solely on workers' compensation data as a source of policy or information. Since workers' compensation rates are based on the number of claims filed there are strong incentives for employers not to file claims. Individuals may also avoid filing legitimate claims either because of the complexity of the process or the perception that their injuries are not that severe. Some data indicate that up to 40 percent of injuries remain unreported. In terms of the insurance function of workers' compensation it might seem acceptable to report only the most serious injuries (thereby reducing the costs of compensation). However, when workers' compensation claims become the main source of accident statistics it means that our understanding and monitoring of workplace safety is systematically biased. In effect, we may be underestimating the number and type of workplace incidents and, as a result, mismanaging occupational health and safety.

Sources: Azaroff, L. S., Levenstein, C., & Wegman, D. (2002). Occupational injury and illness surveillance: Conceptual filters explain underreporting. *American Journal of Public Health, 92,* 1421–1429; Rosenman, K. D., Gardiner, J. C., & Wang, J. (2000). Why most workers with occupational repetitive trauma do not file for workers' compensation. *Journal of Occupational and Environmental Medicine, 42,* 25–34; Shannon, H., & Lowe, G. S. (2002). How many injured workers do not file claims for workers' compensation benefits? *American Journal of Industrial Medicine, 42,* 467–473; and Thompson, A. (2007). The consequences of underreporting workers' compensation claims. *CMAJ, 176(3),* 343–344.

Workers' Compensation is a form of insurance governed by an act of Parliament to help workers who are injured on the job to return to work. Consider the example of a construction labourer who has sustained an injury on the job and is now unable to work because of a disability. Workers' Compensation will ensure that the injured worker receives (1) first-aid treatment, either on the job or at the nearest local treatment facility, (2) benefits while at home recuperating, and (3) proper treatment for any injuries. If necessary, rehabilitation will be provided to help the worker return to his or her former job or some modified version of it, if circumstances dictate.

Historical Roots

Workers' Compensation has its origin in Germany in 1884 but was not established in Canada until 1914, when the Ontario Workmen's Compensation Act was passed by Parliament. This time lag was something of an advantage, because it allowed for consideration of the American and European experience (the federal Employers' Liability Act was passed in the United States in 1908). In 1900, the Ontario government inquired into the German system. This was followed in 1912–1914 by an intensive and prolonged study of the existing laws in other European countries and in the United States, under the guidance of Sir William Ralph Meredith, Chief Justice of Ontario. On the basis of his findings, the first act in Canada was passed.

Acts were subsequently passed in all provinces and territories, and although they have been amended many times (largely for the purpose of increasing coverage and benefits), they have retained many of the principles set forth in the Ontario act of 1914:

1. collective liability for employers, with some recognition of risk in the amount of contribution paid by individual employers
2. compensation for workers regardless of the financial condition of the employer
3. compensation based on loss of earnings
4. a "no-fault" system
5. a nonadversarial process: little or no recourse to the courts (in Ontario, Schedule 2 can allow legal recourse)

In essence, the implementation of Workers' Compensation systems is a tradeoff for both workers and employers. Workers receive an assurance that they will be compensated for injury without having to undertake expensive and lengthy lawsuits, but in return they accept the authority of the Workers' Compensation Boards to determine the amount of any compensation. Employers take on the obligation of paying for the Workers' Compensation system but are protected from litigation that could drive them into bankruptcy.[1]

Workers' Compensation in Canada

Administration and Responsibilities

RPC 3.2

The provincial and territorial acts throughout Canada are administered by Workers' Compensation Board (WCB) members who are appointed by the lieutenant governor in council within each jurisdiction and who hold office at the lieutenant governor's pleasure. The various boards are empowered to fix and collect assessment, determine the right to compensation, and pay the amount due to the injured worker. In all these matters, the Workers' Compensation system has exclusive and final jurisdiction. The Ontario act is representative of the type of legislation that exists in all jurisdictions in terms of its authority and power.

The regulations and responsibilities of Workers' Compensation Boards are as follows:

- The injured worker will receive payment while off work and will have all medical bills paid if the injury happened at work and because of work.
- The injured worker will receive a pension if the disability is or becomes permanent.
- The injured worker will receive benefits if he or she cannot earn the same amount of money earned before the accident.
- The injured worker's immediate family and dependants will be entitled to benefits if the worker is killed or dies as a result of an injury on the job.
- The Workers' Compensation Boards classify employers to ensure consistency.
- The Workers' Compensation Boards decide whether an individual is classified as a worker, a subcontractor, or an employer, as each class has different conditions.
- The Workers' Compensation system can pay benefits if a worker is affected by an industrial disease that has resulted from his or her occupation.

In addition to these regulations and responsibilities, the Board—now the WSIB following the passage of the Workers' Compensation Reform Act in 1998—added a prevention emphasis to the traditional compensation functions.

The addition of prevention to the mandate of Workers' Compensation Boards is increasingly common across Canada. WCBs have focused on prevention by offering premium reductions based on safety records. For example, Alberta reduced premiums in 2006 to a provincial average of $1.57/$100 of payroll, with a further reduction forecast for 2007—approximately the same rate as was levied more than 20 years ago. Most jurisdictions are either reducing their rate or holding it steady (see Occupational Health and Safety Today 3.1). In addition to the reduction in general premiums, employers in Alberta (and some other provinces—see the discussion in this chapter on the use of experience rating) can achieve further premium reductions of up to 20 percent from the industry rate based on their safety performance. Conversely, organizations with a poor safety record may be charged a surcharge to reflect the increased costs of insurance.

A mandate for prevention also means that WCBs are actively involved in trying to prevent accidents. WCBs provide a wide range of information for employers and employees on safety-related matters. For example, WorkSafeBC maintains a large online library of safety-related publications. The WCB in Alberta offers a Certificate of Recognition (COR) to organizations that have implemented safety programs that meet its standards. In many jurisdictions in Canada, Workers' Compensation Boards provide extensive resources to both employers and individuals interested in health and safety issues.

Occupational Health and Safety Today 3.1

Workers' Compensation Premiums (averages per $100 of payroll)

	2006	2007 (forecast)
Alberta	$1.57	$1.43
British Columbia	$1.90	$1.69
Manitoba	$1.68	$1.68
New Brunswick	$2.14	$2.10
Newfoundland and Labrador	$2.75	Unavailable
Northwest Territories/Nunavut	$1.87	$1.71
Nova Scotia	$2.65	$2.65
Ontario	$2.26	$2.26
Prince Edward Island	$2.23	Unavailable
Quebec	$2.32	$2.24
Saskatchewan	$1.84	$1.84
Yukon	$2.16	$2.64

Source: Association of Workers' Compensation Boards of Canada, "Provisional average assessment rates, per $100.00 payroll." Retrieved from http://www.awcbc.org/english/Assessment_provisional_rates.asp, February 7, 2007.

In relation to most of the industries within the scope of the provincial or territorial acts, the system of compensation is one of compulsory and collective liability. Under collective liability, the various industries are classified according to their size and end product, and each employer is assessed a rate that is a percentage of its payroll. The percentage is determined by the injury cost of its classification. From the accident fund thus collected, payments are made for compensation, medical aid, rehabilitation, accident prevention, and administrative expenses. Each employer is liable for assessment, irrespective of the cost of injuries sustained by its workers. As a result, each is relieved of individual liability. In most jurisdictions, liability is further distributed by a disaster reserve fund.

Public authorities and certain large corporations such as railways and shipping or telegraph companies have a different liability approach from the collective liabilities scheme and are individually liable for compensation; however, all disputes are settled by the WCB. Such corporations contribute their portion of the cost of administering the various acts.

Most WCBs, at one time, had responsibility for the accident-prevention or OH&S aspects of Workers' Compensation. In the 1970s and 1980s, the combined role was seen as a conflict of interest by some governments, and these WCB functions were placed under a government department in most provinces and territories (e.g., the Department of Labour). Although the OH&S function is separate in most jurisdictions (with B.C. being an exception), all WCBs cooperate with the responsible government department by sharing information. Several WCBs have input into the experience rating or

Occupational Health and Safety Notebook 3.1

Contact Information for the Provincial and Territorial Workers' Compensation Boards

Workers' Compensation Board of Alberta
P.O. Box 2415
9912-107 Street Edmonton AB T5J 2S5
Tel: 780-498-3999 Fax: 780-498-7999
Home page: http://www.wcb.ab.ca

Workers' Compensation Board of British Columbia
P.O. Box 5350 Vancouver BC V6B 5L5
Tel: 604-273-2266 Fax: 604-276-3140
Home page: http://www.worksafebc.com

Workers Compensation Board of Manitoba
333 Broadway Winnipeg MB R3C 4W3
Tel: 204-954-4321 Fax: 204-954-4968
Home page: http://www.wcb.mb.ca

Workplace Health, Safety and Compensation Commission of New Brunswick
1 Portland Street P.O. Box 160 Saint John NB E2L 3X9
Tel: 506-632-2200 Fax: 506-632-4999
Home page: http://www.whscc.nb.ca

Workplace Health, Safety and Compensation Commission of Newfoundland and Labrador
146-148 Forest Road P.O. Box 9000 Station B St. John's NL A1A 3B8
Tel: 709-778-1000 Fax: 709-738-1714
Home page: http://www.whscc.nf.ca

Workers' Compensation Board of the Northwest Territories & Nunavut
P.O. Box 8888 Yellowknife NT X1A 2R3
Tel: 867-920-3888 Fax: 867-873-4596
Home page: http://www.wcb.nt.ca

Workers' Compensation Board of Nova Scotia
5668 South Street P.O. Box 1150 Halifax NS B3J 2Y2
Tel: 902-491-8000 Fax: 902-491-8002
Home page: http://www.wcb.ns.ca

Workplace Safety and Insurance Board of Ontario
200 Front Street West Toronto ON M5V 3J1
Tel: 416-344-1000 Fax: 416-344-3999
Home page: http://www.wsib.on.ca

Workers Compensation Board of Prince Edward Island
14 Weymouth Street Charlottetown PEI C1A 4Y1
Tel: 902-368-5680 Fax: 902-368-5705
Home page: http://www.wcb.pe.ca

Commission de la santé et de la sécurité du travail
1199 rue de Bleury C.P. 6056 Succursale "centre-ville" Montréal QC H3C 4E1
Tel: 514-873-7183 Fax: 514-873-7007
Home page: http://www.csst.qc.ca

Workers' Compensation Board of Saskatchewan
200, 1881 Scarth Street Regina SK S4P 4L1
Tel: 306-787-4370 Fax: 306-787-2513
Home page: http://www.wcbsask.com

Yukon Workers' Compensation Health & Safety Board
401 Strickland Street Whitehorse YK Y1A 5N8
Tel: 867-667-5645 Fax: 867-393-6279
Home page: http://www.wcb.yk.ca

merit/demerit program and work with government in developing programs designed to reduce workplace injuries. Employers or injured workers who disagree with a WCB decision can turn to various appeal bodies and mechanisms. In Prince Edward Island, Saskatchewan, and Yukon, the WCB is the final level of appeal.

Because jurisdictions sometimes provide different benefits, most WCBs within Canada enter into agreements among themselves to avoid duplicate assessments and to assist the worker in claiming and receiving compensation when two or more jurisdictions are involved. These agreements are intended to ensure that the worker receives the best possible benefits and that coverage is extended in a province or territory, often at the request of the injured worker.

The provincial or territorial acts generally cover all employment in industries such as lumbering, mining, fishing, manufacturing, construction, engineering, and transportation. Covered occupations include operation of electrical power lines, employment in waterworks and other public utilities, navigation, operation of boats and ships, operation of elevators and warehousing, street cleaning, painting, decorating, renovating, and cleaning. Those types of employment that are exempted from this list may be admitted at their own request.

Personal injuries resulting from accidents arising out of and in the course of employment are compensated, except in cases in which the accident is attributed to the worker's serious and willful misconduct and does not result in serious disablement. Workers' Compensation systems also compensate for certain specified occupational diseases.

Compensation Rates and Methods

Two standards are in place for determining the rate for payment of compensation. Eight jurisdictions base the payment on a percentage (generally 90 percent) of **net earnings;** the other four base payments on 75 percent of average earnings. Jurisdictions like Nova Scotia have used both methods depending on the date of the accident. A worker's average earnings are generally calculated on the basis of his or her earnings during the past 12 months. Since a large number of workers have not worked for the same employer for 12 months, other ways of establishing earnings are sanctioned. Each act also stipulates a maximum amount of earnings that can be used to determine the maximum amount of compensation. Although there are procedural variations across jurisdictions, Workers' Compensation is based on the individual's past salary record—not on the loss or potential loss of future earnings.

net earnings
salary after mandatory deductions (income tax, Canada Pension, and Employment Insurance)

RPC 3.2

RPC 3.3

One of the underlying premises of Workers' Compensation systems is that people do not want to work.[2] As a result, boards try to provide reasonable compensation without creating an incentive for individuals to stay off work. There is some empirical evidence that raising benefit rates does lead to longer absences from work.[3,4]

The method used to determine the average wage of a worker is the one that gives the best representation of the worker's weekly earnings and seems fair and reasonable. When work is made available and the worker still suffers an earnings loss, the payment for the continuing disability may be adjusted, whether or not the worker accepts the work. A payment for noneconomic loss (functional impairment) is also made in several jurisdictions. This figure is based on such factors as the worker's age, degree of impairment, and number of dependants. For example, a 40-year-old worker with three children would receive a larger payment than a 60-year-old worker with no children.

Compensation may take two forms: cash benefits or wage or earnings loss. Cash allowance is based on the degree of severity of the impairment. Payments continue as long as a disability lasts, in accordance with the entitlement established by the province or territory. In cases of permanent partial impairment, the worker receives a life pension based on rating scales established by the boards. There are allowances for economic losses and non-economic losses. An injured worker could receive noneconomic loss if he or she were unable to perform some of the things that he or she was able to do before the accident. For instance, if a worker were unable to golf as a result of the accident, a benefit could be paid for that noneconomic loss.

Wage or earnings loss refers to situations in which workers can no longer earn the same amount of money that they were earning before the accident as a result of their impairment. For a worker who was earning $20 per hour before the accident and now, as a result of the injury, is capable of earning only $10 per hour, the potential compensation is $10 per hour. The earnings loss is calculated and paid as long as the worker is unable to return to work paying the same wages as before the accident.

In the event of the death of a worker, the spouse may receive a pension in accordance with the schedules established by the various jurisdictions, and allowances are given to children. In addition, most provincial and territorial boards may allow an immediate lump-sum payment and variable expenses.

Medical Aid and Accident Prevention

 3.4

loss of functional capacity
limit of ability or dexterity depending on the seriousness of an injury

Accompanying compensation in all cases is the provision of medical aid. This aid includes medical and surgical care, hospitalization, nursing care, drugs and supplies, physical and occupational therapy, and the provision and maintenance of prostheses. An employee who sustains a work-related injury is compensated not only for loss of earnings but also for **loss of functional capacity**. Workers who, as a result of their injury, are no longer able to perform some of their duties on the job, such as lifting, twisting, or bending, are considered to have suffered loss of functional capacity for which benefits are payable.

Employers within a particular industry may form safety associations and make rules for accident prevention that, on approval of the WCB and the lieutenant governor in council in the jurisdiction, are binding on all employers in that industry. WCBs pay the expenses of these associations out of the accident fund and have the authority to investigate the premises of employers to ensure compliance with safeguards required by law. The goal of safety associations is to provide training in the area of accident prevention and health and safety.

Social Goals of Workers' Compensation

Workers' Compensation is driven by two main social goals: (1) to provide services intended to prevent injuries or reduce the psychological impact of injuries when they occur, and (2) to provide the training and development necessary to prepare an injured worker to return to work. The various WCBs have come to look on compensation as a means for society to share with the worker the consequences of industrial accidents and to ensure the restoration of the worker to active participation in the life of the community. The focus is more on restoring earning power than paying for its loss. In no sense is compensation considered a reward for being injured.

Occupational Health and Safety Today 3.2

Spiralling Disability Costs

An aging workforce and an expanded definition of disabling conditions have resulted in a greatly increased number of individuals receiving disability compensation. Some estimate that the costs of long-term disability increased almost 30 percent between 2003 and 2005. Employee illness and disability is estimated to cost Canadian employers $16 billion each year.

Changes in the composition of the workforce and, in particular, the elimination of mandatory retirement is expected to affect these already escalating costs, and organizations need to consider how they will approach this new class of older workers.

Sources: Clark, T. (2007, January). Benefit trends: Will you still need me. *Benefits Canada, 33*; and Sharratt, A. (2006, April). In the balance. *Benefits Canada*, 65–77.

This social conception of compensation is grounded in the following standard provisions contained in the various acts:

1. unlimited medical aid
2. artificial prostheses
3. a fund to encourage reemployment (known as Second Injury and Enhancement Fund [SIEF] in some jurisdictions)
4. liberal compensation
5. rehabilitation maintenance income

Not only does the compensation system in Canada provide greater benefits than most insurers in other countries, but it also ensures that benefits are not prejudiced by earnings after rehabilitation. In Canada, permanently injured workers draw compensation for life and are able to keep their pensions, even if the sum of their pensions and supplements to earnings amounts to more than their wages before they were hurt. In contrast, many compensation laws in the United States hinder rehabilitation, either by cutting off compensation for permanent injury as soon as workers begin to earn as much money as they did before the injury or by paying compensation for only a limited period, leaving workers stranded before they can be retrained.

Provision for Second Injuries

The Canadian Workers' Compensation system provides for a "second injury fund," the purpose of which is to facilitate the reemployment of disabled workers. Without a provision for multiple injuries, employers might be tempted to discriminate against workers with disabilities, as an additional injury could make the employer responsible for a far more serious disability than if the worker had not had a prior injury. Thus, a worker who has lost one arm will be given a total disability rating if he or she loses the second arm. By charging the excess liability resulting from the cumulative effect of a prior disability and the subsequent injury to a disaster reserve fund, the various acts distribute the burden throughout industry as a whole rather than letting it rest on one particular class. In this way, employers are relieved of the extra risks associated with the employment of workers with disabilities. RPC 3.5

Occupational Health and Safety Today 3.3

Return-to-Work Programs

In response to spiralling disability costs, many firms are adopting an active approach to managing disability and return to work. Such programs typically try to get the individual back to the workforce as soon as possible. Although there is an obvious economic incentive to return individuals to the workforce, there is also a therapeutic incentive. Data from private insurers suggest that the average length of disability is about four-and-a-half years; after the individual has been on disability compensation for two years, the expected length more than doubles to 11 years. These data point to the need for early and effective intervention.

This need is identified under Ontario legislation that requires both workers and employers to maintain contact during the period of recovery from a disability and to cooperate in a return to work. Employees are specifically obligated to cooperate in health care and other return-to-work measures required by the WSIB. Employers are obligated to identify suitable employment consistent with the individual's abilities and, where possible, to ensure a return to preinjury earnings.

Sources: Workplace Safety and Insurance Board of Ontario, "Return to work." Retrieved from http://www.wsib.on.ca/wsib/wsibsite.nsf/public/EmployersESRW, February 7, 2007; and WorkSafeBC, "Understanding return-to-work program." Retrieved from http://www.worksafebc.com/health_care_providers/related_information/understanding_return-to-work/default.asp, February 7, 2007.

Rehabilitation

Before World War I, persons with disabilities were left to fend for themselves. Some were placed in poorhouses, while others survived through begging. Gradually, society realized that just because people had disabilities did not mean they could not be productive; however, first attempts at drafting persons with disabilities into the workplace proved to be a difficult and frustrating experience for the workers. Persons with disabilities found that although they were given an opportunity to earn a living, they could do so only by accepting menial jobs that no one else wanted. When thousands of injured soldiers returned from World War I, the need to provide rehabilitation programs was finally recognized. Rehabilitation is a financial necessity as well as a moral and social obligation. Only with the assistance of effective rehabilitation can the future cost of the Workers' Compensation system be maintained at a reasonable level. There are three types of rehabilitation. **Vocational rehabilitation** refers to the steps undertaken by WCBs to help injured workers return to their place of employment or find similar or suitable work elsewhere. Placement services, vocational testing, and retraining or training may all be part of this process. **Physical rehabilitation** refers to the steps taken to restore, whether fully or partially, the worker's physical function. **Social rehabilitation** refers to the psychological and practical services that help workers with severe disabilities cope with daily life (e.g., assistance with cooking, bathing, household chores). A scenario in which the full range of compensation benefits was provided to an injured worker is outlined in Occupational Health and Safety Today 3.4.

vocational rehabilitation
the steps undertaken by WCBs to help injured workers return to their place of employment or find similar or suitable work elsewhere

physical rehabilitation
the steps taken to restore, whether fully or partially, the worker's physical function

social rehabilitation
the psychological and practical services that help workers with severe disabilities cope with daily life

Occupational Health and Safety Today 3.4

Workers' Compensation at Work

In 1987, Mr. X lost his left hand in an industrial accident. Over the previous 10 years, he had risen from the position of delivery-truck driver to plant manager at a small aluminum fabricator in northwest Toronto.

Mr. X recalled the accident. "We were having problems with the alignment. The mechanic was on lunch and repairs had to be made. I had done the same thing a thousand times before. It was a stupid accident. There was a piece of paper on the floor, and I instinctively kicked it out of the way. Unfortunately, I didn't know that the foot pedal was beneath the paper. The press came down in the blink of an eye and my hand was left attached to my wrist by a single tendon."

Mr. X had been thinking about a career change before the accident. In addition to his duties as plant manager, he had begun to do some selling and marketing and found it was something he enjoyed. After the accident, Mr. X knew that he would not be able to work in the plant again, so he began to consider retraining.

After his surgery, Mr. X spent four weeks in hospital recovering. A WCB representative came to see him two days after the accident and initiated his claim so that he could continue to pay his bills. Before Mr. X could be fitted with a prosthesis, his physical wounds had to heal. He spent the next couple of months getting better and receiving treatment.

Around this time, Mr. X decided to pursue a marketing career. Thanks to the sponsorship of the WCB, he enrolled in a marketing program. On graduation, Mr. X received further assistance from a WCB placement adviser. Within months, a job was located. After completing a training program with his new employer, Mr. X began work as a full-time marketing representative.

In this scenario, the full range of compensation benefits was provided, including monetary benefits, medical aid, prosthetic device, vocational rehabilitation, placement services, and counselling in social services.

Occupational Diseases and Workplace Stress

A significant issue facing Workers' Compensation today concerns occupational diseases and the degree to which they are work related. Examples of occupational diseases would include various cancers, skin diseases, and allergic reactions to materials and components within the workplace. Occupational disease compensation has been part of Workers' Compensation ever since six specific diseases were cited in Ontario's act of 1914. The past 30 years have seen a broadening of the definition of "accident" and "injury," which has allowed for greater consideration of occupational disease claims. Today, many occupational disease claims can be considered in the same way as any other claim. The need to isolate the point at which the disease was contracted has given way to a recognition that the disease could be the result of exposure or injury over time. Occupational disease claims, unless very straightforward, are often adjudicated by a special claim unit and may require additional expert medical opinion as well as exposure and employment histories. Some WCBs use separate claim forms for specific occupational diseases. The **latency period** is quite often a major factor in determining the acceptability of the claim.

latency period
the time between exposure to a cause and development of a disease

Stress-related disabilities can be divided into three groups: (1) physical injury or occupational disease leading to a mental disability, (2) mental stress resulting in a physical disability, traumatic occurrence, or series of occurrences, and (3) mental stress resulting in a mental condition. Generally, stress claims in the first group have been dealt with in the same way as any other claims. Those in the second group have been subject to some selection. If the disability (say, a cardiac attack) is acute, it will be considered for compensation. If the disability (say, an ulcer) is a result of accumulated stress, it will likely not be considered for compensation. With respect to the third group, an unusual incident that provokes the mental reaction and results in a disability will probably be considered for compensation; chronic stress resulting in a mental disability is seldom compensated. The adjudication of stress claims is currently receiving a great deal of attention from all insurance parties. The courts and human rights tribunals have been consistent in maintaining that stress-related disorders or other psychological disabilities are to be treated the same as physical disabilities in employment settings.[5] It remains to be seen whether Workers' Compensation schemes can defend their exclusion of some stress-related disorders in the face of this accumulated experience.

Assessments

RPC 3.5

Employers are grouped together according to the type of operation or industry in which they are engaged, and they are assessed on that basis. The groups are referred to as industries, classes, subclasses, or classifications. In some jurisdictions, the terms "unit" and "sector" are used; employers are not grouped by occupation, although occupation may help determine a subdivision of an industry or class.

Separate accounts are generally used when an employer is involved in more than one industry or when an industry or employer's operation includes several departments. Assessments are determined by the WCB at least once a year when the board sets a percentage or rate to be applied to the payroll of the employer. Payrolls are estimated and then the employer is required to submit a certified payroll statement.

The Workers' Compensation system in Canada is based on the concept of dividing employers into three categories: (1) those who contribute to the accident fund and benefit from its collective liability, (2) those who are individually liable for their own employees' accidents, and (3) those in certain low-risk industries who are excluded under various acts across the country. Employers who pay directly for the accidents of their employees are generally public enterprises such as provincial or territorial and municipal governments and certain transportation and communication companies within Crown corporations.

All employers within a particular industry group are assessed at the same rate based on the injury experience of the group as a whole. In most jurisdictions, within the general accident fund, a provision is made for a rate stabilization and disaster reserve fund. One group by itself cannot sustain the heavy costs associated with a major disaster that might occur in any one year, or with a sharp decline in assessable payroll due to massive layoffs in the industry. Continued financing can be provided by the rate stabilization and disaster funds, which are maintained by the various WCBs.

Occupational Health and Safety Notebook 3.2

Illustrative Industry Assessment Rates

The average Workers' Compensation assessment in Ontario for 2007 was $2.26 for every $100 in insurable earnings. However, there are dramatic differences in assessment across occupational groups. For some sample rates, see the table below.

Sample of WBC Assessments across Occupational Groups

Rate Group	Description	Assessment per $100 of insurable earnings
031	Logging	$10.81
728	Roofing	$12.98
741	Masonry	$11.15
335	Publishing	$0.56

Source: Workplace Safety and Insurance Board of Ontario, "2007 premiums." Retrieved from http://www.wsib.on.ca/wsib/wsibsite.nsf/public/employersrates2007, February 7, 2007.

Experience Rating

RPC 3.5

Experience rating in Workers' Compensation refers to an accident insurance premium pricing scheme that takes into account the clear cost experience of the individual employer. Under experience rating, the assessment for each firm may be higher or lower than the basic rate for the relative industry group. Firms with lower-than-average accident costs per worker pay lower premiums than firms with above-average accident costs. In essence, experience rating reduces or eliminates the cross-subsidization of relatively unsafe firms by relatively safe firms. Given two otherwise similar firms, a safer employer will face lower Workers' Compensation costs and hence lower production costs. Thus, the primary effect of the experience rating is to create a financial incentive for relatively unsafe firms to begin caring for their workforce.

Experience rating is intended to offer an incentive to employers to reduce injuries and to return workers to their jobs as early as possible. In this way, employers benefit because the amount of money spent on compensation is reduced, and workers benefit because they are returned to their job quickly. Experience rating is thus a process of rewarding good performers and penalizing those organizations that are not making efforts to reduce accidents and return workers back to work as quickly as possible.

Generally, if an employer has an experience rating of a three-year average injury cost lower than that of the entire group, that employer will receive a rebate on the annual assessment. Conversely, employers who have an average injury cost higher than the group will receive demerit charges on top of their regular assessments.

One of the most important reasons for mandatory experience rating is the reduction of industrial accidents and injuries and their costs. The profit-maximizing, cost-minimizing firm will respond to the incentive by investing in activities that reduce its Workers' Compensation claim costs to the point at which the expected marginal benefits (i.e., incremental reduction in the expected cost of injuries and accidents) equal the marginal cost. Given the existence of workplace risk, and assuming full information about such risk, the firm may allocate resources to safety practices or pay the costs associated with work injury. Profit-maximizing firms operating in competitive markets will strive to minimize some of the costs associated with workplace injuries and accidents, such as Workers' Compensation premium payments (including experience rating service charges/refunds as well as material costs), fixed employment costs, lost production time, and damage to equipment, by preventing accidents (i.e., reducing the probability of a hazardous state) as well as by engaging in activities that minimize costs once accidents do occur. Post-accident employer actions that can result in claim cost reduction include implementing early return-to-work programs and appealing WCB decisions on workers' benefits.

The Workers' Compensation Boards in several jurisdictions (e.g., Ontario, Alberta, B.C.) operate experience-rating plans with the goal of creating incentives for firms to reduce their claim rate. That is, the experience rating systems attempt to reward safe firms (through a rebate of assessment premiums) and to penalize unsafe firms (through a surcharge on premiums). Such programs provide some leverage to firms seeking to reduce their Workers' Compensation costs—to the extent that firms can establish and maintain better than average safety records, costs will be decreased.

Occupational Health and Safety Notebook 3.3

Experience Rating Programs in Ontario

New Experimental Experience Rating Program (NEER)

NEER automatically applies to companies that pay more than $25,000 per year in premiums and are not in a construction rate group. NEER allows companies to earn rebates on premiums by maintaining a good health and safety record. Alternately, if companies have a poor health and safety record, they will be assessed a surcharge. To establish whether a company's record is better or worse than average, it is compared with similar companies (i.e., a company's costs are compared within its rate group over the past three years). Companies are not penalized for long-term conditions such as hearing loss or asbestosis.

CAD-7

CAD-7 applies to employers in the construction sector whose average annual premiums are more than $25,000. Similar to NEER, a company's claim history is compared with similar firms within a rate group to determine whether a surcharge or rebate is applicable.

Merit Adjusted Premium (MAP) Plan for Small Business

MAP is similar to the foregoing programs but applies to small businesses (those paying between $1,000 and $25,000 in annual WCB premiums). Generally, MAP decreases or increases to premiums do not take effect until after three years of continuous operation (although increases may be applied earlier if a significant number of claims are filed).

Sources: Workplace Safety and Insurance Board of Ontario, "New experimental experience rating program (NEER)." Retrieved from http://www.wsib.on.ca/wsib/wsibsite.nsf/Public/NEER, February 7, 2007; Workplace Safety and Insurance Board of Ontario, "CAD-7." Retrieved from http://www.wsib.on.ca/wsib/wopm.nsf/Public/130206, February 7, 2007; and Workplace Safety and Insurance Board of Ontario, "Merit adjusted premium (MAP) plan for small business." Retrieved from http://www.wsib.on.ca/wsib/wopm.nsf/Public/130204, February 7, 2007.

Occupational Health and Safety Today 3.5

Integrated Disability Management

In Canada, a clear distinction has been made between programs designed to provide compensation for injuries that occur at work (i.e., Workers' Compensation) and programs designed to provide income to employees who are ill or disabled because of non-occupational injuries. Non-occupational illnesses or injuries are typically dealt with through short-term and long-term disability plans paid for by the employer, the employees, or both (i.e., rate-shared plans). Unions and union members may also participate in rate-shared plans. Integrated disability management is based on the belief that rising disability costs can be managed if disability programs (long- and short-term disability, sick leave, and Workers' Compensation) are managed in their entirety.

The evidence for such integrated programs is convincing–implementing integrated disability management has resulted in cost savings in many firms.

Source: Scott, L. (2003, February–March). Time for integrated disability management has arrived. *HR Professional Magazine*.

Empirically, then, the question is whether experience rating schemes actually work—that is, do they decrease accidents or injuries in the workplace? This is an exceedingly complex question and there does not appear to be a clear answer thus far.[6] However, the best evidence available to date looked at the incidence of claims before and following the implementation of experience rating plans and suggests that such plans are effective in improving workplace safety.[7]

How Organizations Can Manage Disability

Although minimizing costs, such as Workers' Compensation premiums, is one goal of human resources, another is to ensure that injured workers return to the workplace as quickly as possible. Ensuring a prompt return to work helps both the individual and the organization. The individual returns to his or her full income as quickly as possible. The organization minimizes costs associated with replacing employees and retains the valuable skills of current employees.

Not surprisingly, a great deal of attention has been focused on the two issues involved in disability management: minimizing disability-related costs through integrated disability management and ensuring a prompt return to work.

Strategies for managing disability include the following:

1. *Create and run an effective corporate culture that values employees and establishes them as an integral part of the workforce.* An effective disability management program cannot conflict with the organizational culture. Specifically, it is the culture that makes it easier to create a disability management program. The corporate culture best able to enhance a disability management program is one that includes the following:

   (a) regular collaborative communication between supervisors and employees

(b) helpful cooperative relationships among coworkers
(c) training for new managers on how to handle personnel issues effectively, including evaluating employee performance
(d) favourable work conditions
(e) opportunities for career growth
(f) clearly defined and flexible work roles
(g) a willingness on the part of senior management to invest money up front in order to save money in the near and distant future
(h) incentive for local managers to make disability management part of their decision-making process

2. *Ensure senior management support.* To be successful, a disability management program requires support and cooperation from staff at all levels of the company. At times, the most effective way to obtain this cooperation is to enlist senior management support.
3. *Intervene early and regularly.* All corporations should have a policy of contacting employees early and regularly throughout the disability absence. Contacting employees sooner rather than later produces three distinct benefits:

   (a) Employees tend to come back to work more quickly.
   (b) Employees who return to work tend to stay at work.
   (c) Employees generally return to earn a higher wage.

   The early return and regular contact strategy must be supplemented with an effective return-to-work policy in place before an employee becomes disabled.
4. *Develop case management capacities.* Case management refers to the coordination of health and social services so that injuries or disabilities receive care that is appropriate, timely, and efficient. The goals of case management are to enhance the injured worker's quality of life and, if possible, reduce the costs associated with care. Case management should therefore begin early in the process to ensure that injured workers are receiving the most effective and most cost-efficient services available.
5. *Create modified and light duty jobs to allow an early return to work.* The most cost-saving strategy is to bring employees back to work when they can perform at least some of their tasks. This concept can speed up recovery by giving an employee practical goals to achieve during the rehabilitation process. It can serve as a work-hardening function by gradually strengthening the employee's ability, thereby reducing the risk of injury on the first day back at work.
6. *Train supervisors to encourage and facilitate an early return to work.* This is perhaps the most difficult step in any disability management program. The company can begin by expanding the role of the supervisors to include assistance for employees with disabilities.
7. *Create data systems.* An effective disability management system can greatly minimize costs by identifying problem areas, creating a baseline for measuring improvement, and increasing the efficiency with which Workers' Compensation absences are tracked. Companies can

obtain a system tailored to individual needs and budgets. Up-to-date data allow a company to track trends and identify problem areas within the corporation.

Return to Work

RPC 3.6

RPC 3.7

It is common to classify disability-related absence into three stages: acute (1–30 days), subacute (31–90 days), and chronic (91+ days).[8] Clearly the costs of disability increase as a worker progresses through the stages. Return-to-work programs are aimed at getting people back to work early in the process. Even if the individual cannot perform his or her original job, it is possible for the individual to return to work in some capacity.

One of the first steps in creating an effective return-to-work program is creating the environment. One study found that disability leave was shortened among a sample of 197 workers following carpal tunnel surgery when the organizational culture (manifested in policies and procedures) supported strong interpersonal relations and emphasized safety as a value (e.g., worker training, proactive return-to-work programs, and an emphasis on communication).[9]

Return to work often involves a modified job assignment. Traditionally, injured workers might be assigned to light duties or to some job that they were capable of doing while injured without fear of making their condition worse. Research has consistently identified physical demands of the job as an important predictor of return to work. For example, engaging in heavy physical labour such as construction or work that requires working in awkward positions (e.g., bending, twisting, crouching) is associated with delayed return to work after injury.[10,11] If jobs can be modified to eliminate or reduce the physical demands, then an early return to work may be facilitated. Given these findings, it is not surprising that return-to-work programs that include some ergonomic redesign of the workplace tend to be the most effective.[12]

In light of our discussion of psychosocial hazards in the workplace (see Chapter 6), it is interesting to note that these factors also affect return to work. As might be expected, low-quality jobs are associated with delayed return to work, where "low quality" refers to high demands, job stress, or a lack of control.[13]

Although employers will generally benefit from return-to-work provisions, employees may resist their implementation. Employees may fear loss of their job (i.e., If I take a modified job, I'll never get back to my real job), fear reinjury or exacerbation of their condition, or may simply feel unable to return to work. Concerns about stigma and threats to career prospects have been identified as barriers to workers taking stress leave.[14] Additionally, coworkers and supervisors who might have to "take up the slack" for the injured individual may accuse him or her of malingering or "working" their injury to get an easy job. The fear of such reactions may delay return to work. For example, fear of discrimination was found to be one factor that inhibited workforce reentry among a sample of individuals with HIV/AIDS.[15] This shows the need to make return to work a standard policy that deals with these concerns up front.

Occupational Health and Safety Today 3.6

The Duty to Accommodate

Although return-to-work programs are increasingly promoted as a means of managing disability cases, Canadian human rights legislation also imposes obligations on employers to accommodate workers with disabilities. That is, there is a legal obligation to accommodate injured workers to facilitate their return to work. Moreover, case law has increasingly placed the onus on employers to accommodate workers. In the well-known case of *British Columbia (Public Service Employees Relations Commission) v. BCGSEU*, 3 S.C.R. 3, commonly referred to as the "Meiorin decision," the Supreme Court of Canada established that employers had an obligation to accommodate individuals and to be proactive in removing discriminatory workplace practices. Based on a recent review of court cases,* the duty to accommodate appears to be defined by 10 general principles:

1. An employer has the obligation to accommodate employees who suffer from a disability to the point of undue hardship.
2. Employees must produce medical or psychological evidence that they are suffering from a disabling condition if they expect to be accommodated by their employer.
3. Disruptive behaviour associated with a disability or failure to perform assigned duties by an employee with a disability is not sufficient cause to terminate the employee, provided he or she makes known the disorder.
4. Failure of an employee to adhere to a medical regi-men and therapy that may be prescribed to address the disability may be sufficient grounds for termination of the employee.
5. The risk associated with the position occupied by a person with a disability may mitigate the nature of the accommodation.
6. The severity and stability of the condition can be considered as part of an employee's return to work and accommodation.
7. The employee can make reasonable objections, including economic loss, to the accommodation that is offered by the employer; however, the employee must accept reasonable accommodation offered by the employer, even though that accommodation may not be perfect from the employee's perspective.
8. Accommodation cannot be made on the basis of a stereotype held by the employer about the employee with a disability. The employer must investigate to determine what the individual employee is capable of doing.
9. Large organizations, particularly government departments, will be held to a higher standard with respect to their duty to accommodate employees with disabilities and with respect to the point where undue hardship begins.
10. The BFOR (bona fide occupational requirement) defence outlined in the Meiorin decision will be used to assess any arguments of undue hardship.

---

*. Kelloway, E. K., Francis, L., Catano, V. M., Cameron, J., & Day, A. (2004). *Psychological disorders in the Canadian Forces: Legal and social issues. Contractor's report.* National Defence Headquarters, Ottawa: Director Human Resources Research and Evaluation.

Summary

Workers' Compensation was established in Canada in 1914 with the passage of Ontario's Workmen's Compensation Act. Since then, coverage and benefits have increased, as have the associated costs. The thrust of the Workers' Compensation system today is to create more safety-conscious work environments and to work actively to reduce the number of work-related accidents, disabilities, and diseases. Primary responsibility rests with the employer to ensure that the compensation system is administered efficiently and funded equitably through assessments of employers. The underlying philosophy of Workers' Compensation is that employers are as accountable to their employees as they are for the bottom line.

Key Terms

latency period 63
loss of functional capacity 60
net earnings 59
physical rehabilitation 62
social rehabilitation 62
vocational rehabilitation 62

Weblinks

"Workers' Compensation Past, Present and Future—An Historical Overview"

http://www.awcbc.org/english/history.asp (p. 55)

WorkSafeBC

http://www.worksafebc.com (p. 56)

National Institute of Disability Management and Research

http://www.nidmar.ca (p. 67)

Workers' Compensation Board of Nova Scotia

http://www.wcb.ns.ca (p. 69)

RPC Icons

RPC 3.1 Provides input on matters related to the drafting and/or application of legislation or regulations related to health, safety security, and Workers' Compensation.

- legislation
- process and means of influencing legislative change
- linkages with change agents (e.g., HR Associations, interest groups, politicians, bureaucrats)
- report writing
- common and statutory law (e.g., employment standard: labour relations)
- Worker Protection (including health and safety and Workers' Compensation)
- theories and practices for protection of individuals and groups
- Occupational health and safety legislation (e.g., Occupational Health and Safety Act of Ontario, Workplace Safety & Insurance Act—Bill 99, Workplace Hazardous Materials Information System, Transportation of Dangerous Goods legislation, environmental legislation, smoking in the workplace legislation, civil rights legislation)

RPC 3.2 Establishes and implements strategies to minimize compensation costs.

- relevant legislation
- cost/benefit techniques

- Workers' Compensation billing, rate structures, and claims adjudication processes
- industry best practices
- modified return to work program
- ergonomics and physical demands analysis
- training and development
- policy, procedure and program development
- Worker Protection (including health and safety and Workers' Compensation)
- measurement bases and underlying methodologies used in finance departments
- Occupational health and safety legislation (e.g., Occupational Health and Safety Act of Ontario, Workplace Safety & Insurance Act—Bill 99, Workplace Hazardous Materials Information System, Transportation of Dangerous Goods legislation, environmental legislation, smoking in the workplace legislation, civil rights legislation
- ergonomics
- management techniques for OH&S Programs
- types of employee assistance and wellness programs

RPC 3.3 Coordinates Workers' Compensation benefits with other employee benefits (e.g., sick leave, long-term disability, and pension).

- relevant legislation
- employer-sponsored benefits
- statutory benefits
- program/policy development
- the culture of the organization
- conflict resolution
- record keeping and reporting
- technical terminology
- group insurance benefits
- pension plans
- Worker Protection (including health and safety and Workers' Compensation)
- theoretical and applied aspects of compensation functions
- types of employee benefits (e.g., standardized and flexible benefits plans)
- methods of managing compensation systems (including budgeting, cost control, and monitoring, auditing and evaluating effectiveness of pay system)

Task & Knowledge Requirements

- Occupational health and safety legislation (e.g., Occupational Health and Safety Act of Ontario, Workplace Safety & Insurance Act—Bill 99, Workplace Hazardous Materials Information System, Transportation of Dangerous Goods legislation, environmental legislation, smoking in the workplace legislation, civil rights legislation)

RPC 3.4 Establishes effective programs for accident prevention, incident investigation, inspections, fire and emergency response, and required training.

- relevant legislation
- workplace inspection and accident investigation techniques
- nature of the business and physical work environment
- potential risks and hazards in the workplace
- emergency response planning
- community emergency response services
- training and development
- industry best practices
- Worker Protection (including health and safety and Workers' Compensation)
- training and development program design and administration
- hazard identification and control
- accident investigation procedures
- emergency preparedness procedures
- management techniques for OH&S Programs

RPC 3.5 Analyzes rate grouping costs, early intervention and return to work programs, claims management programs, and claims appeals.

- capability of available resources such as rehabilitation centers, physiotherapists, ergonomists, and medical consultants
- relevant legislation including rate structures (e.g., Workers' Compensation, HR, occupational health)
- cost/benefit methods
- intervention processes
- Workers' Compensation billing and claims processes and guidelines
- industry best practices
- range of job functions within the organization's structure
- company benefit plans and policies
- Worker Protection (including health and safety and Workers' Compensation)
- objectives, processes, and conceptual foundations of financial and management accounting
- issues in identifying relevant costs (e.g., cost accuracy vs. relevance; costs & pricing; irrelevant costs; costing collective; bargaining proposals; cost-benefit analysis)
- the economic, legal, technical, and moral impact of OHS
- types of employee assistance and wellness programs

TASK & KNOWLEDGE REQUIREMENTS

- conceptual definition and implications of occupational stressors (e.g., potential stressors, methods of identifying potential stressors and strain outcomes, response to organizational stressors, and management of employee strain outcomes)

RPC 3.6 Ensures accommodation and graduated return to work programs are in place to meet the needs of disabled employees.

- relevant legislation
- collective agreements
- external factors such as arbitration awards, judicial reviews
- program/policy/procedure development
- best practices outside the organization
- claims and case management
- conflict resolution
- report writing and record keeping
- jobs which may be available for modified work
- physical demands analysis
- ergonomics
- available medical services and outside resources
- the organization's culture
- the economic, legal, technical, and moral impact of OHS
- methods of accommodating employee needs (e.g., flexible hours, job sharing, child care)
- Worker Protection (including health and safety and Workers' Compensation)

RPC 3.7 Ensures that modifications to the work environment are consistent with the nature of worker disability (e.g., total vs. partial and temporary versus permanent).

- relevant legislation
- collective agreements
- arbitration awards, judicial reviews
- industry best practices
- problem solving techniques
- claims and case management
- conflict resolution
- report writing and record keeping
- technical terminology
- physical demands analysis
- ergonomics
- Worker Protection (including health and safety and Workers' Compensation)

Task & Knowledge Requirements

- methods of accommodating employee needs (e.g., flexible hours, job sharing, child care)
- the economic, legal, technical, and moral impact of OHS
- ergonomics

Discussion Questions

1. Outline the responsibilities of WCBs today. Describe how these

responsibilities have changed over the years since the inception of Workers' Compensation in 1914.

2. Imagine you are a truck driver. An accident on the road has left you with two broken legs and a head concussion. What type of assistance might you expect from Workers' Compensation? What could your manager do to expedite your return to work?
3. If you are employed, talk with the health and safety manager in your organization. (If you are a student, ask to speak to the safety officer at your school.) Obtain information about the organization's sector, assessment, and record of experience ratings.

Using the Internet

1. Check the Workers' Compensation Board in your area. What cost savings are available to firms that improve their health and safety record? What obligations exist to implement return-to-work procedures?
2. Most WCBs publish their current rates online. Pick a single industry and find the appropriate rate group assessment across the provinces and territories. Who pays the highest assessments? Who pays the lowest?

Exercises

1. Various jurisdictions have struggled with how employees should be compensated for stress-related disabilities. Using the Workers' Compensation websites listed in Occupational Health and Safety Notebook 2.3 in the preceding chapter, check to see how the following scenarios are handled in your jurisdiction:

    a. mental/mental—stress at work results in a psychological disorder (e.g., depression)
    b. mental/physical—stress at work results in a physical disorder (e.g., heart attack)
    c. physical/mental—an accident at work results in a psychological disorder (e.g., anxiety attacks)

2. Company X operates one 12-hour shift per day for 220 days per year. They employ 315 people. The company records show a history of accidents and injuries:

    - 3 medical-aid injuries with no days lost
    - 15 property-damage accidents with a total of 35 days lost
    - 11 equipment failures that caused a total of 20 days lost
    - 19 injuries requiring medical attention with a total of 75 days lost

Calculate the following (see the appendix at the end of this chapter for the formulas):

a. frequency   b. severity

Explain how the company's severity rate can have a significant increase while the frequency rate has a very minor increase.

Case 1

The Employer's Duty

Sulleman has worked for Speedy Courier for the past three years. Last Tuesday, he was loading his truck when he suddenly screamed in pain. Apparently, Sulleman had injured his back while lifting a box that exceeded the weight limits. Sulleman was rushed to the hospital, where they could find no evidence of injury other than the pain expressed by Sulleman. Knowing that the lack of hard evidence is common in these types of injuries, you can assume that Sulleman will be off work for a considerable period. As the HR representative for Speedy Courier, you have been charged with fulfilling the company's responsibilities under the act. Moreover, senior management has expressed concern with the number of disability claims and the fact that most recent claims were for extended periods (e.g., several exceeding 12 months). What do you need to do?

Case 2

A Stressful Job

Joan is an emergency room nurse at a busy city hospital. She has always enjoyed the hustle of working with emergencies and the challenges of dealing with the unexpected. Lately, though, Joan has been worried about her own well-being. She has been very abrupt with her coworkers on several occasions and has had difficulty concentrating on her job. Although there have been no problems to date, Joan is worried that her deteriorating performance might cause a problem given the critical nature of her work. Her doctor suggested that she take an extended leave because of her "nerves" and assured her that Workers' Compensation would cover her lost salary. As an HR person, what would you advise Joan?

Appendix

Calculating Injury Frequency and Severity Rates

Copies of the reports of the accident analysis involving injuries should accompany the firm's Workers' Compensation claim forms. Compensation Boards issue injury frequency and severity rates for injuries resulting from accidents in order to determine the assessment for the organization.

Frequency is the number of medical-aid injuries relative to the number of hours worked expressed in a ratio of 200,000. Some firms and jurisdictions use a factor of 1,000,000 rather than 200,000. Using the 200,000 figure, the relationship becomes

$$\text{frequency} = \frac{\text{number of injuries}}{\text{total hours worked}} \times 200{,}000$$

Take, as an example, a company that employs 300 people who work 8-hour shifts for 250 days in one year. The total number of hours worked is

$$250 \times 300 \times 8 = 600{,}000$$

This company has a record of 6 medical-aid injuries with no lost time, 15 minor injuries with 5 days lost, 3 major injuries with 55 days lost, and 6 property-damage accidents with no lost time. The total number of injuries is

$$(6 + 15 + 3) = 24$$

The frequency is calculated as

$$\text{frequency} = \frac{24}{600{,}000} \times 200{,}000 = 8$$

Therefore, this organization has an injury frequency ratio of 8 per 200,000 or 8.

Property-damage accidents are not considered since there is no associated injury.

Severity of work-related injuries is the ratio of the number of days lost due to injuries to a factor of 200,000. Severity is calculated by using the relationship

$$\text{severity} = \frac{\text{number of days lost to injury}}{\text{total hours worked}} \times 200{,}000$$

The severity based on the total number of days lost due to injury in the above example would be calculated as

$$\text{total lost days} = (5 + 55) = 60$$

$$\text{severity} = \frac{60}{600{,}000} \times 200{,}000 = 20$$

The injury severity for this company is 20, or a ratio of 20:200,000. If the company works two or three shifts instead of one, as the examples show, then the total hours worked will be increased twofold or threefold and the relationship will be the same.

These figures facilitate comparison between various years of the company and between other companies within the same product and size group. These values can help to identify trends. Records of injuries caused by accidents can also be used as a basis for risk and fault-tree analyses.

Endnotes

1. Roberts, K. (2003). Using workers' compensation to promote a healthy workplace. In D. A. Hoffman & L. E. Tetrick (Eds.), *Health and safety in organizations: A multilevel perspective*. San Francisco, CA: Jossey Bass.
2. Roberts, K. (2003). Using workers' compensation to promote a healthy workplace. In D. A. Hoffman & L. E. Tetrick (Eds.), *Health and safety in organizations: A multilevel perspective*. San Francisco, CA: Jossey Bass.
3. Hyatt, D. E. (1996). Work disincentives of workers' compensation permanent partial disability benefits: Evidence for Canada. *Canadian Journal of Economics, 29,* 289–308.
4. Meyer, B., Viscusi, W. K., & Durbin, D. (1996). Workers' compensation and injury duration: Evidence from a natural experiment. *American Economic Review, 85,* 322–340.
5. Kelloway, E. K., Francis, L., Catano, V. M., Cameron, J., & Day, A. (2004). *Psychological disorders in the Canadian Forces: Legal and social issues. Contractor's report*. National Defence Headquarters, Ottawa: Director Human Resources Research and Evaluation.
6. Roberts, K. (2003). Using workers' compensation to promote a healthy workplace. In D. A. Hoffman and L. E. Tetrick (Eds.), *Health and safety in organizations: A multilevel perspective*. San Francisco, CA: Jossey Bass.
7. Durbin, D., & Butler, R. (1998). Prevention of disability for work-related sources: The roles of risk management, government intervention and insurance. In T. Thomason, J. F. Burton, & D. E. Hyatt (Eds.), *New approaches to disability in the workplace*. Madison, WI: IRRA.
8. Krause, N., & Lund, T. (2003). Returning to work after occupational injury. In J. Barling & M. Frone (Eds.), *The psychology of workplace safety*. Washington, DC: APA Books.
9. Amick, B., Habeck, R. V., Hunt, A., Fossel, A. H., Chapin, A., & Keller, R. B. (2000). Measuring the impact of organizational behaviors on work disability prevention and management. *Journal of Occupational Rehabilitation, 10,* 21–38.
10. Krause, N., & Lund, T. (2003). Returning to work after occupational injury. In J. Barling & M. Frone (Eds.), *The psychology of workplace safety*. Washington, DC: APA Books.
11. Krause, N., Lynch, J., Kaplan, G. A., Cohen, R. D., Goldberg, D. E., & Salonen, J. T. (1997). Predictors of disability retirement. *Scandinavian Journal of Work, Environment, and Health, 23,* 403–413.
12. Krause, N., & Lund, T. (2003). Returning to work after occupational injury. In J. Barling and M. Frone (Eds.), *The psychology of workplace safety*. Washington, DC: APA Books.
13. Krause, N., Dasinger, L. K., Deegan, L. J., Brand, R. J., & Rudolph, L. (2001). Psychosocial job factors and RTW after low back injury: A disability phase-specific analysis. *American Journal of Industrial Medicine, 40,* 374–392.
14. Dollard, M. F., Winefield, H. R., & Winefield, A. H. (1999). Predicting work stress compensation claims and return to work in welfare workers. *Journal of Occupational Health Psychology, 4,* 279–287.
15. Martin, D. J., Brooks, R. A., Ortiz, D. J., & Veniegas, R. C. (2003). Perceived employment barriers and their relation to workforce-entry intent among people with HIV/AIDS. *Journal of Occupational Health Psychology, 8,* 181–194.

PART TWO

Hazards and Agents

CHAPTER 4 PHYSICAL AGENTS

CHAPTER 5 CHEMICAL AND BIOLOGICAL AGENTS

CHAPTER 6 PSYCHOSOCIAL HAZARDS

CHAPTER 7 HAZARD RECOGNITION AND ASSESSMENT

Chapter 4

Physical Agents

Chapter Learning Objectives

After reading this chapter, you should be able to

- define the numerous terms relating to physical agents
- explain the human reactions to the various agents, particularly noise and radiation
- discuss the management of physical agents
- outline the actions of these agents on human physiology
- with the use of the chapter appendix, understand the methods of calculating noise levels and exposures

THE ROAR OF THE CROWD

It's every hockey fan's dream: your team makes the playoffs and you have tickets to the series. You'll get to see your favourite players, witness high-calibre hockey, and, possibly, experience noise-induced hearing loss firsthand. This was shown in a study conducted in games 3, 4, and 6 of the 2006 Stanley Cup finals between the Edmonton Oilers and the Carolina Hurricanes.* Researchers wore dosimeters that sampled the noise level near the ear every second for the entire game; they also conducted tests of hearing function before and after. The results showed the average noise exposures for the games were 104.1, 100.7, and 103.1 dB—noise levels peaked at just over 120 dB. The general standard for safety is 85 dB over an 8-hour period before hearing loss is experienced. For every 3 dB increase the exposure time is halved (i.e., at 88 dB it would take 4 hours to reach the maximum exposure). Six minutes of exposure to a Stanley Cup playoff game is sufficient for noise-induced hearing loss! Not surprisingly, researchers experienced some hearing impairment, and one experienced a significant threshold shift (an impairment in hearing that lasts for one to two days).

This research illustrates at least four important facts about physical agents in the workplace. First, such agents may be present in unexpected workplaces. Most discussions of workplace noise focus on heavy machinery and factories—not hockey rinks. While we think of this as recreation, note that the rink is a place of employment for many individuals (e.g., players, officials, etc.). Second, exposure to some physical agents may be inherent in the workplace—how does one host the Stanley Cup without having the fans cheer? Third, legislated standards are best viewed as maximum tolerances—not as the "safe" level of exposure, but rather as the highest tolerable level. Physical harm (such as noise-induced hearing loss) can occur well below the legislated exposure level. Finally, health and safety issues are often complex, and potential solutions also have to be evaluated for the risks they may introduce into the environment.

*. Hodgetts, W. E., & Liu, R. (2006). Can hockey playoffs harm your hearing? Reprinted from *CMAJ, 175(12),* 1541–1542.

RPC 4.1

RPC 4.2

RPC 4.3

RPC 4.4

physical agents
sources of energy that may cause injury or disease

ambient
all-encompassing condition associated with a given environment, being usually a composite of inputs from sources all around us

In this chapter we consider the effects of physical agents in the workplace. **Physical agents** are sources of energy that may cause injury or disease. Examples include noise, vibration, radiation, and extremes in temperature and pressure. Each of these agents may be **ambient** or acute (i.e., resulting from a single exposure).

Noise

Noise is defined as any unwanted sound. Technically, it refers to "the auditory sensation evoked by the oscillations in pressure in a medium with elasticity and viscosity," such as air.[1] Noise is a growing health problem in industry. In British Columbia, for example, approximately 8 percent of 143,000 workers tested in 2003 showed signs of hearing damage (**early warning change**). In the same year, 2,400 new claims for noise-induced hearing loss were filed.[2]

early warning change
a deterioration of hearing in the upper frequency—the earliest detectable sign of noise-induced hearing loss

WWW

One major characteristic of the human ear and hearing is that we do not hear everything in a nice, neat way. If sound were measured electronically, the sound spectrum might appear more or less as a straight line. What the human ear hears or perceives is significantly different. The human hearing range of frequencies is approximately 20 Hz to 20,000 Hz. Thus, a person can hear a bass note from a tuba or a shrill note from a piccolo, but not a dog whistle. This has direct implications for human hearing problems. Just because we cannot hear the sound does not mean that it is not present and possibly causing hearing damage.

The response of the human ear is usually represented as a graph that illustrates the threshold of hearing (see Figure 4.1). The term *threshold of hearing* refers to the envelope or range of sound that the human ear can perceive or hear. The standards for the measurement of noise use the unit of a decibel, or dB (also referred to as sound pressure level). When the human response is involved, the unit becomes dB(A) or A-weighted decibel, represented by the graph in Figure 4.1. This response is built into the sound meters used for measuring noise exposure in the workplace.

FIGURE 4.1

Human Hearing Response Curve

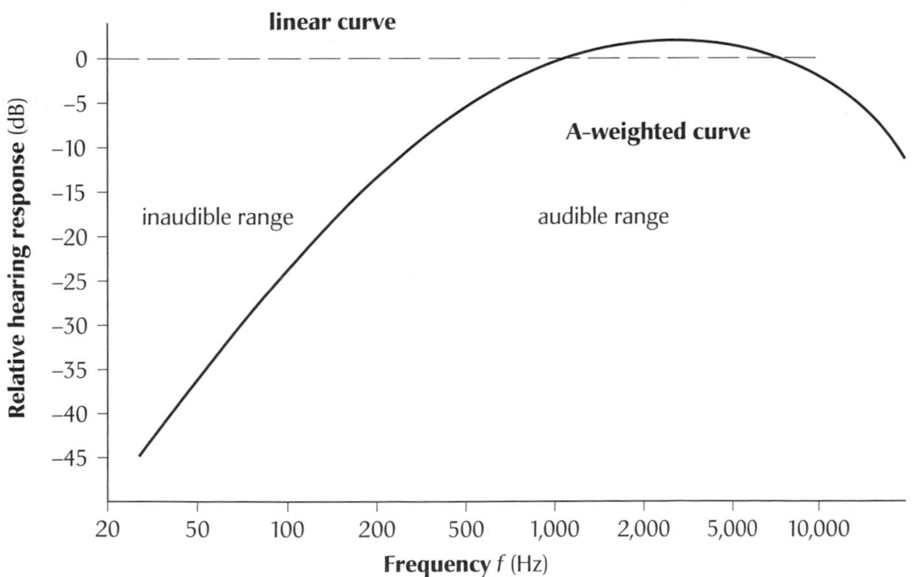

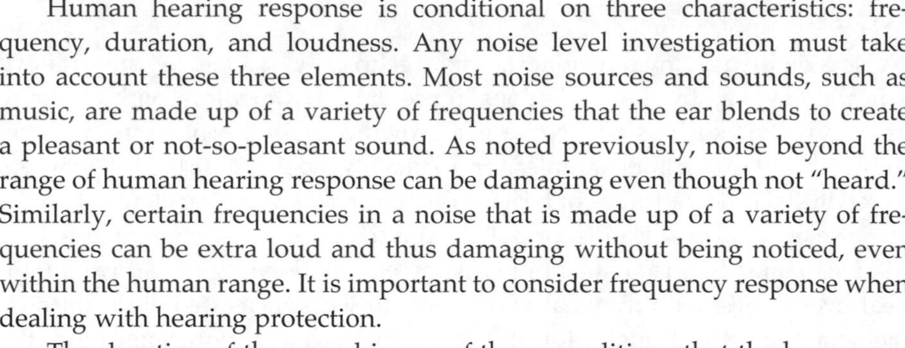

Human hearing response is conditional on three characteristics: frequency, duration, and loudness. Any noise level investigation must take into account these three elements. Most noise sources and sounds, such as music, are made up of a variety of frequencies that the ear blends to create a pleasant or not-so-pleasant sound. As noted previously, noise beyond the range of human hearing response can be damaging even though not "heard." Similarly, certain frequencies in a noise that is made up of a variety of frequencies can be extra loud and thus damaging without being noticed, even within the human range. It is important to consider frequency response when dealing with hearing protection.

The duration of the sound is one of those conditions that the human ear responds to in a strange way. A loud noise of very short duration, like a gunshot, is perceived to be "quieter" than the same sound level heard for a longer duration. They can both be damaging, but only the latter one "sounds" like it. The short-duration noise is referred to as impact or impulse noise, which has a duration of about 1 millisecond (1/1000th of a second). The third characteristic of human response is loudness. This term is self-explanatory. The louder (volume) the noise, the more problems it can cause.

Types of Hearing Loss

Noise can affect humans in three ways: physiologically, sociologically, and psychologically. In terms of the first effect, physiological damage, there are two basic types of hearing loss. The first is *conductive,* which restricts the transmission of sound to the cochlea or inner ear (see Figure 4.2); the second is *sensorineural* (sometimes referred to as nerve deafness), which affects the cochlea and is usually irreversible. Conductive hearing loss can be caused by wax buildup, infection, or trauma. From an industrial standpoint, it can be caused by the non-hygienic application of hearing protectors or the improper cleaning of these devices.

More prevalent in industry, however, is the sensorineural type of hearing loss. It is interesting to note that exposure to excessive noise first affects frequencies in the speech range—approximately 500 Hz to 3,000 Hz. Two indications of exposure to excessive noise levels at work are ringing in the ears (tinnitus) and raising the volume on radios and television after work. The volume of the radio or television will seem very high the next morning because temporary hearing loss diminishes with rest and removal from exposure. Hearing loss is one of the most insidious of disabilities. It is not uncommon for major loss to occur gradually over 5 to 10 years, depending on the type of exposure.

Gradual hearing loss, known as temporary threshold shift (TTS), can sometimes be reversed by removal from the noise source. Permanent threshold shift (PTS) identifies a hearing disability that is permanent and may not be correctable. In many cases, a hearing aid can bring about some improvement.

FIGURE 4.2

The Auditory System

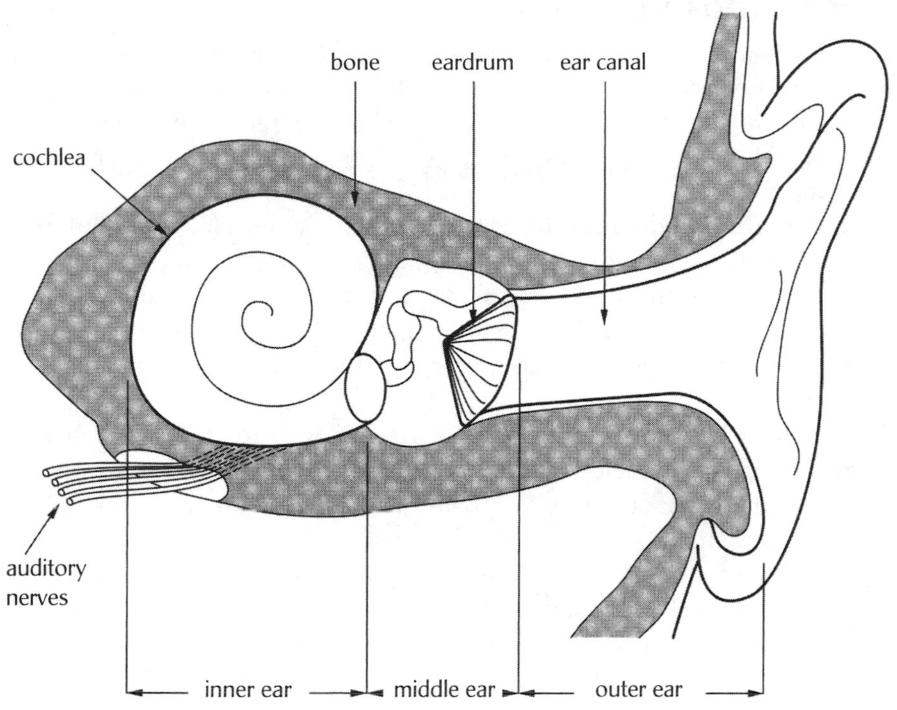

However, such a device is of little assistance when the hearing loss has been caused by noise exposure or sensorineural loss, because the hair cells in the cochlea have been destroyed.

The second effect of noise is sociological. In the past, companies would sometimes hire workers with hearing loss to work in high-noise areas since it was thought that the damage had already been done. However, it is now known that noise can cause extra-auditory effects, including a startled response to a loud, unexpected noise; cardiovascular, neurologic, endocrine, and biochemical changes; and nausea, malaise, and headaches.[3] Other laboratory and field studies have also demonstrated **vasoconstriction, hyperreflexia,** fluctuations in hormonal secretions, and disturbances in equilibrium and visual functions.

The third effect deals with human psychology. Many people are affected and disturbed by certain sounds that are not loud enough to present any serious physiological problem. These are day-to-day noises that tend to bug us, such as a patron talking during a movie, a helicopter flying overhead, or a tap dripping. Although the actual noise level may be well below acceptable

vasoconstriction
the process of causing a constriction of the blood vessels

hyperreflexia
the condition of unusually quick reaction by the nerves to some external stimulus

standards and may not be measurable with a sound level meter, it is nonetheless very real (often referred to as "selective hearing") and can cause stress and other possible nonauditory effects.

Noise Exposure Standards

Noise exposure standards vary across provinces and territories in terms of their relative stringency. The standards are based on worker exposure during a defined time frame. This relationship is referred to as *dose,* which describes the amount of noise absorbed by or impinged on an organ (the ear or the body) in a given unit of time. At the time of this writing the noise standard or threshold limit value (TLV) in Ontario allows for an 8-hour exposure of 90 dB(A) without hearing protection. New regulations introduced in Ontario mean that on July 1, 2007, Ontario will reduce the standard to 85 dB and will introduce a time-weighted average exposure limit as in most other jurisdictions. The 5 dB(A) difference between the two standards represents a difference of twice the noise energy, the 90 dB(A) standard being greater. The exposure limits in Canadian jurisdictions are presented in Table 4.1. Increments of 5 dB are referred to as an exchange rate. The **exchange rate** represents the doubling of the sound power, which in turn requires the halving of the exposure time.

exchange rate
represents the doubling of the sound power

The above standards are based on continuous noise, such as an air compressor or machine running. Impact or impulse noises, such as a punch press operating with more than a one-second interval between strokes, have

TABLE 4.1

Noise Level Exposure Limits in Canadian Jurisdictions

JURISDICTION	MAXIMUM ALLOWABLE 8-HR EXPOSURE
Federal	87 dB(A)
Alberta	85 dB(A)
British Columbia	85 dB(A)
Manitoba	85 dB(A)
New Brunswick	85 dB(A)
Newfoundland and Labrador	85 dB(A)
Northwest Territories and Nunavut	85 dB(A)
Nova Scotia	85 dB(A)
Ontario	90 dB(A)*
Prince Edward Island	85 dB(A)
Quebec	90 dB(A)
Saskatchewan	85 dB(A)
Yukon	85 dB(A)]

* Changes to 85 dB on July 1, 2007

Occupational Health and Safety Notebook 4.1

Noise in the Workplace: Signs and Levels

Given the noise exposure limits presented in Table 4.1, some comparisons are useful:

Normal conversation at 1 metre	55 dB(A)
Passenger car at 20 metres	65 dB(A)
Diesel truck at 20 metres	85 dB(A)
Lawnmower at 1 metre	92 dB(A)
Handheld circular saw at 1 metre	115 dB(A)

Although nothing will replace accurate measurement of noise levels in the workplace, the Canadian Centre for Occupational Health and Safety suggests a workplace might be too noisy if

a. people have to raise their voices to be understood

b. employees have ringing in the ears at the end of the workday

c. employees find they have to turn their radio up on the drive home (compared with the volume on the way to work)

d. individuals who have worked in the workplace for years have difficulty understanding conversations at parties or restaurants

If any of the above statements are true, a noise assessment or survey of the workplace should be undertaken.

Source: Canadian Centre for Occupational Health and Safety. Retrieved from http://www.ccohs.ca, February 7, 2007.

a totally different method of measurement based on the number of impacts per day. Another widely applied or referenced set of standards is that established by the American Conference of Governmental Industrial Hygienists (ACGIH). ACGIH recommends a noise TLV of 85 dB(A) for eight hours. This organization's standards are updated annually.

Occupational Health and Safety Today 4.1

Hearing Protection for Fire Fighters

Although we recognize the many hazards involved in firefighting, we might not think of noise as a particular concern for fire fighters. However, fire fighters use power tools, work around noisy fire engines and pumpers, and, of course, are close to loud sirens. Although this seems like a clear case calling for hearing protectors, it is also important that fire fighters be able to communicate with one another. One solution is an earmuff-type hearing protector with a built-in microphone and headset. These commercially available devices allow fire fighters to communicate with one another while protecting hearing. However, this is not a total solution as there is now evidence that hearing protection may be less effective when worn in conjunction with hard hats, eye protection, and respirators–all equally essential to the fire fighter's role.

Sources: Abel, S. M., Sass-Kortsak, A., & Kielar, A. (2002). The effect on earmuff attenuation of other safety gear worn in combination. *Noise & Health, 5,* 1–13; and Fire Fighters' Association of Ontario, "Issue: Hearing protection during emergency operations." Retrieved from http://www.ffao.on.ca/Section%2021.htm#hearing, February 7, 2007.

Noise exposure tests can be done by an outside specialist or a trained person on staff using a **sound pressure level meter,** an **octave band analyzer,** a **dosimeter,** or an **audiometer.**

sound pressure level meter
measures gross noise level

octave band analyzer
measures the noise level in each frequency range

dosimeter
measures a person's exposure to noise as a percentage for one shift

audiometer
an instrument used to determine the sensitivity of a person's hearing or degree of hearing loss

Noise Control

Noise can be controlled by using logical methods. The process for control follows the source–path–human strategies used by health and safety professionals. The first strategy used to reduce noise is to make the *source* quieter. There are a number of possible approaches. If the problem consists of a noisy machine, for instance, it may be possible to make the machine quieter by adding sound-absorbing materials, placing vibration padding under it, redesigning the operation so that the machine performs in a different manner, isolating the machine in a separate room or sound-deadening enclosure, or purchasing a new machine. All these alternatives can be expensive and may not be enthusiastically endorsed. However, a cost–benefit analysis, which takes into account such factors as noise-based illness, absenteeism, and Workers' Compensation costs, may paint a more positive and dramatic picture.

The second strategy—*path*—involves moving the worker away from the source or erecting sound barriers between the noise and the worker, or both. Based on the physics of noise, as the distance from the sound source is doubled, the noise level will drop by a fixed amount. For example, if a noise level of 90 dB is measured 5 metres away from a machine (a point source) and the distance is increased to 10 metres, the noise level will be **attenuated** or lowered by 6 dB. This is called a "free field effect," which simply means that nothing like walls is around to reflect the sound back on the worker. Objects such as the walls of the building and other machines will cause reflections that can reduce the amount of attenuation from this fixed amount. Nevertheless, the principle is still valid, and this process is usually less costly than the source approach.

attenuated or attenuation
reduction of noise at one location compared to another farther from the source

The third strategy—*human*—involves the use of personal protective equipment. This approach is the least costly and the one that is most commonly used. It is not always the best method, but many companies are not well enough informed to undertake other approaches such as job rotation, relocation, isolation, automation, rest periods, and site design. The two basic classes of hearing protection available are earplugs, which are inserted into the ears, and circumaural muffs or earmuffs, which are worn over the ears. A description of the various types of industrial hearing protection is provided in Table 4.3 in the chapter appendix. It should be noted that whatever strategies are used to decrease noise exposure, personal protective devices may still be necessary in conjunction with other methods.

Occupational Health and Safety Notebook 4.2

Choosing Hearing Protectors

For each application and to be properly fitted for maximum protection, there are ten factors to consider when deciding on the most effective hearing protection.

1. *Comfort*. Earmuffs in particular can be hot in warm conditions. The spring band can generate a feeling of the head being squashed. Workers who are claustrophobic may experience feelings of confinement.
2. *Visibility*. It is important that hearing protection be visible, so that supervisors can ensure the worker is wearing the protection and using it in the required manner.
3. *Size*. People have heads of different sizes and shapes. It is imperative that hearing protective devices be fitted properly. Additional types of paraphernalia such as face shields used in conjunction with hearing protection must also be examined.
4. *Weight*. Generally, the lighter the protection, the greater the comfort.
5. *Ease of donning*. A device that is easy to put on will gain more acceptance among workers.
6. *Cost*. The actual dollar cost will depend on the application, the required degree of attenuation, and the style of device. Earmuffs are more costly than earplugs. The specific noise protection required could necessitate both plugs and muffs.
7. *Effective attenuation*. Most modern hearing protection devices use a noise reduction rating (NRR) system to indicate the degree of attenuation based on laboratory evaluation. The NRR value is usually accompanied by a chart showing attenuation by octave band frequencies. Generally, the higher the number, the greater the level of attenuation. A good rule of thumb relationship is expressed with the equation below:

   $$NRR = L_{\text{actual}} - L_{\text{standard}} + 7$$

   where L_{actual} is the noise level measured in the workplace, and L_{standard} is the noise standard for an eight-hour period. Thus, if a worksite has a noise level of 97 dB(A) and the standard is 90 dB(A) for eight hours, the required NRR for hearing protectors would be 97 − 90 + 7, or 14 dB(A).
8. *Hygiene*. This requirement is the most critical and most abused. It is not uncommon to observe a hearing protection device hanging from a hook in a dirty environment. Care must be taken to keep the personal item clean and stored in a sanitary location to avoid ear infections, which could cause more damage than the noise does.
9. *Useful life*. Disposable plugs or inserts do not last long but require no maintenance, while muffs last longer but require maintenance.
10. *Maintenance*. All nondisposable hearing protection devices require ongoing maintenance and care. They must be cleaned regularly with soap and warm water, not alcohol, and checked periodically for wear. The foam seal pads on circumaural units must be regularly maintained because skin oils and sweat will cause embrittlement and surface failure. Once the seal is damaged, the attenuation effectiveness is reduced.

Sources: Berger, E. H., Ward, W. D., Morrill, J. C., & Royster, L. H. (Eds.). (1988). *Noise and hearing conservation manual* (4th ed.). Akron, OH: American Industrial Hygiene Association; Chandler, H. (2004). "An earful of sound advice," *Occupational Health and Safety Canada.* Retrieved from http://www.ohscanada.com/SafetyPurchasing/HearProt.asp, February 7, 2007; and Canadian Centre for Occupational Health and Safety, "What is personal protective equipment?" Retrieved from http://www.ccohs.ca/oshanswers/prevention/ppe/designin.html, February 7, 2007.

Vibration

Vibration refers to the oscillating motion of a particle or body moving about a reference position.[4] Vibration has a number of mechanical causes, including the dynamic effects from machine tolerances, clearances, rolling or rubbing contact, and out-of-balance conditions with rotary or reciprocating parts. Vibration can be accidental (a car wheel that is out of balance) or intentional (a vibrating feeder on a dry bulk material conveyor).

Vibration is a health hazard for three reasons. It can cause whole body vibration, segmental vibration, and noise. As with noise, vibration is transmitted through a medium, although in this case the medium is usually solid (e.g., steel or brick). The health effects will vary depending on the frequency and amplitude of the vibration. At low frequencies, say up to 15 Hz, the body will experience what is known as **whole body vibration.** In this instance, the complete human body will "shake" with the source. We have all experienced this condition in an automobile or on board a ship—the condition is called car- or seasickness. As the frequency of the vibration increases, parts of the body—not the whole body—will be affected by a process called **segmental vibration.**

whole body vibration
affects the whole body as a unit

segmental vibration
affects only parts of the body

resonance
the effect that occurs when an object reacts strongly to some particular frequency

One term that frequently comes up in discussions of vibration is **resonance,** which refers to the effect that occurs when an object reacts strongly to some particular frequency. If you sing in a tiled shower stall, you will occasionally hear a note that sounds louder than most, which means that the space is resonant to that note. Parts of the human body can resonate when exposed to some lower frequencies. For instance, the head and shoulders can resonate at 20 Hz to 30 Hz, while the eyeballs resonate at 60 Hz to 90 Hz.[5] If your vision becomes blurry when you have been working with a power tool such as a belt sander, you are experiencing minor levels of eyeball resonance, which is harmless unless prolonged.

Vibrations are classified into two categories: low frequency (discussed above) and high frequency. Vibrating effects fall into two separate conditions. As noted, the first concerns low-frequency vibrations. The second deals with higher-frequency vibrations that can happen so fast the body cannot respond. When the higher frequencies occur, the effects of wave velocity and acceleration take precedence. Vibratory effects are evaluated using measurements of velocity and acceleration caused by the source using a vibration meter, which is often a variation on a sound-level meter.

The health effects of whole body vibration include inhibition of muscular reflexes, impaired or blurred vision, and alterations of brain electrical activity. Segmental vibration effects include sore neck and shoulder muscles and sore joints; Raynaud's phenomenon, or white fingers, caused by restricted blood circulation in the fingers; neuritis and degenerative alterations of the central nervous system; fragmentation, **necrosis,** and **decalcification** of the carpal bones; and muscle atrophy and tenosynovitis.

necrosis
death or decay of tissue

decalcification
loss of lime salts (calcium) in the bones

The frequency response associated with vibrating systems is directly related to the mass of the system. In the simplest terms, if the mass or weight is increased, the effects of vibration can be lowered through a dampening

Occupational Health and Safety Notebook 4.3

Hand–Arm Vibration Syndrome (HAVS)

Working with handheld power tools (particularly in cold weather) can result in vibration-induced white finger (VWF)—or, more generally, hand–arm vibration syndrome.* HAVS results from changes in blood circulation and the nervous system associated with vibration and is characterized by

- tingling in the fingers
- loss of sensation in the fingers (numbness)
- loss of sense of light touch
- whitening (blanching) of the fingers when exposed to cold
- loss of grip strength
- development of cysts in fingers and wrists

HAVS is a progressive disorder and is also known as Raynaud's phenomenon. Prevention efforts focus on reducing vibration, using ergonomically designed tools, keeping hands warm and dry, and taking rest breaks.

*. Mason, J. (2003). Bad vibrations. *Occupational Health*, 55(7), 24.

Sources: Mason, J. (2003). Bad vibrations. *Occupational Heath, 55*(7), 24; and Weir, E., & Lander, L. (2005). Hand-arm vibration syndrome, *CMAJ, 172*(8), 1000–1001.

action. An example would be the increased weight on the outer flange of a flywheel that smoothes out much of the machine vibration. Using a flywheel is one method of control to reduce the health effects.

Whole body vibration effects can result from driving a motorcycle, truck, or tractor, or working near large machines such as air compressors or punch presses. Segmental vibration effects are caused by using vibrating tools such as riveters, sanders, saws, air hammers, or hammer drills. The most serious segmental effects are those associated with hand–arm vibrations. Using vibrating hand tools produces a Catch-22 situation. To properly control a vibrating hand tool, it is necessary to grip it securely; however, the tighter the hand grips the tool, the more severe the effects of segmental damage from vibration. The human resource professional should also be aware that vibration has chronic effects that must be managed.

Occupational Health and Safety Notebook 4.4

Controlling Vibration

Strategies for whole body and segmental vibration control include

- avoiding the source by revising the task
- using equipment that produces lower vibrations
- adding dampening devices to equipment to reduce vibrations
- decreasing worker exposure time
- isolating the worker from the source

Source: Canadian Centre for Occupational Health and Safety, "How can you measure vibration?" Retrieved from http://www.ccohs.ca/oshanswers/phys_agents/vibration/ vibration_measure.html, February 7, 2007.

Thermal Stress

homeostasis
the balance of heat generation

Thermal stress conditions involve cold and hot temperature extremes, usually coupled with high humidity. The human body can be seen as a machine that takes in chemical energy (food) and converts it to mechanical energy (muscles) and heat (see Figure 4.3). The balance of this heat generation, referred to as **homeostasis,** is the basis for examination of the effects of heat and cold on the body. Simple thermodynamic theory shows that temperature, like water, flows from the high point to the low point. Thus, in cold climates, heat will flow from the body into the surrounding environment, thereby making the person feel cold. Similarly, in hot climates, heat will be absorbed by the body, making the person feel hot. Adding physical work to either of these situations will increase body heat and shift the thermal balance. When an imbalance occurs, the body is stressed thermally. This body thermal balance can be illustrated by the mathematical model below:[6]

$$\boldsymbol{S = (M - W) \pm R \pm C \pm V - E}$$

where S is the body heat storage or loss, M is the metabolic heat production of the body, W is the work output, R is the radiative heat gain or loss, C is the convective heat gain or loss, V is the respiratory heat gain or loss, and E is the evaporative heat loss.

When there is heat, the body will gain heat if R, C, and V are positive; similarly, if there is heat loss, then R, C, V, and E are negative. In medical terms, heat gain is referred to as hyperthermic; heat loss is referred to as hypothermic; and a condition of neither gain nor loss is known as balance.

conduction
heat transfer occurring when two surfaces are in contact

convection
heat transfer occurring when one surface adds heat to the surroundings

There are three methods of heat transfer that apply to the body, as well as to any other thermal condition. The first method, **conduction,** occurs when two surfaces are in contact (e.g., the skin touches a hot stove, resulting in a local burn). The second method, **convection,** occurs when one surface adds

FIGURE 4.3

The Body as a Machine System

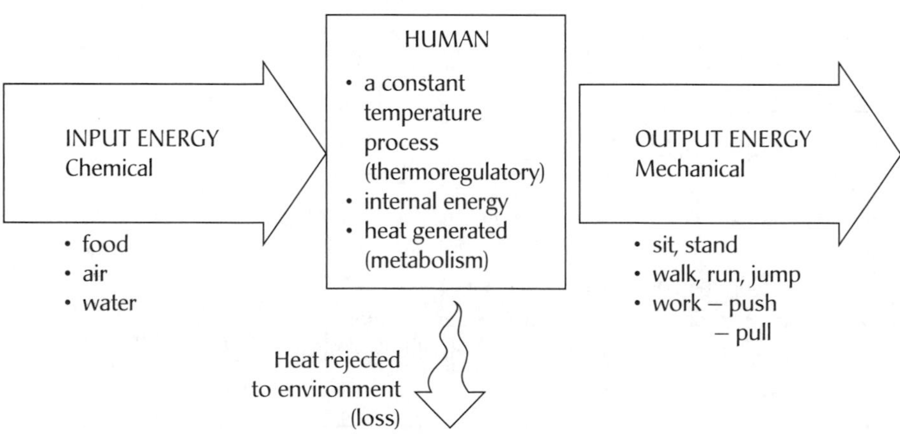

heat to the surroundings (e.g., the skin is close to air flow emanating from a flame or a heater). The third method, **radiation,** occurs when energy is transmitted by electromagnetic waves (e.g., the skin is exposed to sunlight).

radiation
heat transfer occurring when energy is transmitted by electromagnetic waves

The body has remarkable temperature control, with the blood system and the skin being the major players. As body heat increases, blood flow increases, capillaries move closer to the surface of the skin (they actually open up), and sweating increases, thereby allowing increased heat exchange to the atmosphere. As body heat decreases, blood flow slows and the capillaries withdraw from the skin surface, thus reducing the amount of heat transferred to the atmosphere.

The effects of heat and cold on health are well recognized by anyone who spends a lot of time outside in summer and winter. The focal point of most thermal stress and control is at the body core—from the neck to the groin and between the shoulders. The body core temperature range is 35°C to 38.5°C, with "normal" being 37°C. When the core temperature goes outside this range, serious problems can result. Heat-related illnesses include heat stroke (the body loses control of its thermal balance), heat hyperpyrexia (the body temperature rises), heat syncope (heat-induced fainting), heat exhaustion, heat cramps, heat rash, and heat fatigue. Cold-related illnesses include chilblains, caused by reduced circulation in the extremities; trench foot, caused by cold, wet conditions; frostbite, caused by local freezing of tissue; and hypothermia, which occurs when cold causes the body's thermal regulation to fail.

Occupational Health and Safety Today 4.2

Beat the Heat

Occupational health and safety legislation such as that in British Columbia now obligates employers to pay close attention to the dangers of heat exposure. If workers are at risk of heat-related disorders, employers are required to conduct a heat-stress assessment. If it is not possible to reduce the level of heat or to implement engineering controls, the employer must either (a) adjust work–rest schedules to reduce exposure or (b) provide personal protective equipment such as air-cooled or water-cooled vests. Employers must also ensure a supply of cool drinking water near the worksite.

Tips for reducing the adverse consequences of working in the heat include the following:

- Drink cool water at least every 15–20 minutes (remember that thirst is not a good indicator of fluid loss).
- Wear personal protective gear such as cooled vests or bandanas when working in high temperatures on a regular basis.
- Use sunblock and wear a hat.
- Wear suitable eye protection.
- Schedule work–rest regimens.

Similar controls also apply to cold exposure.

Source: WorkSafeBC, "Preventing heat stress at work." Retrieved from http://www.worksafebc.com/publications/health_and_safety/by_topic/assets/pdf/heat_stress.pdf, February 7, 2007.

Occupational Health and Safety Notebook 4.5

Measuring Thermal Stress

Thermal stress is measured using the wet bulb globe temperature (WBGT) index. This index measures the effect of heat and humidity on a worker.

WBGT °C	Description
< 27	No complaints of heat discomfort
27–29	Varying complaints
> 29	Sedentary work for unacclimatized workers
> 31	Continuous work suspended; work–rest schedules implemented
> 38	Threshold limit value; no work without protection

Source: Workers' Compensation Board of BC, "WCB of BC occupational health and hygiene issue sheet: Issue–Heat stress measurement standards." Retrieved from http://www.bcpsea.bc.ca/public/ohs/OHandSManual/Gen_Hazard_Requirements/07_Noise_Vibration/Heat_Stress/WCB_Issue_Sheet_Heat_Stress_Measurement.html, February 7, 2007.

Radiation

Radiation is divided into two distinct groups—ionizing and nonionizing. These two types of radiation are identified primarily by wavelength range—short for ionizing and long for nonionizing—and by their action on tissue. This section will be general since any worker employed by a company involved in radiative processes or materials must undergo extensive, specialized training.

Ionizing Radiation

Ionizing radiation is any form of electromagnetic energy capable of producing ions through interaction with matter. Types of ionizing radiation include X-rays, gamma rays, alpha particles, beta particles, and neutrons. X-radiation is most commonly found in medical facilities. The other forms of ionizing radiation are commonly found in nuclear operations or research companies. All of these forms, except X-rays, occur naturally as well as in manufactured states. Natural radiation is found in ground-grown food, cosmic bombardment, building materials such as concrete, and fertilizers such as phosphorus. Most of these sources are measurable with very sensitive instruments but are insignificant from a health standpoint. Some harmful ionizing radiation, which might occur in basements and mines, is radon gas.

Radiation exposure or dosage is usually measured in a unit called a rem (*r*oentgen *e*quivalent *m*an). Natural radiation is approximately 125 mrem (millirem) per year. A dose of approximately 75 rem (75,000 mrem) per year can cause serious health effects.

Manufactured ionizing radiation can be found in a number of products or operations other than nuclear energy. Most home smoke detectors use a source that emits alpha particles, which are harmless; older "glow-in-the-dark" watch faces were painted with very low radioactive paint. In industry, ionizing radiation can be found in bulk-material measuring devices, high-voltage electronic devices, and medical equipment such as X-ray machines or scanners; none of these poses a health hazard to the general population.

The biological effects of equal amounts of different radiations depend on several factors, including whether the exposure is whole body or local (for example, the arm), acute or chronic. Genetic effects can include cell mutation, burns, and radiation sickness. Control of exposure will include regular monitoring, shielding, job rotation, protective equipment, and extensive training. This is why the dentist places a lead apron over your body and neck when taking X-rays.

Nonionizing Radiation

Nonionizing radiation refers to electromagnetic radiation that does not have energies great enough to ionize matter. Types of nonionizing radiation include ultraviolet radiation, visible (white light) radiation, infrared radiation, microwave radiation, and radio waves. The sun can be a source of all these radiations. The eye is the primary organ at risk from nonionizing radiation (see Figure 4.4).

Control of nonionizing radiation exposures usually includes isolation or separation, protective equipment, and training. With respect to separation, a pregnant computer worker should be offered another job where she is not exposed to a VDT. Even though there is no hard evidence of fetal risk, and such a move may be impractical in a small firm, the company should not put itself in the position of subjecting one of its employees to a possible health risk.

Occupational Health and Safety Notebook 4.6

Effects of Nonionizing Radiation

Specific health effects of nonionizing radiation forms can be itemized as follows:

1. *Ultraviolet radiation* (originating from mercury vapour lamps and fluorescent tubes): conjunctivitis and keratitis (inflammation of the cornea), reddening of the skin (sunburn), skin cancer.
2. *Infrared radiation* (originating from incandescent, fluorescent, high-intensity discharge lights, and hot metals and glass): corneal and retinal burns, overheating of the iris, cataracts, skin burns.
3. *Microwave radiation* (originating from microwave ovens, radar, induction heating equipment, and diathermy equipment): deep tissue damage (cooking), surface skin rash, cataracts and eye lens opacities, biochemical changes and central nervous effects, pacemaker interference.
4. *Radio waves* (originating from radio and television broadcasting, most electronic devices—e.g., video-display terminals [VDTs] and power lines): a number of conditions, including tumours, none of which have been conclusively proven.

Sources: Ontario Ministry of Labour, "Radiofrequency and microwave radiation in the workplace." Retrieved from http://www.labour.gov.on.ca/english/hs/guidelines/radiation/index.html, February 7, 2007; Manitoba Department of Labour, "Work Safe bulletin: Radiation, July 1997, Bulletin #180." Retrieved from http://www.gov.mb.ca/labour/safety/pdf//bltn180.pdf, February 7, 2007.

FIGURE 4.4

General Absorption Properties of the Eye for Electromagnetic Radiation

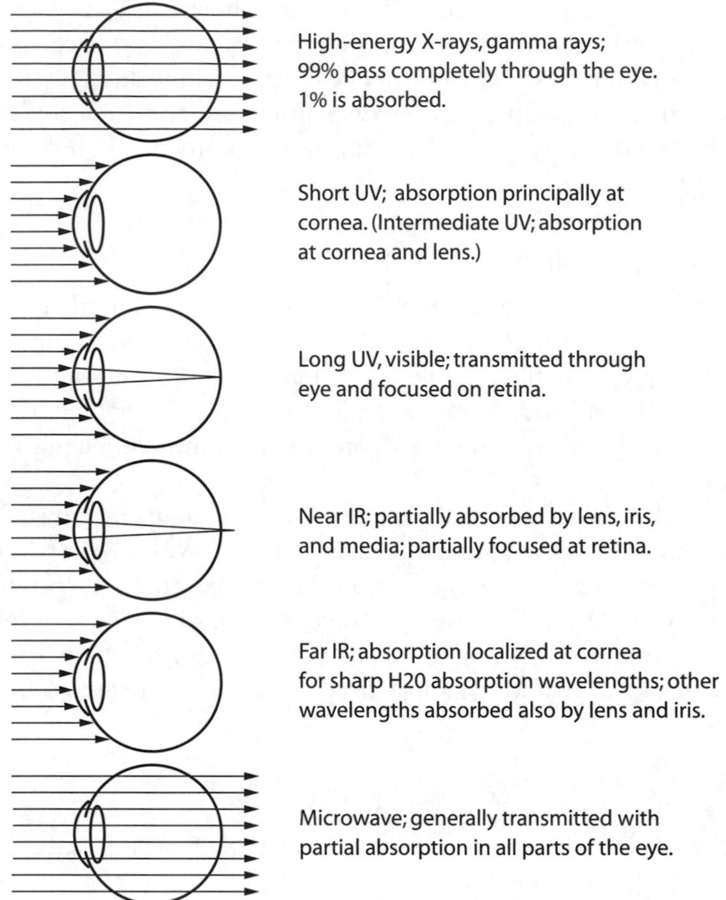

Summary

This chapter has focused on four physical agents that are commonly encountered in industry—noise, vibration, thermal stress, and radiation. Industries in which agents like ionizing radiation are encountered have implemented extensive, specialized training programs and procedures. In most situations, however, simple prevention policies and programs are adequate for reducing and controlling worker exposure to physical agents.

Occupational Health and Safety Today 4.3

Is Your Cell Phone a Physical Agent?

The proliferation of cell phones for personal and business use has given rise to concerns that cell phones may pose a risk factor for diseases such as brain cancer. The concern emerges from the observation that cell phones are essentially radio transceivers that emit and receive electromagnetic signals.

Many reviews of the scientific literature examining the impact of cell phone radiation have been conducted. Every review has concluded that there is no clear evidence of adverse health effects associated with cell phone usage. Nonetheless consumer concern has led cell phone manufacturers to print the specific absorption rate (SAR)—a measure of how much radiation is given off—on each phone. Moreover, the recommendations for the safe use of cell phones typically advocate limiting cell phone usage.

Sources: Health Canada, "It's your health: Safety and the safe use of cell phones." Retrieved from http://www.hc-sc.gc.ca/iyh-vsv/prod/cell_e.html, February 7, 2007; CBC, "Cellphone radiation." Retrieved from http://www.cbc.ca/news/background/cellphones/radiation.html, February 7, 2007; and Krewski, D., Byus, C., Glickman, B. W., Lotz, W. G., Mandeville, R., McBride, M., Prato, F. S., & Weaver, D. F. (2003). Recent advances in radio-frequency fields and health. *Journal of Toxicology and Environmental Health*.

Key Terms

ambient 82
attenuated or attenuation 88
audiometer 88
conduction 92
convection 92
decalcification 90
dosimeter 88
early warning change 83
exchange rate 86
homeostasis 92
hyperreflexia 85
necrosis 90
octave band analyzer 88
physical agents 82
radiation 93
resonance 90
segmental vibration 90
sound pressure level meter 88
vasoconstriction 85
whole body vibration 90

Weblinks

CBC News, "Noise"

http://www.cbc.ca/consumers/market/files/home/noise/ (p. 83)

National Research Council Canada, "Noise Control in Buildings"

http://irc.nrc-cnrc.gc.ca/pubs/bsi/85_e.html (p. 84)

Hearing Center Online, "Name that sound—What does hearing loss sound like?"

http://www.hearingcenteronline.com/sound.shtml (p. 84)

American Conference of Governmental Industrial Hygienists

http://www.acgih.org (p. 87)

WorkSafeBC, "Part 7 Noise, Vibration, Radiation and Temperature"

http://regulation.healthandsafetycentre.org/s/Part7.asp (p. 90)

Ontario Paramedic Association, "Public Service Announcements"

http://www.ontarioparamedic.ca/communications/ pr_ideas.html (p. 92)

The Radiation Safety Institute of Canada, "Issues in Radiation Safety"

http://www.radiationsafety.ca/Issues.htm (p. 94)

RPC Icons

RPC 4.1 Analyses risk to the health and safety of employees and determines appropriate preventative measures, including training, provision of required safety equipment, and administrative practices.

- relevant legislation
- nature of the business and physical work environment
- hazard recognition
- workplace inspection techniques
- safety programs, equipment, and emergency procedures
- ergonomics
- functions of the JHSC
- training and development/presentation techniques
- industry best practices
- relevant technical terminology
- the collective agreement
- services and equipment available in the community
- Worker Protection (including health and safety and Workers' Compensation)
- Training and development program design and administration

Task & Knowledge Requirements

- Occupational health and safety legislation (e.g., Occupational Health and Safety Act of Ontario, Workplace Safety & Insurance Act—Bill 99, Workplace Hazardous Materials Information System, Transportation of Dangerous Goods legislation, environmental legislation, smoking in the workplace legislation, civil rights legislation)
- hazard identification and control
- emergency preparedness procedures

- management techniques for OH&S Programs
- types of employee assistance and wellness programs

RPC 4.2 Implements and evaluates practices in the areas of health, safety, security, and Workers' Compensation.

- investigative techniques
- hazard recognition
- disaster recovery techniques
- relevant legislation
- resource information
- common health and safety practices
- company policies and procedures
- Worker Protection (including health and safety and Workers' Compensation)
- theories and practices for protection of individuals and groups
- Occupational health and safety legislation (e.g., Occupational Health and Safety Act of Ontario, Workplace Safety & Insurance Act—Bill 99, Workplace Hazardous Materials Information System, Transportation of Dangerous Goods legislation, environmental legislation, smoking in the workplace legislation, civil rights legislation)
- hazard identification and control
- management techniques for OH&S Programs

RPC 4.3 Analyses risk to the health and safety of employees and determines appropriate preventative measures, including training, provision of required safety equipment, and administrative practices.

- relevant legislation
- nature of the business and physical work environment
- hazard recognition
- workplace inspection techniques
- safety programs, equipment, and emergency procedures
- ergonomics
- functions of the JHSC
- training and development/presentation techniques
- industry best practices
- relevant technical terminology
- the collective agreement
- services and equipment available in the community
- Worker Protection (including health and safety and Workers' Compensation)
- training and development program design and administration

Task & Knowledge Requirements

- Occupational health and safety legislation (e.g., Occupational Health and Safety Act of Ontario, Workplace Safety & Insurance Act—Bill 99, Workplace Hazardous Materials Information System, Transportation of Dangerous Goods legislation, environmental legislation, smoking in the workplace legislation, civil rights legislation)

- hazard identification and control
- emergency preparedness procedures
- management techniques for OH&S Programs
- types of employee assistance and wellness programs

RPC 4.4 Ensures due diligence and strict liability requirements are met, e.g. records are kept and formal procedures established.

- relevant legislation and common law
- company policies and procedures
- industry best practices
- program and policy development
- training and development techniques
- risk analysis
- common and statutory law (e.g., employment standard: labour relations)
- Worker Protection (including health and safety and Workers' Compensation)
- theories and practices for protection of individuals and groups

TASK & KNOWLEDGE REQUIREMENTS

- Occupational health and safety legislation (e.g., Occupational Health and Safety Act of Ontario, Workplace Safety & Insurance Act—Bill 99, Workplace Hazardous Materials Information System, Transportation of Dangerous Goods legislation, environmental legislation, smoking in the workplace legislation, civil rights legislation)
- management techniques for OH&S Programs

Discussion Questions

1. Workers in a manufacturing division in your jurisdiction have made a formal complaint that three machines are too noisy. Noise measurements are taken: the results are 83 dB, 87 dB, and 88 dB. Do the workers have a legitimate complaint?
2. Name three sources of UV radiation in an office. Then describe the effects of UV radiation on health.
3. All jurisdictions in Canada have access to the same science. Yet jurisdictions vary in legislated standards (e.g., for noise exposure; see Table 4.1). Why might different standards apply in different jurisdictions?
4. Many occupations involve an inherent exposure to a physical agent resulting in excessive exposure to noise, vibration, thermal conditions, and so on. Outline the steps an employer can take to protect employees when avoiding the exposure is not possible.

Using the Internet

1. Working outside in the Canadian winter can be a hazard for many workers. Using Internet resources, determine the health and safety regulations and guidelines for outdoor work in your jurisdiction. Compare regulations across several provinces or territories. Which jurisdictions have developed the most extensive sets of guidelines for outdoor work?

Exercise

1. Occupational health and safety legislation establishes standards for exposure to various forms of physical agents in the workplace. Think of common forms of after-work entertainment (e.g., movies, bars, restaurants, malls). What physical agents are present in these settings? What risks do they pose for customers? for employees of these establishments?

Case 1

Monty's Problem

The newly appointed corporate medical director, a physician, paid an initial visit to one of the branch plants of the company. For the first time, he met the occupational health nurse, an RN and recent CCOHN, who had been appointed from the local community some years previously. Occupational hygiene and safety at the plant was the responsibility of one of the senior production engineers, a P.Eng., who had been at the plant for many years. Neither of these individuals had received any formal instruction in occupational health nursing or occupational health and safety, respectively, since such training had not been available when they were appointed to these positions. The director was disturbed to note that medical records maintained by the nurse appeared to be available to the personnel department and that there was no defined occupational health and safety program. The manager of the plant was absent on the day of the director's visit and therefore unavailable to discuss these concerns.

On returning to corporate headquarters, the physician sent a directive to the occupational health nurse instructing her that medical records were to be regarded as private and that information was not to be released without his express permission. He also asked the occupational health and safety person to purchase a simple class 2 sound-level meter and to carry out a survey of noise levels at the branch plant. This information was to be available for discussion when the director next visited the operation.

Unfortunately, these requests caused considerable difficulties. The nurse had an argument with the personnel department over the availability of medical records and this led to intense internal friction. The production engineer/health and safety specialist resented the interference of the physician and complained to the plant manager, whom he had known personally for many years. The plant manager, Monty James, called head office to ensure the director did not visit the plant without his permission or at least giving notification so that Monty would be available.

In reply, the physician pointed out that the noise levels at the site were clearly excessive and that the so-called occupational health and safety specialist was not capable of carrying out his duties.

When Monty James heard this response, he telephoned his superior, the general manager at corporate. If you were Monty, what would you say to your superior and how would you go about resolving the situation?

Case 2

Expensive Jewellery

As a newly hired HR specialist, you are touring the floor of the manufacturing plant. You are surprised to see that many workers are wearing their hearing protectors around their neck like a necklace instead of covering their ears. Moreover, the style seems to be to wear safety glasses perched on top of the head rather than in a position that would protect eyes. Employees working with acids are doing so in street clothes and barehanded despite the fact that rubber gloves and safety aprons are hanging on hooks next to the workstation. Even from your brief tour, it is clear that the company has invested in the best personal protective equipment available. Yet workers do not seem to use the equipment to protect themselves. One of your new responsibilities is health and safety programming. What do you do?

Appendix

This appendix illustrates some of the techniques and calculations for noise and hearing protection that could prove useful to the HR practitioner when examining workplace conditions, adding new noise-generating equipment, or working with a consultant, government inspectors, or certified members of the Joint Health and Safety Committee. Noise calculations deal with the combining of noise levels from various operating machines or purchase of new equipment. Some of this material may be required as defined in the specific course of study of the academic institution involved.

Calculating Noise Levels

Noise level is measured in units of decibels or dB. This is a unit of measure of sound pressure level (SPL), which is the technical name for noise level or the "amount" of noise that we hear. This relationship can be mathematically expressed as

$$\text{dB} = 20 \log (\boldsymbol{p}/\boldsymbol{p_0}) \quad \text{(equation 5.1)}$$

where dB is the sound pressure level (SPL), p is the sound pressure, and p_0 is a reference pressure, usually 0.00002 Pascal (N/m^2) or 0.0002 microbars.

Although equation 5.1 has little practical application other than identifying the basics of noise, a variation of it can assist in noise-level evaluation. The variation is expressed as

$$\text{total dB} = 10 \log (10\ \text{dB}^{1/10} + 10\ \text{dB}^{2/10} + \ldots + 10\ \text{dB}^{n/10}) \qquad \text{(equation 5.2)}$$

where the various dB values are for any number of machines or noise sources in an area. For example, one manufacturer had a machine with a noise level, or SPL, of 88 dB. The manufacturer decided to purchase an additional machine. The supplier insisted that the noise level of the new machine was 85 dB, below the current noise standard. However, when the values for each of these machines were entered into the relationship expressed in equation 5.2, the result was the total dB $= 10 \log (10^{88/10} + 10^{85/10}) = 89.8$ or 90 dB, which reached the current limit and could possibly create some hearing problems. Any other ambient noise in this workplace could cause the noise level to exceed the safety standards. This calculation can be used for decibels (dB) as above, or A-weighted decibels [dB(A)].

An easier way to make this same calculation is shown in Table 4.2. In our example, the difference in noise level between the two machines is 88 − 85, or 3 dB. Using the table, find the line that shows a difference of 3. The line at

TABLE 4.2

Measuring Noise Levels

Difference between High and Low Noise Levels	Amount to Be Added to Higher Noise Level	Difference between High and Low Noise Level	Amount to Be Added to Higher Noise Level
0.0 to 0.1	3.0	4.1 to 4.3	1.4
0.2 to 0.3	2.9	4.4 to 4.7	1.3
0.4 to 0.5	2.8	4.8 to 5.1	1.2
0.6 to 0.7	2.7	5.2 to 5.6	1.1
0.8 to 0.9	2.6	5.7 to 6.1	1.0
1.0 to 1.2	2.5	6.2 to 6.6	0.9
1.3 to 1.4	2.4	6.7 to 7.2	0.8
1.5 to 1.6	2.3	7.3 to 7.9	0.7
1.7 to 1.9	2.2	8.0 to 8.6	0.6
2.0 to 2.1	2.1	8.7 to 9.6	0.5
2.2 to 2.4	2.0	9.7 to 10.7	0.4
2.5 to 2.7	1.9	10.8 to 12.2	0.3
2.8 to 3.0	1.8	12.3 to 14.5	0.2
3.1 to 3.3	1.6	14.6 to 19.3	0.1
3.4 to 3.6	1.5	19.4 to ∞	0.0
3.7 to 4.0	1.5		

which the difference ranges from 2.8 to 3.0 gives a factor of 1.8, which is to be added to the highest noise level. Thus, 88 + 1.8 gives a total of 89.8, or 90 dB, as before.[7]

This table can be used for more than two sound sources. When there are more than two, the sound sources must be dealt with in pairs. For example, there are four machines in an area that are running and causing noise. The ratings are 82 dB, 85 dB, 88 dB, and 88 dB. Take these noise levels in pairs, 82 and 85, 88 and 88. In the first instance, the difference is 3 dB, which from the table, as above, gives a factor of 1.8, which is added to the highest value. Thus 85 + 1.8 = 86.8. Perform this same operation with the second pair, 88 and 88. The difference between these is 0. From the table for 0.00 to 0.1, the factor is 3.0, which when added to the highest value gives 88 + 3.0 = 91.3. Now we have two new pairs—86.8 and 91.3. The same operation is again performed. The difference is 4.5. From the table for 4.4 to 4.7, the factor is 1.3, which is added to the higher of the two values. Thus 91.3 + 1.3 = 92.6. The total noise level in this example becomes 92.6 dB, which by any standard is too high.

If equation 5.2 is used, then

$$\text{total dB} = 10 \log (10^{82/10} + 10^{85/10} + 10^{88/10} + 10^{88/10}) = 92.4 \text{ dB}$$

Shift Adjustment for Noise Exposure

All of the TLV values for chemical and noise exposure are based on an 8-hour shift. If the shift is longer, say 12 hours, or shorter, say 4 hours, then the time weighted average (TWA) should be adjusted. This adjustment for noise uses the equation:

$$\boldsymbol{L_{eq}, t = L_{eq}} - 10 \log \boldsymbol{T_1 / T} \qquad \text{(equation 5.3)}$$

where L_{eq} is the noise exposure level limit for an 8-hour shift; L_{eq}, t is the noise exposure level limit for the time exposure t; T_1 is the time period worked; and T is the nominal time period.

Example: If a worker works a 12-hour shift at a location where the limit for an 8-hour period is 85 dB(A), then the exposure limit for the 12-hour shift will be

$$\boldsymbol{L_{eq}}, 12 = 85 - 10 \log 12/8 = 83.2 \text{ dB(A)}$$

In a similar fashion, if the worker spent only 4 hours at the job, then the new TWA will become

$$\boldsymbol{L_{eq}}, 4 = 85 - 10 \log 4/8 = 88.0 \text{ dB(A)}$$

Although these calculations are mathematically correct, conditions such as long-term exposure, physical condition, and a 40-hour workweek must be considered.

Hearing Protection Types or Classifications

The early part of this chapter noted that there were two basic styles of hearing protection devices—plugs and muffs. The following table shows a more detailed breakdown of the styles and their designations.

TABLE 4.3

Types of Industrial Hearing Protection

CLASS	TYPE	DESCRIPTION
Earplugs	A1	Pre-formed earplug, the fitting of which should be done professionally.
	A2	User-formable earplug made of soft sponge-like materials that the user rolls between the fingers for insertion into the ear canal.
	B1	A stethoscope configuration with the spring headband holding earplugs in position in the ears. Easy to observe, and the band may be worn in several positions on the head.
Circumaural	D1	An earmuff that surrounds the complete ear with a headband that sits only on the top of the head. Often best for comfort and optimum attenuation.
	D2	An earmuff similar to D1 but with a headband system that can be worn in many positions on the head. Attenuation may vary with headband position.
	D3	An earmuff attachment for a hardhat, which can be permanently attached or field applied. Usually used in construction settings.
Nonlinear Protectors	F1	A specialty device with an electronic amplifier. A system that allows only certain sound levels and frequencies to pass unimpeded.
	F2	A specialty device with a mechanical "ear valve" on each ear that responds to impact noise and causes attenuation.
Combination		Many of the above types may be used in combination.

Endnotes

1. Berger, E. H., Ward, W. D., Morrill, J. C., & Royster, L. H. (Eds.). (1988). *Noise and hearing conservation manual* (4th ed.). Akron, OH: American Industrial Hygiene Association.
2. WorkSafeBC Health and Safety Centre. *Hearing conservation in British Columbia—2003*. Retrieved from http:// hearingconservation.healthandsafetycentre.org/s/Statistics .asp, August 5, 2004.
3. Key, M. M., Henschel, A. F., Butler, J., Ligo, R. N., Tabershaw, I. R., & Ede, L. (1977). *Occupational diseases: A guide to their recognition* (rev. ed.). Cincinnati, OH: U.S. Department of Health, Education, and Welfare.
4. Broch, J. T. (1980). *Mechanical vibration and shock measurements* (2nd ed.). Nærum, Denmark: Brüel and Kjær.
5. Soule, R. D. (1973). Vibration. In *The industrial environment–Its evaluation and control*. Cincinnati, OH: U.S. Department of Health, Education, and Welfare.
6. Hammer, W. (1989). *Occupational safety management and engineering* (4th ed.). Englewood Cliffs, NJ: Prentice Hall.
7. Michael, P. L. (1988). Physics of sound. In *The industrial environment–Its evaluation and control* (2nd ed.). Cinninnati, OH: U.S. Department of Health, Education, and Welfare.

Chapter 5

Chemical and Biological Agents

Chapter Learning Objectives

After reading this chapter, you should be able to

- define the numerous terms relating to chemical and biological agents
- explain the interactions of various chemical and biological groups
- discuss the management of chemical and biological agents
- describe the monitoring requirements and instrumentation used
- outline the actions of chemical and biological agents on human physiology
- explain the health and safety risks of airborne respirable contaminants and aerosols
- discuss the methods of measuring airborne contaminants

BIOTERRORISM IN CANADA

Anthrax is an infection caused by the bacterium *Bacillus anthracis*. Since the terrorist events of September 11, 2001, some people in the United States have received letters or packages that contain anthrax spores. Inhaling anthrax results in death in 50 percent of the cases if untreated (a vaccine is 93 percent effective). There have been no such events in Canada, although concerns regarding anthrax are still relevant.

A traffic accident in Winnipeg in March 2005 resulted in the mobilization of a hazardous materials team when it was learned that the Federal Express truck involved in the accident was transporting containers of anthrax. In September 2006 emergency procedures were invoked at Brock University when the university received a postcard insinuating a threat and discovered an unknown white powder in the athletic complex. The events turned out to be unrelated (and the powder was whey protein).

Events such as these illustrate both the possibility of a biological or chemical agent being released and the need to implement effective emergency procedures.

Sources: CTV, "Traffic accident prompts Winnipeg anthrax scare." Retrieved from http://www.ctv.ca/servlet/ArticleNews/story/CTVNews/1109789080407_105198280/?hub=CTVNewsAt11, February 7, 2007; and *The Gazette*, "Brock suffers anthrax scare." Retrieved from http://www.gazette.uwo.ca/article.cfm?section=News&articleID=770&month=09&day=26&year=2006, February 7, 2007.

RPC 5.1

RPC 5.2

RPC 5.3

RPC 5.4

chemical agents
hazards created by one or more chemicals

biohazard
hazard created by exposure to biological material

Most occupational health and safety legislation, as noted in Chapter 2, now includes specific sections dealing with chemical and biological agents. Chemical and biological agents are also dealt with under WHMIS regulations. Virtually all occupational diseases, such as asbestosis, silicosis, various types of dermatitis, and respiratory problems, and many occupational injuries, such as chemical splashes, spills, and burns, are related to chemical or biological exposures. The results of these exposures can range from minor irritation to death. Dealing with these materials requires complete training. There have been too many deaths, among young people in particular, to ignore these facts. This chapter will provide an overview of the problems associated with chemical and biological substances and the requirements for management and control. The term **chemical agents** is used to describe hazards that are created by any one or any combination of a very large number of chemicals and their physical reactions. A *biological agent* or **biohazard** can be as subtle and as deadly as some chemical agents. Biological agents include hazards such as mould, fungus, bacteria, and viruses. Each of these agents may be **ambient** or acute (i.e., a single exposure).

ambient

all-encompassing condition associated with a given environment; usually a composite of inputs from sources all around us

Chemical Agents

More than 70,000 different chemicals are currently in use in North America, and approximately 800 new ones are introduced every year. No toxicity data are available for about 80 percent of the chemicals that are used commercially.[1] Increasingly, physicians are seeing patients who complain of physiological reactions to low-level chemical exposures in the environment, such as headaches, dry nasal passages, and nausea, to name but a few. These complaints have been variously labelled as multiple chemical sensitivity (MCS), twentieth-century disease, total allergy syndrome, and environmental illness.[2] Certain industrial chemicals have been linked to cancer, lung disease, blood abnormalities, nervous-system disorders, birth defects, sterility, and skin problems. The specific effects of some chemicals are well documented, while those of many others are still unknown.

For example, vapours entering the atmosphere from solvents such as paint thinners are included in the chemical-reaction category, because the vapours from the solvents can have a reaction to such things as heat and pressure. Airborne particulates (e.g., dust created by mechanical means such as sanding or grinding) are included in the physical-reaction category in that the contaminant is caused by an expenditure of energy or work. These categories account for most of the health hazards found in industry and at home.[3]

Although such agents may be a hazard in and of themselves, they can also interact synergistically with other lifestyle or environmental factors. Synergistic effects occur when the result of two factors taken together is greater than the sum of the two. For example, a lifestyle factor such as smoking can have a synergistic effect on some materials. An asbestos worker is four times more likely to develop lung cancer than is a non-asbestos worker; the probability rises to 80 to 90 times more likely if the asbestos worker smokes.

It has been estimated that 80 percent of all occupational illnesses are the result of chemical exposures.[4] Health problems created by chemical exposures are more prevalent in the workplace than in any other location. Although for the sake of simplicity this chapter will discuss single chemical exposures, most of the exposures that take place in the workplace are more complex.

To understand chemical agents, we must be familiar with the associated hazards each possesses. The hazard associated with a material is defined as the likelihood that it will cause injury in a given environment or situation. The potential degree of seriousness of the hazard is determined by its **toxicity** (i.e., its ability to cause injury to human biological tissue) or its explosive properties, which are defined in terms of flammability and reactivity. The

toxicity

ability to cause injury to human biological tissue

Occupational Health and Safety Today 5.1

Deadly Fires Burning: Fire Fighters at High Risk for Occupational Cancer

Each day Canadian fire fighters risk their lives in flaming buildings as a service to their community. Although the immediate risk of death from an injury sustained during an active fire is obvious, other health risks associated with firefighting may not be as obvious. In reality, fire fighters are also at high risk for certain types of cancer because of long-term exposure to carcinogenic chemical fumes and smoke. For instance, the chemical fumes released from burning plastic are toxic. In fact, some relatively rare forms of cancer are far more common among fire fighters than among the general population. For instance, glial blastoma, a primary brain cancer, is three times more likely among fire fighters than it is in the general population.

Some provincial and territorial jurisdictions recognize particular forms of cancer as an occupational illness stemming from fighting fires. In 2002, Manitoba became the first province to pass legislation linking cancer to full-time firefighting. Such legislation is called *presumptive*—if workers in a certain occupation develop a disease it is presumed to have been caused by their occupation and there is no need for the worker to prove the link. In Manitoba, for example, under an amendment to the Workers' Compensation Act, if a past or present fire fighter is diagnosed with "(a) a primary site brain cancer; (b) a primary site bladder cancer; (c) a primary site kidney cancer; (d) a primary non-Hodgkin's lymphoma; (e) a primary leukemia; (f) a primary site colorectal cancer; (g) a primary site ureter cancer; or (h) a primary site lung cancer" (The Manitoba Workers' Compensation Act 4(5.2) the illness will be presumed to be caused by employment as a fire fighter. This amendment means that fire fighters who suffer these conditions and their families are qualified to receive Workers' Compensation. Manitoba set a high bar for other jurisdictions. Since the Manitoba legislation passed, other provinces have followed with legislation linking firefighting to certain forms of cancer. Others, such as British Columbia, continue to treat the issue on a case by case basis.

The availability of financial compensation for fire fighters suffering from cancer is certainly a large move forward—in fact, the Manitoba legislation follows years of lobbying on the part of the Manitoba Professional Firefighters Association. However, fire fighters are also focused on the prevention of occupational cancers. In terms of chemical exposure, the most dangerous time is when the flames have been put out, but the fire is smouldering and fire fighters are engaged in site cleanup. This is a time when individuals may be less vigilant about the use of protective breathing apparatus. Education programs about the importance of protective equipment may help reduce the incidence of these deadly cancers.

Sources: McLauchlin, D., & Bartlett, S. (2002, Summer). "Deadly duties." *Media Magazine*. Retrieved from http://www.caj.ca/mediamag/summer2002/award-radio.html, February 7, 2007; Legislative Assembly of Manitoba. (n.d.). Bill 5, "The workers compensation amendment act." Retrieved from http://web2.gov.mb.ca/laws/statutes/ccsm/w200e.php, February 7, 2007; and *The Tyee*, "Firefighters demand cancer benefits." Retrieved from http://thetyee.ca/News/2005/02/07/FirefightersDemand/, February 7, 2007.

extent to which a potentially toxic substance is an actual health hazard will depend on other factors, such as the concentration of the chemical and the length of time the employee is exposed to it.

All chemicals have different melting, freezing, and boiling points. In most situations, more than one of these states is present at the same time. Consider an open container of boiling water: The water is in the liquid state, while the steam is in the water entering the gas state. Similarly, ice will feel hard (solid), be wet (liquid), and actually have evaporated water surrounding it (vapour). The majority of chemical-related health problems result from contact with

Occupational Health and Safety Notebook 5.1

Types of Contaminants

Listed below are seven types of contaminants:

1. *Dust:* Airborne respirable particulate that is solid particles generated by some mechanical means such as grinding, crushing, or sanding. The heavier particles tend to settle out of the air under the influence of gravity. The lighter or smaller the particle, the longer or greater the settling rate.
2. *Fume:* Airborne respirable particulate formed by the evaporation of some solid materials (e.g., steel where the parent metal will vaporize on the application of weld-level heat and the vaporized metal will condense on contact with cooler ambient air). This condensed particulate is a fume. (This term is often confused with vapour.) Particle size is usually less than one micron or micrometre in diameter. Other examples of fume include plastic extrusion and automobile exhaust, which can include fumes (from the metallic additives) and vapours (from the unburned fuel).
3. *Smoke:* Airborne respirable particulate originating from the products of combustion, usually less than 0.1 micron in size. An example would be tobacco smoke or smoke from a fire.
4. *Mist:* Airborne respirable particulate in the form of liquid droplets generated by condensation from the gas state or by the breaking up of a liquid into a dispersed state of finely divided droplets. Spray paint and hair spray are two sources of mist generation.
5. *Vapour:* The airborne respirable contaminants in a gaseous form of any substances that are normally in the solid or liquid state at room temperature and pressure. Usually caused by evaporation. An example would be the airborne contaminant present above any solvent.
6. *Gas:* An airborne respirable contaminant that is one of the three states of matter created where the temperature is above the boiling point. Carbon dioxide and oxygen are two examples.
7. *Liquid:* Chemicals are sometimes found in a liquid form that, although not airborne respirable particulate, can come in contact with the skin and the eyes, when there is a splash or spill during manual mixing or pouring operations, for instance.

Source: Olishifsky, J. B. (1995). Overview of industrial hygiene. In B. A. Plog (Ed.), *Fundamentals of industrial hygiene* (4th ed.). Chicago, IL: National Safety Council.

chemicals in the liquid and gas or vapour states. Most of the negative effects of exposure are derived from airborne respiratory contaminants known as **aerosols**.

aerosols
airborne respirable contaminants, such as liquid droplets or solid particulate, dispersed in air, that are of a fine enough particle size (0.01 micrometres to 100 micrometres) to remain suspended for a time

A workplace health hazard is posed by exposure to one or more of these airborne respirable particulate forms. For instance, the white cloud that rises from a welding operation usually consists of fumes resulting from the condensation of the parent metal and the weld rod metal and coating, smoke resulting from the combustion of oil and other surface contamination, and vapours resulting from the evaporation of some of the oils and solvents on the metal surface.

Toxicology: An Overview

Toxicology is the scientific study of poisons. For the purposes of this chapter, toxicology will refer to the study of chemical-related occupational illnesses.

Chemicals may enter the body by one of four routes, referred to as **routes of entry.** In order of risk and normal contact, they are respiration (inhalation), skin absorption, ingestion, and skin penetration.

routes of entry
respiration (inhalation), skin absorption, ingestion, and skin penetration

Occupational Health and Safety Today 5.2

Occupational Asthma: The Case of Snow Crab Workers

If we asked you to think about someone with a shellfish allergy, you would likely recall a person with a food allergy diagnosed in childhood, rather than a person with an adult-onset occupational illness. However, this less well known reaction to shellfish is a reality for many people who work in snow crab processing plants. Snow crab processing employees are at risk for developing a specific type of occupational asthma called crab asthma. This form of asthma may develop following exposure to airborne fumes and dust that materialize when processing (cooking, crushing, or cutting) crab. SafetyNet, a community research alliance on health and safety in coastal and marine work, led by Memorial University of Newfoundland researchers Dr. Barbara Neis and Dr. Stephen Bornstein, has launched a long-term research program on crab asthma.

The symptoms have two major categories: asthma symptoms and allergy symptoms. The asthma symptoms include coughing, wheezing, tightness of the chest, and shortness of breath. The allergy-type symptoms include itchy, watery eyes, running nose, and skin rash. These symptoms are strongest while at work but can persist when the person goes home at night or takes vacations.

Although not all processing workers develop crab asthma, it can be a devastating diagnosis for those who develop the condition. The symptoms, which can occur anywhere from a few weeks after starting work in a plant to a few years after exposure, can mean the individual has to leave the job. In many coastal communities, the crab processing plant may be the only employment option. As such, alternative employment is difficult to find and unemployment may follow. Due to this, some individuals with crab asthma may continue to work in crab processing plants while their condition worsens. As an occupational illness, crab asthma is a compensable claim.

Sources: SafetyNet: A Community Research Alliance on Health and Safety in Coastal and Marine Work. Retrieved from http://www.safetynet.mun.ca/, February 7, 2007; and Howse, D., Neis, B., & Horth-Susin, L. (2003, October). All out of breath and nowhere to go: The social, economic and quality of life impacts of occupational asthma to snow crab. Paper presented at the SafetyNet Conference, St. John's.

Respiration (Inhalation)

An average-sized human breathes approximately eight litres of air per minute while at rest; this quantity increases with any activity.[5] Most human exposure to chemicals comes from breathing airborne contaminants. The respiratory system, illustrated in Figure 5.1, does a very efficient job of distributing these contaminants throughout the body during the normal air exchange process.

There are five basic levels of protection or defence within the respiratory tract. The first level of defence is the nose. The nose, or upper respiratory tract, is lined with hairs, or cilia, that act as a coarse filter medium. The interior of the nasal passage is the second level of defence; here **turbinates** are found, which act as a humidification and heat exchange source. The third level of defence is further back in the throat where the hairs or cilia are coated with a thick fluid called mucus. This mucus/cilia system will entrap the finer particulate. The trapped contaminant is removed by blowing the nose and/or clearing the throat. Everyone has experienced these conditions after cleaning the garage, dusting a room, or sanding wood for refinishing. The fourth level of defence is the aerodynamic characteristics of the lung passages such as the bronchi and the bronchiole. Here, the flow of air and its turbulence from

turbinates
spiral or spongy sections of the respiratory system that have a centrifugal effect to help remove aerosols

Figure 5.1

The Respiratory System

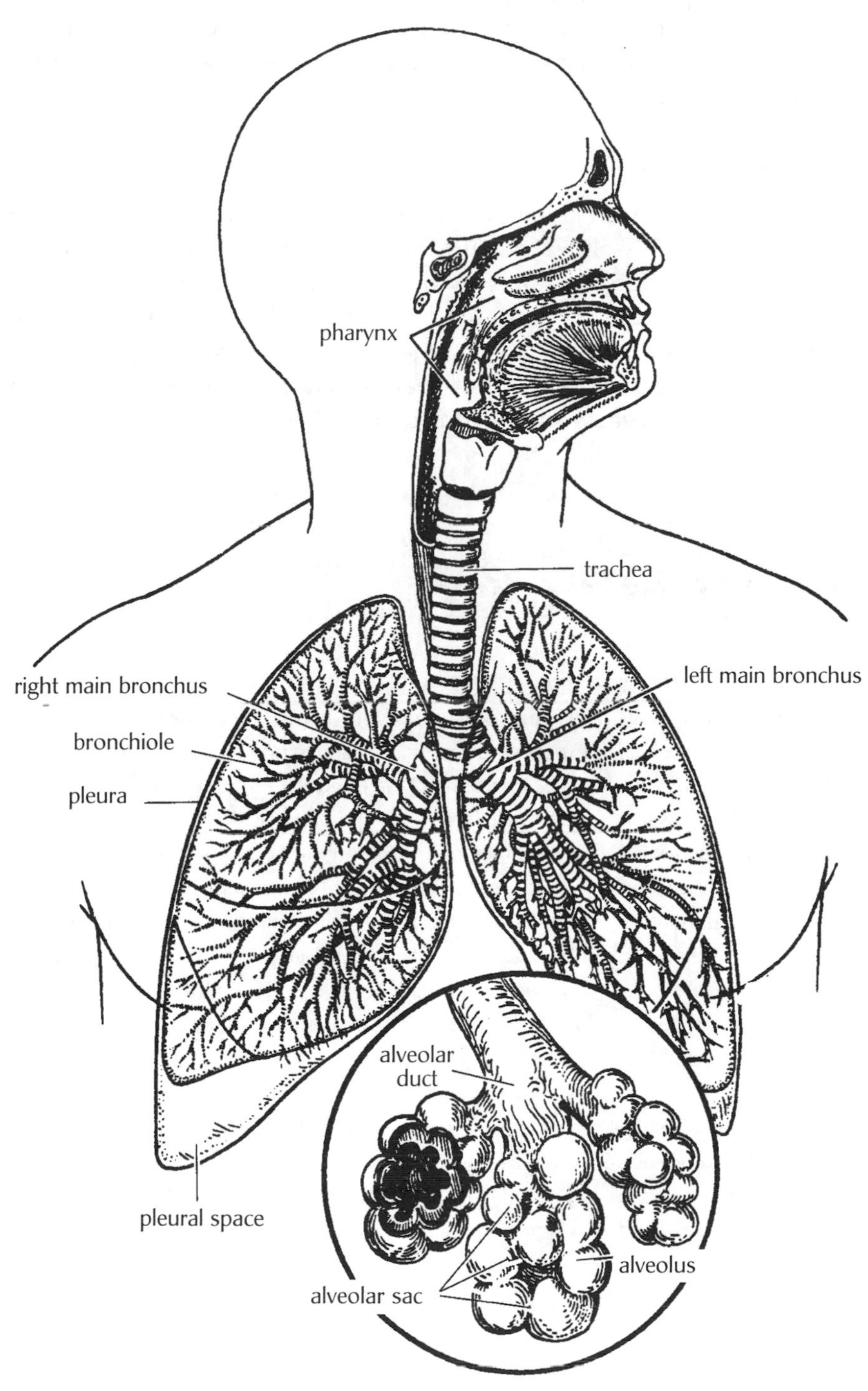

breathing will allow much of the larger particulate that bypassed the earlier defences to be expelled with normal exhalation. The fifth level of defence consists of myriad tiny air sacs, called **alveoli,** that are located at the ends of the lung's air passage, called the alveolar ducts. These sacs (which are the source of oxygen transfer from the lungs to the bloodstream) contain small cells called macrophages (Greek for "big eater") that dispose of any impurities via the lymph system.

alveoli
tiny air sacs

Skin Absorption

In many workplaces and at home, chemical contact with the skin is a common occurrence. Many fat-soluble chemicals can be readily absorbed and most gases can pass through the skin very quickly. Chlorinated solvents such as carbon tetrachloride can pass through the skin into the blood and eventually reach the liver, where tissue damage may occur. Dimethyl sulphoxide can be absorbed through the skin in less than a minute following contact, and most people can detect a garlic-like taste in the back of the throat from this exposure.

Occupational Health and Safety Today 5.3

Good Scents?

Environmental illness (EI) involves seemingly healthy individuals experiencing long-lasting symptoms of physical distress in their work settings. EI contaminants are estimated to exist in 20 to 30 percent of all work settings in North America. This illness has generally been associated with newly constructed and renovated buildings designed for energy efficiency and, until recently, was thought to be related solely to the inadequacy of mechanical ventilation systems. Recent findings suggest that other factors contribute to poor indoor air quality (e.g., car exhaust fumes from indoor garages, and heat and chemicals released by laser printers, computers, and photocopiers).

The effects of EI are variable and nonspecific, affecting building occupants both physically and psychologically. Physical symptoms include mucous-membrane irritation affecting the eyes, nose, and throat; skin ailments; and unpleasant odour and taste perceptions. Other commonly reported symptoms include fatigue, headaches, nausea, confusion, and dizziness, as well as asthma-like symptoms. Typically, symptoms increase with exposure to the affected environment, but usually dissipate once the occupant leaves the building (i.e., evenings, weekends, and holidays). In some cases symptoms do not abate. They may recur on exposure to chemicals found in home products and in non-work environments. Moreover, an increasing number of individuals have developed sensitivities to fragrances such as perfumes, scented deodorants, and hair spray.

In recognition of this growing phenomenon, an increasing number of organizations are adopting scent-free policies. Typically, workplaces post notices requesting both employees and visitors to refrain from using scented products while on the premises. Although aimed at a health and safety issue, such policies can be quite controversial, with some individuals maintaining their right to wear fragrances of their choice. Adopting a scent-free workplace policy should be preceded and accompanied by an educational campaign pointing out the reality of EI chemical/fragrance sensitivities and the types of physical symptoms some individuals experience when exposed to such fragrances.

Source: Canadian Centre for Occupational Health and Safety, "Can scents cause health problems?" Retrieved from http://www.ccohs.ca/oshanswers/hsprograms/scent_free.html, February 7, 2007.

Occupational Health and Safety Notebook 5.2

Illnesses Linked to Asbestos Exposure

Asbestos exposure is killing Canadian workers. Diseases stemming from asbestos exposure dominate occupational illness claims processed by the Workers' Compensation Boards across the country. For example, from 1992 to 2001 in B.C., 18.9 percent of the fatality claims accepted by the WCB were related to asbestos. All other occupational diseases combined accounted for only 12.9 percent of the claims. Asbestos continues to account for a majority of workplace illnesses causing death.

What is asbestos? The term actually describes a class of strong and flexible mineral fibres. It was the strength and flexibility of asbestos that made it a popular component for building and construction materials. In fact, before the 1970s asbestos was widely used in building materials such as cement and insulation. However, as the long-term health consequences of asbestos exposure have become known, its use has become increasingly controlled and limited. Nonetheless, products containing asbestos do remain on the market. Today, asbestos products are bonded with other materials, thus reducing the health threat. However, damage to these products, such as automotive brakes or some floor tiles, may release dangerous particles into the air.

The first signs of asbestos-related illness tend to arise many years after exposure. Some of the conditions that have been linked to asbestos include the following:

- *Asbestosis*. A scarring of the lung tissues that arises 10 to 15 years following exposure to airborne asbestos. This condition is characterized by respiratory difficulty. The damage is irreversible. This condition can result in respiratory failure and ultimately death.
- *Mesothelioma*. A form of cancer that attacks the linings of the chest cavity, lungs, and abdomen. It spreads rapidly and survival following diagnosis is very rare. The only known cause of mesothelioma is asbestos exposure.
- *Lung cancer*. Asbestos is an acknowledged cause of lung cancer. Even though it takes years to develop, changes to the lungs start soon after exposure to asbestos.

Sources: Health Canada, "Health risks of asbestos." Retrieved from http://www.hc-sc.gc.ca/iyh-vsv/environ/asbestos-amiante_e.html, February 7, 2007; and Sharpe, A. & Hardte, J. (2006). Five deaths a day: Workplace fatalities in Canada 1993–2005. CSLS Research Report 2006-04. Ottawa: Centre for the Study of Living Standards.

The ability of a chemical to easily pass through the skin is often closely associated with its level of toxicity. For example, the toxicity of DDT is about the same for insects and humans when it is injected. However, it is much less toxic to a person when applied to the skin, because it is poorly absorbed through the skin. Other pesticides are much more rapidly absorbed through human skin. Many agricultural workers have died following skin absorption of pesticides, particularly the organophosphate insecticides.

Chemicals that are not rapidly absorbed through the skin may produce a localized irritation (dermatitis) at the point of contact through a process called defatting, which causes the skin to become white and dry (e.g., when cleaning your hands with paint remover) and thus more permeable to water vapour, leading to tissue water loss and cracking. Burns or blisters can result from contact with acids or alkalis (chemical action). Skin disorders can result from contact with certain plants (biological action). Skin damage can result from contact with radiation or heat (physical action).

Occupational Health and Safety Notebook 5.3

Toxicity Terminology

* *Dose.* The degree of exposure and possible reaction with time. The dose is usually the basis for the values that are developed for threshold limit values (TLV), which are used as a control measure in the workplace. For example, the TLV for carbon dioxide is 5,000 parts per million (ppm), based on an 8-hour exposure time.
* *Acute toxicity.* An effect that manifests itself immediately following exposure or very shortly thereafter. Burning your hand on a hot surface, for example, results in immediate pain and discoloration, and, later, blisters.
* *Chronic toxicity.* An effect that manifests itself some time after the exposure (possibly months or even years). Some examples are cirrhosis of the liver from prolonged alcohol exposure; sensitization from isocyanates; occupational cancer, such as leukemia, from benzene exposure; or mesothelioma from asbestos exposure.
* *Local toxicity.* The effect of an exposure at the point of contact. Cleaning your hands with paint thinner will cause dry, grey skin at the point of contact; this will be an immediate reaction.
* *Systemic toxicity.* An effect that occurs at some location remote from the point of contact. For example, inhaling a chlorinated solvent such as trichloroethylene can cause damage to the liver, or inhaling carbon monoxide, which interrupts oxygen transfer to the blood, can cause asphyxiation and death.

Source: ACGIH. (1994). *Threshold values for chemical substances and physical agents in the workplace.* Cincinnati, OH: American Conference of Governmental Industrial Hygienists.

target organs
tissues or organs that are most affected by exposure to a particular substance

surfactant layer
layer of liquids in the digestive tract and elsewhere (e.g., the cardiovascular system) that modify or reduce the surface tension within the conductors—intestine, blood vessels—to allow material—blood, food, stools, and so on—to move easily

Ingestion

For many solvents, entry through the mouth and digestive system is not as important as entry through the skin or the lungs. Poor personal hygiene can contribute to poisoning, as can eating, drinking, or smoking in an area where solvents are used. Ingestion of most solvents will cause damage to the lining of the digestive system. The ingested solvent may also be absorbed into the bloodstream and carried to **target organs,** where it will produce toxic effects. Worse still, the ingested solvent may be aspirated into the lungs where it can destroy the **surfactant layer,** cause a chemical pneumonitis, and collapse the alveoli.[6]

Occupational Health and Safety Notebook 5.4

Classification of Toxic Substances

Toxic materials are many and varied and have a variety of health effects on humans. In this section, organic and inorganic solvents are enumerated, because they are common at home and at work, and they can have widespread health effects based on their properties. The overall effects of toxic materials can be grouped under the following 12 classifications.

1. *Irritants*. Irritants, sometimes referred to as "primary irritants," produce tissue or other damage at the point of contact. They are divided by route of entry into two groups:
   a. *Inhaled irritants*. Inhaled irritants refer to airborne respirable contaminants or aerosols (including vapours, gases, and solid particulate) that are inhaled into the lungs causing damage wherever they settle. Ammonia is dissolved into body fluids and absorbed by the mucous membranes of the upper airways, and can result in symptoms such as headache, nausea, salivation, and burning of the throat. Bronchitis may follow a very severe exposure, if the patient survives.
   b. *Contact irritant*. A contact irritant is any material that causes some sort of irritation, such as a rash or itch, at the point of contact. An example would be using Varsol to clean paint from your hands or coming into contact with poison ivy. In most cases, the skin is the organ most affected.
2. *Asphyxiants*. Any material that interferes with the oxygen supply to the blood and body tissues is referred to as an asphyxiant. Normal air contains approximately 21 percent oxygen and 79 percent nitrogen. The average person uses about 3 percent of the oxygen in air when breathing. If the oxygen content of the air falls below 15 percent, the body will be asphyxiated. There are two major types of asphyxiants:
   a. *Simple asphyxiants*. Any airborne respirable chemical that reduces the quantity of oxygen in the inhaled air by displacement is referred to as a simple asphyxiant. Examples are methane, propane, and nitrogen.
   b. *Chemical asphyxiants*. If an airborne and inhaled chemical interferes with the transport of oxygen by the blood hemoglobin or with the ability of the body cells to use oxygen, it is called a chemical asphyxiant. Examples of such chemicals are carbon monoxide, which interferes with the ability of the hemoglobin to transport oxygen and can result in tissue hypoxia and death, and hydrogen sulphide (rotten gas), which can interfere with the ability of the body cells to use oxygen and can result in immediate coma with acute exposure and possible death.
3. *Anesthetics and narcotics*. Any chemical that affects the central nervous system (CNS) can be considered to belong to this class. Most of these chemicals can, on exposure, cause headaches, interfere with the ability to concentrate, and act as a depressant. Examples include ethyl alcohol, acetylene, acetone, and toluene. In fact, all organic solvents can produce narcotic effects. Many of us have experienced some of these symptoms after consuming alcohol.

(continued)

Classification of Toxic Substances (continued)

4. *Systemic poisons*. Systemic poisons can cause damage to one or more internal organs, as well as cell and neuron damage. Chlorinated materials such as DDT, endrin, chloroform, or trichloroethylene can cause damage to the liver and kidneys, usually as a result of chronic exposure. Benzene can cause damage to the blood-forming cells (the homeopathic system). Carbon disulphide is believed to damage the neurons. Other common systemic poisons include heavy metals such as lead, cadmium, and mercury, and chemicals such as arsenic and fluoride.
5. *Liver toxicants*. This grouping includes any chemical that will cause direct damage to the liver. The toxic action may be chemical (caused by alcohol) or metabolic (caused by benzene). In most instances, slight damage can be repaired. Cirrhosis is the most common disease.
6. *Kidney toxicants*. Kidney toxicants, like liver toxicants, include chemicals that cause damage to the kidneys, usually through the process of metabolic transformation whereby harmless chemicals are rendered harmful or vice versa. Heavy metals such as lead, cadmium, and mercury, in addition to some solvents, can have this effect.
7. *Neurotoxins*. As the name indicates, these chemicals can cause damage to the nerves in the body. Hexane, a component of gasoline, can produce a condition called peripheral neuropathy–a disease affecting the nerves of the extremities–that can result in numbness and loss of feeling. This condition is dose-related.
8. *Sensitizers*. Sensitizers, whether chemical or biological, cause the body's immune system to respond abnormally and produce antibodies against chemicals such as isocyanates and poison ivy. The result is an allergy to the specific chemical in which even casual exposure to the material will cause an allergic reaction. Workers thus affected may have to change jobs, if not employers. Although sensitization is usually a chronic process, a very large acute exposure can sometimes bring it on. Farmer's lung, humidifier fever, nickel itch, and nickel fume fever are some common examples of sensitization.
9. *Lung toxicants*. Toxic chemicals that can affect the lungs include irritant gases such as hydrogen chloride and ammonia, vapours such as isocyanates, and respirable solids such as asbestos, platinum, and silica. These materials can cause a variety of diseases, from simple pneumoconiosis (an accumulation of dust in the lungs and the tissue reaction to the presence of such dust) to cancer.
10. *Mutagens*. Any chemicals that can lead to changes or mutations in DNA. The actions of chemicals like lead, nickel, zinc, and manganese usually cause the death of cells but may in some cases allow the distorted cell to multiply and create a potentially malignant tumour.
11. *Teratogens*. Chemicals such as lead, DDT, and PCB can cause damage to germ cells or create defects in a developing fetus. The most infamous chemical–thalidomide–is well known to cause gross abnormalities or birth defects in the fetus.
12. *Carcinogens*. Carcinogens are agents that cause or promote the formation of cancers. Well-known carcinogens include vinyl chloride, which can cause a liver cancer called angiosarcoma; benzene, which can result in leukemia; and asbestos, which can lead to mesothelioma. Following exposure to the carcinogenic chemical, there can be a latency period of 5 to 15 or more years.

Sources: Key, M. M., et al. (Eds.). (1977). *Occupational diseases: A guide to their recognition* (rev. ed.). Cincinnati, OH: U.S. Department of Health, Education, and Welfare; and WorkSafe Saskatchewan, *Ontario's basic certification training program participant's manual* (Chemical hazards chapter). Retrieved from http://www.worksafesask.ca/files/ont_wsib/certmanual/ch_08.html?noframe, February 7, 2007.

Penetration

Penetration occurs when the skin is cut or punctured by any sharp object. The type of contamination on the source, such as a knife or needle, will determine the possible trauma or illness. Cuts can occur when contact is made with sharp metal, glass materials, or other pointed instruments. Workers such as doctors, nurses, and veterinarians can easily be punctured by a hypodermic needle. The disorders range in seriousness from low-grade infections to HIV (human immunodeficiency virus).

Characteristics and Properties of Solvents

Solvents were created, for the most part, by the science of organic chemistry, and they are the most prevalent of products that we use both at work and at home. There are eight general characteristics or properties that make solvents effective but at the same time hazardous and toxic.

1. *Low surface tension*. This property allows a solvent to spread evenly and quickly and to provide excellent wetting of the contact surface. The higher the wetting factor, the better the wetting effect. But the wetting factor allows a spilled solvent to flow into cracks and joints and remain there, creating vapours that may be toxic. It also allows for more effective skin absorption.
2. *High vapour pressure*. The fact that vapour pressure increases with temperature increases the volume or concentration of a generated vapour or gas. This solvent property allows efficient cleaning in processes such as degreasing systems because of the high vapour generation at the high operating temperatures. It can, however, create an inhalation hazard, the risk of which increases with temperature. This is not considered a problem as long as the container is kept closed. In a fire situation, the pressure increase can cause an explosion.
3. *Low boiling point*. The lower the **boiling point**, the greater the rate of evaporation or generation of vapours from a liquid. This property is useful when cleaning or painting because the solvents can evaporate quickly at room temperature allowing the article to dry or tack off efficiently. The lower the boiling point, the greater the health risk since vapour can be generated at lower temperatures. Chemicals with boiling points close to room temperature or lower, such as ammonia (BP = 22 °C) or hydrogen cyanide (BP = 25 °C), can be a special problem since they can evaporate readily and are very toxic.

boiling point
temperature at which the vapour pressure of a liquid equals atmospheric pressure

4. *Low heat of vaporization*. This characteristic defines the amount of heat or energy that is required to change a liquid into a gas or vapour. The less heat required, the less costly the process is in an industrial environment. Similarly, the lower the amount of heat necessary, the greater the risk of exposure if the material is not properly controlled.

5. *High volatility*. The main test of a solvent's effectiveness is the speed at which it will evaporate. The greater the volatility, the faster the evaporation, the greater the health and fire risk.
6. *Ability to dissolve fats*. The more effectively a solvent dissolves fats or oils, the more useful it can be. However, when solvents are in contact with the skin, the skin's surface oils are dissolved. The unprotected skin then becomes susceptible to infection and other trauma. Skin contact with solvents is one of the major causes of **dermatitis.**

dermatitis
the inflammation of the skin from any cause

7. *Flammability*. It is one of the main hazards associated with solvent use since all organic solvents are flammable. Care must be taken to ensure that there are no sources of ignition present during use. Chemical specifications usually list four characteristics that relate to flammability.

   (a) *Flash point*. Defined as the lowest temperature at which a liquid gives off enough vapour to form an ignitable mixture with air and produce a flame with a source of ignition. If the flash point is close to room temperature, the danger of ignition can be very great.
   (b) *Lower explosion limit* (LEL) also known as lower flammability limit (LFL). Defined as the smallest fuel–air mixture that is ignitable, expressed as a percent. Carbon monoxide has an LEL of 12.5 percent by volume, which is equivalent to 125,000 parts per million (ppm). The upper exposure value for health exposure is 50 ppm, as shown in various standards. If the exposure to carbon monoxide in the workplace is maintained well below the health limit, there is no risk of ignition to that source.
   (c) *Upper explosion limit* (UEL) also known as the upper flammability limit (UFL). Defined as the highest fuel–air mixture that is ignitable, expressed as a percent. Carbon monoxide has a UEL of 74 percent by volume or 740,000 ppm. The LEL and UEL spread indicates that carbon monoxide could be ignited through a wide range of fuel–air mixtures, which could be an advantage if the gas were to be used for some heat application.
   (d) *Auto-ignition temperature*. Defined as the lowest temperature at which a flammable fuel–air mixture will ignite from its own heat source. An example is spontaneous combustion in moist hay in a barn or in paint-soaked rags stuffed in a pail.

8. *Vaporization*. Most solvents will form very large volumes of vapour from a small amount of liquid. For instance, turpentine can form 112 litres of vapour for each litre of liquid at standard temperature and pressure conditions.

Inorganic Solvents

Inorganic solvents fall into two classes: acids and bases. These are the simplest of chemical groups and are the oldest known forms. The difference between an acid and a base is expressed in terms of pH, a unit that notes the degree of acidity or alkalinity of a solution, having a scale of 1 to 14. A pH value of 7 is considered as neutral (i.e., neither an acid nor a base). A pH of 1 indicates extreme acidity, while a pH of 14 indicates extreme alkalinity.

1. *Acids*. Materials such as hydrochloric acid (HCl), sulphuric acid (H_2SO_4), and chromic acid (H_2CrO_4) are some of the most common. All are very corrosive and are used for refining and processing metals. The plating process makes extensive use of these acids. The health effects are predominantly burns resulting from inhalation and skin contact. The eyes are the most susceptible body part, and are exposed usually as a result of splashing. Chromic acid is a known carcinogen and a sensitizer. The most common sign of chromic acid exposure is the presence of chrome holes in the surface of the skin. These are ugly, black holes left when the skin has been corrosively attacked. Their size depends on the amount of exposure and personal hygiene practices.
2. *Bases*. Sometimes referred to as alkalines, these chemicals include potassium hydroxide (KOH), sodium hydroxide (NaOH), and sodium chloride (NaCl) or table salt. Sodium chloride in its refined state is a requirement of a normal diet. In its less refined form, it is used to keep roads free of ice. The other two alkalines are used to etch or dissolve a variety of materials. All are toxic in certain concentrations.

Organic Solvents

RPC 5.5

Organic solvents, which are petrochemically based, are manufactured by combining the carbon atom with a great many other elements. These solvents can be identified by their molecular structure and can be grouped under 10 classifications, as shown in Table 5.1.

Biological Agents

Biological agents or biohazards are natural organisms or products of organisms that present a risk to humans. Two of the better-known diseases resulting from biological agents are Legionnaires' disease (*Legionella pneumophilia*) and AIDS (acquired immunodeficiency syndrome). Although exposure to biohazards is not as common as exposure to chemical agents, the results can be just as deadly. The acute and chronic exposure effects described previously for chemical agents apply to biohazards as well, although the sources of exposure are different and the physiological reactions vary. The majority of exposures occur through inhalation.

biological agents
natural organisms or products of organisms that present a risk to humans

Most biohazards encountered in the workplace fall into BSL 1. Viral agents such as hepatitis B would be included in BSL 2. People most at risk of exposure to biohazards are employed in unique or specialized fields, such as medicine, research, and farming. In the case of salmonella food poisoning, however, members of the general public could be at risk through food contamination (see Table 5.2).

TABLE 5.1

Organic Solvents

Number	Classification	Example	Toxic Effects	Uses
1	Aliphatic hydrocarbons	Paraffin, acetylene, methane	Simple asphyxiants, CNS, irritants	Fuels, refrigerants, dry cleaning, propellants
2	Aromatic hydrocarbons	Benzene, toluene, xylene	CNS, dermatitis, leukemia (benzene)	Plastics, resins, dyes, pharmaceuticals
3	Halogenated hydrocarbons	Chlorine, iodine, fluorine, carbon tetrachloride	CNS, dermatitis, cancer (carbon tetrachloride)	Fire extinguishers, fumigants, aerosol propellants
4	Nitro-hydrocarbons	Nitroglycerin, pitric acid	Irritants, skin sensitizers	Explosives
5	Esters	Methyl acetate, banana oil	Irritants	Plastics, resins, artificial flavours, perfumes
6	Ethers	Ethylene oxide	Irritants, anesthetics, nausea, respiratory difficulties	Antifreeze, chemical synthesizers, cancer treatment (ethyl ether—anesthetic)
7	Ketones	Acetone, methyl ethyl ketone (MEK)	Narcotic, irritants, vertigo, nausea	Acetate rayon, artificial silk, lubricants
8	Alcohols	Ethyl alcohol (grain alcohol), methyl alcohol (wood alcohol)	Narcotic, dermatitis, headache, nausea, tremors, blindness	Ethyl—liquors; methyl—solvent for inks, embalming fluids
9	Glycols	Ethylene glycol, cellosolve	Intoxication; blood, brain, and kidney disorders	Antifreeze, disinfectants, drugs
10	Aldehydes	Formaldehyde	Sensitizers, CNS, allergic response	Dyes, perfumes, flavourings, vinegar

TABLE 5.2

Biological Agents

AGENT GROUP	AGENT	SOURCE	OCCUPATION
Bacterial	Anthrax *(bacillus anthracis)*	Direct contact with infected animals, hides, and wool	Veterinarians, farmers, butchers, wool workers
	Brucellosis (*brucella* species)	Exposure by ingestion or cuts from excretions or secretions of infected animals, microbiology	Livestock handlers, meat inspectors, farmers, lab workers
	Salmonellosis (*salmonella* species)	Oral exposure, usually from unsanitary food conditions (food poisoning)	Travellers, patient-care workers, amateur chefs
	Staphylococcal food poisoning (*staphylococcus* species)	Ingestion of improperly stored or leftover food or food infected by workers	Food workers, health care workers, home storage
	Lyme disease *(borrelia burgdorferi)*	Tick bites	Outdoor workers
Chlamydiae	Psittacosis or ornithosis *(chlamydia psittaci)*	Inhalation or exposure to infected bird droppings	Zoo workers, taxidermists, pet owners
Rickettsia	Q fever *(coxiella burneth)*	Contact with sheep, cattle, goats, birth by-products, and contaminated dusts	Farmers, veterinarians, slaughterhouse workers, laboratory workers
	Rocky Mountain spotted fever *(rickettsia rickettsii)*	Tick bites	Outdoor workers—lumberjacks, ranchers
Viruses	Cat scratch disease	Breaks in skin, usually from animal scratch	Pet owners and breeders
	Serum hepatitis (hepatitis B virus–HBV)	Direct contact with infected material by puncture, abraded skin, or onto mucous membrane surfaces	Hemodialysis workers, surgeons, dentists, health care workers
	Infectious hepatitis (hepatitis A virus–HAV)	Fecal–oral transmission (from contaminated water)	Travellers, primate handlers, dentists
Fungal	Dermatophytosis (*trichophyton* species)	Contact with people infected by soil, animals, or humans	Gardeners, military personnel (athlete's foot), farm workers (cattle ringworm), health care workers
	Histoplasmosis *(histoplasma capsulatum)*	Inhalation or ingestion of dust from areas that have been bat or bird habitats	Construction workers, bird or chicken farm workers
	Farmer's lung (*aspergillus* species)	Inhalation or ingestion of dusts containing spores from mouldy hay or grain or compost piles	Mushroom workers, brewery workers, bird hobbyists
	Humidifier lung (*penicillium* species)	Inhalation of airborne spores from sources of mould such as cheese, wood, HVAC system water	Cheese workers, HVAC (heating, ventilating, and air-conditioning) workers, tree cutters

Control of Exposures

 5.5

The safe use and handling of chemical and biological agents can be ensured only through the active employment of a variety of control measures. Figure 5.2 outlines the various control measures used to ensure the safe handling of solvents. Controls for low-level biohazards can follow similar measures. These controls are the subject of the sections that follow.

FIGURE 5.2

Engineering, Work Practices, and Medical Control Measures

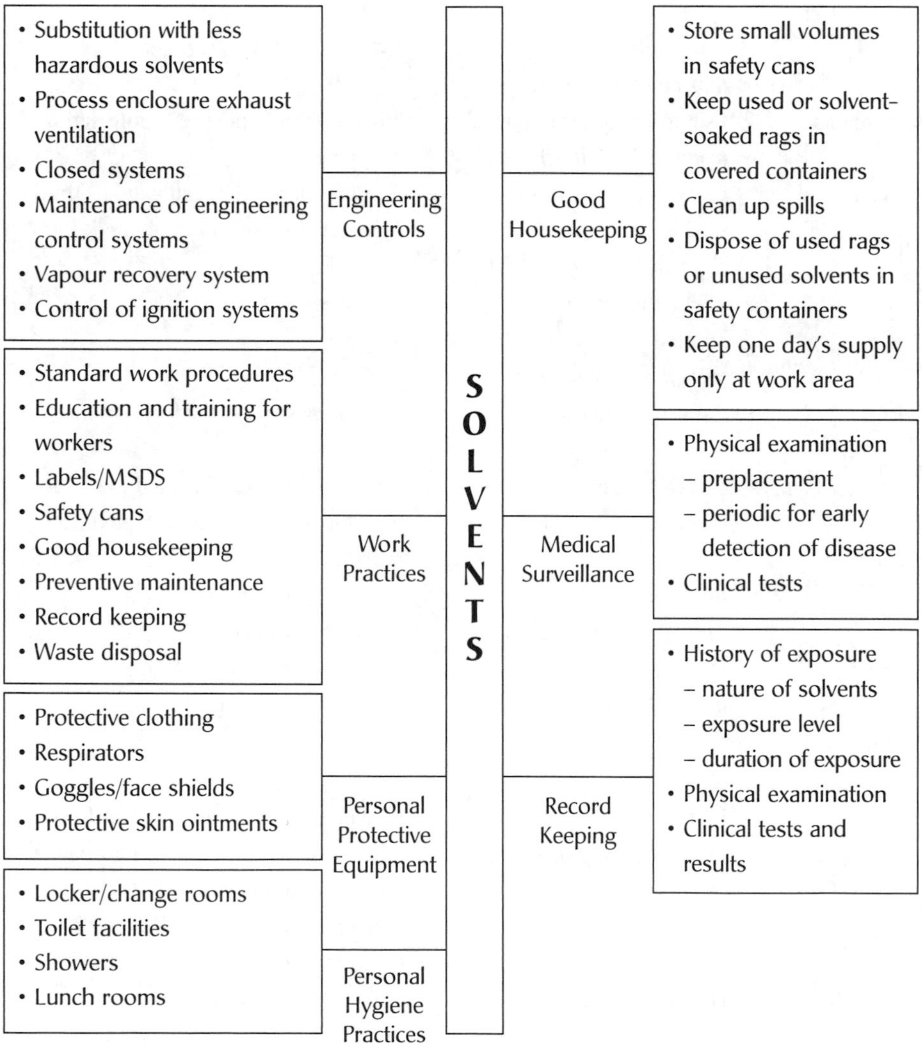

SOLVENTS

Engineering Controls
- Substitution with less hazardous solvents
- Process enclosure exhaust ventilation
- Closed systems
- Maintenance of engineering control systems
- Vapour recovery system
- Control of ignition systems

Work Practices
- Standard work procedures
- Education and training for workers
- Labels/MSDS
- Safety cans
- Good housekeeping
- Preventive maintenance
- Record keeping
- Waste disposal

Personal Protective Equipment
- Protective clothing
- Respirators
- Goggles/face shields
- Protective skin ointments

Personal Hygiene Practices
- Locker/change rooms
- Toilet facilities
- Showers
- Lunch rooms

Good Housekeeping
- Store small volumes in safety cans
- Keep used or solvent-soaked rags in covered containers
- Clean up spills
- Dispose of used rags or unused solvents in safety containers
- Keep one day's supply only at work area

Medical Surveillance
- Physical examination
  - preplacement
  - periodic for early detection of disease
- Clinical tests

Record Keeping
- History of exposure
  - nature of solvents
  - exposure level
  - duration of exposure
- Physical examination
- Clinical tests and results

Occupational Health and Safety Notebook 5.5

Classification of Biological Agents

All biological agents are classified in four groups on the basis of their degree of risk to humans. The higher the class number, the greater the risk.

- *Biosafety Level 1 (BSL 1)*. Agents of no or minimal hazard that can be handled safely using techniques for nonpathogenic materials and are harmless to healthy humans. An example is *E. coli* K12. Effective control is maintained through cleanliness and ventilation in which air is conducted through a high-efficiency particulate air (HEPA) filter in a biological safety cabinet (a well-ventilated room or space in which a worker is isolated from contact with biological agents). The degree of sophistication of the biological safety cabinet depends on the biosafety level.
- *Biosafety Level 2 (BSL 2)*. Agents that may produce diseases of varying degrees of seriousness through accidental skin penetration for which preventive or therapeutic interventions are often available. Examples are bacteria such as salmonella, legionella, and streptococcus; fungi; parasites; and viruses such as hepatitis A, B, C, and D. Control involves the use of a well-ventilated, sealed, filtered space with an air wall to keep workers from contacting the biohazard.
- *Biosafety Level 3 (BSL 3)*. Agents involving special hazards that require special conditions for containment. Agents are indigenous or exotic with potential for infection following aerosol transmission. Agents are associated with serious or lethal disease for which preventive or therapeutic interventions may be available. These agents can pose a high risk to the individual but not the community. Examples include rabies, yellow fever, and HIV types 1 and 2. Containment involves specialized facility design and equipment, with cabinets with HEPA filters externally exhausted back to the room and containment spaces under negative pressure.
- *Biosafety Level 4 (BSL 4)*. Organisms that are extremely dangerous or exotic, that pose a life-threatening disease, and for which preventive or therapeutic interventions are usually not available. Examples include Lassa fever virus, Ebola virus, and tickborne encephalitis virus. Containment locations are rare and usually involve a totally enclosed room that is gas-tight and well ventilated. OH&S practitioners should not be involved at this level.

Sources: DiNardi, S. R. (ed.). (1997). *The occupational environment–Its evaluation and control*. Fairfax, VA: AIHA Press; Canadian Council on Animal Care, "Biosafety guidelines and levels of containment." Retrieved from http://www.ccac.ca/en/CCAC_Programs/ETCC/Module04/15.html, February 7, 2007; and Office of the Auditor General of Canada, "Biosafety and laboratory containment levels." Retrieved from http://www.oag-bvg.gc.ca/domino/reports.nsf/html/9807xe01.html, February 7, 2007.

Engineering Controls

One of the best ways to reduce the risks associated with handling solvents is to find alternatives. A thorough investigation should be conducted to ensure that the proposed substitute meets the intended purpose, does not contain dangerous properties, and is compatible with existing materials in use. However, if solvents are being used, areas should be properly enclosed to prevent or minimize the escape of vapours, and an effective exhaust system should also be in place. Because some of the chemicals used may be a source of ignition, it is equally important to ensure that appropriate fire-extinguishing equipment is on hand and that combustibles are isolated from sources of ignition. Materials should not be stored adjacent to highly reactive chemicals.

Work Practices and Procedures

All employees must be properly trained in the identification and handling of dangerous substances. Senior management must ensure that policies and procedures are accompanied by an appropriate discipline system for dealing with those employees who willfully choose to neglect these practices. Standards must be communicated, in writing, to all employees. (This is also a requirement of WHMIS.)

agents
any substances—chemical, biological, or physical—to which a human may be exposed at work or at home

Good housekeeping is essential when handling, storing, or using **agents.** If containers are leaking, they must be transferred immediately to sound containers. Spills must be cleaned up properly, and employees who may be exposed to the hazard must wear protective equipment. Solvent-soaked rags should be disposed of in airtight, all-metal containers and removed daily. Each municipality has its own guidelines for the disposal of wastes, and employees must be familiar with the guidelines that apply to them.

Preventive maintenance must be conducted regularly to ensure that no potential dangers exist. For example, air filters on exhaust or ventilation equipment may become damaged or plugged and pose a potential danger in an enclosed area in which solvents or biohazards are used. Employees should understand the procedures for maintaining equipment and documenting all repairs.

Occupational Health and Safety Today 5.4

Needlestick Injuries: A Spreading Health and Safety Concern

Needlestick injuries have been a health and safety concern for many years. A needlestick injury occurs when a sharp object, such as a needle, that is potentially carrying blood-borne pathogens punctures the skin of a care provider. For example, a nurse changing an intravenous (IV) may inadvertently stick the used needle in her own hand. It is estimated that more than 800,000 needlestick injuries occur each year in North American health care systems—approximately 30 percent of such injuries carry the potential of transmitting diseases such as hepatitis or HIV.

Health care workers have developed procedures for handling and disposing of "sharps" that minimize the chance of a needlestick injury. However, the potential for needlestick injuries has now spread to a new occupation—workers at recycling centres.

Many communities have adopted recycling programs that involve (at least in part) individuals working at a recycling centre sorting through various types of recyclable material (e.g., glass, plastic, etc.). Items such as syringes are frequently discarded in the recycling bins, and recycling plant workers run the risk of a needlestick injury as they sort through the material to identify what can be recycled.

The solution to the problem lies in both prevention and protection. First, communities with recycling programs must educate citizens in the proper procedures for disposing of needles and similar items. Second, employees should be provided with protective gear (e.g., heavy leather gloves over latex) to offset the exposure to needles.

Source: Canadian Centre for Occupational Health and Safety, "What are needlestick injuries?" Retrieved from http://www .ccohs.ca/ohsanswers/diseases/needlestick_injuries.html, February 7, 2007.

Thorough record keeping is essential. Although provinces and territories vary in terms of record-keeping requirements, all demand that records be kept of employee exposure, workplace air monitoring, and equipment breakdowns and repairs.

Administrative Controls

Perhaps the single most important administrative function is the education and training of all employees in safe work practices. Employees should receive training in safe operating and emergency procedures, in the use and care of personal protective equipment, and in the handling and control of agents. Training must be conducted on an ongoing basis, given the fact that new solvents and other agents are constantly entering the workplace. Finally, workers must be familiar with all aspects of Workplace Hazardous Materials Information System (WHMIS) legislation, which was discussed at length in Chapter 2.

Personal Protective Equipment

Personal protective equipment (PPE) is specifically designed to protect workers from particular hazards. PPE should be used only when there is no feasible or practical way to enclose a process, provide local exhaust, or apply other control measures. *PPE must not be used as an alternative to putting in the proper controls.*

Because inhalation is the most common and hazardous route of entry, the most commonly used protection device is a respirator. Respiratory protection is more specialized for biohazards than it is for chemical agents, since a biological airborne contaminant can be much smaller than a chemical one. PPE for hands, face, and other body parts must be provided where necessary. No single protective device, such as a facemask, will adequately address all conditions for all workers. Each device must be matched to the chemical or biological exposure, and it is imperative that the device be properly fitted to the individual. (One size does not fit all!)

Personal Hygiene Practices

The ingestion of chemicals or biological particulate is often due to poor hygiene practices. Individuals who handle agents without wearing proper protective gear, such as gloves, are at risk of food contamination. In other such instances, chemicals that are not adequately removed at the workplace can be transferred to the worker's home. To ensure that this and similar types of incidents do not occur, individuals who handle toxic substances must adhere to the following:

- Remove outer protective clothing and clean hands, arms, face, and nails before entering rest areas or lunchrooms.
- Avoid touching lips, nose, and eyes with contaminated hands.
- Wash hands before eating, drinking, or smoking, and eat, drink, and smoke only in designated areas.
- Remove work clothes and wash or shower before leaving work.

Medical Surveillance

Medical surveillance programs, an administrative control, are implemented to ensure that employees who are exposed to agents are not subjected to situations in which their health will be jeopardized. To be effective, pre-employment and preplacement medical examinations should be conducted to establish a baseline of the employee's health or exposure to agents in previous workplaces. Follow-up medical examinations should be conducted periodically. Examinations may include chest X-ray, pulmonary function tests, and blood workups. Finally, record keeping is an important aspect of the medical surveillance program. The types of exposures employees face and their health records before and after exposure should be included in this process.

Summary

Chemical agents and, to a lesser extent, biological agents are the major causes of occupational diseases. Despite their associated risks, these agents are easily controlled if guidelines such as those provided in the WHMIS and OH&S legislation are rigorously followed. This chapter has focused on the types, characteristics, measurement, and control of chemical and biological agents. All workers who are exposed to these agents should be knowledgeable about their potential health effects as well as trained in their proper use and handling.

Key Terms

aerosols 111
agents 126
alveoli 114
ambient 109
biohazard 108
biological agents 121
boiling point 119
chemical agents 108
dermatitis 120
routes of entry 111
surfactant layer 116
target organs 116
toxicity 109
turbinates 112

Weblinks

Toxicology Resources

http://home.nas.net/~dbc/cic_hamilton/toxic.html (p. 111)

Crop Protection Institute, "Pesticide Safety Handbook"

http://www.croplife.ca/english/pdf/Pesticide_Handbook.pdf (p. 114)

Poison Control Centres of Canada

http://www.acpo.on.ca/safety/poison-a.htm (p. 116)

WorkSafeBC, "Resources—Fungi and Microorganisms"

http://indoorair.healthandsafetycentre.org/s/FungiandMicroorganisms.asp (p. 121)

Office of Health and Safety, "The 1, 2, 3's of Biosafety Levels"

http://www.cdc.gov/od/ohs/symp5/jyrtext.htm (p. 125)

RPC Icons

RPC 5.1 Analyses risk to the health and safety of employees and determines appropriate preventative measures, including training, provision of required safety equipment, and administrative practices.

- relevant legislation
- nature of the business and physical work environment
- hazard recognition
- workplace inspection techniques
- safety programs, equipment, and emergency procedures
- ergonomics
- functions of the JHSC
- training and development/presentation techniques
- industry best practices
- relevant technical terminology
- the collective agreement
- services and equipment available in the community
- Worker Protection (including health and safety and Workers' Compensation)
- Training and development program design and administration

TASK & KNOWLEDGE REQUIREMENTS

- Occupational health and safety legislation (e.g., Occupational Health and Safety Act of Ontario, Workplace Safety & Insurance Act—Bill 99, Workplace Hazardous Materials Information System, Transportation of Dangerous Goods legislation, environmental legislation, smoking in the workplace legislation, civil rights legislation)
- hazard identification and control
- emergency preparedness procedures
- management techniques for OH&S Programs
- types of employee assistance and wellness programs

RPC 5.2 Implements and evaluates practices in the areas of health, safety, security, and Workers' Compensation.

- investigative techniques
- hazard recognition
- disaster recovery techniques
- relevant legislation
- resource information
- common health and safety practices
- company policies and procedures
- Worker Protection (including health and safety and Workers' Compensation)

- theories and practices for protection of individuals and groups
- Occupational health and safety legislation (e.g., Occupational Health and Safety Act of Ontario, Workplace Safety & Insurance Act—Bill 99, Workplace Hazardous Materials Information System, Transportation of Dangerous Goods legislation, environmental legislation, smoking in the workplace legislation, civil rights legislation)
- hazard identification and control
- management techniques for OH&S Programs

RPC 5.3 Analyses risk to the health and safety of employees and determines appropriate preventative measures, including training, provision of required safety equipment, and administrative practices.

- relevant legislation
- nature of the business and physical work environment
- hazard recognition
- workplace inspection techniques
- safety programs, equipment, and emergency procedures
- ergonomics
- functions of the JHSC
- training and development/presentation techniques
- industry best practices
- relevant technical terminology
- the collective agreement
- services and equipment available in the community
- Worker Protection (including health and safety and Workers' Compensation)
- training and development program design and administration

TASK & KNOWLEDGE REQUIREMENTS

- Occupational health and safety legislation (e.g., Occupational Health and Safety Act of Ontario, Workplace Safety & Insurance Act—Bill 99, Workplace Hazardous Materials Information System, Transportation of Dangerous Goods legislation, environmental legislation, smoking in the workplace legislation, civil rights legislation)
- hazard identification and control
- emergency preparedness procedures
- management techniques for OH&S Programs
- types of employee assistance and wellness programs

RPC 5.4 Ensures due diligence and strict liability requirements are met, e.g. records are kept and formal procedures established.

- relevant legislation and common law
- company policies and procedures
- industry best practices
- program and policy development
- training and development techniques

- risk analysis
- Common and statutory law (e.g., employment standard: labour relations)
- Worker Protection (including health and safety and Workers' Compensation)
- Theories and practices for protection of individuals and groups

Task & Knowledge Requirements

- Occupational health and safety legislation (e.g., Occupational Health and Safety Act of Ontario, Workplace Safety & Insurance Act—Bill 99, Workplace Hazardous Materials Information System, Transportation of Dangerous Goods legislation, environmental legislation, smoking in the workplace legislation, civil rights legislation)
- management techniques for OH&S Programs

RPC 5.5 Contributes to policy on the workplace environment (e.g., smoking, workplace violence, scent-free, communicable diseases, and addictions).

- relevant legislation
- program and policy development
- the culture of the organization
- conflict resolution
- record keeping and reporting
- technical terminology
- environmental hazards
- Common and statutory law (e.g., employment standard: labour relations)
- Worker Protection (including health and safety and Workers' Compensation)
- Theories and practices for protection of individuals and groups
- Occupational health and safety legislation (e.g., Occupational Health and Safety Act of Ontario, Workplace Safety & Insurance Act—Bill 99, Workplace Hazardous Materials Information System, Transportation of Dangerous Goods legislation, environmental legislation, smoking in the workplace legislation, civil rights legislation)
- management techniques for OH&S Programs
- trends in occupational health and safety

Discussion Questions

1. This chapter lists the types of contaminants found in industrial workplaces. Consider the typical office setting—to what types of chemical hazards might office workers be exposed?
2. Explain the concept of a "synergistic effect" as used in this chapter.
3. What are the major ways of controlling the potential adverse effects of exposure to chemical and biological agents?

Using the Internet

1. Using a search engine, such as Google, find reports of the SARS outbreak in Canadian cities (especially Toronto) during 2003. What procedures did workplaces (i.e., hospitals) implement to minimize exposure or reaction to this biological hazard?
2. Cases of environmental illness or environmental sensitivity seem to be becoming more common. Search out contemporary cases in which employees have been exposed to chemical or biological agents with long-term consequences. Could these exposures have been prevented? Could the workers have been protected?

Exercise

1. Although exposure to various workplace hazards is never a good thing, some individuals may be more sensitive to some exposures than others. For example, pregnant women may be more at risk when exposed to certain chemicals than are other employees. To what extent can we use HR tools such as selection and placement to offset this problem? Is it appropriate to refuse to hire women of childbearing age to work in environments in which exposures are possible?

Case 1

Mass Hysteria?

It's the first week of the semester in the new school building and already Principal LeBlanc is ready to quit. For years, parents in her district have been campaigning for a new school and teachers have been complaining about outdated classrooms. Now they have a new multimillion-dollar building with all the latest technology.

"You'd think that everyone would be happy," groused LeBlanc to her vice principal, "but all I've heard all day are complaints."

"What kind of complaints?"

"Well, for starters, we have five teachers off sick claiming that they get migraines every time they enter their classrooms. And now parents have started to complain that their kids have sore eyes and are feeling nauseated all the time they're in the building."

"Maybe they're really sick," stated the concerned vice principal.

"Yeah, sick of school," replied LeBlanc. "At least that's what I think."

As a health and safety expert what do you think? What actions would you take?

Case 2

Unexpected Gas

A man was killed by an explosion when another worker attempted to cut through the top of one of two old steel drums using a hand-held grinder. Both barrels had contained a fruit concentrate but were never cleaned. The sparks generated by the grinder ignited hydrogen gas that had been generated from the contents' residue after standing for many years. Because there was a defective sterile coating separating the walls of the drum from the concentrate, the acid in the fruit concentrate reacted with the metal of the drum and formed hydrogen gas. The gas accumulated and the pressure caused the drum ends to bulge. This deformation made it impossible to open the drum with the drum opener and a hole was punched into the top of each drum. One worker was attempting to add water to one drum in order to displace the remaining gas, while another worker attempted to open the other drum with a grinder. Sparks ignited the hydrogen gas, causing an explosion and a fire. The fire was extinguished, but one worker lost his life. The defective drums had been recalled years before by the supplier, and only three remained unaccounted for before the accident.

What steps would you take to ensure that this event was never repeated?

Endnotes

1. Workplace Safety and Insurance Board of Ontario. (2000). *Annual Report*. Toronto: WSIB.
2. Genesove, L. (1995). *Multiple chemical sensitivity syndrome*. Toronto: Healthwise, Accident Prevention.
3. DiNardi, S. R. (Ed.) (1997). *The occupational environment–Its evaluation and control.* Fairfax, VA: AIHA Press.
4. Workplace Safety and Insurance Board of Ontario. (2000). *Annual Report*. Toronto: WSIB.
5. Williams, P. L., & Burson, J. L. (Eds.). (1985). *Industrial toxicology–Safety and health applications in the workplace*. New York: Van Nostrand Reinhold.
6. Pilger, C. W. (1994). *Toxic solvents*. 23rd Intensive Workshop in Industrial Hygiene, Toronto.

Chapter 6

Psychosocial Hazards

Chapter Learning Objectives

After reading this chapter, you should be able to

- describe and distinguish among the concepts of stressor, stress, and strain
- explain the transactional model of stress and its implications
- identify major sources of stress in the workplace
- discuss the psychological, physical, behavioural, and organizational consequences of stress
- describe and distinguish among primary, secondary, and tertiary stress interventions
- discuss violence, sexual harassment, injustice, and technology as emerging workplace stressors

VIOLENCE AT WORK

Workplace violence is an all too common experience in many professions. For instance, those in the health care professions deal with aggressive behaviour from patients, patients' family members, as well as their own coworkers. Teachers report that aggressive behaviour from students and parents threatens their well-being at work. Those who work alone late at night, such as cab drivers and retail clerks, are also at risk.

A recent report from one Canadian health care district, Nova Scotia's Capital District Health Authority, illustrates the extent of aggression among coworkers in the hospital setting. A year-long study in this health care district found that unprofessional conduct and bullying are widespread, contributing to an unpleasant work environment, and that little is being done to address the problem. The report concluded that persistent aggression among coworkers contributed to poor employee morale, high levels of stress, and increased absenteeism. These outcomes occur in concert with rising benefits costs for anti-depressant drugs.

Four major public unions in Nova Scotia—the Nova Scotia Government Employees' Union (NSGEU), the Nova Scotia Nurses' Union (NSNU), the Nova Scotia Teachers' Union (NSTU), and the Canadian Union of Public Employees (CUPE) Nova Scotia—have teamed as the Coalition Against Workplace Violence. They have launched a public awareness campaign on this issue. The group is calling on the provincial government to develop legislation that protects workers from workplace violence. Draft regulations have been available for more than 10 years, but have not been acted upon.

The president of the NSNU notes the irony that the province has introduced legislation to protect patients from abuse by staff, but has not put into place protections for workers who experience violence in the course of their jobs. Glen French, CEO of the Canadian Initiative on Workplace Violence, commented that if one identifies workplace violence as an occupational health and safety matter, it should be treated as such by regulations against the hazard that are enforceable under the law.

The province indicates that it is not recommending changes to the OHS Act because it believes the Act provides workers with protection from hazards relating to violence. The Department of Environment and Labour is instead seeking public input on the issue with the aim to develop a strategy on workplace violence—including a definition of the hazard—that will help employers and employees address workplace violence.

Sources: CBC, "'Blatant' bullying a problem at Capital Health" (February 6, 2007). Retrieved from http://www.cbc.ca/canada/nova-scotia/story/2007/02/06/capital-bullying.html, February 11, 2007; Canadian Occupational Health & Safety News, "Public input sought on NS anti-violence strategy" (January 8, 2007). Retrieved from http://lists.cupe.ca/pipermail/ont-health-safety/2007-January/000022.html, February 11, 2007; and Canadian Healthcare Manager, "Nova Scotia unions favour tougher approach" (December 2006). Retrieved from http://www.chmonline.ca, January 14, 2007.

In 1990, the United States' National Institute of Occupational Safety and Health (NIOSH) declared occupational stress to be one of the 10 leading causes of workplace death, and it is now common to speak of occupational stress as an epidemic.[1] The Conference Board of Canada has estimated that workplace stress costs the Canadian economy $12 billion annually. In the U.S. this figure rises to a staggering $300 billion.[2] In 1997, cost estimates of absenteeism stemming from work–life conflict in Canada were in the range of $2.7 billion annually, a number that has most certainly grown in the interim.[3]

Although we recognize that estimates of the cost of work stress involve considerable guesswork, it is clear that workplace stress is a large and growing problem with considerable consequences for individuals and organizations. The workplace is replete with factors that contribute to stress, and many Canadian workers experience the reality of stress. In the 2003 General Social Survey, Canadian workers reported that work overload and poor interpersonal relations at work were major sources of stress.[4] A recent survey of employed Nova Scotians indicated that a large percentage of them experienced such stressors as high work loads (60%), role conflict (70%), and work–family conflict (50%). Furthermore, about 20 percent of the sample reported health-related symptoms that commonly manifest after the experience of stress.[5]

So, what exactly is stress? One way to discuss stress is in terms of the **psychosocial model of health.** The term *psychosocial* is used to highlight the importance of both the social environment and the psychological or individual factors that affect a person's health and well-being. Social factors that may influence a person's health include supportive family members, exposure to violence, and workplace policies. Psychological factors that affect a person's health include self-esteem, anxiety levels, and ability to cope with pressure.

psychosocial model of health
approach to the study of health that highlights the importance of both the social environment and psychological factors

In everyday conversation, we use the term *stress* in several different ways. We talk about feeling stress and about stress as something we're exposed to. Even the scientific literature demonstrates considerable confusion over the precise meanings of stress-related terms.[6] Most researchers now agree on a general stress model that distinguishes among three closely related terms: stressors, stress, and strain.

Stressors

stressor

an objectively verifiable event that occurs outside the individual that has the potential to cause stress

A **stressor** is an objectively verifiable event occurring in the environment that has the potential to cause stress. For example, congested traffic would constitute a stressor. Stressors, then, exist outside the individual and reflect some of the social factors that affect a person's health. Stressors may vary along several dimensions: frequency of occurrence, intensity, duration, and predictability (time of onset).[7] The combination of these dimensions has led researchers to distinguish among four categories of stressors: acute stressors, chronic stressors, daily stressors, and catastrophic stressors (see Table 6.1).

Acute stressors have a specific time onset (i.e., you know exactly when it began), are typically of short duration and high intensity, and have a low frequency. For example, a traffic accident is an acute stressor. In terms of the work environment, a performance review meeting or a conflict with a supervisor may be acute stressors. In contrast, a *chronic* stressor has no specific onset, may be of short or long duration, repeats frequently, and may be of either low or high intensity. Many individuals today are experiencing job insecurity as a chronic stressor. Most cannot point to a specific event or time that triggered the insecurity, but the nagging worry that their job is at risk is always with them.

Daily stressors have a specific onset, are of short duration, are low in intensity, and are typically infrequent. Getting caught in a traffic jam is an example of a daily stressor. To use a work-related example, dealing with a broken piece of office equipment may be a daily stressor for some employees. Finally, we need to recognize the existence of *catastrophic* stressors or disasters. Much like acute stressors, catastrophic stressors have a specific onset, occur infrequently, have a high intensity, and may be of either long or short duration. The main distinction between acute and catastrophic stressors is in the intensity of the stressor. Catastrophic stressors typically involve a direct threat to life, loss of life, or major property damage. Again, the complexity of categorizing stressors is indicated by the observation that catastrophic stressors can become chronic stressors over time. For example, the events of September 11, 2001 constituted a catastrophic stressor for those directly involved, but also have long-term consequences for those individuals who live with the fear of terrorism.

TABLE 6.1

Categories of Stressors

TYPE	FREQUENCY	DURATION	INTENSITY	TIME OF ONSET
Acute	Rare	Short	High	Specific
Chronic	Frequent	Short or long	Low or high	Non-specific
Daily	Infrequent	Short	Low	Specific
Catastrophic	Very rare	Short or long	Extremely high	Specific

Stressors in the Workplace

RPC 6.1

Although the categorization of stressors presented above provides a general overview of stressors, other researchers have focused on defining the content or sources of stressors that exist in the workplace.[8] The NIOSH model identifies the following major categories of workplace stressors.

- *Workload and work pace*. This category refers to the amount of work that has to be completed and the speed at which employees have to work to complete their tasks.
- *Role stressors* (conflict, ambiguity, and interrole conflict). Role conflict exists when individuals face incompatible demands from two or more sources. Role ambiguity reflects the uncertainty employees experience about what is expected from them in their jobs; the opposite of role ambiguity is role clarity. Interrole conflict exists when employees face incompatible demands from two or more roles. The most common form of interrole conflict is work–family conflict, in which the demands of work conflict with the role of parent or spouse.
- *Career concerns*. This category includes worries about job security, fear of job obsolescence, underpromotion and overpromotion, and, more generally, concerns about career progression.
- *Work scheduling*. Working rotating shifts or permanent night shifts results in a disruption of physiological circadian rhythms, as well as a disruption of social activities.
- *Interpersonal relations*. Poor interpersonal relations in the workplace are consistently identified as a source of stress. Conversely, having well-established sources of social support (i.e., receiving support from coworkers and supervisors) may actually reduce the effects of other workplace stressors.
- *Job content and control*. Jobs that are highly repetitive or do not make use of a variety of workers' skills or give workers a measure of control over how and when they complete their tasks can be a source of stress.

Stress

Although stressors are objective events, the individual's response to or evaluation of these events also has an important role to play. Researchers have typically referred to this response or evaluation as **stress.** Stress is an internal response to stressors and is often characterized by negative feelings of arousal. Stress, then, reflects some of the psychological factors that affect a person's health. In contrast to the objective stressors we have discussed, stress is an internal event that is subjectively defined. Stress is a consequence of any action, situation, or event that places special demands on a person. The stress response is an adaptive reaction to these demands and is influenced by differences between people.

stress
an individual's internal response to, or evaluation of, stressors; often characterized by negative feelings of arousal

Occupational Health and Safety Notebook 6.1

Occupational Health Psychology

Occupational health psychology applies psychology to questions of occupational stress, illness, and injury. Developing throughout the 1990s, the recent growth of this field has brought considerable attention to psychosocial risk factors for workplace injury and illness.

Occupational health psychology aims to improve quality of work life and *protect* and *promote* the safety, health, and well-being of workers. Occupational health psychologists consider both organizational and individual factors in occupational health and believe that the transformation of the work environment can carry positive effects for employee health.

In 1990 the U.S. National Institute of Occupational Safety and Health (NIOSH) presented its national strategy for the prevention of work-related psychological disorders (Sauter, Murphy, & Hurrell, 1990). These four components continue to provide direction for researchers and practitioners of occupational health psychology. The components are as follows:

1. *A focus on organizational change.* The strategy recognized that organizational change is possible and is at times necessary to reduce psychosocial hazards in the workplace.
2. *A focus on information.* Workers should be provided with information, education, and training regarding psychosocial hazards and psychological health at work.
3. *A focus on psychological health services.* Enriched services for the promotion of psychological well-being and the treatment of psychological symptoms (e.g., employee assistance programs, inclusion of preventive services in benefits plans) should be provided to employees.
4. *A focus on surveillance.* The surveillance and monitoring of psychosocial risk factors and psychological disorders should be routine in organizations.

Sources: Occupational Health Psychology Homepage. Retrieved from http://www.cdc.gov/niosh/ohp.html, February 1, 2007; and Sauter, S. L., Murphy, L. R., & Hurrell, J. J. (1990). Prevention of work-related psychological disorders: A national strategy proposed by the National Institute for Occupational Safety and Health (NIOSH). *American Psychologist, 45,* 1146–1158.

general adaptation syndrome
the body's way of gearing up for fight or flight (i.e., to confront or run away from a predator)

Stress is an adaptive response. The stress response is our way of mobilizing resources to deal with stressors in the environment. Viewed in an evolutionary context, stress is the product of millions of years of evolution. The **general adaptation syndrome** (stress response) is the body's way of gearing up for fight or flight (i.e., to confront or run away from a predator).[9] The syndrome has three stages: alarm, resistance, and exhaustion. The alarm phase begins when a person is confronted with a stressor (i.e., the body prepares for fight or flight). Resistance is the body's attempt to restore homeostasis (i.e., to return to normal). Exhaustion occurs if the stressor is not dealt with and strain reactions set in. Some of the physiological changes that occur as the body prepares for fight or flight include increased blood supply to the brain and major muscle groups, decreased blood supply to the digestive system and skin, increased heart rate and breathing, and increased activity in the stomach, bowels, and bladder. If the stress reaction is prolonged, the resulting symptoms include headaches, dry mouth, skin rashes, heartburn, hypertension, stomach ulcers, and asthma.

Stress is moderated by individual differences. Psychologists have recognized for many years that our responses to events in the environment are largely determined by our interpretation of the events. Some people are less vulnerable to stressors in their environment than others. In fact, one of the most popular models of stress, the transactional model, is based on the notion that individuals may perceive and respond differently to the same stressors.[10] According to this model, people appraise the stressors in their environment and assess their ability to manage them. For example, a person may determine that although he or she has heavy work demands, he or she can manage the workload by setting up a comprehensive "to do" list and delegating some of the tasks to coworkers. Stress occurs when an individual realizes that a pertinent stressor is present and that he or she does not have the resources or ability to manage that stressor. Thus, it is clear that stress does not always follow exposure to a stressor; rather, it results when an appraisal process indicates that the stressor is indeed an unmanageable threat to the person's well-being.

Researchers often talk about stressors as events that have the potential to cause change, harm, or loss, or to pose a threat or a challenge. Even events that are viewed as positive can be stressors. For instance, a promotion can be a stressor because it involves considerable change (e.g., in job duties), challenge (e.g., increased job responsibilities), and threat (e.g., the potential to be a failure in the new job). Stress is the body's way of coping with the environment, and the response is the same whether these demands are positive or negative.

Stress Moderators

Many factors affect people's evaluations of stressors as well as how they react to them (degree of stress experienced). We often call these factors **moderators.** A moderator is a variable that changes the relationship between two other variables. Some moderators *aggravate* or increase the effects of stressors. These types of moderators are called **risk factors** for stress. Other moderators can *protect* an individual from the adverse effects of stressors. Because of their role in breaking the chain of response, these moderators are sometimes referred to as stress **buffers.**

Two well-accepted general classes of moderators in the stress process are the enduring properties of the individual (i.e., personality characteristics) and the social context (i.e., social support, individual relationships). We will consider each type of moderator.

moderator
a variable that changes the relationship between two other variables

risk factor
a variable that increases the negative effects of stress

buffer
a variable that protects people from the negative effects of stress

Type A behaviour
action–emotion complex that can be observed in any person who is aggressively involved in a chronic, incessant struggle to achieve increasingly more in increasingly less time

The Individual—Personality

A considerable amount of research has examined the role of personality in stress. Personality is the relatively stable set of characteristics, responses, thoughts, and behaviours of a given individual.[11] Two personality characteristics of particular relevance in a consideration of stress are the **Type A behaviour** pattern and negative affectivity.

Type A Behaviour Type A individuals are people who try to achieve increasingly more in increasingly less time. Their struggle is chronic and, if necessary, is carried out against the will of others.[12] Individuals who exhibit Type A behaviour are hard-driving, competitive, and time-urgent. There are two components of Type A behaviour: achievement-striving and impatience-irritability.[13] An individual who is high on achievement-striving is typically very goal directed and action oriented. Individuals high on impatience-irritability are typically very time conscious, hostile, impatient, and irritable. In general, achievement-striving is associated with performance but not health outcomes. That is, those high on achievement-striving perform well, but this aspect of themselves is not related to their health. Conversely, impatience-irritability is associated with health outcomes. Those high on impatience-irritability experience more stress and have poorer health, but this aspect is not related to their work performance.[14]

negative affectivity
a dispositional dimension reflecting persistent individual differences in the experience of negative emotion

Negative Affectivity **Negative affectivity** is a mood factor that reflects persistent individual differences in the experience of negative emotion. A simpler way to interpret this is the difference between an optimist and a pessimist. The latter demonstrates negative affectivity across situations; that is, some individuals seem predisposed to see the negative side of everything. Such individuals may seem to react negatively or adversely to all stressors, and it is in this sense that negative affectivity may serve as a risk factor in the stress process.

The Social Context—Social Support

Although the preceding discussion has focused on the qualities and personality traits of the individual, a considerable body of evidence also suggests the importance of social relationships as a moderator of the stress process. Having sources of support can help reduce a person's vulnerability to stressors.[15] In other words, having people who provide support is a buffer for stress. Alternatively, a lack of social support can intensify the impact of stressors and may be a potential risk factor for stress. You might be surprised to learn that a low degree of support from one's organization and supervisor places an individual at risk for work-related musculoskeletal injuries.[16]

Support can come from a number of sources, including supervisors, coworkers, and family members. Support can also be offered in a number of ways. For instance, a coworker may provide *tangible* support by giving a new employee needed information about a job task. This same coworker might also show *emotional* support by offering positive feedback and encouragement to the new hire.

strain
the result of stress; it is classified into four categories of reactions: psychological, physical, behavioural, and organizational

Strain

The result of stress is **strain.** When people encounter a stressor and experience persistent stress, ultimately strain will result. We will discuss four categories of strain reactions: psychological, physical, behavioural, and organizational.

Psychological Strain

Psychological strain reactions typically include either a disturbance in affect (e.g., mood) or a disturbance in cognition (e.g., concentration). Feeling irritable, anxious, overwhelmed, moody, depressed, and angry are all common *affective* strain reactions. Indeed, we often describe these moods as "feeling stressed out." Disturbances in mood resulting from stress can range from short-lived periods of feeling blue, down, or irritable to longer-term and more serious diagnoses of psychological disorders such as depression and anxiety disorders.[17]

Although most people recognize affective or emotional reactions to stress, cognitive reactions often go unnoticed. Typical strain-related cognitive disturbances include difficulty in making up your mind (often on trivial matters), difficulty in concentrating and staying with one task, not being able to remember people's names even though you know them quite well, and other small mistakes. These small mistakes are generally not very important, but they can be devastating for an individual under considerable strain. For instance, in some situations, making even small mistakes in the workplace can have negative consequences for employee safety and performance.[18]

Occupational Health and Safety Today 6.1

Depression and Work

Depression affects a large number of Canadian employees. Estimates suggest that as many as half a million Canadian employees experience depression. A recently released analysis of the 2002 Canadian Community Mental Health Survey found that 80 percent of those employees who experienced depression reported that their symptoms negatively affected their work performance; almost 20 percent of those indicated the impairment was very severe. Common impairments associated with depression are trouble concentrating, reduced productivity, and poor time management. Workers who have recently experienced a depressive episode are twice as likely to have been absent from work in the prior week than those who have never experienced depression. These negative effects of depression can persist up to two years after the episode.

It thus seems clear that depression negatively affects work. However, perhaps ironically, it is sometimes the work itself that increases the risk of depression. The same survey also illustrates that many workplace stressors are associated with depressive symptoms. For instance, those who work shift work, particularly evening and night shifts, are more likely to be depressed than others. Further, those who reported they were exposed to many workplace stressors most days on the job were also at increased risk for depression.

Source: "Study: Depression and work impairment," from the Statistics Canada publication "The Daily," Catalogue 11-001, Friday, January 12, 2007. Available at http://dissemination.statcan.ca/Daily/English/070112/d070112a.htm.

Physical Strain

Many physical strain reactions have been identified throughout this chapter (e.g., stomach upsets, headaches). Some of these symptoms may seem quite trivial, but considerable evidence now suggests that stress is implicated in more serious physical conditions. Most prominently, coronary heart disease (CHD) has been consistently linked to increased stress, as has high blood pressure (hypertension), strokes, ulcers, asthma, and even some forms of cancer.[19]

The mechanisms through which strain manifests itself physically are not yet clearly understood, although well-documented changes in hormone and enzyme secretion occur under stress. Moreover, stress may play a dual role as a cause of serious physical illness. First, individuals exposed to a stressor may experience stress and ultimately develop a physical strain response—illness (e.g., you are constantly under pressure to meet deadlines and make clients happy; as a result, you have developed hypertension). Second, increased strain may also lower the body's resistance (by impairing the immune system), thereby opening the door to physical illness.[20] In fact, recent evidence suggests work-related stress is a risk factor for the common cold, such that those experiencing heavy psychological job demands reported increased incidence of colds.[21]

Behavioural Strain

Behavioural strain reactions can take a variety of forms. Individuals under increased stress may develop nervous habits (e.g., nail biting or nervous tics). Other forms of behavioural strain reactions may include avoidance of certain situations, or a reduction in individual involvement, either because of a lack of interest or as a means of reducing the demands on the individual's time. Evidence also suggests that individuals may increase their smoking, consumption of alcohol, or reliance on psychotherapeutic drugs under periods of increased stress.[22] Given the known health outcomes associated with smoking, excessive alcohol consumption, and overmedication, these are very dangerous ways of coping with increased stress.

Organizational Strain

Stress researchers interested in organizations identify increased absenteeism, decreased performance, disturbances of interpersonal relationships at work, and an increased likelihood of looking for alternative employment as some of the most common organizational outcomes of stress. Consistent evidence suggests that high levels of stress are also associated with an increased risk of workplace accidents. This increased risk may be a consequence of other strain reactions (e.g., increased cognitive failures, impaired ability to concentrate). We should also note that the causal direction of this relationship is not certain. Although accidents and increased stress are certainly correlated, it may be that working in a dangerous or risky environment is, in itself, a stressor.

Managing Psychosocial Hazards

It is clear that work-related stressors, stress, and strain have substantial negative consequences for both employees and organizations. Fortunately, individual employees and organizational management can work together to offset or avoid these negative outcomes by using an approach known as **preventive stress management.** The basic principle of preventive stress management is that the health of an organization and the health of its employees are interdependent.[23] In other words, organizations whose employees are in good health are more likely to be successful. Alternatively, employees who work for organizations that provide pleasant working conditions are more likely to be healthy, productive individuals.

RPC 6.1

RPC 6.2

preventive stress management
an approach to managing stress in the workplace that emphasizes that the health of an organization and its employees are interdependent; encourages the reduction of stressors in the workplace as well as the recognition and management of occupational stress and strain

Ideally, stress management programs will include both organizational and individual interventions that are designed to reduce exposure to stressors, reduce the experience of stress when stressors are unavoidable, and swiftly provide treatment options to those individuals who are experiencing the negative consequences of stress. In the following paragraphs, we describe three categories of interventions (primary, secondary, and tertiary) and provide illustrative examples of organizational and individual efforts to manage stress in the workplace for each type of intervention.

Primary Interventions

Primary interventions involve the reduction or removal of the actual stressors and are highly effective in reducing work-related stress and strain.[24] The idea is that the removal of sources of stress from the workplace should reduce employee stress and strain. Despite the supporting evidence, primary prevention strategies are not broadly implemented in Canadian organizations, presumably because organizational decision makers believe that the cost and logistics of primary preventive strategies would be excessive; therefore, they prefer to focus on interventions that target the employees' ability to cope with existing stressors.[25] However, the costs associated with primary preventive efforts can be reasonable and, given resulting reduction in employee stress, worth the effort involved in their implementation. Tables 6.2 and 6.3 provide examples of primary stress prevention strategies at the individual and organizational levels.

primary interventions
stress interventions that involve the reduction or removal of actual stressors

RPC 6.3

RPC 6.4

RPC 6.5

Secondary Interventions

Secondary interventions focus on minimizing negative outcomes once a person is feeling stress. Techniques such as stress management and relaxation training help people to identify the negative health effects of stress and teach effective coping strategies, with the intention that appropriate strategies for managing stress can lessen the negative effects of stress on health.[26] Common examples of secondary intervention programs are relaxation training, stress management training and counselling, physical fitness programs, and balanced nutrition. Secondary interventions are more widely used than primary preventive techniques. However, secondary strategies are less desirable than

secondary interventions
stress intervention techniques that focus on minimizing negative consequences once a person is feeling stress

primary approaches because they target stress only after it has occurred. See Tables 6.2 and 6.3 for examples of ways that organizations and individuals can engage in secondary stress interventions.

TABLE 6.2

Stress Intervention Strategies: Individual Level

LEVEL OF INTERVENTION	EXAMPLES
Primary	Avoid taking on an overload of work
	Take adequate leisure time
	Try to reduce Type A behaviour
Secondary	Talk with friends and coworkers
	Make time to exercise
	Use relaxation techniques
Tertiary	Seek medical treatment
	Participate in psychological counselling

TABLE 6.3

Stress Intervention Strategies: Organizational Level

LEVEL OF INTERVENTION	EXAMPLES
Primary	Redesign particularly demanding jobs
	Respect employees' opinions in management decision-making process
	Provide flexible working conditions
Secondary	Provide comprehensive benefits programs that include provisions for such options as employee assistance programs (EAPs), personal leave, massage therapy
	Offer on-site fitness centres
	Ensure balanced nutrition on the cafeteria menu
Tertiary	Offer benefits packages with sick days and leave options
	Provide counselling services following major stressors, such as a violent episode at work or major acts of terrorism
	Support employee efforts to find appropriate medical or psychological care

Tertiary Interventions

Tertiary interventions include strategies such as psychological therapy and medical attention that are used after the fact to help those individuals who have not been able to manage workplace stress effectively and are now experiencing symptoms of strain.[27] In the "best of all organizations, primary and secondary prevention would be enough to manage the demands of work life."[28] However, in the event that stressors and stress are not adequately dealt with via primary and secondary efforts, it is important to consider potential tertiary intervention strategies that organizations and individuals can use to treat their symptoms of strain. What is important at the tertiary level is that individuals experiencing strain are aware that the symptoms are a real threat to their overall health and well-being and seek treatment. The organization can facilitate tertiary interventions by providing education about strain-related illnesses for employees. Tables 6.2 and 6.3 outline the individual and organizational strategies that contribute to successful tertiary stress interventions.

tertiary interventions
stress intervention techniques that are used to help those individuals who have not been able to effectively manage workplace stress and are now experiencing symptoms of strain

RPC 6.6

RPC 6.7

Emerging Stressor: Workplace Violence

Workplace violence is a critical health and safety issue facing North American organizations. Homicide, the most severe form of violence, is the third leading cause of work-related death in the United States, with 631 such deaths occurring in 2003.[29] Although occupational homicide occurs more frequently in the United States, Canadian organizations are not immune from this phenomenon. For example, in 1999 a former employee of Ottawa-Carleton Transpo shot and killed four transit workers and seriously wounded two others. In 2002 a worker who had been recently fired shot and killed two former colleagues and himself at B.C.'s Environmental Protection Agency.

Less severe forms of workplace violence such as pushing and shoving occur more frequently than homicide. In Ontario, for example, the most frequent forms of workplace violence are hitting, kicking, and biting. Researchers interested in workplace violence also consider the effects of non-physical forms of aggression; non-physical or psychological aggression includes such things as bullying, threats, or being sworn at in the course of one's workday. Estimates suggest that the prevalence of psychological aggression in the U.S. workforce is about 40 percent, while the overall prevalence of physical violence is 6 percent.[30] A recent survey conducted in Nova Scotia provides some insight on violence in the Canadian workplace. Approximately 4 percent of respondents indicated they had recently experienced violence from a supervisor, about 10 percent indicated they had experienced violent behaviour in a coworker, and more than 16 percent reported being targets of violence by clients.[31] These numbers suggest that the prevalence of workplace violence may be somewhat higher in Canada than in the U.S.

Workplace violence has been categorized into four major types based on the assailant's relationship to the workplace.[32] These categories are described in Table 6.4. By far the most common type of workplace violence is that

TABLE 6.4

A Categorization of Workplace Violence Incidents

CATEGORY	RELATIONSHIP OF THE ASSAILANT TO THE ORGANIZATION
Type 1	Member of the public with no legitimate relationship to the organization, usually committing a criminal act
Type 2	Member of the public who receives legitimate service from the organization (e.g., client, patient)
Type 3	An employee or former employee of the organization
Type 4	The spouse or partner of an employee

where the perpetrator has no legitimate business relationship with the targeted workplace and enters the work environment to commit a criminal act (e.g., robbery). Most workplace homicides are robbery related.[33] Individuals at risk include taxicab drivers, convenience store employees, and gas station attendants. The type of workplace violence in which a "disgruntled employee" threatens a coworker or supervisor for what is perceived as unfair treatment captures a large amount of media attention. Only a small portion, 4 to 7 percent, of workplace homicides occur between coworkers.[34]

Researchers have attempted to identify the job characteristics that increase the risk for violence from both members of the public and coworkers. In 2002, LeBlanc and Kelloway developed a risk assessment instrument that focused on occupational characteristics.[35] Some of the job characteristics that they found placed people at a high risk to experience workplace violence included, but were not limited to, the following:

- Interacting with the public
- Denying the public a service or request
- Making decisions that influence other people's lives (e.g., an HR manager terminates an employee, or a teacher assigns a student a failing grade)
- Supervising others
- Exercising physical control over others (e.g., law enforcement officers and private security personnel)
- Handling firearms and similar weapons (e.g., law enforcement, retail workers who sell guns)
- Working alone (particularly working alone at night or working alone with money, as is the case with taxi drivers)
- Handling cash (e.g., retail jobs)
- Collecting or delivering items of value (e.g., armoured car drivers)
- Contact with individuals who are under the influence of mind-altering substances (e.g., bartenders)
- Caring for the physical needs of others (e.g., health care workers)
- Going to clients' homes (e.g., home care health workers)

Consequences of Workplace Violence

The immediate consequences of workplace violence (i.e., someone is physically injured or killed) are obvious. However, it is becoming increasingly apparent that the consequences of violence in the workplace may be even more widespread. Workplace aggression is associated with a number of negative outcomes for organizations and employees, including lost productivity, decreased employee psychological and somatic health, decreased commitment to the organization, and a decline in the performance of organizational citizenship behaviours.[36] Plus, research on the consequences of workplace violence has identified a wider circle of victims than originally thought, with the impact of workplace violence extending beyond the primary victims. Vicarious exposure to workplace violence (i.e., witnessing workplace violence or hearing about a violent incident in the workplace) may also have long-term consequences for individuals.[37]

Exposure to violent episodes in the workplace seems to have more long-lasting consequences for the individuals involved and their employing organizations than originally thought. Numerous research studies show that exposure to workplace violence results in individuals fearing the recurrence of violence. We might describe this fear of future incidents of violence as stress. In turn, that fear results in both personal strain (i.e., impaired mental and physical health) and organizational strain (i.e., decreased commitment, increased intent to leave the organization, neglect of job duties).[38]

Occupational Health and Safety Notebook 6.2

Tips for Dealing with Workplace Violence

The Canadian Centre for Occupational Health and Safety (CCOHS) offers workers the following tips for dealing with threats of workplace violence:

1. Know the risks involved in your job.
2. Trust your instincts.
3. Be ready to respond.
4. Remain calm.
5. Report all incidents.

These tips point to the need for individuals to recognize that workplace violence can and does happen. Individuals need to be prepared for potential violence. Similar cautions apply to employers. The legal requirement of due diligence and the experience of companies that have dealt with workplace violence suggest the following tips for employers:

1. Know the risk factors present in the workplace; minimize risk whenever possible.
2. Have a written policy prohibiting violence and ensure that employees are trained in the application of the policy.
3. Have a plan—know how to respond to actual or threatened violence.
4. Take all threats of violence seriously.
5. Stay within your area of competence; get the proper authorities involved.

Source: Canadian Centre for Occupational Health and Safety, "Violence in the workplace." Retrieved from http://www.ccohs.ca/oshanswers/psychosocial/violence.html, February 10, 2007.

Emerging Stressor: Sexual Harassment

RPC 6.8

RPC 6.9

Several studies have identified sexual harassment as a workplace stressor of increasing importance. Most forms of sexual harassment involve unwelcome, intrusive sexual attention and verbal comments. A recent estimate, based on an evaluation of numerous research studies, is that 58 percent of women have experienced behaviours that are potentially harassing and 24 percent of American women agree that they have experienced sexual harassment in the workplace.[39] Data collected in Canada suggest similar exposure rates: 56 percent of working women who responded to a large survey on sexual harassment indicated that they had experienced sexually harassing behaviour in the previous year.[40] The most commonly reported behaviours in the Canadian survey were insulting jokes and staring. Physically violent actions such as rape do occur in the workplace but only rarely.[41]

Section 247.1 of the Canada Labour Code prohibits sexual harassment and defines sexual harassment as any conduct, comment, gesture, or contact of a sexual nature

> (a) that is likely to cause offence or humiliation to any employee; or
> (b) that might, on reasonable grounds, be perceived by the employee as placing a condition of a sexual nature on employment or on any opportunity for training or promotion.[42]

sexual harassment
intentional, persistent, and unwelcome sexual conduct or remarks that occur despite resistance from the victim

Sexual harassment, then, is any intentional, persistent (i.e., repeated), and unwelcome sexual conduct or remark that occurs despite resistance from the victim. Note that in cases of severe misconduct (e.g., sexual assault) a single incident meets the definition and constitutes sexual harassment. The act or conduct must be deliberate and intentional. In other words, the offender must be aware that the behaviour is offensive. To alleviate the potential loophole of offenders who could say during a sexual harassment hearing that they were unaware their behaviour was offensive, tribunals use what they call the "reasonable person" test. Basically, this test determines whether a reasonable person would be aware that the behaviour is offensive.

This description of sexual harassment seems to point to two different types of sexual harassment:[43]

RPC 6.2

RPC 6.9

RPC 6.10

1. *Sexual coercion* (or "quid pro quo" harassment) is an attempt to extort sexual cooperation. This extortion can take the form of subtle or explicit job-related threats (e.g., job loss, loss of promotion), or the form of promising job-related rewards (e.g., promotions, raises). The Ontario Human Rights Code specifically prohibits job-related rewards or punishment in exchange for sexual favours by a person in authority.
2. *Hostile environment* is sexual harassment that occurs without any coercion or extortion, but the occurrence of sexual harassment creates a hostile, intimidating, and discriminating environment. Sexually harassing behaviours of this nature can range from insulting, misplaced comments, through pervasive sex-related verbal or physical conduct, to life threats or physical attacks. According to most research on the incidence of sexual harassment, it is the "hostile environment" type of sexual harassment that is most prevalent.

Occupational Health and Safety Today 6.2

Prototypical Cases of Sexual Harassment: Not What You Expect?

You'd likely agree that prototypical stories of workplace sexual harassment call to mind an attractive young woman being pursued by an older man in a relative position of power. In the face of persistent, unwanted advances from the man, the woman ultimately makes an accusation of sexual harassment.

Recent research conducted by Dr. Jennifer Berdahl from the Rotman School of Business at the University of Toronto finds that such assumptions about sexual harassment are in fact wrong. The most frequent targets of sexual harassment are not meek, young, attractive women dealing with sexually coercive actions from men. Dr. Berdahl found that outspoken women who do not comply with gender stereotypes and who work in male-dominated jobs are the most frequent victims of sexual harassment. In essence, these women are more likely to experience hostile work environments where they are the recipients of rude remarks, made fun of, and face obstacles to their career progression.

Dr. Berdahl suggests that her research has implications for organizational interventions on sexual harassment. Policies that rely on such things as dress codes and proscribing dating rules do not address the realities of sexual harassment in today's workplaces. She suggests that workplaces should instead focus on achieving work environments where skilled men and women are viewed as equals.

Sources: Berdahl, J. (2007). The evolution of harassment in the workplace. *Rotman Magazine*, Winter 2007, 48–51; and Goar, C. "True face of sexual harassment," *Toronto Star* (January 24, 2007). Retrieved from http://www.thestar.com/article/174064, February 10, 2007.

Sexual Harassment as a Health and Safety Issue

Sexual harassment becomes a health and safety issue for two primary reasons. First, studies show that being the victim of sexual harassment is a stressful experience that is associated with several organizational strains, including increased job dissatisfaction, decreased loyalty to the organization, and increased intent to leave the organization. Some women who have reported being a victim of sexual harassment to their organization experienced the formal process as unjust—in fact, some report that they have been fired after making a sexual harassment claim. There are also personal consequences of sexual harassment, with victims significantly more likely to experience dissatisfaction with life in general and to experience psychosomatic disorders (e.g., respiratory, stomach, and sleep problems; headaches and migraines; weight loss or gain). Thus, exposure to sexual harassment is associated with impaired employee well-being and becomes a health and safety issue.

Second, the courts have increasingly viewed workplace sexual harassment as the responsibility of the employer. Before 1981, sexual harassment on the job was not prohibited by any human rights statute in Canada. A groundbreaking step occurred in 1989, when the Supreme Court of Canada concluded that sexual harassment is a form of sex discrimination and is therefore prohibited in employment. Sex discrimination had been prohibited by human rights statutes for some time in Canada, but sexual harassment was not initially recognized in those statutes.[44] This was an important progression from simply acknowledging that sexual harassment was a serious problem to taking steps to prevent it from occurring.

Another major change occurred when the Supreme Court of Canada stated that an employer is liable for the discriminatory acts of its employees. This decision had great implications, as employers now had a legal motive to prohibit sexual harassment in their companies. Legal liability translates into a strong financial incentive to prevent an illegal act from occurring. For example, in one of the largest lawsuits of its type, Mitsubishi Motors in the United States paid $34 million to settle allegations of sexual harassment filed by the Equal Employment Opportunities Commission on behalf of 300 female employees. Essentially, the allegations were that the women were subjected to sexual comments, innuendo, and unwanted groping, and that plant managers knew of, but did nothing to correct, these problems.

The ruling that employers are liable for discriminatory acts including harassment has several implications for organizations:[45]

1. Employers are responsible for the due care and protection of their employees' human rights in the workplace.
2. Employers are liable for the discriminatory conduct of and sexual harassment by their agents and supervisory personnel.
3. Sexual harassment by a supervisor is automatically attributed to the employer when such harassment results in a tangible job-related disadvantage to the employee.
4. Explicit company policy forbidding sexual harassment and the presence of procedures for reporting misconduct may or may not be sufficient to offset liability.
5. Employers will be pressured to take a more active role in maintaining a harassment-free work environment.
6. Employers will feel a greater discomfort with intimate relationships that develop between supervisors and their subordinates because of the legal implications, and this may motivate employers to discourage such office relationships.
7. Employers' intentions to have effective sexual harassment policies are insufficient. To avoid liability, the policies must be functional and must work as well in practice as they do in theory.

As you can see, the Supreme Court has made employers responsible for any sexual harassment that occurs in the organization. As a result, employers are more likely to initiate interventions to eliminate or at least reduce the occurrence of sexual harassment in their workplace.

Emerging Stressor: Injustice at Work

Recent studies show that employees who experience unfairness in their workplace report higher levels of strain.[46] Researchers have long known that unfairness negatively affects employee attitudes including their intentions to leave their workplace and their commitment to the organization. However, investigations of the relationship between the experience of unfairness at work and employee health are relatively new.

In organizational justice research, "fairness" is not treated as a one-dimensional construct. Researchers in this area focus on three separate categories of fairness judgments that a person can make: (1) the fairness of outcomes, or **distributive justice,** (2) the fairness of processes, or **procedural justice,** and (3) the fairness of interpersonal treatment, or **interactional justice.**[47] All three types of injustice have been associated with increased work stress and strain. In fact, perceived injustice has been associated with increased risk of psychiatric symptoms, high blood pressure, and sickness-related absences from work.[48]

distributive justice
the perceived fairness of outcomes

procedural justice
the perceived fairness of decision-making processes

interactional justice
the perceived fairness of interpersonal treatment

Employees are likely to judge an outcome as unfair when they do not receive a reward or recognition they feel they deserve. For example, Joe, an employee who has recently put in many extra hours on a project at work, may feel that he deserves a bonus in recognition of his extra effort. If he does not receive a bonus, he may feel that he has been the victim of a distributive injustice.

With respect to procedural injustice, people arrive at perceptions regarding the fairness of a procedure by examining several aspects of the process. Procedures that allow employee input and are consistently implemented across conditions, unbiased, accurate, ethical, subject to appeals on the part of those involved, and representative of all relevant parties are viewed as more fair than those that are not.[49] For instance, Ellen may judge the decision to change her work hours from 8 a.m. to 4 p.m. to 9 a.m. to 5 p.m. as more fair if she was consulted about the reason for the decision and permitted to give her opinion about the potential change.

In terms of interactional fairness, individuals judge the fairness of the interpersonal treatment they receive on several levels. For instance, they examine the extent to which their supervisors treat them with kindness and consideration, provide adequate explanations for decisions, and give useful and timely feedback. As an example, Tom is likely to have a better reaction to a negative performance review if his boss delivers that information in a sensitive manner and gives helpful tips on how he can improve his performance before the next performance appraisal.

Creating a Fair Workplace

Organizations can engage in primary stress interventions by working to reduce the occurrence of injustice at work. Organizational leaders should be given training on the importance of fairness at work. Leadership training programs that include a discussion of the value of fair treatment are likely to help leaders see the value of fairness and the damage associated with injustice. The provision of appropriate feedback in a kind and sincere manner can go a long way toward improving an employee's perceptions of interactional justice at work and may have a positive impact on that individual's health.

Organizations can also make an effort to use decision-making processes that are procedurally fair. In that case, organizations may want to consider allowing employee representation on committees or decision-making bodies for important organizational procedures. For instance, if an HR manager is considering changing the employee review process, striking a committee that includes representatives from the various stakeholder groups may increase the perceived fairness of the new evaluation process and ultimately the well-being of the employees who undergo the performance review.

Emerging Stressor: Technology

Innovations in both computer hardware and software have largely changed the workplace, including the way that people do their work and interact with other people on the job.[50] Researchers in occupational health and safety recognize the health risks involved with the increasing presence of technology in the workplace. For instance, increased reliance on computers in the modern work environment is associated with increased risk for physical health problems. The repetitive movements involved with computer use, such as keyboarding and mouse control, place people at risk for musculoskeletal injuries. Carpal tunnel syndrome is an example of a common work-related musculoskeletal disorder that may stem from computer usage. In carpal tunnel syndrome, the median nerve of the arm and hand is compressed.[51]

Musculoskeletal injuries are a prevalent and costly problem. Individuals with these disorders are sometimes in such chronic pain that they are forced to seek disability leave or early retirement.[52] Workers' Compensation claims

Occupational Health and Safety Today 6.3

Too Much Mail?

The advent of electronic mail was originally hailed as a revolutionary tool that would save time and streamline organizational communication. However, few might have predicted just how popular email would become. Daily, worldwide email traffic is now at 141 billion messages.

The results of a 2005 Hewlett Packard–sponsored survey illustrated that workers are highly distracted and pressured by the onslaught of work-related email. The interruptions and information overload that come with large amounts of email can leave people feeling tired and reduce their productivity. About two-thirds of the respondents indicated they checked work email while out of the office and on vacation. About half reported they respond to emails they receive within an hour of receipt. Some reported stepping out of social engagements to check email on handheld devices—others report doing so while in face-to-face meetings. Checking email on PDAs in public is perceived by some as very rude indeed. Others prefer to use email to communicate with colleagues rather than picking up the phone or even walking to the next office.

Some companies are lashing out at the proliferation of email. Jon Coleman of Pfizer Canada has requested that staff in his department substantially reduce the number of emails they send over a one-year period. By providing tips on the appropriate and efficient use of electronic communication, email trainers are helping employees reach this challenging goal. Pfizer has also introduced a program called Freedom Six to Six, banning email messages between 6 p.m. and 6 a.m. and on weekends. The idea is to allow employees to really disengage from their work and to promote work–life balance—with the goal that employees will thus be more productive while at work.

Sources: CNN, "E-mails hurt IQ more than pot." Retrieved from http://www.cnn.com/2005/WORLD/europe/04/22/text.iq/, February 1, 2007; *Maclean's*, "You've got too much mail." Retrieved from http://www.macleans.ca/topstories/business/article.jsp?content=20060130_120699_120699, February 1, 2007.

Occupational Health and Safety Notebook 6.3

Technology-related Stressors

The increasing role of technology in the workplace affects the psychological as well as the physical well-being of workers. Several technology-related factors have been implicated as psychosocial stressors:

- *Control.* We have all likely experienced the frustration of an ill-timed computer crash. In these types of situations, our increasing reliance on technology to help us complete our work tasks can in fact be associated with reduced control at work. When our control over our work environment is reduced, increased stress and strain can result.
- *Isolation.* Our increasing reliance on technology has been associated with increased isolation in the workplace, reducing the incidence of positive social interactions among workers. For instance, employees who rely on computers are often "tied to their desks" to complete their work and therefore are available for fewer social interactions with their coworkers.
- *Privacy.* The advanced state of technology in today's workplaces provides new means of employee surveillance and monitoring. Increasingly, organizations are turning to watchdog systems to keep track of such things as the amount of time an employee spends on the phone or email, the number of keystrokes a worker makes at the keyboard in a given amount of time, or the extent to which people use office technology (e.g., the Internet) for non–work-related tasks. In some cases these systems are used for performance monitoring.
- *Increased job demands.* The increasing role of technology in the workplace can also increase the demands associated with a job. (Recall that workload and work pace can be potent psychosocial stressors.) With respect to work pace, technological advances have increased the pace of many jobs. For example, the prevalence of technology such as email and fax has shortened the expected turnaround time for work-related communication. Plus, the need to keep pace with quickly advancing technology increases the workload of some employees.

Source: Based on Coovert, M. D., & Thompson, L. F. (2003). Technology and workplace health. In J. C. Quick & L. E. Tetrick (Eds.), *Handbook of occupational health psychology* (pp. 223–248). Washington, DC: American Psychological Association.

surrounding musculoskeletal disorders can place large financial demands on companies and government compensation systems. Preventive solutions are available to employers. A field of study called ergonomics emphasizes the importance of creating workstation arrangements that fit the needs of the worker. For instance, one might consider the design of the computer keyboard and mouse, and the positioning of the computer monitor, with the aim of reducing the likelihood of musculoskeletal strain while working at the computer.

Summary

In this chapter we have distinguished among the concepts of stressors in the work environment, the experience of stress, and the possible strain consequences. Whether or not someone perceives an event as stressful, or as a stressor, is individual. Not everyone will react to the same situation in the same way. People must perceive the event to be demanding in some way (e.g., a threat or a challenge) for it to be deemed stressful. As we've discussed, stress is an adaptive and individualistic response to the demands of the objective environment (i.e., stressors). We have also demonstrated that these demands take a variety of forms (acute, daily, chronic, catastrophic).

Stress can also have serious consequences. Individuals exposed to continued or high levels of stress develop strain reactions that may be psychological, physical, behavioural, or organizational. In turn, these forms of strain reactions can affect the organization and people's lives. Both the human and the monetary costs of occupational stress warrant our attention.

Both organizationally and individually driven interventions to reduce the extent to which stressors exist in the workplace or to minimize the damage caused by unavoidable stressors are important. These programs involve primary preventive techniques, secondary interventions to help people avoid the negative consequences of stress, and tertiary programs that help people find the appropriate treatment when they are experiencing strain. The most successful stress management initiatives involve both the individual employee and the organization as a whole.

Workplace violence and sexual harassment are critical issues facing employees in many organizations. Recent research and theorizing has supported the suggestion that both violence and harassment are properly viewed as workplace stressors. Although there are certainly other forms of abusive behaviour occurring in organizations, most attention has focused on workplace violence and sexual harassment because of the dramatic nature of these events and their consequences.

Both injustice and technology are introduced as emerging workplace stressors. Recent research suggests that exposure to unfairness at work and the technological demands placed on today's employees are potential sources of workplace stress. In these sections we highlighted the individual nature of stress. Not all employees reach the same conclusions about the fairness of a single situation, nor are all employees bothered by the increasing technological demands of modern workplaces. However, both these issues are starting to be recognized as potential health and safety issues in the workplace.

Key Terms

buffer 141
distributive justice 153
general adaptation syndrome 140
interactional justice 153
moderator 141
negative affectivity 142
preventive stress management 145
primary interventions 145
procedural justice 153
psychosocial model of health 137
risk factor 141
secondary interventions 145
sexual harassment 150
strain 142
stress 139
stressor 138
tertiary interventions 147
Type A behaviour 141

Weblinks

Coalition Against Workplace Violence

www.stopworkplaceviolence.ca (p. 137)

Canadian Centre for Occupational Health and Safety, "OSH Answers: Health Promotion / Wellness / Psychosocial"

http: / / www.ccohs.ca / oshanswers / psychosocial / (p. 137)

Healthy Ontario, "Job Stress"

http: / / www.healthyontario.com / Health_Feature / Job_Stress.htm (p. 139)

Canadian Fitness and Lifestyle Research Institute, "Lifestyle Tips"

http: / / www.cflri.ca / eng / lifestyle / index.php (p. 145)

Canadian Centre for Occupational Health and Safety, "Violence in the Workplace"

http: / / www.ccohs.ca / oshanswers / psychosocial / violence.html (p. 148)

RPC Icons

RPC 6.1 Implements and evaluates practices in the areas of health, safety, security, and Workers' Compensation.

- investigative techniques
- hazard recognition
- disaster recovery techniques
- relevant legislation
- resource information
- common health and safety practices
- company policies and procedures
- worker protection (including health and safety and Workers' Compensation)
- theories and practices for protection of individuals and groups
- Occupational health and safety legislation (e.g., Occupational Health and Safety Act of Ontario, Workplace Safety and Insurance Act—Bill 99, Workplace Hazardous Materials Information System, Transportation of Dangerous Goods legislation, environmental legislation, smoking in the workplace legislation, civil rights legislation)
- Hazard identification and control
- Management techniques for OH&S programs

RPC 6.2 Ensures due diligence and strict liability requirements are met, e.g. records are kept and formal procedures established.

- relevant legislation and common law
- company policies and procedures
- industry best practices
- program and policy development
- training and development techniques
- risk analysis
- common and statutory law (e.g., employment standard, labour relations)
- worker protection (including health and safety and Workers' Compensation)
- theories and practices for protection of individuals and groups

Task & Knowledge Requirements

- Occupational health and safety legislation (e.g., Occupational Health and Safety Act of Ontario, Workplace Safety & Insurance Act—Bill 99, Workplace Hazardous Materials Information System, Transportation of Dangerous Goods legislation, environmental legislation, smoking in the workplace legislation, civil rights legislation)
- management techniques for OH&S programs

RPC 6.3 Contributes to policy on the workplace environment (e.g., smoking, workplace violence, scent-free, communicable diseases, and addictions).

- relevant legislation
- program and policy development
- the culture of the organization
- conflict resolution
- record keeping and reporting
- technical terminology
- environmental hazards
- common and statutory law (e.g., employment standard, labour relations)
- worker protection (including health and safety and Workers' Compensation)
- theories and practices for protection of individuals and groups
- Occupational health and safety legislation (e.g., Occupational Health and Safety Act of Ontario, Workplace Safety and Insurance Act—Bill 99, Workplace Hazardous Materials Information System, Transportation of Dangerous Goods legislation, environmental legislation, smoking in the workplace legislation, civil rights legislation)
- management techniques for OH&S programs
- trends in occupational health and safety

RPC 6.4 Ensures internal environmental concerns such as quality of air and water is addressed.

- relevant legislation
- record keeping and reporting

Task & Knowledge Requirements

- investigative techniques
- hazard identification
- available medical services and other outside resources
- policies and procedures
- the organization's culture
- worker protection (including health and safety and Workers' Compensation)
- theories and practices for protection of individuals and groups
- Occupational health and safety legislation (e.g., Occupational Health and Safety Act of Ontario, Workplace Safety and Insurance Act—Bill 99, Workplace Hazardous Materials Information System, Transportation of Dangerous Goods legislation, environmental legislation, smoking in the workplace legislation, civil rights legislation)
- hazard identification and control

RPC 6.5 Develops or provides for wellness and employee assistance programs to support organizational effectiveness.

- policy/procedure development
- collective agreements
- industry best practices
- outside service providers
- the organization's culture
- conflict resolution techniques
- problem-solving techniques
- report writing and record keeping
- the relationship between employee wellness and productivity
- performance goals of the organization and how these are affected by employee wellness
- key components of an EAP such as intake, assessments, counselling, traumatic incident debriefing, and cap on service
- cost/benefit analysis
- types of employee assistance programs
- types of employee assistance and wellness programs
- conceptual definition and implications of occupational stressors (e.g., potential stressors, methods of identifying potential stressors and strain outcomes, response to organizational stressors, and management of employee strain outcomes)
- trends in occupational health and safety

RPC 6.6 Ensures that mechanisms are in place for responding to crises in the workplace, including critical incident stress management.

- oral and written communication
- training and development techniques
- industry best practices
- the workplace environment, including the availability of emergency equipment
- policy and program development and evaluation
- intervention strategies
- relevant legislation (e.g., fire code, Workers' Compensation)
- investigation techniques
- stress management techniques
- types of employee assistance programs
- Occupational health and safety legislation (e.g., Occupational Health and Safety Act of Ontario, Workplace Safety and Insurance Act—Bill 99, Workplace Hazardous Materials Information System, Transportation of Dangerous Goods legislation, environmental legislation, smoking in the workplace legislation, civil rights legislation)
- hazard identification and control
- accident investigation procedures
- emergency preparedness procedures
- management techniques for OH&S programs
- conceptual definition and implications of occupational stressors (e.g., potential stressors, methods of identifying potential stressors and strain outcomes, response to organizational stressors, and management of employee strain outcomes)

RPC 6.7 Analyses risk to the health and safety of employees and determines appropriate preventative measures, including training, provision of required safety equipment, and administrative practices.

- relevant legislation
- nature of the business and physical work environment
- hazard recognition
- workplace inspection techniques
- safety programs, equipment, and emergency procedures
- ergonomics
- functions of the JHSC [Joint Health and Safety Committee]
- training and development/presentation techniques
- industry best practices
- relevant technical terminology
- the collective agreement
- services and equipment available in the community
- worker protection (including health and safety and Workers' Compensation)
- training and development program design and administration

Task & Knowledge Requirements

- Occupational health and safety legislation (e.g., Occupational Health and Safety Act of Ontario, Workplace Safety and Insurance Act—Bill 99, Workplace Hazardous Materials Information System, Transportation of Dangerous Goods legislation, environmental legislation, smoking in the workplace legislation, civil rights legislation)
- hazard identification and control
- emergency preparedness procedures
- management techniques for OH&S programs
- types of employee assistance and wellness programs

RPC 6.8 Responds to serious injury or fatality in the workplace.

- program and policy development
- investigation procedures

Task & Knowledge Requirements

- relevant legislative requirements
- first-aid training and emergency response equipment
- relevant legislative bodies
- pension and insurance benefits/policies
- common and statutory law (e.g., employment standard, labour relations
- worker protection (including health and safety and Workers' Compensation)
- Occupational health and safety legislation (e.g., Occupational Health and Safety Act of Ontario, Workplace Safety and Insurance Act—Bill 99, Workplace Hazardous Materials Information System, Transportation of Dangerous Goods legislation, environmental legislation, smoking in the workplace legislation, civil rights legislation)
- hazard identification and control
- accident investigation procedures
- emergency preparedness procedures

RPC 6.9 Ensures that security programs and policies minimize risks while considering the obligation of the employer and the rights of employees, union, and third parties.

- nature of the business and physical work environment
- relevant legislation
- industry best practices
- program and policy development
- safety and security equipment in the workplace
- risk assessment/techniques
- cost/benefit analysis

RPC 6.10 Ensures compliance with legislated reporting requirements.

- relevant legislation
- methods of reporting incidents

- accident investigation
- training and development techniques
- report writing and record keeping

Task & Knowledge Requirements

- worker protection (including health and safety and Workers' Compensation)
- technical, legislative, political, and personal implications of OHS
- the economic, legal, technical, and moral impact of OHS
- occupational health and safety legislation (e.g., Occupational Health and Safety Act of Ontario, Workplace Safety and Insurance Act—Bill 99, Workplace Hazardous Materials Information System, Transportation of Dangerous Goods legislation, environmental legislation, smoking in the workplace legislation, civil rights legislation)
- hazard identification and control
- accident investigation procedures
- emergency preparedness procedures
- management techniques for OH&S programs

Discussion Questions

1. Think of at least 5 stressors that you have experienced in the last 12 months. Using the guidelines presented in this chapter, categorize the stressors as daily, acute, chronic, or catastrophic. Which, if any, seemed to lead to strain?
2. If only one individual in a workplace is experiencing strain, are the causes of that strain likely to be in the workplace? Why or why not?
3. What are the major sources of stress in modern workplaces?
4. How does stress manifest itself in behaviour? in organizational functioning?
5. What are some actions that individuals can take to help manage stress? What can organizations do to help employees avoid or manage stress?
6. What are some of the ways in which evolving technology contributes to the experience of workplace stress? What are some interventions that employees and employers might attempt in order to avoid or manage the stress associated with technology?
7. Discuss some emerging stressors in the workplace. How might companies help employees deal with the changing demands of work?

Using the Internet

1. In this chapter we have discussed workplace violence as a very real and growing occupational health and safety issue. Using Internet resources, research recent news stories involving violence in the workplace. Categorize them as Type 1, Type 2, Type 3, or Type 4 (see Table 6.4).

2. Psychological symptoms have been identified as a health-related outcome of stress. Individuals who feel prolonged stress may experience such symptoms as depression and anxiety. Many employees indicate that they would be uncomfortable telling their boss or coworkers that they were experiencing these types of psychological symptoms because of the stigma associated with these types of mental health problems. Using the website resources of the Canadian Mental Health Association (http://www.cmha.ca), the Canadian Psychiatric Association (http://www.cpa-apc.org), the Canadian Psychological Association (http://www.cpa.ca), the Canadian Centre for Occupational Health and Safety (http://www.ccohs.ca), and other websites, design an awareness program that might help reduce the stigma associated with stress-related mental health issues in the workplace.
3. Although worker health has been a concern for many years, one of the new trends in occupational health is the concept of a "healthy organization." Using Internet resources, define what a healthy organization is. How do companies go about achieving this status? Does the concept of health have value when applied to the organization?
4. Research an organization in which employees may experience work-related threats or assaults. Conduct a risk assessment to determine whether there is a risk of violence. Describe the measures that a human resources manager can take to develop and implement a workplace violence-prevention program. There are numerous websites that will be helpful in this exercise. The Workers' Compensation Board of British Columbia's publication entitled "Take Care: How to Develop and Implement a Workplace Violence Prevention Program" may be particularly useful. It can be downloaded from http://www.worksafebc.com/publications/health_and_safety/by_topic/assets/pdf/take_care.pdf. (Based on an exercise by Catherine Fitzgerald)

Exercises

1. Think about your current or most recent job. What are/were some of the pertinent stressors? What actions do/did you take to cope with them? How does/did the organization help you to deal with the stress? Talk to some of your friends or members of your family about the stressors they encounter at work and the strategies that they and their employers use to manage workplace stress.
2. Returning to work after a stress-related leave can be difficult for both the individuals coming back to work and their coworkers. Create and enact two role-plays in which you and your classmates are employees at an organization. In one of the scenarios, one of the employees is returning to work after a leave due to a stress-related mental health problem. In the second scenario, one of the coworkers is returning to work following a leave due to a car accident. Following the role-plays discuss each scenario. How did the returning employee feel? What

were the responses of the coworkers? Was there a greater sense of discomfort in discussing the well-being of the person who had been on stress leave, relative to the person who was in the car accident? Do you think there are taboos about discussing mental health problems in the workplace? In your follow-up discussion, generate ways that organizations and individual employees might make the transition easier for the person returning to work from a stress-related leave.

3. Imagine you are currently the human resources director for a large organization. You have been given the job of designing and implementing a new performance review system. You know that the employees may find the shift to a new system stressful and that employees often think that performance review instruments are unfair. You are also aware that perceived injustice in the workplace is a stressor and you would like to minimize the extent to which your employees are exposed to work stress. What might you do to maximize the perceived distributive, procedural, and interactional fairness of the performance review process?
4. Contact the human resources department of an organization. Interview the HR manager about psychosocial hazards in the workplace. Some of the things you should ask about are
   a. The extent to which he or she considers workplace stress to be a problem in that organization
   b. The types of stressors experienced by the employees in that organization
   c. The types of strain reported by employees
   d. The organizational outcomes of employee stress that the company experiences (e.g., turnover, absenteeism)
   e. The types of interventions the company has to help employees reduce or manage stress

Case 1

A Stressful Job

Joan is an emergency room nurse at a busy city hospital. She has always enjoyed the hustle of working emergency and the challenges of dealing with the unexpected. Lately, Joan has been worried about her own well-being. She has been very abrupt with her coworkers on several occasions and has had difficulty concentrating on her job. Although there have been no problems to date, Joan is worried that her deteriorating performance might cause a problem given the critical nature of her work. Her doctor suggested that she take an extended leave because of her "nerves." As the HR representative, what do you think is going on here? Are Joan's concerns likely to be a result of stress? What stressors are present in the environment? If there are 20 employees in emergency and Joan is the only one complaining, does this mean that her complaints are not real?

Case 2

Violence on the Job

Vic Wagar is the new HR manager at Brandon Financial Services. BFS is a mid-sized company with many branches that provides personal and business banking services. Less than one month into his new job, Vic was faced with a novel and unexpected situation. During an attempted robbery at one of the smaller branches, one of BFS's employees was shot. Despite prompt first aid and evacuation, the employee died in hospital the next day. Vic has been asked by senior management to take charge of the situation. In particular, they have asked Vic to make sure the eight other branch employees are "all right" and are dealing with the tragic event. Vic has been assured that BFS will place all required resources at his disposal to ensure the remaining employees receive whatever care they need. Knowing of your expertise in these areas, Vic has contacted you for advice. He needs to know what types of reaction to expect from the eight remaining employees. Most important, he wants to know what action, if any, he should be taking. What do you tell him?

Case 3

Technology at Work

SmithCorp is a quickly growing organization specializing in pharmaceuticals. The management of SmithCorp prides itself on being on the cutting edge. Accordingly, it ensures that all its employees are provided with the latest advances in technology. Employees have laptops, wireless Internet access, BlackBerry devices, and cell phones. SmithCorp also frequently upgrades its software and network systems. Many of the employees rely heavily on this technology and these programs in their daily work. A large portion of SmithCorp's staff works in sales and product management. They are frequently on the road visiting client sites and making sales calls. As such, much of the communication among coworkers and between coworkers and their managers is technologically mediated. What are some of the potential psychosocial hazards that employees at SmithCorp might face? As an HR manager at SmithCorp's head office, what types of programs could you implement to help employees manage the stress and strain that may result from exposure to these psychosocial hazards?

Case 4

The New Leader

Tyrell Brown is an HR manager at a medium-sized medical research firm. Lately he has been receiving complaints from some employees in the finance division. Ella Chen, the newly appointed Director of that division, has a different management style. Employees report that she is unpredictable, inconsistent, and clearly plays favourites among the staff. Many report that Ella is abrupt and does not respect the employees. They are particularly frustrated that she expects improvements without providing any feedback on employees' performance. How might you describe Ella's actions? What are the possible outcomes for the employees in the finance division if things don't change? What might Tyrell do to improve the situation?

Endnotes

1. Sauter, S. L., Murphy, L. R., & Hurrell, J. J. (1990). Prevention of work-related psychological disorders: A national strategy proposed by the National Institute for Occupational Safety and Health (NIOSH). *American Psychologist, 45,* 1146–1158.
2. American Institute of Stress. (2002). *Job stress*. New York: Author.
3. Duxbury, L., Higgins, C., & Johnson, K. L. (1999). *An examination of the implications and costs of work-life conflict in Canada.* Health Canada.
4. Williams, C. (2003). Sources of workplace stress. *Perspectives on Labour and Income, 4(6),* 5–12.
5. Kelloway, E. K., & Francis, L. (2006, February). *Stress and Strain in Nova Scotia Organizations: Results of a Recent Province-wide Study.* Paper presented at the Nova Scotia Psychologically Healthy Workplace Conference, Halifax.
6. Pratt, L. I., & Barling, J. (1988). Differentiating between daily events, acute and chronic stressors: A framework and its implications. In J. J. Hurrell, L. R. Murphy, S. L. Sauter, & C. L. Cooper (Eds.), *Occupational stress: Issues and development in research* (pp. 41–53). London: Taylor & Francis.
7. Pratt, L. I., & Barling, J. (1988). Differentiating between daily events, acute and chronic stressors: A framework and its implications. In J. J. Hurrell, L. R. Murphy, S. L. Sauter, & C. L. Cooper (Eds.), *Occupational stress: Issues and development in research* (pp. 41–53). London: Taylor & Francis.
8. Sauter, S. L., Murphy, L. R., & Hurrell, J. J. (1990). Prevention of work-related psychological disorders: A national strategy proposed by the National Institute for Occupational Safety and Health (NIOSH). *American Psychologist, 45,* 1146–1158.
9. Selye, H. (1946). The general adaptation syndrome and diseases of adaptation. *Journal of Clinical Endocrinology, 6,* 117; and Theorell, T. (2003). To be able to exert control over one's situation: A necessary condition for coping with stressors. In J. C. Quick & L. E. Tetrick (Eds.), *Handbook of occupational health psychology* (pp. 201–220). Washington, DC: American Psychological Association.
10. Lazarus, R. S., & Folkman, S. (1984). *Stress, appraisal, and coping*. New York: Springer.
11. Gazzaniga, M. S., & Heatherton, T. F. (2003). *Psychological science*. New York: W. W. Norton.
12. Friedman, M., & Rosenman, R. (1974). *Type A behavior and your heart*. New York: Knopf.
13. Helmreich, R. L., Spence, J. T., & Pred, R. S. (1988). Making it without losing it: Type A, achievement motivation and scientific attainment revisited. *Personality and Social Psychology Bulletin, 14,* 495–504.
14. Landsbergis, P. A., Schnall, P. L., Belkic, K. L., Baker, D., Schwartz, J. E., & Pickering, T. G. (2003). The workplace and cardiovascular disease: The relevance and potential role for occupational health psychology. In J. C. Quick & L. E. Tetrick (Eds.), *Handbook of occupational health psychology* (pp. 265–287). Washington, DC: American Psychological Association; and Bluen, S. D., Barling, J., & Burns, W. (1990). Predicting sales performance, job satisfaction, and depression using the achievement striving and impatience-irritability dimensions of Type A behavior. *Journal of Applied Psychology, 75,* 212–216.
15. Speilberger, C. D., Vagg, P. R., & Wasala, C. F. (2003). Occupational stress: Job pressures and lack of support. In J. C. Quick & L. E. Tetrick (Eds.), *Handbook of occupational health psychology* (pp. 185–200). Washington, DC: American Psychological Association.

16. Warren, N., Dillon, C., Morse, T., Hall, C., & Warren, A. (2000). Biomechanical, psychological, and organizational risk factors for WRMSD: Population based estimates from the Connecticut Upper-Extremity Surveillance Project (CUSP). *Journal of Occupational Health Psychology, 5,* 164–181.
17. Sauter, S. L., Murphy, L. R., & Hurrell, J. J. (1990). Prevention of work-related psychological disorders: A national strategy proposed by the National Institute for Occupational Safety and Health (NIOSH). *American Psychologist, 45,* 1146–1158.
18. Wallace, J. C., & Vodanovich, S. J. (2003). Can accidents and industrial accidents be predicted? Further investigation into the relationship between cognitive failures and reports of accidents. *Journal of Business and Psychology, 17,* 503–514.
19. Kristensen, T. S. (1996). Job stress and cardiovascular disease: A theoretical critical review. *Journal of Occupational Health Psychology, 3,* 246–260; and Wager, N., Fieldman, G., & Hussey, T. (2003). The effect on ambulatory blood pressure of working under favourably and unfavourably perceived supervisors. *Occupational and Environmental Medicine, 60,* 468–474.
20. Segerstrom, S. C., & Miller, G. E. (2004). Psychological stress and the human immune system: A meta-analytic study of 30 years of inquiry. *Psychological Bulletin, 130,* 601–630.
21. Mohren, C. L., Swaen, G. M. H., Borm, P. J. A., Bast, A., & Galama, J. M. D. (2001). Psychological job demands as a risk factor for common cold in a Dutch working population. *Journal of Psychosomatic Research, 50,* 21–27.
22. Frone, M. R., Cooper, M. L., & Russell, M. (1994). Stressful life events, gender and substance use: An application of Tobit regression. *Psychology of Addictive Behaviors, 8,* 59–69.
23. Quick, J. C., Quick, J. D., Nelson, D. L., & Hurrell, Jr., J. J. (1997). *Preventive stress management in organizations*. Washington, DC: APA Books.
24. Burke, R. J. (1993). Organizational-level interventions to reduce occupational stressors. *Work and Stress, 7,* 77–87; and Hepburn, C. G., Loughlin, C. A., & Barling, J. (1997). Coping with chronic work stress. In B. H. Gottleib (Ed.), *Coping with chronic stress*. New York: Plenum Press.
25. Hepburn, C. G., Loughlin, C. A., & Barling, J. (1997). Coping with chronic work stress. In B. H. Gottleib (Ed.), *Coping with chronic stress*. New York: Plenum Press.
26. Hepburn, C. G., Loughlin, C. A., & Barling, J. (1997). Coping with chronic work stress. In B. H. Gottleib (Ed.), *Coping with chronic stress*. New York: Plenum Press.
27. Hepburn, C. G., Loughlin, C. A., & Barling, J. (1997). Coping with chronic work stress. In B. H. Gottleib (Ed.), *Coping with chronic stress*. New York: Plenum Press.
28. Quick, J. C., Quick, J. D., Nelson, D. L., & Hurrell, Jr., J. J. (1997). *Preventive stress management in organizations*. Washington, DC: APA Books.
29. Schat, A. C. H., Frone, M. R., & Kelloway, E. K. (2006). Prevalence of workplace aggression in the U.S. workforce: Findings from a national study. In E. K. Kelloway, J. Barling, & J. J. Hurrell (Eds.), *Handbook of workplace violence* (pp. 47–89). Thousand Oaks, CA: Sage.
30. Schat, A. C. H., Frone, M. R., & Kelloway, E. K. (2006). Prevalence of workplace aggression in the U.S. workforce: Findings from a national study. In E. K. Kelloway, J. Barling, & J. J. Hurrell (Eds.), *Handbook of workplace violence* (pp. 47–89). Thousand Oaks, CA: Sage.
31. Kelloway, E. K., & Francis, L. (2006, February). *Stress and strain in Nova Scotia organizations: Results of a recent province-wide study.* Paper presented at the Nova Scotia Psychologically Healthy Workplace Conference, Halifax.
32. LeBlanc, M. M., & Barling, J. (2005). Understanding the many faces of workplace violence. In S. Fox & P. E. Spector (Eds.), *Counterproductive workplace behavior: An integration of both actor and recipient perspective on causes and consequences* (pp. 41–64). Washington, DC: American Psychological Association Press.
33. National Institute for Occupational Safety and Health. (1996). *Violence in the workplace*. Retrieved from http://www.cdc.gov/niosh/violphs.html, January 7, 2005.
34. Braverman, M. (1999). *Preventing workplace violence: A guide for employers and practitioners* (1st ed.). Thousand Oaks, CA: Sage.

35. LeBlanc, M. M., & Kelloway, E. K. (2002). Predictors and outcomes of workplace violence. *Journal of Applied Psychology, 87,* 444–453.
36. Schat, A. C. H., & Kelloway, E. K. (2005). Workplace aggression. In J. Barling, E. K. Kelloway, & M. R. Frone (Eds.), *Handbook of work stress* (pp. 189–218). Thousand Oaks, CA: Sage Publications.
37. Schat, A. C., & Kelloway, E. K. (2000). The effects of perceived control on the outcomes of workplace aggression and violence. *Journal of Occupational Health Psychology, 4,* 386–402.
38. Rogers, K., & Kelloway, E. K. (1997). Violence at work: Personal and organizational outcomes. *Journal of Occupational Health Psychology, 2,* 63–71; and Schat, A. C., & Kelloway, E. K. (2000). The effects of perceived control on the outcomes of workplace aggression and violence. *Journal of Occupational Health Psychology, 4,* 386–402.
39. Ilies, R., Hauserman, N., Schwaohau, S., & Stibal, J. (2003). Reported incidence rates of work-related sexual harassment in the United States: Using meta-analysis to explain reported rate disparities. *Personnel Psychology, 56,* 607–631.
40. Crocker, D., & Kalemba, V. (1999). The incidence and impact of women's experiences of sexual harassment in Canadian workplaces. *Canadian Review of Sociology and Anthropology, 46,* 541–558.
41. Fitzgerald, L. F. (1993). Sexual harassment: Violence against women in the workplace. *American Psychologist, 48,* 1070–1076.
42. Aggarwal, A. P. (1992). *Sexual harassment in the workplace*. Toronto: Butterworths Canada Ltd.
43. Aggarwal, A. P. (1992). *Sexual harassment in the workplace*. Toronto: Butterworths Canada Ltd.; and Hesson-McInnis, M. S., & Fitzgerald, L. F. (1997). Sexual harassment: A preliminary test of an integrative model. *Journal of Applied Social Psychology, 27,* 877–901.
44. Aggarwal, A. P. (1992). *Sexual harassment in the workplace*. Toronto: Butterworths Canada Ltd.
45. Aggarwal, A. P. (1992). *Sexual harassment in the workplace*. Toronto: Butterworths Canada Ltd.
46. Elovainio, M., Kivimaki, M., & Helkama, K. (2001). Organizational justice evaluations, job control, and occupational strain. *Journal of Applied Psychology, 86,* 418–424; Francis, L., & Barling, J. (2005). Organizational injustice and psychological strain. *Canadian Journal of Behavioural Science, 37,* 250–261; and Tepper, B. J. (2001). Health consequences of organizational injustice: Tests of main and interactive effects. *Organizational Behavior and Human Decision Processes, 86,* 197–215.
47. Cropanzano, R., & Greenberg, J. (1997). Progress in organizational justice: Tunneling through the maze. In C. L. Cooper & I. T. Robertson (Eds.), *International review of industrial and organizational psychology*, vol. 12 (pp. 317–372). London: John Wiley & Sons.
48. Ferrie, J. E., Head, J., Shipley, M. J., Vahtera, J., Marmot, M. G., & Kivimäki, M. (2006). Injustice at work and incidence of psychiatric morbidity: The Whitehall II study. *Occupational and Environmental Medicine, 63,* 443–450; and Kivimäki, M., Elovainio, M., Vahtera, J., & Ferrie, J. E. (2003). Organizational justice and the health of employees: Prospective cohort study. *Occupational and Environmental Medicine, 60,* 27–34; and Wager, N., Fieldman, G., & Hussey, T. (2003). The effect on ambulatory blood pressure of working under favourably and unfavourably perceived supervisors. *Occupational and Environmental Medicine, 60,* 468–474.
49. Leventhal, G. S., Karuza, J., & Fry, W. R. (1980). Beyond fairness: A theory of allocation preferences. In G. Mikula (Ed.), *Justice and social interaction* (pp. 167–218). New York: Springer-Verlag; and Thibaut, J., & Walker, L. (1975). *Procedural justice: A psychological analysis*. Hillsdale, NJ: Erlbaum.
50. Coovert, M. D., & Thompson, L. F. (2003). Technology and workplace health. In J. C. Quick & L. E. Tetrick (Eds.), *Handbook of occupational health psychology* (pp. 221–241). Washington, DC: American Psychological Association.
51. Coovert, M. D., & Thompson, L. F. (2003). Technology and workplace health. In J. C. Quick & L. E. Tetrick (Eds.), *Handbook of occupational health psychology* (pp. 221–241). Washington, DC: American Psychological Association.
52. Brenner, H., & Ahern, W. (2000). Sickness absence and early retirement on health grounds in the construction industry in Ireland. *Occupational and Environmental Medicine, 57,* 615–620.

Chapter 7

Hazard Recognition and Assessment

Chapter Learning Objectives

After reading this chapter, you should be able to

- identify the sources of workplace hazards
- describe methods to systematically examine these hazards
- list ways to assess the probability, exposure, and consequences of the hazards
- describe the concept of risk assessment
- recognize and define the terminology associated with hazard recognition
- employ the various techniques available to determine risk
- outline the effects of and necessity for task analysis
- be able to discuss various types of trauma, based on human activity
- describe the nature and etiology of repetitive-strain injuries
- describe the techniques of manual lifting
- recognize the ergonomic factors associated with hazard recognition and assessment
- describe the components of a hazard identification program

Caught In, Under, or Between

Occupational health and safety statistics classify some injuries as "caught in, under, or between (CIUB) machinery." For John Rogers, this technical classification is also a tragic reality.

Sixty-eight-year-old Rogers was working at a juice bottling plant in Kings County, Nova Scotia. On February 6, 2007, Rogers was reaching for some bottles that had tipped over. He was caught between the conveyer belt and the machine that places bottles on the belt. The machine arm struck him and pinned him until his coworkers hit the emergency stop button. He was rushed to hospital with a crushed throat, where he remains in serious condition at the time of this writing.

As health and safety professionals, we need to classify and analyze workplace hazards to make safer workplaces. Terminology and classification are often "dry" and "boring," but we should never forget that the hazards are real and the consequences immense for both individuals and organizations.

Source: Adapted from "Worker at N.S. juice plant seriously injured by piece of equipment," *Canadian Occupational Health and Safety News.* Retrieved from http://www.ohscanada.com/issues/ISArticle.asp?id565192&issue502072007, February 7, 2007.

Virtually every workplace has recognizable hazards to which people are exposed. A hazard is classically defined as any existing or potential condition in the workplace that, by itself or interacting with other factors, can result in deaths, injuries, property damage, or other losses.[1] Hazard recognition and evaluation refer to the process of determining those factors likely to cause incidents and accidents. The complete process of recognition, assessment, and control is commonly referred to as RAC.

Terminology

The process of hazard identification and evaluation involves some very specific terms, some of which are incorrectly used interchangeably. Although some terms seem similar, they each have a distinctive use within the OH&S field.

hazard
any condition or changing set of circumstances that has the potential to cause an injury

event
any activity that may occur on a day-to-day basis as a direct or indirect result of some human or human-related undertaking

1. *Hazard*. A **hazard** is any condition or changing set of circumstances that has the potential to cause an injury. A hazardous condition would include a damaged ladder, an icy porch and steps, or a frayed electrical wire. A changing set of circumstances would include the substitution of a toxic solvent for a nontoxic solvent.
2. *Event*. An **event** is any activity that may occur on a day-to-day basis as a direct or indirect result of some human or human-related undertaking; operating a forklift or word processor is an event.

3. *Incident*. An **incident** is any observable human activity that is an unwanted event or occurrence that *might have* had a negative impact on the people, property, or process involved. Thus, an incident includes both accidents and close calls. Examples of close calls include not wearing safety glasses when operating a power saw, wearing loose clothing when operating machinery with moving parts, and brushing against hot objects with unprotected hands without getting burned. Incidents involve the presence of a hazard but may or may not result in an accident.

incident
any observable human activity that is an unwanted event or occurrence that *might have* had a negative impact on the people, property, or process involved

4. *Accident*. An **accident** is any unwanted event that *causes* harm to people, property, or processes. Accidents usually result from direct contact with some form of energy that is greater than the strength of the body or structure to resist. These energies may be

accident
any unwanted event that *causes* harm to people, property, or processes

   - electrical, such as a shock from an electrical fixture or static source
   - mechanical, such as being caught in a machine or slipping while walking
   - thermal, causing burns from extreme heat or cold
   - radiative, from any radiation source including the sun and some artificial lighting
   - gravitational, causing unstable objects to fall
   - kinetic, having to do with a body or device that is moving or stopping suddenly
   - chemical, resulting from contact with any chemical substance causing burns

   In most accidents, several types of energies are involved. For example, when a worker falls off a ladder and breaks an arm, the energies involved are gravity (the fast trip to the ground), mechanical (not enough grip between the worker's feet and the ladder rung), and kinetic (the sudden stop).

5. *Injury*. An **injury** is any trauma, physical or mental, direct or indirect, acute or chronic, experienced by a human being. *Physical injury* includes any damage to tissue (resulting from cutting, abrasion, burning, etc.), and can include the inhalation of a toxic substance. A physical injury is very easy to identify. *Mental injury,* which includes such conditions as anxiety or depression, is more difficult to identify and prove. Both types of injuries can be debilitating and both are compensable under most Workers' Compensation programs. There are several classes of injury.

injury
any trauma, physical or mental, direct or indirect, acute or chronic, experienced by a human being

   (a) **Direct injury** is an injury that is the immediate or primary result of an action, such as leaning against a hot stove and being burned.
   (b) **Indirect injury** is a serious complication, such as an infection resulting from being burned by a stove.
   (c) *Acute* trauma is an injury that occurs quickly (e.g., a burn from a stove).
   (d) *Chronic* trauma is a condition or injury that takes many years to develop and manifest itself, such as the development of a malignant tumour 25 years after exposure to a toxic material such as asbestos.

direct injury
an injury that is the immediate or primary result of an action

indirect injury
a serious complication incurred as a result of an injury

repetitive-strain injury results from ongoing, continuous, and repetitive actions that cause muscle or skeletal strain

6. **Repetitive-strain injury.** A repetitive-strain injury results from ongoing, continuous, and repetitive actions that cause muscle or skeletal strain (e.g., tennis elbow).

Types of Injuries

overt traumatic injuries injuries resulting from coming into contact with an energy source

overexertion injuries injuries resulting from excessive physical effort, repetitive motions, and, possibly, awkward working positions

Considering the nature of workplace injuries will assist us in identifying what type of hazards we are concerned with in the workplace. There are at least two broad classes of injuries that we see occurring in workplaces. **Overt traumatic injuries** (e.g., cuts, fractures, burns) typically result from coming into contact with an energy source (e.g., falling, being struck by material). In contrast, **overexertion injuries** (e.g., sprains, back pain, tendonitis, carpal tunnel syndrome) typically are caused by excessive physical effort, repetitive motions, and, possibly, awkward working positions. From this observation, it follows that hazard identification and control should focus on identifying and controlling sources of energy that can result in injury and conditions of work that may lead to overexertion.

Overt Injuries

One of the most common causes of workplace accidents is individuals coming into contact with objects and equipment in the workplace (see Table 7.1). For example, individuals may be struck by objects that are falling from overhead or may drop materials on themselves, resulting in crush injuries. Material may be flying through the air because of grinding or cutting operations. The use of compressed air in many industrial settings is a particular hazard, as the stream of compressed air may cause small particles of material to accelerate rapidly through the work environment. Individuals may be struck by moving equipment (e.g., vehicles, forklifts).

Another form of contact with equipment occurs when individuals become caught in, under, or between (CIUB) machinery. The use of industrial presses, for example, frequently is associated with crush injuries when individuals

Occupational Health and Safety Notebook 7.1

An Iceberg Model of Health and Safety Costs

As you might know, the visible part of an iceberg is its smallest part. The bulk of the iceberg is below the surface of the water. This is an apt image for health and safety costs. The visible part of the iceberg, which is the smallest part, represents insured costs (sometimes called direct costs), including fire insurance and compensation. The part below the surface—the major portion—represents uninsured costs (or indirect costs), including time for accident investigation, loss of customers, and loss of employees from a resultant layoff. Practice shows that for every dollar of insured costs, there can be 5 to 10 dollars of uninsured costs, making the latter a serious—though often ignored—cost factor. Hazard analysis is directed at preventing these costs from accumulating.

TABLE 7.1

Most Common Injuries among Young Workers

INDUSTRY	MOST COMMON	SECOND MOST COMMON
Hospitality/food service	Struck by object	Contact with hot object
Retail	Overexertion	Struck by object
Transportation	Overexertion	Struck by object
Construction	Struck by object	Overexertion
Forestry	Struck by object	Falls
Manufacturing: wood paper	Overexertion	Struck by object
Manufacturing: metal	Struck by object	Overexertion
Manufacturing: food processing	Overexertion	Struck by object
Wholesale	Overexertion	Struck by object

Source: Workers' Compensation Board of Yukon, "Yukon employers' guide to young workers' safety." Retrieved from http://www.wcb.yk.ca/fileadmin/user_upload/PDF_files/reports_and_publications/handbook.pdf, February 7, 2007. Reprinted with permission.

who are feeding the machine stock get their hands caught in the machinery as it presses. Conveyer belts and other power transmission systems (e.g., belts, pulleys) may have "pinch points" in which individuals become entangled.

Falls also represent a significant source of injury in the workplace. This category includes both falling from a height (e.g., off a ladder, or down a set of stairs) as well as falls on the same level (e.g., slipping on the floor). As we might expect, falls from a height are common in construction, where ladders and other temporary structures (e.g., scaffolding) are frequently used. Falls on the same level frequently result from spilled material (e.g., oil) or by tripping over poorly placed material, uneven surfaces, and so on.

Although frequently overlooked as a type of workplace accident, motor vehicle accidents are a significant health and safety concern. Individuals who drive for a living are exposed to hazardous driving conditions to a much greater extent than are most drivers. Moreover, professional drivers may also deal with shift work and demanding delivery schedules. The equipment they drive is also subject to more rigorous use than the traditional passenger vehicle and requires exceptional ongoing maintenance to ensure safety.

Overt traumatic injuries also result from coming into contact with sources of energy such as electricity, chemicals (e.g., chemical burns), and heat (e.g., touching hot surfaces results in a burn). Using abrasives or prolonged kneeling can result in abrasive injuries in which the skin is torn or rubbed raw.

In each case of overt injury, prevention focuses on (1) recognizing the source of the hazard (i.e., the potential energy source), (2) eliminating the hazard, and (3) protecting workers from exposure to the energy source (i.e., through personal protective equipment).

Overexertion Injuries

Although there are numerous types of overexertion or repetitive strain injuries, most result from one of three basic causes: lifting, working in awkward positions, and repetition.

Materials handling, which involves lifting, carrying, and lowering, is a frequently performed operation in many organizations that can result in high-risk injuries through overexertion and poor posture, both of which are the primary cause of lower back pain. The appendix to this chapter contains a method for estimating lifting tolerances recommended by the National Institute for Occupational Safety and Health (NIOSH) in the United States.[2] Back injuries—from stabbing pain to total disability—can have far-reaching effects for the worker, the worker's family, and the company. Low back pain, frequently associated with materials handling, accounts for more than 50 percent of all musculoskeletal complaints and is the fastest-growing category of disability.[3]

Occupational Health and Safety Notebook 7.2

Twelve Rules for Proper Lifting

1. *Size up the load and check the overall conditions.* Is the load being picked up in the open, or is it surrounded by other boxes? Is it too large to grasp? How far does it have to be carried? How high does it have to be lifted? Is the floor dry or slippery?
2. *Choose the lifting position that feels the best.* There are several "correct" ways to lift a load. Figure 7.1 illustrates two of the more common ones: the straight back leg lift and the stoop lift.
3. *Check for slivers, nails, sharp edges, and so on.* Sustaining a penetration injury while lifting is both painful and awkward.
4. *Lift by gripping the load with both the fingers and the palms of the hand.* The more the hand is in contact with the object, the better the control and the more positive the application of the lifting force.
5. *Keep the back straight.* A straight back (not a vertical back) will reduce stress on the spine and make the load distribution on each vertebral disc uniform.
6. *Maintain good balance.* If you are not steady on your feet, then an off-balance motion can impose significant stress on the discs.
7. *Avoid any unnecessary bending.* Do not place loads on the floor but on a platform or rack if they have to be picked up again later. Bend the knees, and do not stoop.
8. *Avoid unnecessary twisting.* No twisting is acceptable. Turn the feet, not the hips or shoulders.
9. *Avoid reaching out.* Keep all loads as close to the body as possible. The farther away from the body centre, the greater the disc load and hence stress (see Figure 7.2).
10. *Avoid excessive weight.* If the load is too heavy or too awkward, get help. The definition of "excessive" will depend on the individual and his or her physical condition and training.
11. *Lift slowly and smoothly.* Use your body weight to start the load moving and then lift using your legs and arms.
12. *Keep in good physical shape.* The better your physical condition, the easier lifting will be and the lower the risk of sustaining a lower back injury.

Sources: WorkSafe Alberta, "Lifting and handling loads." Retrieved from http://www.hre.gov.ab.ca/documents/WHS/WHS-PUB_bcl001.pdf, February 7, 2007; North American Occupational Safety and Health, "Preventing back injury in manual materials handling." Retrieved from http://www.naosh.org/english/documents/mmh.html, February 7, 2007; and WorkSafeBC, "Top seven dangers for young workers." Retrieved from http://youngworker.healthandsafetycentre.org/s/Top-Seven-Dangers.asp?ReportID533144, February 7, 2007.

FIGURE 7.1

Lift Positions

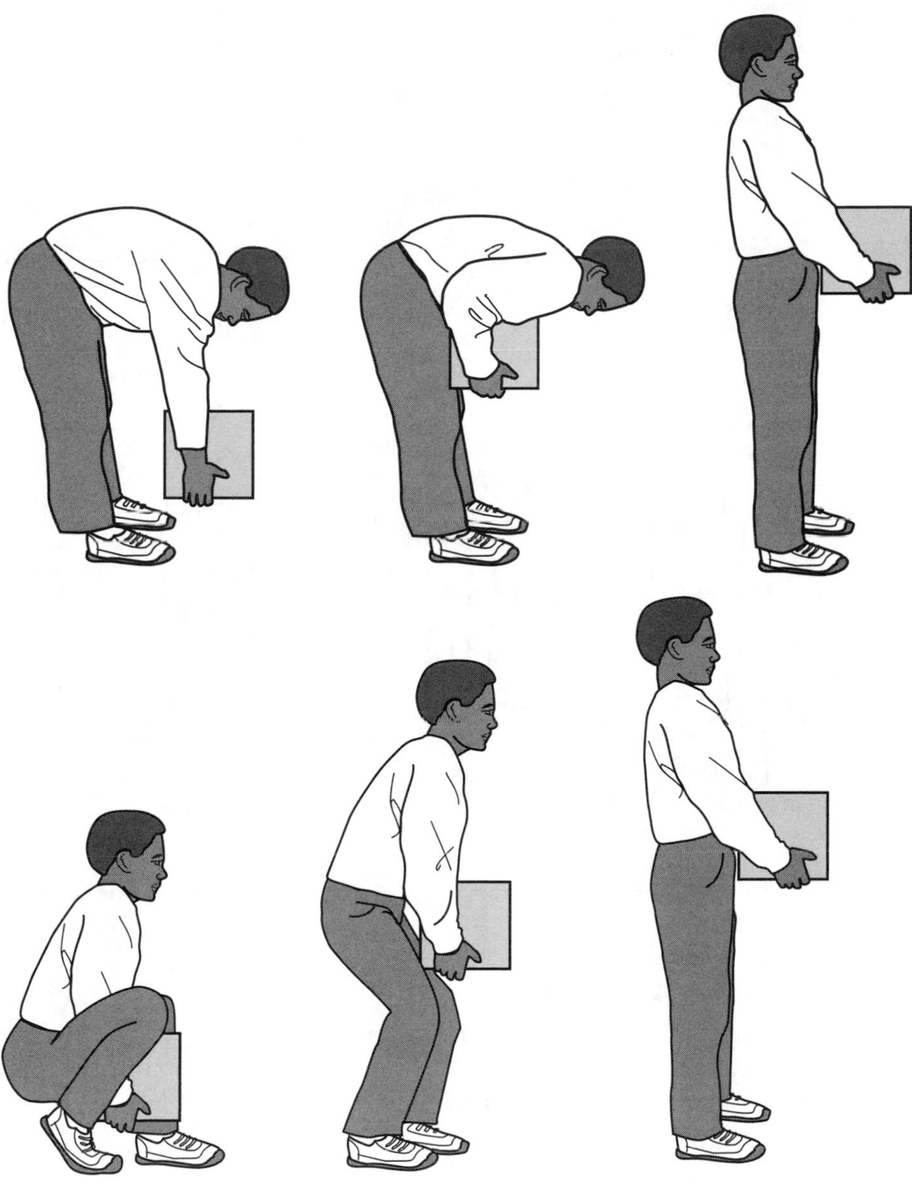

When lifting activities are identified as a workplace hazard, materials handling should be mechanized through the use of conveyors and forklift trucks or other lifting devices, or it can be automated through the use of automated guided vehicles (AGV), which follow sensor lines on the floor, stopping as required to transfer their product, or computer-controlled inventory systems that allow computer-controlled machines to pick up or stock inventory. Thus, many of the risks associated with lifting can be greatly

FIGURE 7.2

Relationship between Load Position and Lower Back Stress

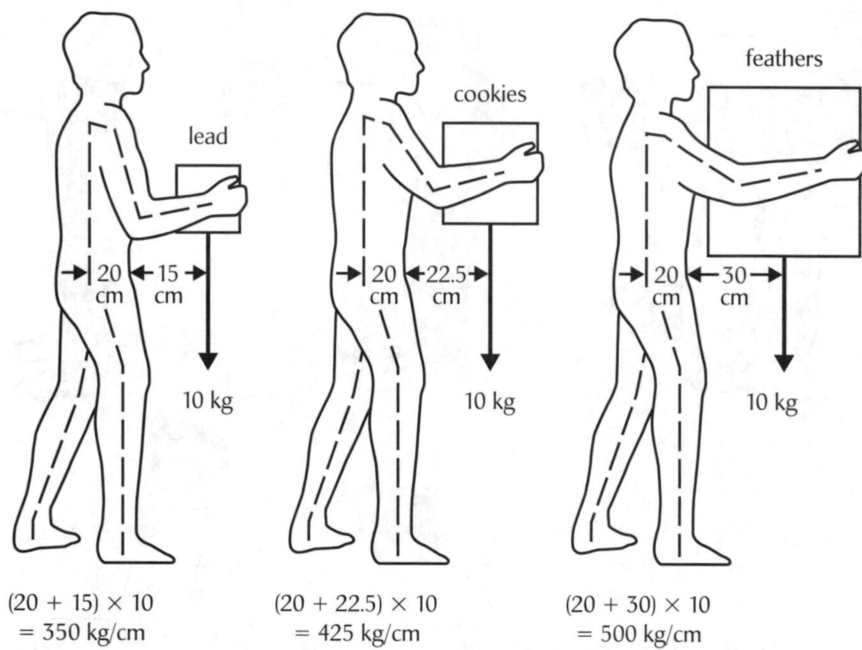

reduced. Supports that force the back to remain straight but do not prevent the worker from lifting or handling heavier loads are used by some workers. Although the logic of using back supports is appealing, agencies such as NIOSH in the U.S. have suggested that there is no scientific support for the use of such devices. The Canadian Task Force on Preventive Health Care found that randomized control trials did not support the use of back supports.[4] Of the five trials reviewed, three found no effect and the remaining two found marginal effects.

Repetitive-Strain Injuries

Repetitive-strain injury (RSI), cumulative trauma disorder (CTD), musculoskeletal injury (MSI), and overuse syndrome (OS) are injuries whose origins can be traced to continuous and repetitive actions that produce muscle or skeletal strain. Because the terms are basically interchangeable, the term RSI will refer to all these conditions in this chapter.

Occupational Health and Safety Notebook 7.3

Recognizing RSI: Risk Factors and Symptoms

Recognizing the risk factors for and symptoms of RSI is the first step toward taking preventive and remedial action. Your job puts you at risk for RSI if

- you spend a large amount of time in continuous computer use or other repetitive action;
- you do not take frequent breaks to stretch;
- your workstation is poorly designed from an ergonomic standpoint;
- you use the computer but have poor typing skills (i.e., poor hand position, excessive force in striking the keys).

The symptoms of RSI can include

- weakness in a limb or limbs
- tingling or numbness in a limb
- pain
- lack of endurance (e.g., hand tires rapidly)
- clumsiness (e.g., difficulty picking things up, buttoning clothing)

Sources: Engineering Electronics, "Computer related repetitive stress injury." Retrieved from http://eeshop.unl.edu/rsi.html, February 7, 2007; and Canadian Auto Workers, "What is RSI?" Retrieved from http://www.caw.ca/whatwedo/health&safety/pdf/03-RSIDayPamphletGeneric1.pdf, February 7, 2007.

Any strain-producing body action that involves use of the fingers, wrists, arms, elbows, shoulders, neck, back, and, to a lesser extent, the lower body and legs, and is repeated over a long period, can cause damage to joints and tissues. Tennis elbow, golfer's elbow, telephone operator's elbow, writer's cramp, and postal worker's shoulder are well-known examples of RSI. More recently named conditions include carpal tunnel syndrome, thoracic outlet syndrome, and white fingers disease or Raynaud's syndrome. The latter, as previously mentioned, is also caused by vibration.

RSI is fast becoming the most common occupational injury. Data from the Canadian Community Health Survey suggest that 1 in 20 Canadians over the age of 20 have experienced RSI.[5] This translates into 2.3 million cases, the majority of which result from work activities.

The origins of RSI can be traced to the following four general conditions:

1. *Unnatural joint position or posture*. Whenever a joint is forced to work in a position that is unnatural or stressed, the risk of RSI is increased. For instance, during keyboarding the wrists are forced out of axial alignment with the arm. The use of a hand tool such as a pair of pliers can force the wrist–arm axes out of line, creating a stress condition that could eventually cause joint irritation.
2. *Force application to hinge joints*. When these joints are forced to carry applied loading, particularly when flexed, the joint load distribution of the cartilage is uneven, causing excessive stress in a small area of the joint. The wrist is a good example of a hinge joint. When performing a task such as lifting while bent, this joint can begin to ache. Repetition of the activity can result in a loss of strength.

3. *Activity repetition*. Tasks such as keyboarding (computer operator) or using a hammer (carpenter) involve a repetitive flexing of the fingers and wrists. The action of typing applies low-load repetition to the fingers (touching the keys) and medium loading to the wrist (supporting the hand). The action of hammering applies a high-impact loading to the wrist, which is flexed into a nonaligned axis on impact. The shock effect increases the potential risk of tissue damage.
4. *Preexisting conditions*. Ailments such as arthritis or circulation disorders can have a synergistic effect on RSI conditions. For example, arthritis is an inflammation condition of the joints that can be aggravated by the stress associated with hammering or keyboarding activity.

Awkward Working Positions

Strains and sprains can also result from bending, twisting, and working in a variety of awkward positions. Frequently, the work position may compound or interact with other factors. For example, an individual may be lifting a load that normally would present no problem but is working in a confined space that prohibits following safe lifting procedures, resulting in an injury.

Perhaps the most common types of injury result from bending or twisting the torso, extending the reach beyond the body, and working overhead with the hands and arms. As a general guideline, individuals should not have to reach below the knees or raise their arms above the shoulder for any length of time. The design of workstations and work procedures should ensure that individuals work in a comfortable position. Moreover, equipment and machinery should be adjustable to accommodate differences in body size.

Occupational Health and Safety Today 7.1

Artistic Occupations at Risk

If you search for RSI on the Web, you will mostly find articles focused on the hazards of computer work and industrial jobs that involve repetitive motions. It may surprise you to know that people in other occupations—such as dancers and musicians—are also at risk for RSI. These occupations involve considerable repetition (practice, practice, practice) and often involve awkward hand or body positions. Intense preparation for a performance, learning new pieces (requiring extensive practice and repetition), changes in techniques or instruments, and prolonged performances are all risk factors for performing artists. Dancers are at risk because of these factors but also because forceful exertions can lead to stress fractures and similar injuries.

Source: Safety and Health in Arts, Production and Entertainment, "Preventing musculoskeletal injury (MSI) for musicians and dancers." Retrieved from http://www.shape.bc.ca/resources/pdf/msi.pdf, February 7, 2007.

Hazard Identification

The identification of hazards includes four areas of analysis: ergonomic factors, human factors, situational factors, and environmental factors. This section is not to be confused with the categories of information to be collected in Chapter 12, which uses the latter three classifications of human, situational, and environmental factors to determine the areas of investigation.

RPC 7.2

RPC 7.3

RPC 7.4

Ergonomic Factors

Ergonomics-related issues are becoming increasingly prominent and important. Over a five-year-period, one-third of compensation claims in British Columbia resulted from ergonomics-related injuries, costing $400 million for more than 100,000 claims.[6] British Columbia was the first province to pass ergonomics legislation.

Studies have indicated that workplaces designed along ergonomic principles not only decrease the risk of physical injury but also increase productivity and efficiency. One airline that introduced ergonomic equipment such as adjustable work surfaces, footrests, and document holders reported a 93 percent reduction in errors, a 50 percent decrease in musculoskeletal problems, a 33 percent drop in visual fatigue, with a 33 percent increase in efficiency.[7] The redesign of computer workstations has been associated with increases in both productivity[8,9] and user satisfaction.[10]

WWW

The goal of an ergonomics program is to design a work system in which the work methods, machines, equipment, layout, and environment (noise, heat, light, and air quality) are matched or are compatible with the physical and behavioural characteristics of the worker to reduce risk.[11] Workplace design has traditionally focused on standardization—one size fits all—despite the wide variations in the physical characteristics of employees. **Anthropometric** factors such as height, weight, reach, and strength influence how the work is done and the likelihood of achieving efficiency and safety. Inexperience and idiosyncratic ways of doing work increase the probability of injuries. Tasks have to be matched to human capabilities to ensure optimal performance and reduction of risk.

anthropometry
study of the measurements of the human body to determine differences in individuals or groups of individuals

Human Factors

Incidents involving humans (often referred to as unsafe acts) fall into two main categories, *predictable* and *random*. An incident that is a result of a predictable action is something that the perpetrator did knowingly. For example, a worker who locks out a machine before making some adjustments is performing a correct, voluntary action, thereby avoiding any possible injury from the operating machine. In most cases, sources of potential accidents are predictable (e.g., a worker knows that it is possible for a ladder rung to break, but uses the ladder anyway). A random event, in contrast, is by its very nature difficult to predict. For example, the worker climbing the ladder could have fallen because another worker walked into the ladder. No one could have predicted this event. However, at times, the same action could also be predictable, depending on circumstances. If the same worker had placed the ladder in a crowded corridor, the event could be considered predictable. A change in conditions can thus transform a random event into a predictable one.

human factor

when a person causes an accident by commission, poor judgment, or omission (failing to do something)

When a worker or another person causes an accident by commission, poor judgment, or omission (failing to do something), the cause is labelled a **human factor.** However, analysts distinguish between fact finding and fault finding. A human action may have been directly or indirectly involved in the event, but "human error" or blame will neither be used nor implied. In a similar vein, no one would willingly or intentionally injure himself or herself, which tends to support the idea that a human action should not be considered "human error" and have blame assigned. No matter how many backup systems are in place, some shortcut or personal foible can cause the system to fail. The intent of hazard recognition, assessment, and control is not to find a scapegoat, but to correct procedures and behaviours so that the likelihood of the accident occurring again is reduced. Similarly there are techniques—see the fault tree analysis in the chapter appendix—that can permit a professional to identify hazardous conditions or activities and implement correct procedures before hazardous events occur.

unsafe act

generally refers to a deviation from standard job procedures or practices that increases a worker's exposure to a hazard

An **unsafe act** generally refers to a deviation from standard job procedures or practices that increases a worker's exposure to a hazard. Unsafe acts may be direct and indirect. A human action that may cause an immediate event of any type, and over which the person has control, is considered a direct, unsafe act (sometimes referred to as a *substandard practice*). An example would be the improper modifications to a respirator used in a paint booth to allow a cigarette to be smoked through the filter cassette. An indirect, unsafe act is one in which the human action is only indirectly involved. Consider the following example. A designer of a machine alters a braking system on a punch press that allows the machine to complete its operating cycle after the emergency stop is activated instead of immediately stopping. In this instance,

Occupational Health and Safety Today 7.2

Safety Policy at Saskferco: "First We Walk the Walk"

Saskferco is a producer of nitrogen fertilizer located in Belle Plaine, Saskatchewan. The company claims an exceptional safety record, which it attributes to a focused commitment to health and safety and the implementation of a comprehensive health and safety program. Their program includes a detailed safety manual, specialized safety training, recognition of safe performance, benchmarking, emergency planning, and regular inspections. Although it is important to have a clearly articulated safety policy, it is arguably more important to "walk the walk" by demonstrating the firm's commitment to safety through tangible efforts and initiatives.

Source: Saskferco Canada, "Safety." Retrieved from http://www.saskferco.com/safety_environ/safety.shtml, February 7, 2007.

there is overlap between an indirect unsafe act and an unsafe condition. The machine defect started as an indirect unsafe act but resulted in an unsafe condition for the operators using the machine.

Some safety professionals differentiate between the terms "unsafe act" and "substandard practice" by suggesting that the latter implies a much broader application. In this text, the term unsafe act will be used to indicate acts or practices that are unsafe or potentially unsafe. Following are some examples of unsafe acts:

- Unauthorized operation of equipment—using after hours or without training
- Improper use of equipment—using a forklift truck to lift a load beyond its weight limit
- Use of defective equipment—using a broken ladder
- Failure to lock out power when servicing equipment
- Removal or disabling of safety devices—removing the guard from a table saw
- Failure to warn or secure—leaving a forklift truck running unattended
- Improper lifting, loading, or positioning—lifting a package that is too long or too heavy
- Failure to use personal protective equipment—not wearing safety glasses when using a table saw
- Improper use of personal protective equipment—using a respirator that is unsuitable for the aerosols involved
- Alcohol or drug abuse—being under the influence at work
- Horseplay—throwing snowballs in a factory

Occupational Health and Safety Notebook 7.4

Interaction of Factors

The four factors discussed in this chapter (ergonomic, human, situational, and environmental) do not happen in isolation–rather they may interact to result in accidents or injury. Consider the case of the Ocean Ranger.

In February 1982 the Ocean Ranger, a giant oil rig, capsized and sank off the coast of Newfoundland, resulting in the loss of the entire crew of 84 men. A subsequent investigation revealed errors on the part of the crew in charge of ballast control. Part of their job was to assess the draft of the rig by looking out a porthole in one of the legs of the rig, which was more than 8 metres above mean water level. To save time and energy, they left the porthole open. During a storm, water entered through the porthole and damaged the ballast control system. The problem was compounded when the crew misread the control manual and opened instead of closed the ballast tanks. This case illustrates the importance of presenting display information in a way that will allow for error-free interpretation.

Although the focus here is on display design, what other factors were at play?

Sources: CBC Archives, "The Ocean Ranger disaster." Retrieved from http://archives.cbc.ca/IDD-1-70-349/disasters_tragedies/ocean_ranger/, February 7, 2007; and Atlantic Oil & Gas Works Online, "Future offshore safety was a prime concern." Retrieved from http://www.oilworks.com/ February2002/NewMag/safety.html, February 7, 2007.

Situational Factors

situational factors

also known as unsafe conditions; exist when a company does not provide proper equipment, tools, or facilities, or when its operations are unsafe

Situational factors, also known as *unsafe conditions,* exist when a company does not provide proper equipment, tools, or facilities, or when its operations are unsafe. The following are examples of unsafe conditions:

- Improper illumination—too dark or too much glare
- Poor exhaust or ventilation systems—the toxic vapours from a process hang in the air rather than being removed
- Defective equipment and materials—not to the required specifications
- Airborne toxic chemical agents—aerosols that are generated by poor control of the process
- Physical agents—machinery noise
- Fire and explosion conditions—improper use or handling of flammable materials
- Poor housekeeping—oil spills and trash allowed to remain
- Adverse temperature conditions—working around a furnace on a hot summer day
- Poor indoor air quality—odours and stuffiness
- Ineffective personal protective equipment—not the correct type of protection for the specific conditions, such as providing dust masks where vapour masks should be used
- Continuance of improper procedures or practices—continuing to allow machine adjustment while the machine is operating

The above situational factors can be grouped into four categories:[12]

1. Defects in design
2. Substandard construction
3. Improper storage of hazardous materials
4. Inadequate planning, layout, and design

Environmental Factors

Environmental factors, including physical factors, chemical factors, biological factors, and ergonomic factors, can play either a direct or indirect role in accidents. For example, physical factors such as noise, vibration, illumination, and temperature extremes have an obvious relation to safety. A noisy work environment may prevent a worker from hearing approaching vehicles or may damage hearing over time. Similarly, chemical factors such as airborne toxic gases not only may cause illness, but also may impair a worker's reaction, judgment, or concentration. Contact with biological agents such as viruses or parasites may cause either minor illness—a cold—or something more serious—hepatitis B. Ergonomic factors such as poor desk-chair design or improper lifting techniques can cause discomfort and muscle strain.

Choosing a Hazard Identification Program

Safety and HR professionals have several choices to make when determining the type of hazard identification program they will undertake. The factors influencing this decision include the source of the request for information, the nature of the hazards to be identified, and the costs associated with the program.

Source of Request

The identification of workplace hazards may be prompted by a request from a Ministry of Labour or a Workers' Compensation Board (resulting from the presence of specific substances or conditions in the workplace) or from the joint health and safety committee (resulting from a complaint or inspection). Alternatively, the program may be initiated as part of an organization's safety program. The person responsible for OH&S may decide to survey one procedure, one area, or the entire plant, depending on the request.

Nature of Hazards

Some tests can be performed on a single employee, while others require samples from many workers. Similarly, some hazards (such as a broken tool) can be identified within minutes; other hazards, such as chemical agents, may require months of testing. All have an injury potential.

Cost

Cost will also determine the extent of the program. For example, to obtain an air sample for benzene contamination, sampling may have to be done in several locations over an eight-hour shift. Several air samples, including blanks, may have to be taken at each location. (A **blank** is an unopened cassette or other sampling device, such as a charcoal tube, that is used as a baseline or zero point for comparison in chemical testing.) The cost of obtaining three samples, plus a blank, in five locations (including the eight hours of the safety professional's time) would be more than $3,000. Unless it is a required legal assessment or a due diligence requirement, then a cost–benefit analysis would have to be done—comparing test costs to a reduction in cost for lost-time injuries.

blank
an unopened cassette or other sampling device, such as a charcoal tube, that is used as a baseline or zero point for comparison in chemical testing

Use of Safety Experts

Most organizations have a network of associations with people who have a great deal of knowledge about OH&S in the workplace. These experts include occupational health and safety inspectors, the suppliers who manufacture the tools and equipment used at the worksite, insurance company loss control specialists, safety personnel in the same occupational sector, labour representatives specializing in safety issues, and agencies such as the Industrial Accident Prevention Association (IAPA) or the Construction Safety Association of Ontario (CSAO).

Components of the Hazard Identification Program

walk-through survey
a survey in which a safety professional walks through a worksite and notes hazards

safety sampling
a systematic survey procedure undertaken by safety personnel who record their observations of unsafe practices on a sampling document

A safety professional can enter a worksite and, by walking through, be able to note hazards. The utility of a **walk-through survey** is increased by arranging to have the supervisor and a worker member of the joint health and safety committee accompany the safety expert. **Safety sampling,** often referred to as *behaviour* or *activity sampling,* is a systematic survey procedure undertaken by safety personnel who record their observations of unsafe practices on a sampling document. They might observe, for example, workers without hardhats where they are required.

Actual and observable exposures to hazards are the focus of the survey. Examples of exposure include chemical substances such as solvents and physical agents such as noise. Safety personnel might observe escaping smoke, or open containers, or the wrong type of personal protective equipment worn by employees. However, potential and inferred exposures would not be ignored. The former includes any substance for which an intended control procedure is being considered. The latter includes any observable accumulation of material such as dust, which might become an airborne hazard.

 7.3

Following the walk-through survey, the safety personnel encode and count their observations. A report is then submitted to management to provide an objective evaluation of the type and number of unsafe acts and conditions.

Management can ask workers who represent a variety of tasks and jobs to identify hazards and unsafe conditions. Employees might report that they are required to adapt tools (thus rendering them potentially hazardous) in order to meet production quotas, or that a machine is dripping oil, rendering a corridor slippery and treacherous. Discussions with both the experts and the employees should be supplemented by an analysis of the job site and the work performed.

Analysis of the Plant, Tasks, and Jobs

Geographical Information

The company should have a detailed layout of the plant or premises, showing the location of processes, machinery, materials storage, shipping, and so forth. A drawing showing the location of any toxic materials and storage arrangement must be available under WHMIS requirements.

job description
the content and hierarchy specific to a particular job

job specifications
the requirements necessary to perform the various functions of a job (e.g., ability to lift weight, education level)

Task and Job Inventory

A description of the job and its associated tasks should be obtained and organized by department, operation, or product. The human resources department can assist by providing the **job description** and **job specifications.** Flow process charts that incorporate standard industrial engineering symbols can clarify the relationships among tasks, jobs, and procedures (see Figure 7.3).

FIGURE 7.3

Flow Chart for Table Tennis Paddle Assembly

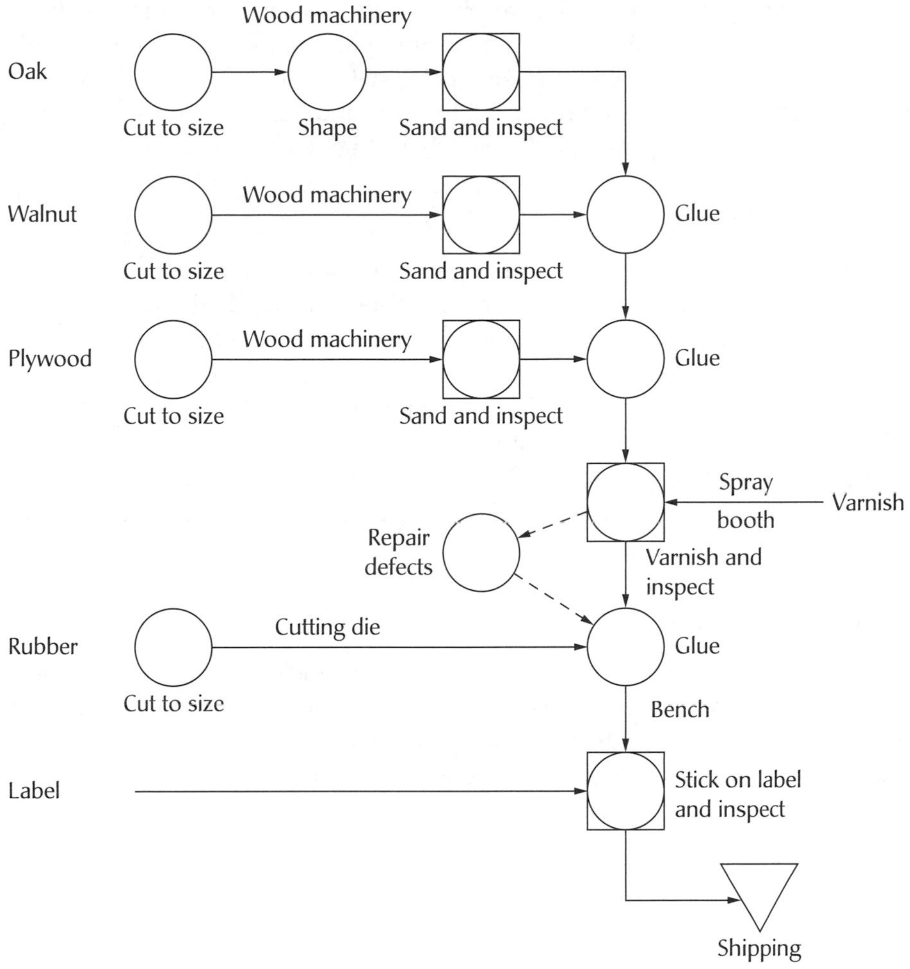

Task Analysis

Task analysis refers to the systematic examination of a job's many components. It consists of a list of tasks and the job of which they are a part, the number of workers who perform the same or similar tasks, the time spent on each task, the importance of the task to the job, the complexity and criticality of the job, the learning curve if complicated and repetitive, and the effort required. The analysis identifies the various demands on the worker, the tasks that are susceptible to worker error and stress, and potentially hazardous conditions. Industrial engineering methods are best for performing this kind of analysis.

Reports and Audits

A review of the reports filed after an incident, accident, injury, or as part of a safety inspection will provide valuable information on hazards. Occupational health and safety departments and safety associations can also provide

written information about the type of accidents in similar industries. Accident and injury rates published by governments are another source of information. Most Workers' Compensation Boards (for a complete list, see Chapter 3), for example, publish regular reports on accident statistics. Audit information, which is obtained by reviewing records of all injuries, accidents, incidents, workplace design changes, and environmental sampling, is an extremely useful source for cataloguing hazards. Most large organizations use computers to store, analyze, and report on hazards and incidents, thus facilitating the identification of hazards by type or department.[13]

Hazard Analysis

hazard analysis
an orderly, analytical technique that examines a system for the most probable hazards having the severest consequences, for the purpose of establishing corrective or control mechanisms

positive tree
shows, graphically, how a job should be done

fault tree
an illustration of things that can go wrong

Hazard analysis is used to acquire specific hazard and failure information about a given system.[14] Hazard analysis is an orderly, analytical technique that examines a system for the most probable hazards having the severest consequences, for the purpose of establishing corrective or control mechanisms. The most common form of hazard analysis is the analytical tree, of which there are two types. The **positive tree** shows, graphically, how a job should be done. The more frequently used tree is the **fault tree,** which provides an illustration of things that can go wrong. A typical fault tree structure is shown in Figure 7.6 in the appendix at the end of this chapter.

Risk Assessment

Once hazards have been identified, the risk of an incident, accident, or injury must be determined. Insurance companies have long used risk evaluation to determine the susceptibility of humans to having accidents and even to dying. The rates that subscribers pay are predicated on this type of evaluation. For

Occupational Health and Safety Notebook 7.5

Job Safety Analysis

One particularly useful means of identifying potential hazards in a job is to conduct a job safety analysis. Typically, this analysis is conducted by a team of subject matter experts, including the workers who do the job, supervisors, and health and safety specialists. The job safety analysis consists of

1. Breaking down the job into its constituent elements (e.g., tasks and sequences of tasks).
2. Analyzing each element to identify potential hazards. This may (and should) include the worker "walking through" each element of the job and explaining the details of each element to the team.
3. Considering "critical incidents" in which accidents or near misses occurred to inform the team's analysis.
4. Making recommendations to change the workstation, process, or method in order to control all the identified hazards.

Source: Canadian Centre for Occupational Health and Safety, "What is a job hazard analysis?" Retrieved from http://www.ccohs.ca/oshanswers/hsprograms/job-haz.html, February 7, 2007.

example, younger drivers pay higher insurance rates because they are involved in a disproportionate number of accidents. Insurers similarly measure the relative risk of such events as theft, fire, flood, and vandalism. The same concept can be applied to health and safety.

RPC 7.2

RPC 7.4

Risk is the probability of an injury expressed as a percentage. The assessment of risk is calculated by determining the probability of an occurrence, the consequences of that occurrence, and the exposure to the cause of the occurrence, expressed as

Risk = Probability × Consequences × Exposure

Probability refers to the chance or likelihood that an event will happen. The range of probabilities for risk runs from about 5 percent to about 95 percent. For management purposes, probability can also be measured in the following terms:[15]

probability
the chance or likelihood that an event will occur

- Likely will occur immediately or shortly after exposure to the hazard
- Probably will occur in time
- Possibly will occur in time
- Unlikely will occur

Any measurement of the risk of an accident occurring will have to take into account the degree of worker **exposure** to the hazard. This estimate includes not only the number of people who are regularly exposed, but also the frequency of the exposure. The more contact one has with a known hazard, the greater the risk. A worker who operates a lathe continuously throughout an eight-hour shift has more exposure than does the worker who uses the lathe only once or twice. However, consideration must also be given to the worker's level of experience. Generally, the more experience a worker has in dealing with a potentially dangerous work situation, the lower the possibility of injury. A professional race-car driver should be at a lower risk of injury when driving on a busy highway than is a regular commuter. Even a driver who has done skid-school training should be at a lower risk on the same roadway. A distracter such as an automobile accident can increase the probability of an accident. The number of workers exposed to a hazard could be used in a ranking or weighting system as part of the risk formula. Thus, probability can be affected by

exposure
how regularly, or the number of times, a contact is made with the event

- experience
- exposure
- proximity
- external stimuli or distraction
- illumination

Factors such as noise and light can increase the probability of an accident. The machine-generated noises in an assembly plant may mask the sound of an approaching vehicle like a forklift truck. Dimly lit workstations and pathways may increase the risks associated with potential hazards such as protruding sharp material and steps. The loud talking of a coworker may distract a worker who is engaged in a potentially hazardous task.

consequences
the results or severity of the injury

Consequences correspond to the severity of the injury, and can range from dust in the eye, to amputation of a finger, to death. Below is a subjective ranking system that can be used to classify the degree of hazard consequence:[16]

1. *Catastrophic:* may cause death or loss of a facility
2. *Critical:* may cause severe injury, occupational illness, or major property damage
3. *Marginal:* may cause minor injury or minor occupational illness resulting in lost workday(s), or minor property damage
4. *Negligible:* probably would not affect personnel safety or health but still in violation of specific criteria

By estimating probability, consequence, and exposure, safety personnel can determine the risk involved in any given job or task. Table 7.2 is a sample layout that can be used for hazard inventory and risk evaluation. The first column includes a brief description of the job or task being inventoried (a weld assembly operation, in our example). The second column shows the hazard or hazards associated with the task (flash burns, skin burns, toxic fumes, lifting sprains, etc.). The third column shows an estimate of the percentage probability for each hazard, and the fourth column lists the corresponding consequences of each hazard (e.g., "vision loss" for flash burns). Under each heading (probability, consequence, and exposure), the hazards can be rated using a scale of 1 to 10.

The factors in Table 7.3 correspond to the numbers shown in Table 7.2. Thus, if the worker's risk of coming in contact with toxic fumes as a result of welding is calculated from the values assigned out of a maximum of 1,000 as a percent, then

$$\textbf{Risk} = 6 \times 4 \times 8 = 192/1000 = 0.192 \text{ or } 19.2\%$$

TABLE 7.2

Sample Hazard Inventory and Risk Evaluation

Job/Task	Hazard(s) Probability		Risk Consequence		Risk Exposure	
Weld assembly	Flash burns	6	Temporary or partial blindness, lost time	4	Daily while welding	8
	Skin burns	2	Discomfort	3	Rarely	3
	Lifting strains	5	Back injury if heavy material lifted, lost time	4	Occasionally	6
	Toxic fumes	6	Respiratory difficulty without personal protective equipment	4	Daily while welding	8

Table 7.3

Factors for Evaluating Risk

	Probability		Consequence		Exposure
10	Predicted or expected	10	Catastrophic	10	Continuous daily
9		9		9	
8	Almost certain	8	Fatality	8	Frequently, daily
7		7		7	
6	Possible	6	Serious injury	6	Occasional (1/wk–1/mo)
5	50/50 chance	5		5	
4	Coincidence	4	Disabling injury	4	Unusual (1/mo–1/yr)
3	Never occurred before	3	Minor	3	Rare
2	Almost impossible	2	Nerves ("close call")	2	Remotely possible

In this example, the worker would have a 19.2 percent risk of contact with toxic fumes while welding. To determine whether this value is too high, the chemical content and toxicity of the fumes would have to be known. This information appears on the labels of hazardous products.

Follow-up

The information obtained through hazard identification and assessment should be communicated to the plant manager, the immediate supervisor, and the health and safety committee. Some reports may be forwarded to the Ministry of Labour (if the substance is under assessment), or the Ministry of Environment, or to the corporation's lawyers. Safety professionals and supervisors who do not pass on information about unsafe conditions to a responsible manager could be charged under the Occupational Health and Safety Act.

When presented with information about hazards, management may decide to (1) take no action, (2) take corrective action, or (3) consider a cost–benefit analysis to determine whether the anticipated losses are worth the cost of correcting the problem.

Summary

The primary goal of hazard recognition and assessment is to reduce incidents, accidents, injuries, and property damage. A variety of methods are used to identify hazards: safety experts; plant, task, and job analysis; reports and audits; and use of monitoring instruments. Hazard analysis is then used to acquire specific information about the hazards in a given system. The hazards are rated according to their degree of risk, and calculations that take probabilities, consequences, and exposures into consideration are formulated. Although accidents and injuries cannot be eliminated, risk assessment can greatly reduce these undesirable events.

The increase in nontraumatic injuries such as back strain and RSI is costing employers in terms of lost production and compensation. Ergonomics, the design of the workplace to accommodate human characteristics and work methods, offers some solutions. The application of ergonomic principles to lifting, sitting, tool, and worksite design reduces the number of injuries and increases productivity.

Key Terms

accident 171
anthropometry 179
blank 183
consequences 188
direct injury 171
event 170
exposure 187
fault tree 186
hazard 170
hazard analysis 186
human factor 180
incident 171
indirect injury 171
injury 171
job description 184
job specifications 184
overexertion injuries 172
overt traumatic injuries 172
positive tree 186
probability 187
repetitive-strain injury 172
safety sampling 184
situational factors 182
top event 196
unsafe act 180
walk-through survey 184

Weblinks

Workplace Health, Safety and Compensation Commission of Newfoundland and Labrador, "Workplace Hazard Analysis Form"

http://www.whscc.nf.ca/resource/SafetyHandouts/hazardanalysis.pdf (p. 170)

Industrial Accident Prevention Association, "Determining Significant Hazards at Work: A Guide for Employers and JHSCs"

http://www.iapa.ca/pdf/SIGHAZWEB.pdf (p. 172)

Construction Safety Magazine, "Crushed/Hit"

http://66.203.200.8/UploadFiles/Magazine/VOL11NO3/fatals.htm (p. 173)

Construction Safety Magazine, "Falls: The Number One Cause of Construction Deaths"

http://66.203.200.8/UploadFiles/Magazine/VOL10NO3/falls.htm (p. 173)

WorkSafe Saskatchewan, "Important Safety Tips on Using Portable Ladders"

http://www.worksafesask.ca/files/naosh_week/w24-13en.htm?noframe (p. 173)

National Institute for Occupational Safety and Health, "Back Belts: Do They Prevent Injury?"

http://www.cdc.gov/niosh/backbelt.html (p. 176)

Shelter Online, "Online RSI Resources"

http://www.shelterpub.com/_fitness/_office_fitness_clinic/OFC_resources.html (p. 177)

WorkSafeBC, "Injury Prevention Resources for Performing Arts & Film—Music"

http://artsandfilm.healthandsafetycentre.org/s/Music.asp (p. 178)

Manitoba Ministry of Labour and Immigration, "Guidelines—Ergonomics"

http://www.gov.mb.ca/labour/safety/ergoguide.html (p. 179)

Health Care Health and Safety Association, "Workplace Inspection Report"

http://www.hchsa.on.ca/products/forms/lap_005.pdf (p. 181)

Association of Workers' Compensation Boards of Canada, "National Work Injuries Statistics Program"

http://www.awcbc.org/english/NWISP_Stats.asp (p. 185)

RPC Icons

RPC 7.1 Implements and evaluates practices in the areas of health, safety, security, and Workers' Compensation.

- investigative techniques
- hazard recognition
- disaster recovery techniques
- relevant legislation
- resource information
- common health and safety practices
- company policies and procedures
- Worker Protection (including health and safety and Workers' Compensation)
- theories and practices for protection of individuals and groups

- Occupational health and safety legislation (e.g., Occupational Health and Safety Act of Ontario, Workplace Safety & Insurance Act—Bill 99, Workplace Hazardous Materials Information System, Transportation of Dangerous Goods legislation, environmental legislation, smoking in the workplace legislation, civil rights legislation)
- hazard identification and control
- management techniques for OH&S Programs

RPC 7.2 Analyses risk to the health and safety of employees and determines appropriate preventative measures, including training, provision of required safety equipment, and administrative practices.

- relevant legislation
- nature of the business and physical work environment
- hazard recognition
- workplace inspection techniques
- safety programs, equipment, and emergency procedures
- ergonomics
- functions of the JHSC
- training and development/presentation techniques
- industry best practices
- relevant technical terminology
- the collective agreement
- services and equipment available in the community
- Worker Protection (including health and safety and Workers' Compensation)
- training and development program design and administration

TASK & KNOWLEDGE REQUIREMENTS

- Occupational health and safety legislation (e.g., Occupational Health and Safety Act of Ontario, Workplace Safety & Insurance Act—Bill 99, Workplace Hazardous Materials Information System, Transportation of Dangerous Goods legislation, environmental legislation, smoking in the workplace legislation, civil rights legislation)
- hazard identification and control
- emergency preparedness procedures
- management techniques for OH&S Programs
- types of employee assistance and wellness programs

RPC 7.3 Establishes effective programs for accident prevention, incident investigation, inspections, fire and emergency response, and required training.

- relevant legislation
- workplace inspection and accident investigation techniques
- nature of the business and physical work environment
- potential risks and hazards in the workplace
- emergency response planning
- community emergency response services
- training and development

- industry best practices
- Worker Protection (including health and safety and Workers' Compensation)
- training and development program design and administration
- hazard identification and control
- accident investigation procedures
- emergency preparedness procedures
- management techniques for OH&S Programs

RPC 7.4 Ensures that security programs and policies minimize risks while considering the obligation of the employer and the rights of employees, union, and third parties.

- nature of the business and physical work environment
- relevant legislation
- industry best practices
- program and policy development
- safety and security equipment in the workplace
- risk assessment/techniques
- cost/benefit analysis

Task & Knowledge Requirements

- available community resources
- Worker Protection (including health and safety and Workers' Compensation)
- unions' role in health and safety and in employee involvement
- Occupational health and safety legislation (e.g., Occupational Health and Safety Act of Ontario, Workplace Safety & Insurance Act—Bill 99, Workplace Hazardous Materials Information System, Transportation of Dangerous Goods legislation, environmental legislation, smoking in the workplace legislation, civil rights legislation)
- emergency preparedness procedures
- management techniques for OH&S Programs
- types of employee assistance and wellness programs

Discussion Questions

1. Select any lifting task at your workplace or simulate one at home. Using the NIOSH lifting equations (provided in the appendix), calculate the acceptability of the lift and recommend ways to make it less risky and more efficient.
2. A worker has to lift a package weighing approximately 16 kg onto a shelf that is 60 cm from where he or she is standing. The worker picks up the load from a point 30 cm from the floor; the final position on the shelf is 170 cm from the floor. The lift is repeated once each minute. Calculate the AL and the MPL, and determine the acceptability of the operation (see appendix).

3. Determine the administrative controls available at your workplace for dealing with potential back problems or RSI.
4. Examine available literature and catalogues to determine how many methods and accessories are available to prevent keyboard-related RSI. How many of these devices do you have in your own workstation?
5. Outline all the methods that a manager of a small plant could use to identify hazards. What could a safety professional add to this manager's hazard-identification program?
6. Choose any operation in your workplace or at school and identify the hazards associated with it. Perform a risk analysis to determine whether or not these hazards are dangerous. Outline the changes that could be made to reduce the level of risk associated with the hazards.

Using the Internet

1. Human resource managers are responsible for ensuring that workplace safety inspections take place regularly. Using your text and online resources, describe how you would conduct an effective safety inspection program. (*Hint:* Go to http://www.worksafebc.com/publications/publication_index/s.asp and scroll down to a publication called *Safety Inspections.*) (Based on an exercise by Catherine Fitzgerald)

Exercise

1. In law, the "thin skull argument" refers to a perfectly healthy person whose minor trauma caused serious injury. Were it not for the trauma, the individual would not have been hurt. However, other individuals who experience the trauma are not hurt. Imagine, for example, four workers who are struck in the head by flying objects. Three workers suffer no injury whatsoever; the other (perhaps because of an abnormally thin skull) suffers serious brain damage. Is the damage a result of the hazard or the individual's preexisting condition? How should health and safety programs account for individual variability like this?

Case 1

Industrial Hazard Assessment

The plant is experiencing some difficulties with a clamping device on a holding fixture that keeps a metal part in position while it is fed into an automatic stamping machine. The clamp does not always allow the metal part to be fed into the machine properly aligned. The worker who was operating the machine had 32 years' experience with this type of equipment. While attempting to make the necessary adjustments for smooth operation without shutting off the power, she had to reach into the machine. She placed her left hand between the feed-in mechanism levers while her right hand was positioning the misaligned part between the open clamps of the fixture.

Unfortunately, the one-button actuating control was located immediately to the left of the worker's body, about hip level. The worker inadvertently depressed the button with her leg while reaching into the machine. The machine cycled—the feed mechanism slid forward while the fixture clamps closed. The worker had a portion of her left middle finger amputated.

List the following:

a. the unsafe acts
b. the unsafe conditions
c. the energies involved
d. the steps to be taken to prevent this situation from recurring

Case 2

Danger in the Grocery Store

Tadao works as a butcher in a large chain grocery store. His primary responsibility is cutting up meat using large (and very sharp) knives. He's been on the job now for four years and never had a health and safety complaint. Lately, though, he's been experiencing some difficulties. Actually, it started a couple of years ago when Tadao noticed that his right hand was painful at the end of the day and that he was unable to use the hand for several hours after work. The pain and fatigue didn't last long, and Tadao assumed that he was just overworking the hand (Tadao is right-handed). In the past month or so, the pain has escalated—it frequently lasts all night and makes sleep difficult. Tadao also experiences numbness and tingling in the hand. Tadao has begun to avoid activities that require using his right hand, including shaking hands with people.

Last Tuesday, Tadao came to work and could not pick up the knife in his right hand—he had to pick up the knife with his left hand and place it in his right hand to begin work. Watching him go through this procedure a coworker observed, "Well, it looks like you've developed butcher's claw—it comes from doing the same motion over and over again. It happens to us all and there's not much you can do about it." As an HR professional responsible for health and safety, do you have a better answer for Tadao?

Appendix

The material covered in this appendix incorporates two major techniques for workplace analysis. The first is a system known as "fault tree analysis," simplified, which allows an analyst to determine the human factor effect of any job or potential hazard condition. The second is a simplified method of measuring the lifting requirements or conditions of any task or job. Either technique may be required in the specific course outline of the academic institution involved.

RPC 7.1

RPC 7.3

Fault Tree Analysis

Fault tree analysis is a useful technique for evaluating hazards and risk.[17] The process, developed from decision tree theory,[18] is unique in that it reasons backward from a series of conditions to some predetermined, undesired result called a **top event.** The key to its success is the determination of the origin of the top event (undesired result) and inclusion of the human element.

top event

a predetermined, undesired result, the origin of which is determined through fault tree analysis

The following are some examples of top events:

1. *Injury to a person.* A worker is injured while performing a task.
2. *Equipment activated.* Some piece of machinery that was shut down is accidentally turned on while work is being done.
3. *Equipment failure.* A piece of equipment fails to start or else operates improperly.
4. *Worker exposure.* Airborne toxic chemicals or harmful physical agents contaminate the worker.
5. *Explosion or sudden release of energy.* High concentrations of solvents or dust may explode, or a source of high pressure may be released into the atmosphere.

Fault tree analysis uses a series of symbols (see Figure 7.4) to illustrate the various conditions, situations, or event sequences that could result in the undesired or top event. The events or conditions that lead into the top event

FIGURE 7.4

Fault Tree Analysis Symbols

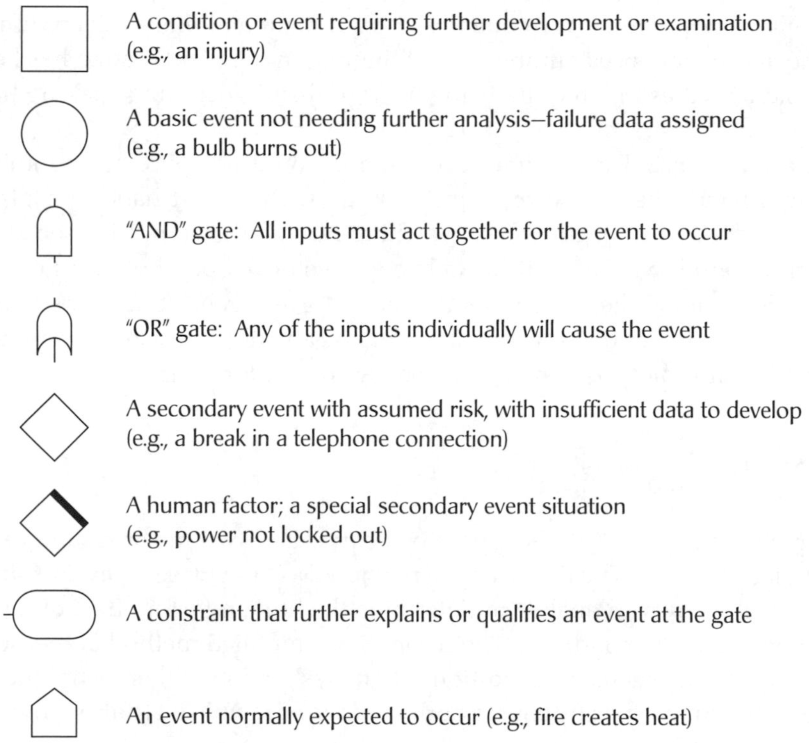

A condition or event requiring further development or examination (e.g., an injury)

A basic event not needing further analysis—failure data assigned (e.g., a bulb burns out)

"AND" gate: All inputs must act together for the event to occur

"OR" gate: Any of the inputs individually will cause the event

A secondary event with assumed risk, with insufficient data to develop (e.g., a break in a telephone connection)

A human factor; a special secondary event situation (e.g., power not locked out)

A constraint that further explains or qualifies an event at the gate

An event normally expected to occur (e.g., fire creates heat)

filter through a gate (see Figure 7.5) that specifies the sequences for the lower conditions and their effect on the top event.

To set up the initial fault tree, follow six steps:

1. Identify the top event (e.g., foreign particle in eye).
2. Identify the possible causes or conditions that could result in the chosen top event, and list them horizontally.
3. Determine whether the gate should be "and" or "or." This will depend on whether the noted conditions will act independently ("or") or in concert ("and").
4. Determine whether the causes or conditions identified in step 2 require further investigation or consideration. A rectangle indicates further information is required.
5. For each rectangle, repeat steps 2 through 4.
6. Once the tree has been constructed (see Figure 7.6 for an example), estimate and note at each event or condition the probabilities of occurrence for each element.

FIGURE 7.5

Gate Arrangements

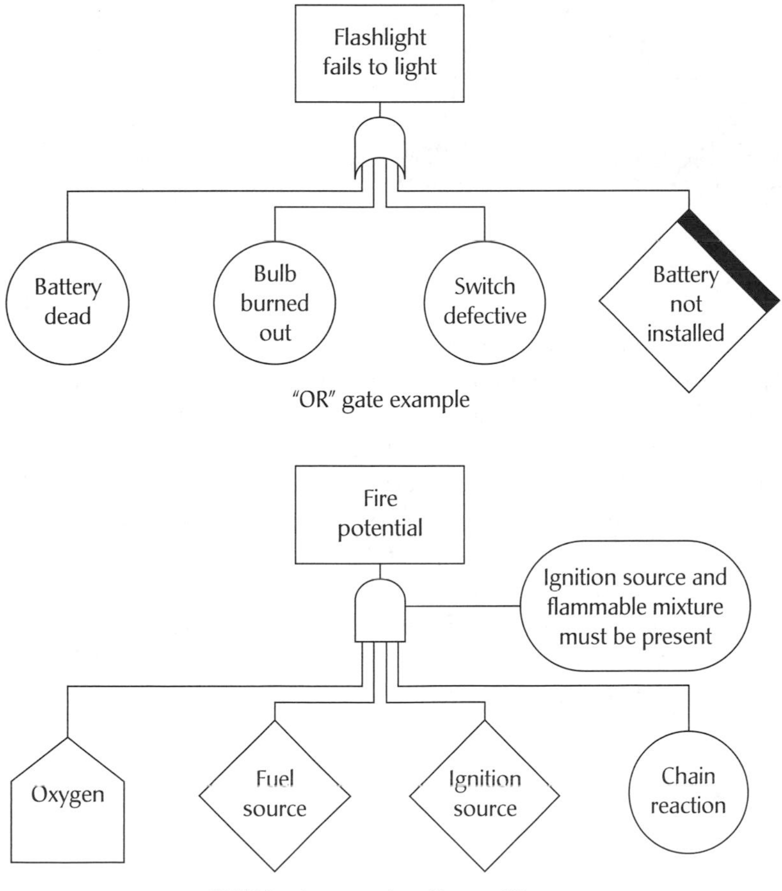

FIGURE 7.6

Example of a Fault Tree

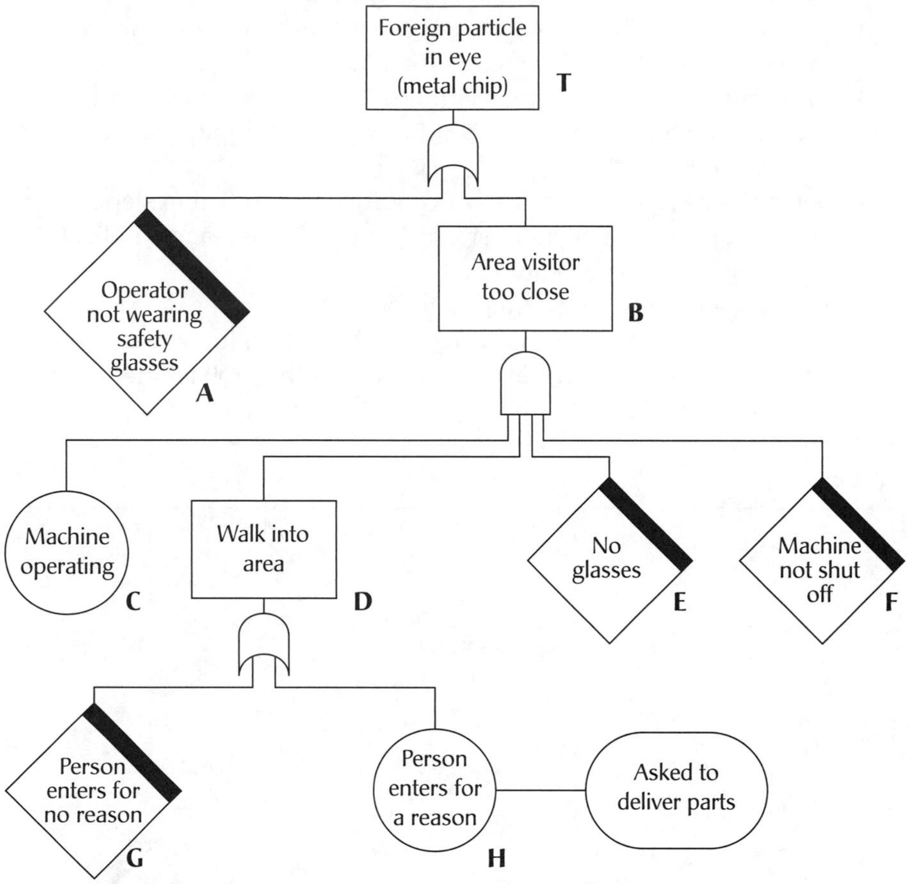

There are two methods of dealing with these probabilities of occurrence. The first (Figure 7.7) considers each row leading into a gate as a separate set of conditions. The probability of occurrence is estimated for each element in the row. The sum of the probabilities must equal 1.00. The critical path can now be highlighted by starting at the lowest element with the highest probability and tracing the path back to the top event. Thus, in this example, the condition at H—the person entering the area for a reason—will be the probable initiating source of the top event.

In the second technique (see Figure 7.8), a probability is assigned to each element randomly. Using the mathematical relationships noted, the probability at each rectangle can then be calculated. The advantage of this method

FIGURE 7.7

Fault Tree with Simplified Probabilities Added

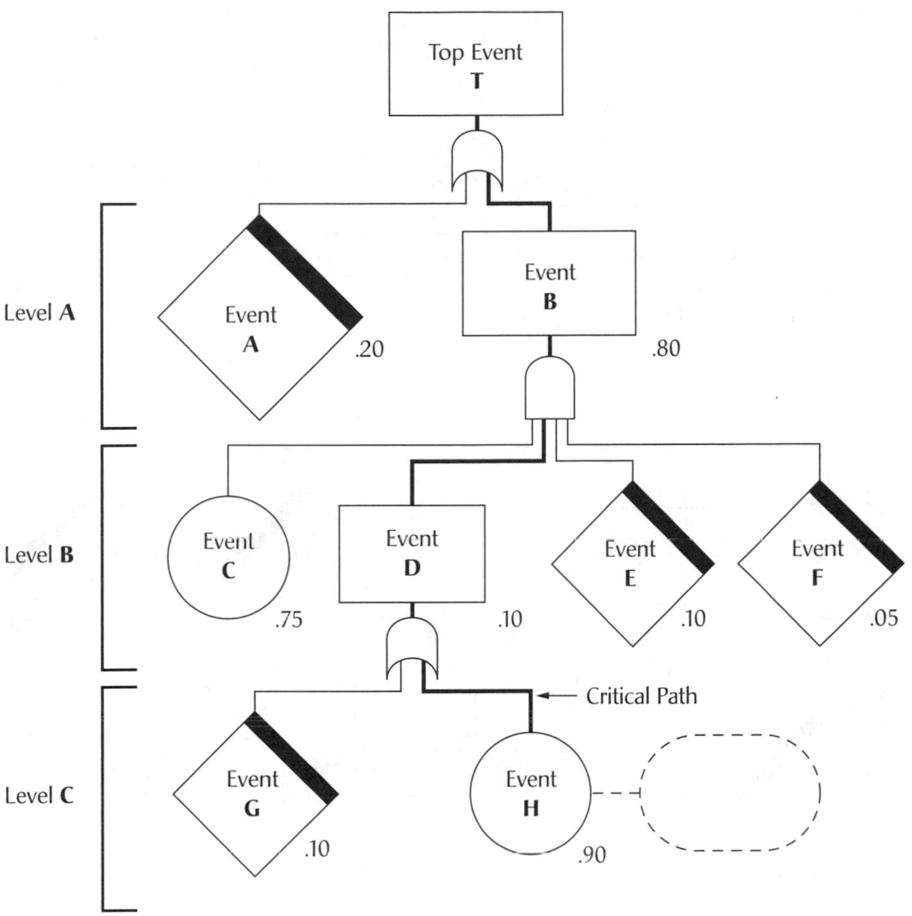

is its flexibility without bias. Once an identification and estimation of the hazard and the associated risk has been made, prevention strategies can be developed.

Obviously, a technical expert is needed to do a fault tree analysis. When should management use such expertise? Any job, operation, or task that has a history of accidents or injuries should receive top priority. Fault tree analysis might also be used in situations in which the severity of the accident is great or where there is a high potential for accidents. When new equipment or operations are introduced, fault tree analysis can be used as a preventive tool.

FIGURE 7.8

Fault Tree Example with Probabilities Added

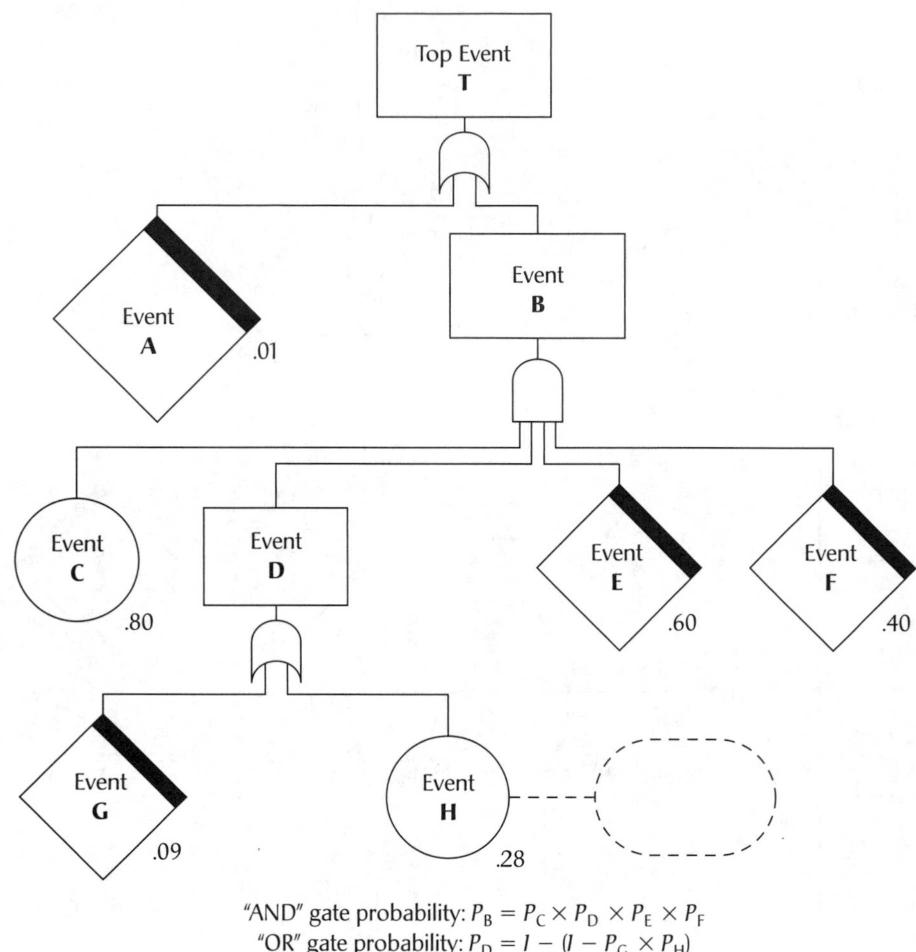

Lifting Calculations Using the NIOSH Method

The NIOSH method examines the weight of the object to be lifted, the height it is to be lifted, the distance from the body, and the location of the load at the start of the lift or pick. Two factors are calculated and compared with the weight of the lifted object. These factors are the action limit (AL) and the maximum permissible limit (MPL).

The action limit is based on the following:

a. Epidemiological data indicating that some workers would be at increased risk of injury on jobs exceeding the AL.
b. Biomechanical studies indicating that lower back, disc-compression forces created at the AL can be tolerated by most (not all) people.

c. Physiological studies showing that the average metabolic requirement for the AL would be 3.5 kcal/min.
d. Psychophysical studies showing that more than 75 percent of women and 99 percent of men could lift loads at the AL.

The maximum permissible limit is based on the following:

a. Epidemiological data indicating that musculoskeletal injury and severity rates are significantly higher for most workers placed on jobs exceeding the MPL.
b. Biomechanical studies indicating that lower back, disc-compression forces created at the MPL cannot be tolerated by most workers.
c. Physiological studies showing that the metabolic expenditure would be excessive for most workers frequently lifting loads at the MPL.

The equations for calculating the AL and the MPL are simple and straightforward and can be easily used on the job. Simply examine a specific lifting task and take a series of measurements (see Figure 7.9). Then enter the data into the two equations and compare the results to the weight of the item being lifted. The equations are

$$AL\ (kg) = 40(15/H)(1 - 0.004\ |V - 75|)(0.7 + 7.5/D)(1 - F/F_{max})$$ for centimetres

$$AL\ (lb) = 90(6/H)(1 - 0.01\ |V - 30|)(0.7 + 3/D)(1 - F/F_{max})$$ for inches

$$MPL = 3(AL)$$

where:

H is the horizontal distance (cm or in.) or reach, measured from the load centre of mass (usually where the hands grasp the load) to the mid-point between the ankles (the ankle bone) at the origin of the lift. *H* is between 15 cm (6 in.) and 80 cm (32 in.). Objects cannot be closer than 15 cm without interfering with the body; objects farther than 80 cm cannot be reached by most people.

V is the vertical distance (cm or in.) measured from the load origin or centre of mass (or to the hands if the object does not have handles) to floor level at the origin of lift. *V* is assumed to be between 0 cm and 175 cm (70 in.), representing the upward-reach envelope of most people.

D is the vertical travel distance (cm or in.) of the object measured between the origin location and the destination location. *D* is assumed a minimum value of 25 cm (10 in.) and a maximum of 200 − V cm (80 − V in.). If the distance is less than 25 cm, then set *D* = 25 cm.

F is the average frequency of lifting (lifts/min.) with a minimum of 0.2 lifts/min., or once every 5 minutes as occasional lifting.

F_{max} is a factor based on duration and operator posture as shown in Table 7.4.

FIGURE 7.9

NIOSH Lifting Calculation Data

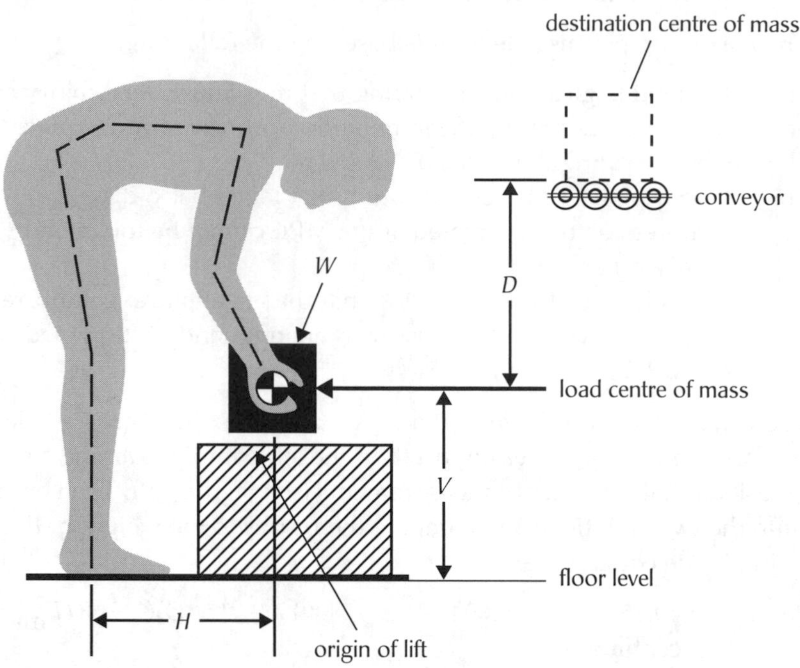

When the AL and the MPL have been calculated, the results are compared with the three lifting regions to determine the acceptability of the lifting task and whether controls will be necessary. Lifting tasks with the weight smaller in value than the AL are considered acceptable. Lifting tasks between the AL and the MPL require administrative controls (e.g., training, employee selection, and placement) or engineering controls. Lifting tasks above the MPL represent an unacceptable condition and require engineering controls (e.g., redesign) for worker protection.

TABLE 7.4

F_{max} Table Average Vertical Location of Lift

DURATION	V > 75 CM (30") (STANDING)	V ≥ 75 CM (30") (STOOPED)
1 hour	18	15
8 hours	15	12

To illustrate the analysis, assume a worker is lifting a 27 kg load from a skid onto a conveyor. The task is performed once each minute. The worker lifts for 8 hours and is required to bend over. The job and lift dimensions, measured using a tape measure, are as follows:

W = 27 kg—the weight of the item to be lifted
D = 56 cm—the vertical distance the item is lifted from rest
H = 53 cm—the reach
V = 30 cm—the vertical distance from the item at rest to the floor
F = 1 lift/min.—lift frequency
F_{max} = 12 from Table 7.4—for 8-hour shift in stooped position

Solving the AL and MPL equations with these values:

$$AL = 40(15/53)(1 - 0.004\,|30 - 75|)(0.7 + 7.5/56)(1 - 1/12)$$

$$= 40(0.28)(0.82)(0.83)(0.92)$$

$$= 7.0 \text{ kg}$$ (The term $|V - 75|$ indicates an absolute value or a value that is always positive even if the arithmetic shows negative.)

$$MPL = 3\ AL = 3(7.0) = 21.0 \text{ kg}$$

The load weight of 27 kg is greater than the AL and the MPL; therefore, the task as noted is unacceptable and engineering controls will be necessary.

If the task is to be redesigned, an analysis of the lifting conditions shows the order of factors, from most to least effective, to be: *H*—reach, *V*—distance to the floor, *D*—vertical lift distance, and *F*—lift frequency. To improve the lifting task in the above example, the workstation can be redesigned by moving the worker closer to the load position (*H*); by presenting the load at a higher level (*V*) standing; and by lifting the load a shorter distance (*D*).

If these revised values are

W = 27 kg
D = 25 cm
H = 30 cm
V = 80 cm
F = 1 lift/min.
F_{max} = 15 from Table 7.4

then substituting these values into the lifting equations for AL and MPL shows

$$AL = 40(15/30)(1 - 0.004\,|80 - 75|)(0.7 + 7.5/25)(1 - 1/15)$$

$$= 40(0.50)(0.98)(1.0)(0.94)$$

$$= 18.4 \text{ kg}$$

$$MPL = 3(18.4) = 55.2 \text{ kg}$$

Even with the redesign, the load weight is still greater than the AL but is now lower than the MPL. Some additional engineering controls may still be necessary (e.g., mechanical assists or reducing the load size). Administrative controls are also necessary (e.g., two-person lifting, work rotation, or weight training).

Previous studies have shown that RSI frequency rates (injuries per hours on the job) and severity rates (hours lost per hours on the job) increase significantly when

- heavy objects are lifted (*W* is large)
- the object is bulky—increased reach (*H* is large)
- distances moved are large (*D* is large)
- objects are lifted frequently (*F* is large)[19]

Any control strategy should consider the variability and the effects of these factors. Lower back discomfort and trauma are the usual results of improper lifting.

Endnotes

1. Firenze, R. J. (1978). *The process of hazard control*. Dubuque, IA: Kendall/Hunt Publishing.
2. National Institute of Occupational Safety and Health. (1983). *A work practices guide for manual lifting: Technical report 81–122*. Cincinnati, OH: U.S. Department of Health and Human Services.
3. Kim, P., Hayden, J. A., & Mior, S. A. (2004). The cost-effectiveness of a back education program for firefighters: A case study. *Journal of the Canadian Chiropractic Association, 48*(1), 13–19.
4. Ammendolia, C., Kerr, M. S., & Bombardier, C. (2002). *The use of back belts for prevention of occupational low back pain: Systematic review and recommendations*. CTFPHC Technical Rep no 02-1. London, ON: Canadian Task Force.
5. Statistics Canada. (2001). *Canadian community health survey*. Ottawa: Author.
6. McDonald, H. (1995, January/February). To regulate or not to regulate. *Accident Prevention,* 9–11.
7. Dolan, S. L., & Schuler, R. S. (1994). *Human resources management: A Canadian perspective*. Scarborough, ON: Nelson Canada.
8. Purdie, J. (1990, November 26). Better offices means greater productivity. *The Financial Post,* p. 35.
9. Smith, M. J., & Bayehi, A. D. (2003). Do ergonomic improvements increase computer workers' productivity? An intervention study in a call center. *Ergonomics, 46,* 3–18.
10. May, D. R., Reed, K., Schwoerer, C. E., & Potter, P. (2004). Ergonomic office design and aging: A quasi-experimental field study of employee reactions to an ergonomics intervention program. *Journal of Occupational Health Psychology, 9*(2), 123–135.
11. Laing, P. M. (Ed.). (1992). *Accident prevention manual for business and industry: Administration and programs* (10th ed.). Washington, D.C.: National Safety Council.
12. Laing, P. M. (Ed.). (1992). *Accident prevention manual for business and industry: Administration and programs* (10th ed.). Washington, D.C.: National Safety Council.
13. Rampton, G., Turnbull, I., & Doran, G. (1996). *Human resources management systems*. Scarborough, ON: Nelson Canada.
14. Firenze, R. J. (1978). *The process of hazard control*. Dubuque, IA: Kendall/Hunt Publishing.
15. Laing, P. M. (Ed.). (1992). *Accident prevention manual for business and industry: Administration and programs* (10th ed.). Washington, D.C.: National Safety Council.

16. Laing, P. M. (Ed.). (1992). *Accident prevention manual for business and industry: Administration and programs* (10th ed.). Washington, D.C.: National Safety Council.
17. Fabrycky, W. J., & Mize, J. H. (Eds.). (1976). *System analysis and design for safety*. Englewood Cliffs, NJ: Prentice Hall.
18. Raiffa, H. (1968). *Decision analysis*. Reading, MA: Addison-Wesley.
19. National Institute of Occupational Safety and Health. (1983). *A work practices guide for manual lifting: Technical report 81–122*. Cincinnati, OH: U.S. Department of Health and Human Services.

PART THREE

Interventions

CHAPTER 8 HAZARD CONTROL

CHAPTER 9 TRAINING

CHAPTER 10 MOTIVATING SAFETY BEHAVIOUR AT WORK

CHAPTER 11 EMERGENCY RESPONSE AND EMERGENCY PREPAREDNESS

CHAPTER 12 ACCIDENT INVESTIGATION

CHAPTER 13 WORKPLACE WELLNESS: WORK–FAMILY AND WORKSITE HEALTH-PROMOTION PROGRAMS

Chapter 8

Hazard Control

Chapter Learning Objectives

After reading this chapter, you should be able to:

- define the many terms used in hazard control
- distinguish between events and actions that constitute precontact, contact, and postcontact control
- describe the requirements for machine guarding
- explain the requirements for lockout procedures and confined space entry
- discuss the necessity of work permits
- explain the concept of source–path–human control
- explain the concept of safety awareness and give examples of awareness campaigns

Caught in the Ice

It was one of the worst tragedies in Canadian occupational health and safety. In March 2004, a 25-km stretch of metre-thick pack ice drifted toward two natural gas rigs located offshore from Nova Scotia. The Venture gas production rig and the exploration rig Rowan Gorilla V stood in imminent danger of having their supporting legs swept out from under them. More than 100 workers on the rigs would be dumped into the North Atlantic almost 300 km offshore.

Not familiar with this tragedy? That's because it never happened. Having recognized the hazard and assessed the danger, both ExxonMobil Canada (owners of the Venture platform) and Canadian Superior (owners of the Rowan Gorilla V) implemented precontact control measures designed to minimize the potential impact of the hazard.

As a first priority, they evacuated the rigs, removing some 100 workers to safety ashore. Rigs were secured against possible damage and both tugboats and Coast Guard icebreakers were on site to try to divert the ice from the rigs. As a result of these actions, nobody was injured and the rigs were not harmed. The companies involved controlled the hazard—hazard control is the focus of this chapter.

Source: "Ice forces evacuation of two offshore rigs near Nova Scotia's Sable Island," *Brockville Recorder and Times*. Retrieved from http://www.recorder.ca/cp/National/040308/n0308137A.html, March 30, 2004.

hazard control
the program or process used to establish preventive and corrective measures

precontact control
addressing issues before an incident or accident occurs

contact control
identifying ways in which a hazardous situation can be prevented from becoming worse and harming workers

postcontact control
putting in place medical and cleanup operations and ensuring that the event cannot be repeated

RPC 8.1

administrative control
management involvement, training of employees, rotation of employees, environmental sampling, and medical surveillance to protect individuals

Hazard control refers to the program or process used to establish preventive and corrective measures as the final stage of hazard recognition, assessment, and control (RAC). The goal is to eliminate, reduce, or control hazards so as to minimize injuries and losses, including accidents, property damage, time lost, and so on. The first step in hazard control is hazard recognition and assessment, the subject of the previous chapter. This chapter will examine the next three steps in the hazard-control process: (1) **precontact control** (addressing issues before an incident or accident occurs), (2) **contact control** (identifying ways in which a hazardous situation can be prevented from becoming worse and harming workers), and (3) **postcontact control** (putting in place medical and cleanup operations and ensuring that the event cannot be repeated).

Administrative Control

Administrative control is the use of management involvement, training of employees, rotation of employees, environmental sampling, and medical surveillance to protect individuals.[1] Administrative control is the second level of priority for worker protection after engineering controls and before

personal protective equipment. Against some negative attitudes, administrative controls can have some effect in minimizing hazardous conditions. The most serious failure of this method is the company's reluctance or lack of appreciation. Using administrative controls, the HR practitioner can be effective by (1) introducing preplacement examinations that can help find an employee with suitable characteristics for the job (e.g., the ability to lift materials), (2) scheduling job rotation that allows a worker to spend time in less hazardous jobs, thereby reducing exposures (e.g., working with toxic materials in the morning and nontoxic materials in the afternoon), (3) moving the worker to another permanent job after exposure to toxic materials, and
(4) performing periodic monitoring. RPC 8.2

Some common examples of administrative control include safety awareness programs, the use of incentives, housekeeping programs, preventive
maintenance, and the development of policies and training for unique situa- RPC 8.3
tions such as confined space entry.

Safety Awareness

Safety awareness refers to programs that attempt to inform workers about health and safety issues and to remind them of the importance of health and safety.

Visible Reminders

Posters and signs at worker entrances and other points of entry are one way to promote safety awareness. A company-designed booklet dealing with health and safety issues can be issued to employees. Safety message inserts can be added to paycheques. Placemats and napkins in the dining area can be imprinted with safety messages. Decals (self-adhesive or magnetic labels) can be applied to specific objects as a safety reminder. In addition, safety displays can be set up at entrances and in cafeterias. These displays can feature photographs of the Safe Employee of the Month or brief statements by workers who were saved from injury by, for example, correct use of personal protective equipment (e.g., safety glasses). Newsletters, bulletin boards, and billboards are other vehicles for promoting safety awareness. Finally, safety campaigns can be used to target a specific hazard or unsafe practice. All these efforts and presentations will not be effective unless the senior managers are fully behind the programs.

Special Events

Numerous special events have been developed to promote safety awareness in the workplace. Table 8.1 presents some of the events in Canada. In general, the intent of these special events is to increase awareness of safety issues in the workplace by focusing on safety or a specific element of safety in the workplace.

Occupational Health and Safety Today 8.1

Young Worker Awareness Program

In response to the high rate of injuries among young workers, virtually every jurisdiction has begun to address the issue of young workers' health and safety. The Young Worker Awareness Program in Ontario is funded by the Workplace Safety and Insurance Board and is delivered through various agencies. The intent of the program is to increase young people's awareness of health and safety issues, the importance of health and safety, and their rights under the law.

Source: Workplace Safety and Insurance Board of Ontario, "Young worker awareness program." Retrieved from http://www.youngworker.ca/english/, February 7, 2007.

Awards and Incentives

Safety awards are another vehicle used to increase awareness of safety. By establishing an award, the sponsoring agency or company creates an "event" comprising a presentation and a media announcement. The resulting publicity can be used to raise safety awareness. Safety award programs have been created by industrial associations, governments, and agencies to recognize achievements in safety (see the Weblinks section at the end of the chapter).

TABLE 8.1

Awareness Events

Event	Date	Purpose
RSI Day	Usually the last day of February	Promote awareness of RSI and related disorders
National Farm Safety Week	March 14–20	Promote awareness of various farm safety issues
National Day of Mourning	April 28	Remember those who have been killed at work; promote safety awareness
North American Occupational Safety and Health Week (NAOSH Week)	First full week of May	Focus the attention of employers, employees, the general public, and all partners in occupational health and safety on the importance of preventing illness and injury in the workplace
National Road Safety Week	May 21–27	Increase awareness of road safety
Healthy Workplace Week	October 25–31	Promote a comprehensive and integrated approach to workplace health in order to improve and sustain the health of Canadian organizations, their work environments, and their employees
National Safe Driving Week	December 1–7	Promote safe driving

Within organizations, individual employees can be given incentives to maintain a good safety performance. These incentives can range from individual payoffs to team rewards. For example, DuPont Canada employees were given special scratch-and-win lottery tickets.[2] Other organizations recognize good safety performance through such incentives as private parking spaces or dinners (see Chapter 10 for a discussion of behaviour-based safety programs, which frequently involve the use of incentives of some form). In addition, supervisors may receive a reward based on the number of employees who attend safety talks or on the number of safety deficiencies that are corrected in an expeditious fashion. Contests may be held in which employees compete to produce the best safety slogan. Finally, safety records can be used as one factor in the evaluation of supervisory and managerial performance. Care must be taken with this approach, since some supervisors may be tempted to hide problems and serious hazards.

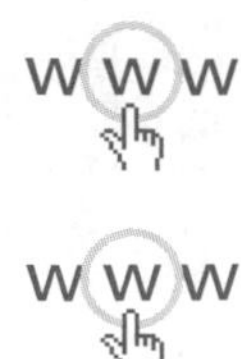

Housekeeping

Ensuring that the worksite is clean and that workers have access to cleaning facilities will contribute to the control of hazards. A clean, orderly workplace can reduce hazards and at the same time increase efficiency. Every worksite contains potentially hazardous tools and equipment. For example, a plant site may have containers of chemicals such as solvents, tools such as drills, and processes that generate dust or scrap material. Maintaining a clean and orderly job site reduces the risk of injury due to falls, fires, and so forth. Furthermore, it is easier to locate first-aid equipment or exits in an environment in which all tools and equipment are in their assigned places.

RPC 8.4

Housekeeping is not just a good practice—it is a legal requirement under most health and safety legislation. Although legislation varies across jurisdictions, the Canadian Health and Safety Regulations under the Canada Labour Code (see the Weblink) are typical:

RPC 8.5

1. Every exterior stairway, walkway, ramp and passageway that may be used by employees shall be kept free of accumulations of ice and snow or other slipping or tripping hazards.
2. All dust, dirt, waste and scrap material in every work place in a building shall be removed as often as is necessary to protect the health and safety of employees and shall be disposed of in such a manner that the health and safety of employees is not endangered.
3. Every travelled surface in a work place shall be

   (a) slip resistant; and
   (b) kept free of splinters, holes, loose boards and tiles and similar defects. (SOR/2000-374, s. 2; SOR/2002-208, s. 6).

The cleaning process itself should be evaluated. Besides the obvious hazards posed by solvents used for cleaning, other hazards may be involved in operations such as dust removal. Workers using compressed air may be tempted to blow dust off work surfaces and even clothing; however, compressed air can be forced through the skin, enter the bloodstream, and cause death.

Occupational Health and Safety Notebook 8.1

Preventing Slips and Falls through Housekeeping

Good housekeeping practices are perhaps the simplest and most effective way to prevent slips and falls in the workplace. These include the following:

- Keeping walkways and stairwells clear of clutter
- Closing drawers, doors, and storage bins after use
- Keeping floors free of debris or spills
- Marking hazards (e.g., spills, debris) until they can be cleaned up
- Ensuring adequate lighting

Source: Canadian Centre for Occupational Health and Safety, "Why should we pay attention to housekeeping at work?" Retrieved from http://www.ccohs.ca/oshanswers/hsprograms/ house.html, February 7, 2007.

Organizations that employ workers who handle toxic materials should ensure washing facilities are located close to the work area. Workers should wash before drinking or eating to prevent the ingestion of toxic materials. No food or drinks should be permitted at the worksite. Workers exposed to chemicals should have showers and change clothes before leaving the worksite. Where appropriate, hazardous materials (hazmat) suits should be available and workers should be trained in their use.

Preventive Maintenance

preventive maintenance
the orderly, continuous, and scheduled protection and repair of equipment and buildings

Preventive maintenance refers to the orderly, continuous, and scheduled protection and repair of equipment and buildings. The primary goals of preventive maintenance are the determination of potential problems and the implementation of corrective action. The primary benefits of this process are uninterrupted production and the reduction of potential hazards caused by equipment failure.

Occupational Health and Safety Notebook 8.2

Administrative Controls for Struck-by-Object Injuries

To reduce injuries attributable to falling objects:

- Provide and require the use of safety helmets.
- Provide safety signage and warning where overhead hazards are present.
- Train and ensure the use of safe-rigging and safe-storage procedures.
- Provide and require the use of safety shoes.

To reduce "caught in, under, or between" (CIUB) injuries:

- Use lockout procedures that require the operator or maintenance provider to turn the power off and to lock the switch in the off position using a personal padlock. Because each worker is the only one with the key to his or her lock, it is impossible to inadvertently start the machine during maintenance.

Source: Canadian Centre for Occupational Health and Safety. Retrieved from http://www.ccohs.ca, October 10, 2004.

Generally speaking, equipment failures do not happen without warning. We are all familiar with the atypical noises our cars or air conditioners produce as a signal that something needs to be fixed. However, maintenance should enter the picture before the emergence of warning signs. It is more cost effective to perform maintenance routinely while the equipment or machines are still operating than it is after they have failed, necessitating shutdown of the entire operation. Checking the level of oil in your car at every second fuel stop is preventive maintenance. To let the oil level drop and the engine seize is expensive and unnecessary. RPC 8.4

Record keeping is an essential part of any preventive maintenance program. Maintenance information should be recorded at the time the maintenance work is done. Pertinent data would include part replacement and frequency, lubrication, bearings and drive repairs, electrical failures, and cleanliness. Once the historical information is available, failure trends—commonly referred to as failure mode analysis or maintenance hazard analysis—can be anticipated and addressed. RPC 8.5

Work Permits

Before any high-risk work is undertaken, a series of work permits must be in place, one for each type of activity. These permits are, in effect, in-house licences to perform dangerous work. Permits are required for confined space entry, electrical work, excavation work, safety-valve work, scaffolding work, radiation work, and equipment disconnecting work (lockout procedures). "Hot work" permits may be required for activities such as cutting, welding, and soldering wherein the heat involved may trigger the fire alarm system or present a fire hazard. A sample work permit for scaffolding is shown in Figure 8.1.

Lockout Procedures

When maintenance or adjustment is performed on any machine, the machine must be shut off and locked out. For example, replacing the signal light on a residential stove involves accessing the interior of the appliance. Shutting off the stove entails turning off the switches; locking it out entails turning off the power at the main fuse box or circuit breaker and removing the appropriate fuses in either the power panel or the stove. With these precautions, no one can turn the stove on and cause an electrical shock or burn injury. Figure 8.2 shows an example of a clamp used for multiple padlocks in a lockout procedure. A more complicated appliance like a furnace necessitates not only the removal of fuses, but also the shutting off of fuel lines and disassembly of a supply flange joint.

The following are some of the precautions that must be taken during the lockout process:

1. Only one person should be in charge of the lockout procedure.
2. The worker must ensure that the machine is shut off completely, that all internal pressure sources (hydraulic, air, and steam) are bled off to atmospheric level and the valves are locked open, and that any movable parts, such as flywheels or rams, are immobilized.

FIGURE 8.1

Example of Scaffold Use Permit

SIRTE OIL COMPANY

SCAFFOLDING PERMIT

DATE | TIME FROM: | TO:

PLANT:

EQUIPMENT & LOCATION:

DESCRIPTION OF WORK TO BE DONE: ☐ ERECTION ☐ REMOVAL

SCAFFOLD DUTY: ☐ LIGHT ☐ ☐ HEAVY

HEIGHT = ___ M WIDTH = ___ M ☐ CONSULT CIVIL ENG. GROUP

ANSWER WITH (X) WHERE APPLICABLE: YES

1. FAMILIAR WITH AREA HAZARDS/SAF. RULES? ☐
2. SCAFFOLD TYPE/MATERIAL AGREED TO? ☐
3. SCAFFOLD ANCHORING POINTS APPROVED? ☐
4. FOUNDATION/FOOTING PREPARED? ☐
5. HAZARD CREATED TO/FROM TRAFFIC? ☐
6. AREA FREE OF COMB./TOXIC GAS? ☐
7. ACCEPTANCE APPROVAL NEEDED? ☐

SPECIAL PROTECTION REQUIRED

☐ MONITOR FOR ______ ☐ SAFETY BELTS/LINE
☐ LIFTING DEVICE APPROVAL ☐ STANDBYS
☐ BARRIERS/ROPING OFF ☐ (SPECIFY)

THE EQUIPMENT AND/OR LOCATION WHERE THE WORK IS TO BE DONE HAS BEEN INSPECTED & POINTS 1-7 ABOVE HAVE BEEN INVESTIGATED TO MY SATISFACTION.

SIGNATURE OF PERSON AUTHORIZING THIS PERMIT

I UNDERSTAND THE HAZARDS INVOLVED IN THE ABOVE PERMITTED WORK AND THE LIMITATIONS REQUIRED HAVE BEEN EXPLAINED TO ME.

7-3 SHIFT | | 11-7 SHIFT

SIGNATURE OF AUTHORIZED CRAFTSMAN

PERMIT CLOSED OUT DATE TIME	WORK COMPLETED ☐ NO ☐		
AUTHORIZED CRAFTSMAN			
APPROVAL FOR USE OF COMPLETED SCAFFOLD	NAME	SIGNATURE	DATE

SIDE 1

CHECKLIST FOR THE AUTHORIZED CRAFTSMAN

PREPARATIONS

☐ SPECIFICATIONS/DRAWING PROVIDED?
☐ FOUNDATIONS/FOOTING PREPARED?
☐ LIFTING DEVICES NEEDED?
☐ ERECTION PERSONNEL EXPERIENCED?
☐ SUPERVISION APPOINTED? COMPETENT?
☐ AREA HAZARDS/SAF. RULES KNOWN?
☐ ADDITIONAL JOB DEMONSTRATION NEEDED?
☐ STRUCTURE INSPECTION/APPROVAL BY A COMPETENT PERSON NEEDED?

STABILITY & CONSTRUCTION

☐ ANCHORING POINTS SELECTED? APPROVED? SUFFICIENT?
☐ SCAFF. MATERIAL INSPECTED? SELECTED? IN GOOD CONDITION?
☐ FOOTING FIRM?
☐ STANDARDS SPACING ADEQUATE?
☐ BRACING USED? SUFFICIENT?
☐ PLATFORMS FULL? TRIPPING? OPENINGS?
☐ GUARDRAILS? TOE BOARDS?
☐ ACCESS ADEQUATE? LADDERS

IN USE

☐ STRUCTURE INSPECTED DAILY?
☐ TRAFFIC HAZARDS?
☐ OVERLOADING?
☐ USE OF PERSONAL PROTECTION?
☐ RESPONSE TO EMERGENCY KNOWN?

DISMANTLING

☐ METHOD AGREED TO?
☐ HAZARD CREATED TO SURROUNDING?
☐ FINAL SITE CLEARING ENSURED?

SPECIAL INSTRUCTIONS

SIDE 2

3. After the machine has been shut down, all the disconnect points, such as the electrical panel, must be left open.
4. Before work begins, complete testing must be undertaken to ensure that all energy sources are inoperative.
5. The worker must use an approved lockout tag and single key padlock (not keyed alike) to secure the equipment.
6. Only the workers who installed each lock are permitted to remove the lock in the reverse order to the lock installation, beginning and ending with the project manager.
7. Each worker must sign off the work permit as his or her lock is removed.

FIGURE 8.2

Clamp Used for Multiple Padlocks

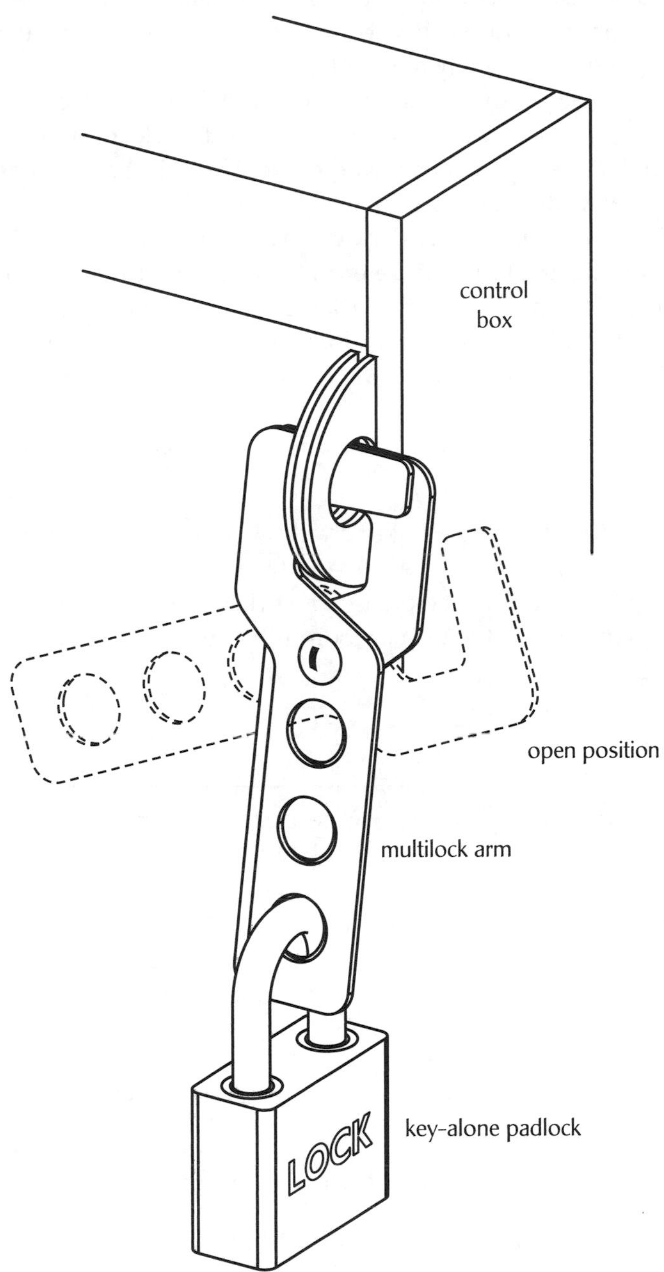

When the project is finished, the equipment will be activated in the reverse sequence to the shutdown. Checks must be made to ensure that guards are in place, isolation devices have been removed, all tools are accounted for, energy controls have been closed and put back into operating condition, and tags and locks have been removed. The last lock removed is that of the manager of the project from the shift on which the lock was applied.

Confined Space Entry

confined space
a space that is potentially deficient in oxygen and could contain toxic aerosols

Confined space refers to a space that is potentially deficient in oxygen and could contain toxic aerosols. Sewers, tanks, and boilers are all examples of confined spaces. Examples also include any long, small tunnel, a shower stall, and some specialty rooms such as computer equipment rooms that are completely independent from any adjacent spaces.

At home, cleaning the bathroom shower stall with the door closed and using a tile cleaner will trap the vapours from the cleanser. These vapours may accumulate near the floor where the work is being done, displace oxygen, and cause drowsiness or fainting.

Entry into industrial confined spaces is addressed in various OH&S regulations. One of the first things to determine is whether the space to be entered is, in fact, a confined space. The flow diagram shown in Figure 8.3 can be used to determine if confined-space procedures are necessary. The diagram shown in Figure 8.4 can be used to determine the extent of the testing that will be required before actual entry.

Once it has been established that a confined space exists, the following steps should be taken:

1. Issue a proper work permit and follow all the lockout procedures.
2. Determine the ease of access to and from the space and develop appropriate contingency plans for worker emergencies.
3. Make sure that all the proper tools and equipment are on hand to do the job.

FIGURE 8.3

Hazard Rating of Confined Space before Entry

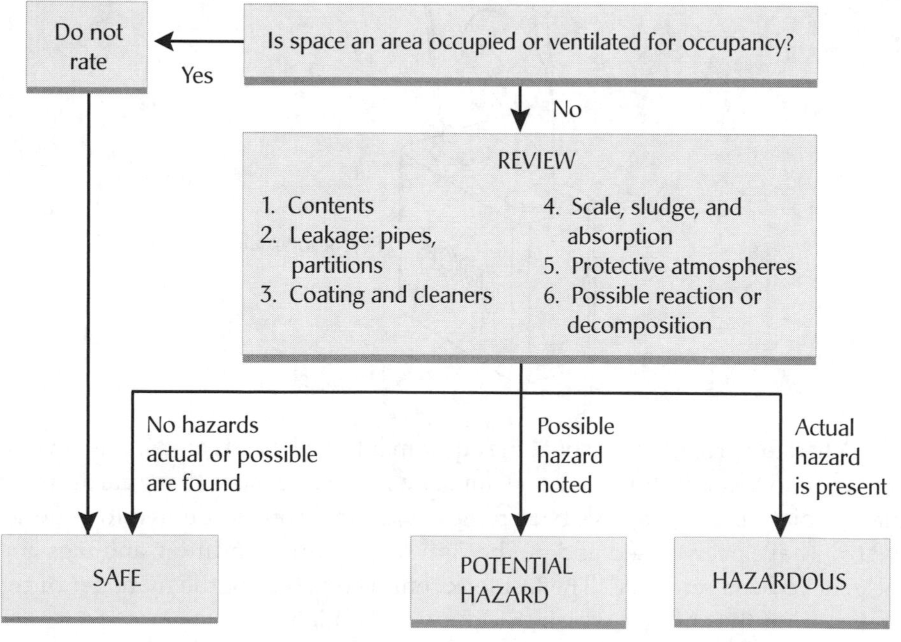

FIGURE 8.4

Review of Confined Space before Entry

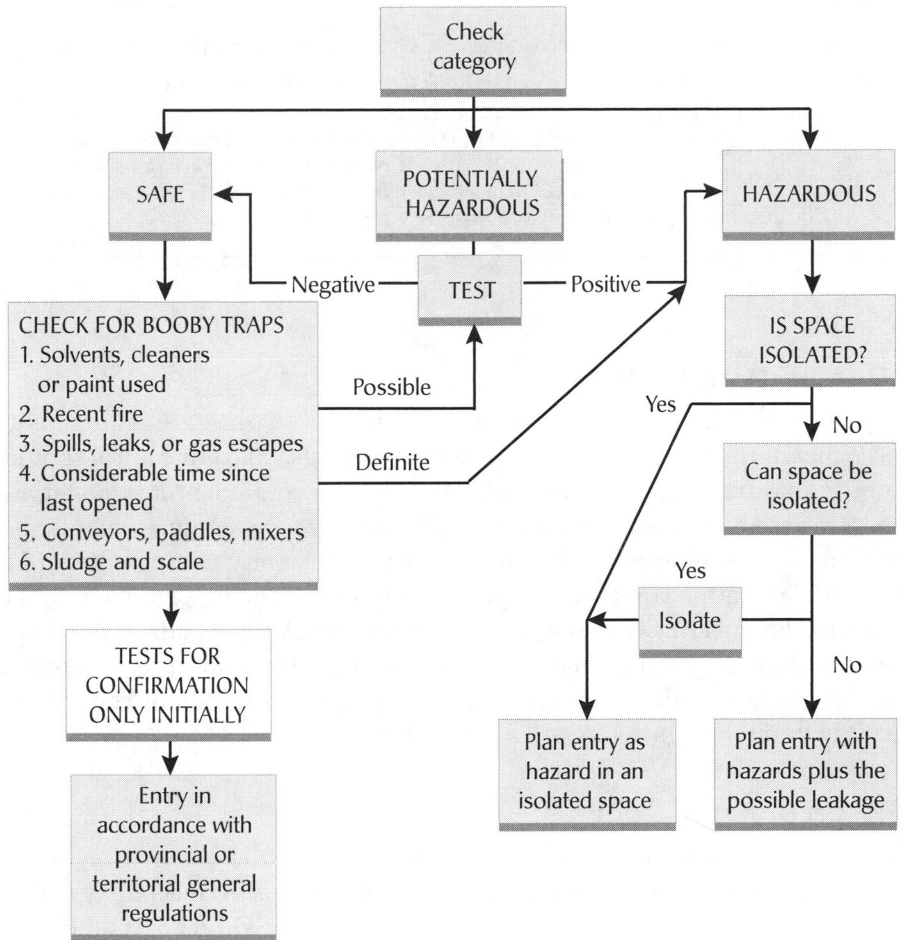

4. Communicate to workers that no smoking or open flames are to be permitted at or near the worksite.
5. Purge the space of all contaminants and test the air quality several times to ensure that all impurities have been removed.
6. Ensure that a constant forced airflow into the space is provided.
7. Clean the interior of the space to ensure that no hazardous scale or deposits are present.
8. Post a trained safety lookout outside the space. (The inside workers should be kept in full view at all times.)
9. Attach a lifeline to each worker in the space. (The free end should be controlled by the safety lookout.)

On completion of the confined-space work, equipment startup can be undertaken in the reverse order to the shutdown. The permit and lockout systems should be followed without deviation.

Occupational Health and Safety Today 8.2

Tragedy on the Farm

On June 13, 2006, two farm workers were in a corn silo in St. Valentin, Quebec, scraping mouldy corn off the walls. When one of the farm owners opened the trap door to drain corn into a truck, Henri-Georges Trahan, who was standing on a pile of grain over the trap door, fell into the grain. He quickly asphyxiated and died. The absence of fall protection gear, respiration units, communication devices, and supervision all contributed to the fatality.

Source: *Canadian Occupational Health and Safety News* (February 5, 2007), "CSST reports on asphyxiation inside silo." Retrieved from http://www.esourcecanada.com/bnn/healthandsafety.asp, February 7, 2007.

Engineering Control

engineering control
modification of work processes, equipment, and materials to reduce exposure to hazards

Engineering control refers to the modification of work processes, equipment, and materials in order to reduce exposure to hazards.[3] Hazard control should be built into the design of the work itself. Before equipment and materials are purchased, specifications for efficient and safe operations should be determined. For example, noise-emission limits for noisy equipment can be specified before the equipment is purchased, thus reducing possible worker exposure. Engineering control also refers to the installation of auxiliary equipment, such as physical barriers and ventilation systems, in order to reduce hazards dealing with the source and path. Various methods of controlling hazards through engineering are discussed below.

Design of Hand Tools

Virtually every activity we undertake that requires the use of our hands involves a tool of some sort. Although a computer-controlled machining centre is not considered a hand tool in the same sense as a screwdriver or toothbrush, each individual piece of production equipment poses its own repetitive-strain injury (RSI) problems. Nevertheless, these items are rarely designed to fit the human hand. The common in-line screwdriver configuration, for example, requires that the hand and wrist be forced out of line. However, the T-bar handle in the ergonomic screwdriver allows the hand and arm to be kept in alignment by producing a lower wrist–arm angle (see Figure 8.5). The key to effective hand tool design is to maintain natural joint alignment such as that illustrated by the ergonomic hammer in Figure 8.6.

Ergonomically designed keyboards, which are available in some computer stores, are constructed to match the natural position of the hands at rest.

Hand-operated tools and devices must allow the hand–wrist–arm group to function in a neutral position (i.e., axes in line). Tools that are used in an assembly operation should be vertically suspended over the workstation on a balancer so that the worker can reach for and grasp the tool without twisting the arm–wrist axis. The tool should be cycled with a handgrip, not a single finger trigger.

FIGURE 8.5

Screwdriver Configurations

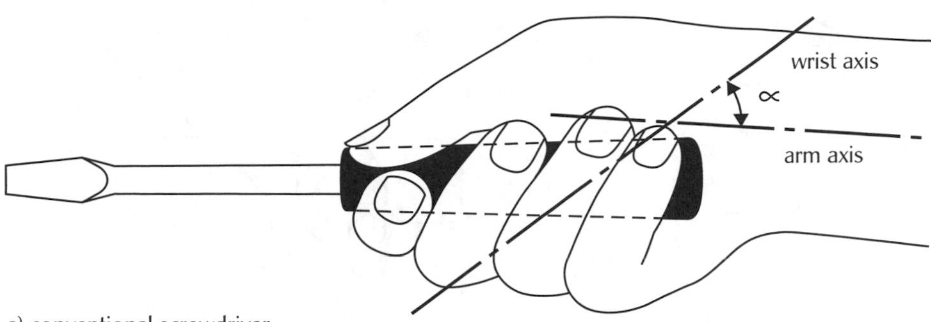

a) conventional screwdriver

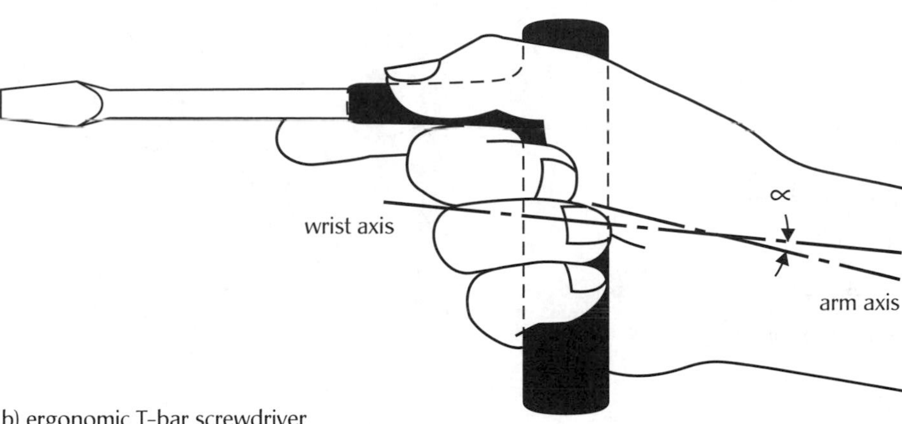

b) ergonomic T-bar screwdriver

Tools should be designed so that excessive holding force to maintain proper control is not required. A vibrating tool can be hard to control without maintaining a very tight and stressful handhold or grip. Workers should move their arms more than their wrists and hands. Greater force can be exerted by the thumb and the middle finger than by the other fingers.

Substitution

Safety professionals can sometimes replace hazardous equipment or materials with those that are less hazardous. For example, replacing a light, fluffy powder with the same material in granular form will result in a reduction of airborne dust levels. Lead paints can be replaced with less toxic material such as water-based coatings. Similarly, electric trucks can be substituted for gasoline-powered ones with a resultant decrease in exposure to carbon monoxide. The substitute should, of course, be checked for other types of hazards. The introduction of electric trucks will reduce the serious risk of carbon monoxide exposure but increase less serious exposure to flammable hydrogen or electric shock from batteries.

FIGURE 8.6

Hammer Configurations

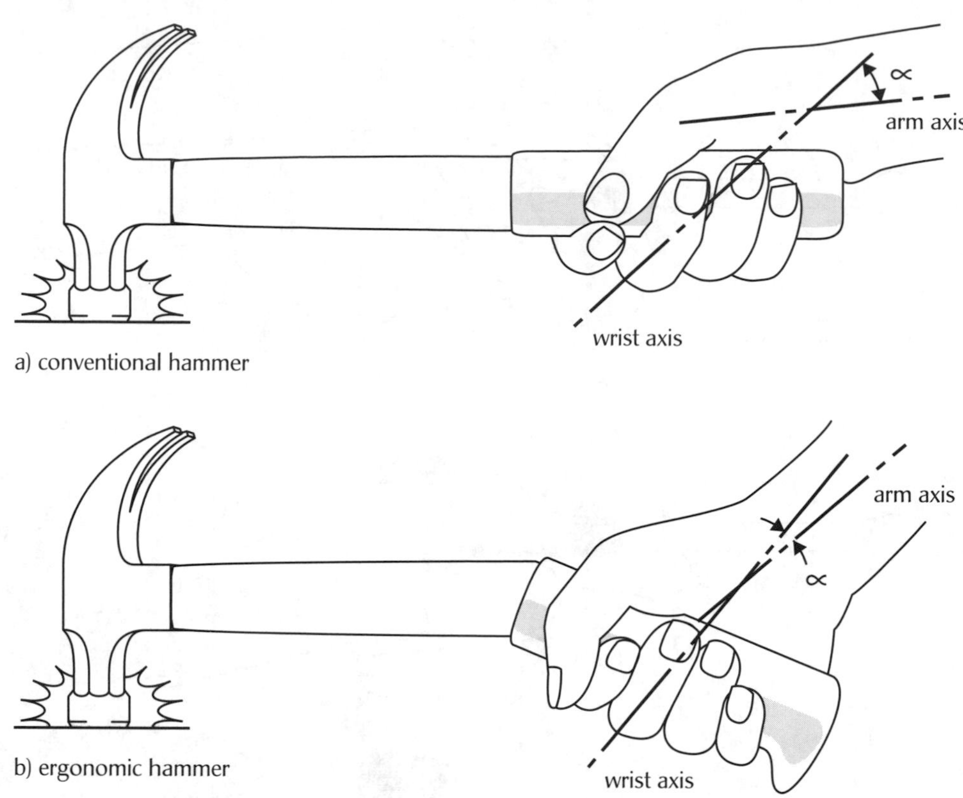

Occupational Health and Safety Notebook 8.3

Controlling RSI through Workspace Design

The application of ergonomic design principles to the design of workspaces, and more specifically to the prevention of RSI, is an example of engineering control of workplace hazards. The predominant method of control involves keeping joints in their natural position or aligned with the connecting limb. To illustrate the joint alignment argument, place your right hand flat on a table, thumb extended to the left. In the natural position, the hand and arm axes will be in line. Now, without moving your arm, flex your wrist to the left in the direction of the thumb. This position is known as "radial deviation." Flex your wrist in the opposite direction. This position is called "ulnar deviation." Raising your fingers off the table, while keeping your arm on the table, will create a position known as "dorsiflexion." If the hand and fingers are flexed downward, the resulting position is "palmar flexion." Each of these positions, if held for any length of time, will become uncomfortable. The radial deviation position and possibly the dorsiflexion position are associated with keyboarding.

Sources: StraightGoods, "February 28 is RSI Awareness Day." Retrieved from http://www.straightgoods.ca/ViewFeature7.cfm?REF=101, February 7, 2007; and Workers' Compensation Board of Alberta, "Office ergonomics." Retrieved from http://www.wcb.ab.ca/pdfs/ergobk.pdf, February 7, 2007.

Workstation Design

The four major components of workstation design are layout, control and display panels, seating, and lighting.

Layout

Design the workstation so that the arm is not used in an extended or reaching position. The farther the hand is from the body, the less power it can exert and the smaller load it can handle. The arm can push and pull greater loads at a worktable if the action is to or from the body than it can if pushing or pulling transversely.

Tasks should be designed so that the preferred hand (left or right) can do the most critical tasks. Foot motions can be used for minor operations, thereby relieving the hands from some repetitive actions. Avoid simultaneous hand-and-foot motions when the task requires close attention. Arm motions are faster and more accurate than foot motions. The hand and arm can be used for fine control or operation; the foot can be used to stop or start a cycle that involves no accuracy of placement.

Tasks that require frequent arm movements should be carried out with the elbows bent and close to the body. Arm movements should be smooth rather than jerky. The hand and arm can pull down with more strength than they can push up. The push power of the arm is greater when the hand is 50 cm in front of the body; the pull power of the arm is greater when the hand is 70 cm in front of the body.[4] The greatest push power for the legs occurs when the angle at the knee is 140–165 degrees—close to standing. The greatest bending strength occurs when the angle of the elbow is 80–120 degrees—close to a right angle.[5] Pushing power is greater than pulling power.

Control and Display Panels

Controls and displays such as an automobile instrument panel or a machine operating panel must exhibit the following four characteristics:

1. *Visibility*. The display must be within the worker's field of vision, with no obstructions. Characters should be of a readable size, with high contrast.
2. *Legibility*. Characters must be adequately spaced as well as distinguishable (a "3" should not look like an "8"). No more than one line or pointer should appear on each display.
3. *Interpretability*. The displays must be interpreted in the same way by all observers. Universal symbols help but can lead to misunderstandings. For example, the red exit symbols may be confused with the red glow that means "stop." In Europe, exit symbols are green.
4. *User-friendliness*. Each control must be a different shape and have a different operating direction in order to be easily distinguished from adjacent controls. Picture the controls in your car: the radio volume rotates, while the station-change button is pushed; the most important controls—the fuel gauge and the speedometer—are displayed most prominently.

Seating

Employees can spend long periods seated at their workstations. Poor sitting positions or posture can restrict blood circulation, increase blood pooling in the legs and feet, and add to the compressive load on the spine. Correct chair design will minimize the concentration of pressures under the thigh and the back of the knee. The most commonly recommended sitting posture is illustrated in Figure 8.7.

Work seating must be completely adjustable in all directions and planes. A forward-tilting seat may be preferred by employees who must lean over a workstation. (Interestingly, a study by Ontario Hydro revealed that only

FIGURE 8.7

Side View of Chair Dimensions

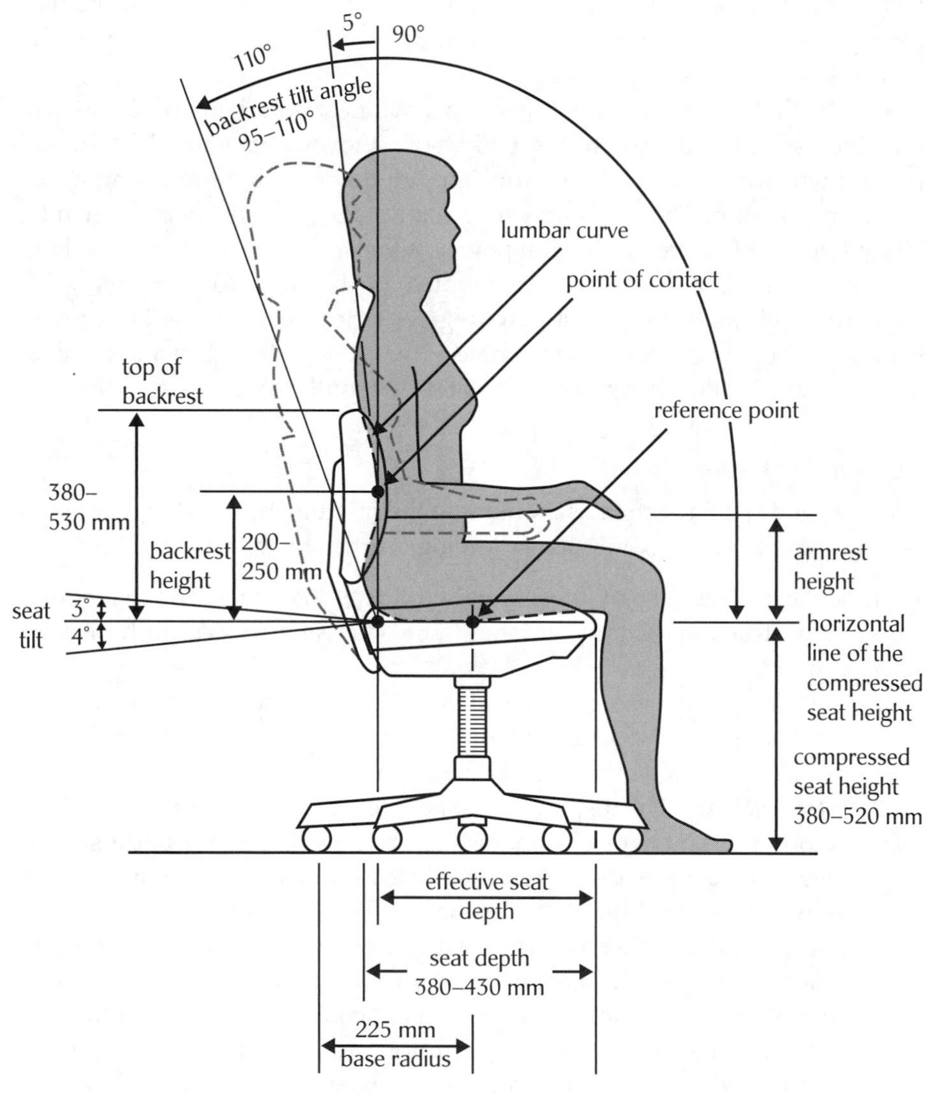

5 percent of users adjust their furniture.[6]) Seat cushions should have about a 2.5 cm compression, with minimal contouring to allow ease of position shift. Permeable fabrics allow ventilation and absorption of perspiration.

The backrest should be curved in the vertical and horizontal planes. It should also be vertically adjustable (so that the point of contact fits the small of the back in the lumbar region) as well as horizontally adjustable. Armrests are recommended unless a wide variety of arm movements are required. The chair base should provide stability and mobility. Five casters with a wide spread will prevent tipping.[7]

Lighting

Lighting has two main purposes: to illuminate the tasks and to increase the safety and comfort of the worker. Bright overhead lighting can produce glare and annoying reflections on a computer screen, resulting in eyestrain and headaches. Choosing the correct lighting for a workplace will involve consideration of the following factors:

- *Intensity:* the amount of light given off by a source
- *Luminance:* the amount of light uniformly reflected or emitted from a surface and the background
- *Reflectance:* the amount of light reflected from a surface (luminance) and the amount of light falling on the surface (illuminance), as in Figure 8.8. A dull black surface has 9 percent reflectance, while a shiny white surface has closer to 100 percent reflectance.
- *Luminaire:* a complete lighting device

FIGURE 8.8

Reflectance Schematic

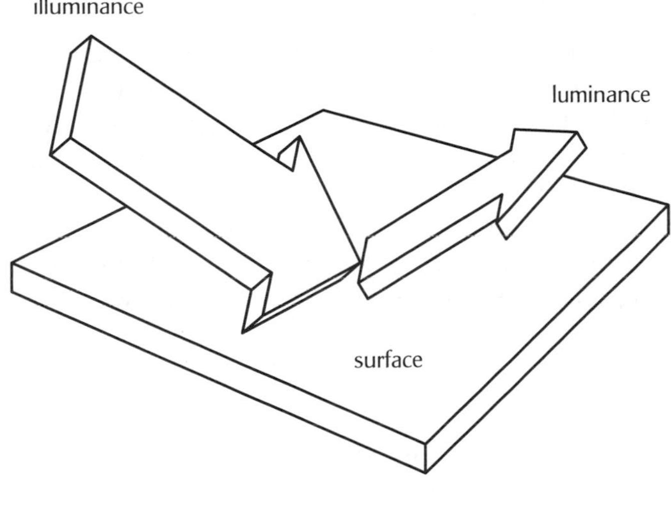

$$\% \text{ Reflectance} = \frac{\text{Luminance}}{\text{Illuminance}}$$

- *Contrast:* the relationship between the amount of light from a surface and the background
- *Glare:* the reduction of visibility caused by brightness differences between an object and its background

Both the quantity and quality of light must be considered. In the context of workstation design, quantity refers to the correct amount of light needed to perform a task. Quality is more complex and includes measures of distribution (or spread), glare, diffusion, shadows, contrast, and colour.

Process Modification

Sometimes changing the manner in which the work is done can increase safety. Moving from a manual operation to an automated one, or from batch processes to continuous processes, may result in fewer hazards.

Effective job design is key to worker safety and efficiency. Frederick Taylor (1856–1915), the founder of industrial engineering, tried to increase both by breaking a job into its basic components and then assigning to each task specific times and methods (motions). Taylor's ideas were applied to the shovelling of coal at the Bethlehem Steel Company in what was to become a classic motion study. This application demonstrated that a stoker could shovel more coal into the blast furnace by using a larger shovel and engaging in fewer work cycles. Decreasing the repetition of the task served to reduce fatigue and back strains.

Subsequent efficiency experts addressed the tedium associated with simple task repetition. Inspired by the Hawthorne studies of the 1920s, the sociotechnological approach to work design was concerned with enhancing worker involvement and satisfaction. What has this to do with health and safety? The more interested and motivated the worker, the lower the probability of a serious accident or injury.

Isolation or Segregation

In this approach, the hazardous job or task is isolated from the employees in order to reduce their exposure. Isolation strategies may be as simple as putting a physical barrier around a chemical or noise source, or removing a hazardous operation to a separate facility. Robots can handle tasks that are too dangerous for humans.

Segregating the hazardous operation in time as well as space is also advisable. Cleanups, maintenance, and particularly hazardous tasks such as spray painting can be done on weekends or at night, when fewer workers are present.

Purchasing

Purchasing agents have an important role to play in the control of hazards. In addition to price, quality, and efficiency, the purchasing agent must consider safety. At a minimum, the equipment must meet the regulatory requirements of the Canadian Standards Association and Ministry regulations.

Purchasing machinery without proper or minimal safety specifications or compatibility can result in equipment failure or injury. Workers can have their toes crushed if they wear safety shoes with inadequate metal caps, or they can suffer from headaches because their safety goggles have imperfections in the lenses. The idea that one size of personal protection equipment fits all is a major fallacy. The best time to eliminate hazards is at the design stage, with input from the company OH&S function.

Once specifications have been met, the safety features of competing brands can be compared. The purchasing agent should consult the company safety specialist and safety records for accidents and incidents that resulted from defects in equipment, machinery, or materials. He or she can use the information contained in these records to defend certain purchasing decisions on a cost–benefit basis.

Machine Guarding

Machine guarding is necessary to protect a worker from the hazards and energies created by moving machinery. According to Ontario's Ministry of Labour, more orders citing problems are written for nonexistent or improper guarding than for any other.[8] The problem is serious enough to have prompted the Canadian Standards Association to issue standard Z432–94, *Safeguarding of Machinery*,[9] which thoroughly covers the topic of machine guarding.

machine guarding
protection for workers from the hazards and energies created by moving machinery

The following basic guidelines for machine guarding apply, regardless of the type or operation of the equipment:

1. The guard must be sturdy enough to resist external source damage that will interfere with the operation of the machine, such as being struck by a forklift truck.
2. The guard must permit required maintenance tasks without excessive dismantling or reassembly labour.
3. The guard must be properly and securely mounted to prevent rattling, which is a distraction, or part interference, which can cause snags and force the operator to attempt to free them, possibly without proper precautions.
4. There should be no parts that, if removed, will compromise the protection provided by the guard—there should always be some guarding left.
5. Construction should be relatively simple so that problems can be immediately identified and corrected during an inspection.

Thoroughness in guard design is essential. An incomplete guard may be as much of a hazard as no guard at all. The guard must not create a false sense of security that may cause accidents and possible injuries. When the guard is in operation, all parts of the body must be excluded, and no access is permitted. The barrier or guard will prevent a worker from being caught in, on, or between moving equipment (kinetic energy), or from being struck by flying, sliding, or falling objects (gravity energy).

Floor barriers installed around pumps and other hazardous equipment must be strong enough to resist damage by, for example, forklift truck impact (mechanical energy), and high enough so that a worker will not trip or fall over them. Expanded metal should fill the open spaces to prevent parts from rolling into the hazard area and fingers from being poked through.

Several devices can be used to control point-of-operation hazards. *Barrier* or *enclosure guards* prevent workers from entering a hazardous area. The barrier may be mechanical (a cage that covers the work action) or electrical (a photocell that will not permit the machine to cycle while the beam is broken). The emergency stop button is another form of guard; for it to be effective, the machine must be equipped with a braking system that will stop the machine in mid-cycle.

Guarding by distance involves keeping workers physically removed from the machine hazard. One of the most common methods is the two-handed trip guard or control, which is located near but not in the midst of the hazard site. Both hands are required to press each button simultaneously for the machine to cycle.

Hand-removal devices are designed to physically remove the worker's hands and arms from the activated machine. The "hand pullout" is a harness-like system fastened to the worker's wrists at one end and to the machine at the other end. When the machine (say a punch press) is activated, the harness mechanism physically pulls the worker's hands out of the way. Short of removing the harness, the worker cannot win the ensuing tug of war.

The "sweep away" is a device with one or two arms (single sweep or double sweep) that, when activated by the machine cycle, will swing across in front of the worker, forcibly removing his or her hands from the danger area. A small panel attached to each arm screens the swept area to keep the worker's hands from reentering the danger zone after the sweep arm passes. The sweep away device is not a recommended guard.

The *photoelectric eye* is a light beam that, when broken, will not allow the machine to cycle. This type of device has the advantage of not adding to the machine any obstructions that can make maintenance difficult. It is generally expensive to install and maintain but very effective.

Feeding tools include hand-held tongs, push sticks, or clamps that allow the operator access to the machine while keeping his or her hands out of the way. Metal tools are usually made of aluminum or magnesium, which will crush easily if caught in the machine, thereby saving the die sets and not allowing the type of **kickback** that could direct the worker's hands into the machine. A press forge operator will use a set of special tongs to hold a red-hot piece of metal in place in the dies while the machine forms the part. In a similar manner, a set of handles secured to sheet glass or metal by vacuum will permit a worker to handle the material without being cut by sharp edges.

kickback
action of having a work piece suddenly thrown backward into the operator

Occupational Health and Safety Today 8.3

Death in a Bakery

David Ellis was 18 years old when he reported to work for his second day at New Sun Cookies in Oakville, Ontario, on February 11, 1999. His job assignment was to run the industrial-sized cookie dough mixer (imagine a 2-metre-high version of a mixer used in a home kitchen that can process 90 kg of dough at a time). The mixer had no lockout features and no machine guards to protect people from the blades while the mixer was in action. These issues had been pointed out to the employer by a provincial health and safety inspector 18 months before the accident. However, the inspector did not issue a written order and nothing was done. About halfway through the shift on February 11, David was removing dough from the mixer bowl when somehow the mixer was turned on, and he was caught in the blades, suffering severe injuries to his head and hands. As a result of the head injuries, David died on February 17, 1999. The company and the company owner received fines; the supervisor was sentenced to 20 days in jail to be served on weekends.

Seven months later, 16-year-old Ivan Golyashov was in almost exactly the same type of accident while working at the Fiera Food Bakery in Toronto. He too died of his injuries.

Sources: Beharie, N. (2001, October/ November). "Young workers: Profile of an accident victim." *OHS Canada*; and CBC, "Second dough mixer death." Retrieved from http://www.cbc.ca/story/news/?/news/1999/09/27/dough270999, February 7, 2007.

Contact Control

If the machine, equipment, or plant becomes damaged from accidental causes or emergencies then control of the hazard site is necessary so the worker can be protected. The main purpose of contact control is to ensure that the workers and emergency crews—fire fighters—are not added to the possible injury list. Steps to be taken can be grouped into the five following categories:

1. *Suppression*. Reduce or eliminate the ongoing hazard condition by using standard fire-fighting techniques: install fans to help clear the contaminants from the surrounding air and turn off the power and utilities to the area. For example, dust from an explosion in a mining operation can be controlled by spraying water at the rock surface.
2. *Barriers*. Install barriers between workers and sources of the emergency to keep unauthorized personnel out of the area.
3. *Modifications*. Identify and modify equipment or structures that need to be strengthened to prevent further damage from occurring, such as adding shoring to weakened walls to prevent collapse.
4. *Substitution*. Eliminate potentially harmful energies that have been unleashed by the event and replace with safer, independent devices—use portable flood lighting to replace the existing plant lighting if there is a possibility that damaged electrical equipment could cause a fire.

5. *Isolation*. Isolate energy sources from the emergency personnel and plant workers. Shut off all energy sources in the plant to prevent additional problems and replace with outside equipment if possible, such as a portable air compressor to replace the one in the damage area. Shut down any expensive equipment that could be damaged by energy surges.

Postcontact Control

The following are some steps that should be taken in the aftermath of an event:

1. Ensure that any injured worker receives immediate and thorough emergency care. The injury could be anything from a blow to the head to exposure to a hazardous chemical. Provisions for first aid and emergency care should be made during the precontact control process. The extent of these provisions will depend on the number of workers in an organization and the types of hazards they face.
2. Lock out the machinery involved until the accident investigation is complete and the damage repaired.
3. Keep unauthorized people out of the area.
4. Determine what can be salvaged and what waste must be disposed of. Environmental regulations may prohibit the easy removal of certain hazardous waste (e.g., PCB-contaminated oils from a damaged power transformer).
5. Apprise the joint health and safety committee, affected managers, and government agencies of the event—fire, police, and paramedics will probably already know.
6. Complete all accident reports to determine what happened. Use report recommendations to ensure the accident will not be repeated.
7. Review all company procedures and revise where appropriate.
8. Communicate with workers about the event. If necessary, implement safety retraining and possibly trauma counselling depending on the seriousness of the event.

Points 2 to 5 are requirements of the Ministry of Labour in most provinces and territories, and the Workers' Compensation Board in B.C.

Source–Path–Human

Hazards can be controlled or eliminated by identifying and attacking the source of the hazard, the path it travels, and the employee or recipient of the hazard. The strategies discussed in this chapter can be regrouped along these lines, as shown in Figure 8.9. This schematic provides a useful summary of the information on hazard control. Placing control strategies in categories is less important than having a thorough understanding that hazard control is necessary and possible.

FIGURE 8.9

Source–Path–Human Controls

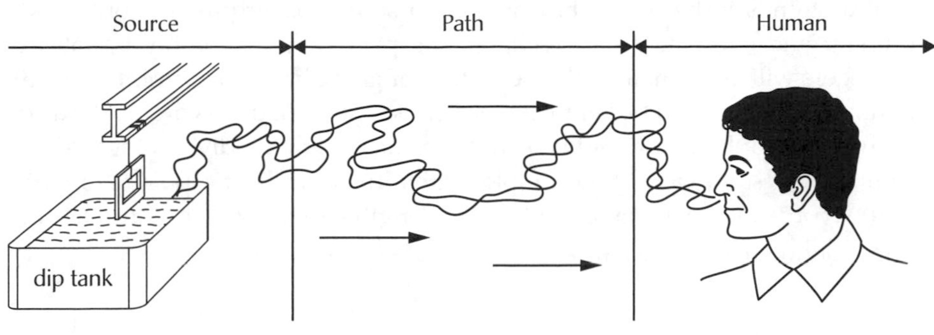

Monitoring / Auditing

RPC 8.4

RPC 8.5

Monitoring is an important part of the hazard-control process. Audits are done to ensure that hazard controls are functioning effectively, as well as to identify new hazards. Monitoring can be done daily by supervisors and maintenance personnel, weekly by department heads, monthly by health and safety committees, and as needed by compliance officers.[10] The auditing process itself affects safety. A 50-percent decrease in accidents in one organization over a 2-year period was attributed to the fact that managers began to audit.[11]

An audit program can be used to evaluate health and safety performance in the workplace. A number of audit methods are available. One very effective technique, which involves the application of total quality control methodologies and trend analysis, relates the number of incidents to some predetermined goal. If it seems from the number of events in a particular time frame that a safety goal failure is imminent, then steps can be taken to prevent the occurrence.

The audit program should do the following:

1. Ensure that safety programs are being carried out without restrictions
2. Ensure that safety programs are up to date and that deficiencies are documented
3. Be carried out by people with some understanding of both the audit methods and the material being examined (the various members of the joint health and safety committee should be able to carry out this inspection)
4. Stimulate discussion among all managers and workers, and ultimately produce conclusions and recommendations
5. Be conducted at least annually by companies with high-risk hazards
6. Include all documentation (WSIB / WCB statements, Ministry of Labour citations, air-sampling results, first-aid and incident reports, hazard analyses, discipline records, cost–benefit studies, etc.).

Record Keeping

Information obtained at all stages of the hazard-control process should be stored in a database. These records are used to identify frequency of events as well as trends in hazards. They are also a source of information on worker training and equipment maintenance. The provision of monthly updates to managers will assist them in their efforts at ongoing hazard control. The length of time records should be kept varies with the nature of the record. Records on individual employees should be kept for as long as that individual is with the company. In some cases (for example, individual records of exposure to radiation) records may have to be kept for the length of employment plus an additional period (e.g., 10 years).

RPC 8.2

Summary

The control of hazards has multiple payoffs for organizations. Planning for, eliminating, or controlling hazards can be done at the precontact stage through training, safety awareness, administrative controls, engineering controls, purchasing, housekeeping, preventive maintenance, and machine guarding. Strategies at the contact stage include how easily and quickly the event can be stabilized. Postcontact control is intended to minimize the damaging effects of hazards by instituting actions that greatly reduce the possibility of recurrence.

Key Terms

administrative control 210
confined space 218
contact control 210
engineering control 220
hazard control 210
kickback 228
machine guarding 227
postcontact control 210
precontact control 210
preventive maintenance 214

Weblinks

Safe Communities Foundation

http://www.safecommunities.ca/home.htm (p. 212)

Industrial Accident Prevention Association, "IAPA's Health and Safety Awards: Start the Journey Towards Health & Safety Excellence"

http://www.iapa.ca/awards/awards_intro.asp (p. 212)

National Quality Institute, "Canada Awards for Excellence"

http://www.nqi.ca/caeawards/default.aspx (p. 213)

Canadian Legal Information Institute, "Canada Occupational Health and Safety Regulations [SOR/86–304]"

http://www.canlii.org/ca/regu/sor86-304/ (p. 213)

RPC Icons

RPC 8.1 Implements and evaluates practices in the areas of health, safety, security, and Workers' Compensation.

- investigative techniques
- hazard recognition
- disaster recovery techniques
- relevant legislation
- resource information
- common health and safety practices
- company policies and procedures
- Worker Protection (including health and safety and Workers' Compensation)
- theories and practices for protection of individuals and groups
- Occupational health and safety legislation (e.g., Occupational Health and Safety Act of Ontario, Workplace Safety & Insurance Act—Bill 99, Workplace Hazardous Materials Information System, Transportation of Dangerous Goods legislation, environmental legislation, smoking in the workplace legislation, civil rights legislation)
- hazard identification and control
- management techniques for OH&S Programs

RPC 8.2 Ensures due diligence and strict liability requirements are met, e.g. records are kept and formal procedures established.

- relevant legislation and common law
- company policies and procedures
- industry best practices
- program and policy development
- training and development techniques
- risk analysis
- common and statutory law (e.g., employment standard: labour relations)
- Worker Protection (including health and safety and Workers' Compensation)
- theories and practices for protection of individuals and groups

Task & Knowledge Requirements

- Occupational heal th and safety legislation (e.g., Occupational Health and Safety Act of Ontario, Workplace Safety & Insurance

Act—Bill 99, Workplace Hazardous Materials Information System, Transportation of Dangerous Goods legislation, environmental legislation, smoking in the workplace legislation, civil rights legislation)
- management techniques for OH&S Programs

RPC 8.3 Ensures that mechanisms are in place for responding to crises in the workplace, including critical incident stress management.

- oral and written communication
- training and development techniques
- industry best practices
- the workplace environment including the availability of emergency equipment
- policy and program development and evaluation
- intervention strategies
- relevant legislation (e.g., fire code, Workers' Compensation)
- investigation techniques
- stress management techniques
- types of employee assistance programs
- Occupational health and safety legislation (e.g., Occupational Health and Safety Act of Ontario, Workplace Safety & Insurance Act—Bill 99, Workplace Hazardous Materials Information System, Transportation of Dangerous Goods legislation, environmental legislation, smoking in the workplace legislation, civil rights legislation)
- hazard identification and control
- accident investigation procedures
- emergency preparedness procedures
- management techniques for OH&S Programs
- conceptual definition and implications of occupational stressors (e.g., potential stressors, methods of identifying potential stressors and strain outcomes, response to organizational stressors, and management of employee strain outcomes)

RPC 8.4 Analyses risk to the health and safety of employees and determines appropriate preventative measures, including training, provision of required safety equipment, and administrative practices.

- relevant legislation
- nature of the business and physical work environment
- hazard recognition
- workplace inspection techniques
- safety programs, equipment, and emergency procedures
- ergonomics
- functions of the JHSC
- training and development/presentation techniques
- industry best practices
- relevant technical terminology
- the collective agreement
- services and equipment available in the community

- Worker Protection (including health and safety and Workers' Compensation)
- training and development program design and administration

Task & Knowledge Requirements

- Occupational health and safety legislation (e.g., Occupational Health and Safety Act of Ontario, Workplace Safety & Insurance Act—Bill 99, Workplace Hazardous Materials Information System, Transportation of Dangerous Goods legislation, environmental legislation, smoking in the workplace legislation, civil rights legislation)
- hazard identification and control
- emergency preparedness procedures
- management techniques for OH&S Programs
- types of employee assistance and wellness programs

RPC 8.5 Establishes effective programs for accident prevention, incident investigation, inspections, fire and emergency response, and required training.

- relevant legislation
- workplace inspection and accident investigation techniques
- nature of the business and physical work environment
- potential risks and hazards in the workplace
- emergency response planning
- community emergency response services
- training and development
- industry best practices
- Worker Protection (including health and safety and Workers' Compensation)
- training and development program design and administration
- hazard identification and control
- accident investigation procedures
- emergency preparedness procedures
- management techniques for OH&S Programs

Discussion Questions

1. Explain why hazard control at the precontact stage is better than hazard control at the other stages.
2. In recent years there has been a move to make ergonomic design and ergonomic standards mandatory in workplaces. Should your jurisdiction implement legislation requiring ergonomic analysis and design of work processes? Why or why not?
3. A maintenance crew has been hired to enter an underground sewer line to do some minor repair work. They call and ask you for advice about necessary equipment and procedures. Briefly outline your response.

Using the Internet

1. Table 8.1 presents a series of special awareness events. Use the Web to determine (a) how these events are celebrated or implemented in your local area and (b) what other safety awareness events are held in your area.

Exercise

1. Identify a hazard at your workplace (or a workplace with which you are familiar). List all the approaches you could undertake to control or minimize the hazard.

Case

Hazard Control

A new plating machine had been installed and was being checked for proper operation. During this check it was discovered that the bearings on the caustic-solution circulating pump were defective and had to be replaced. The pump was removed, repaired, and was being reinstalled. An electrician was assigned to make the electrical connections, while a plumber performed the necessary pipe connections on the same pump.

The electrician finished the assignment except for checking the direction of shaft rotation. Since the plumber was out of the area, the electrician asked the company representative supplying the equipment if the pump was ready to be tried out. The representative stated that it was. The electrician walked to the end of the plater to start the motor, just as the plumber appeared. The plumber's shouts to the electrician not to start the pump were too late because the pump had already been turned on. At that moment, hot caustic solution showered out of the pipe flange, which had not been tightened after reassembly. The solution splashed onto the plumber, two engineers in the area, another plant engineering employee, and the vendor representative. The plumber received burns requiring immediate hospitalization and was off work for about two months. One engineer required subsequent hospitalization for eye burns and was off work for more than a week. The other three involved received minor burns. The accident occurred at 10:45 a.m. on a Wednesday.

What would you recommend for contact and postcontact control?

Endnotes

1. DiNardi, S. (Ed.). (1997). *The occupational environment–Its evaluation and control* (2nd ed.). Fairfax, VA: American Industrial Hygiene Association.

2. Schuler, R., & Dolan, S. (1994). *Human resources management: A Canadian perspective*. Scarborough, ON: Nelson Canada.
3. Pilger, C. W. (1994). Hazard control procedures. Presentation at the 23rd Intensive Workshop in Industrial Hygiene, September 27.
4. Grandjean, E. (1988). *Fitting the task to the man* (4th ed.). London, England: Taylor & Francis.
5. Astrand, P. O., & Rodahl, K. (1986). *Textbook of work physiology* (3rd ed.). New York: McGraw-Hill.
6. McDonald, H. (1995, March/April). Know thy users. *Accident Prevention*, 11–12.
7. Canadian Standards Association. (1995). *Office ergonomics*. CSA Standard, CAN/CSA Z412-M89, section 5.
8. Somasunder, S. (1993, September/October). Machine safeguarding. *OH&S Canada*, *9*(5), 30–31.
9. Canadian Standards Association. (1994). *Safeguarding of machinery*. Standard Z432–94.
10. Laing, P. (Ed.). (1992). *Accident prevention manual for business and industry: Administration and programs* (10th ed.). Washington, D.C.: National Safety Council.
11. Taylor, J. (1991). Guide to health and safety management: 20 proven programs. *Safety Auditing*. Don Mills, ON: Southam Business Communications Inc.

Chapter 9

Training

Chapter Learning Objectives

After reading this chapter, you should be able to:

- discuss the importance of occupational health and safety training
- identify the components of a training program
- explain the role of a needs analysis when designing a training program
- discuss issues that arise in training design and delivery
- describe various options for the delivery of health and safety training programs
- discuss the role of evaluation in any training program
- evaluate the measurement concerns surrounding organizational measures of occupational safety training effectiveness
- describe some common health and safety training initiatives including safety orientation, first-aid training, and WHMIS

ENGLISHTOWN FERRY ACCIDENT

On February 8, 2003, Donald LeBlanc died on the job. The 38-year-old drowned when the tractor he was operating to clear snow and ice from the ramp to the small cable ferry in Englishtown, Nova Scotia slid into St. Ann's Bay. His body was not discovered until August 2003.

The employees at the Englishtown Ferry operation were responsible for clearing the dock and had received training on driving the tractor. However, the trainer did not provide any training on operating the tractor on the ramp itself or under poor weather conditions, having determined that such conditions were too dangerous for individuals who were learning this skill. Mr. LeBlanc had struggled in the training, failing his first test and barely passing on a second attempt.

Following the accident, investigations determined that chains that should have been on the tractor's tires were in fact sitting on the dock. There was also no life preserver or survival gear in the tractor. The Nova Scotia Provincial Government ultimately launched a public inquiry into this incident, which started in October 2005. Preliminary reports from the inquiry point to several recommendations including improved emergency procedures, improved performance evaluation, and extensive improvements to the training provided to employees, including the addition of hazard assessment and emergency response to the training domain.

The circumstances surrounding this tragic incident illustrate the importance of occupational health and safety training in organizations. Failure to provide training or offering inadequate training content and evaluation can place workers in hazardous situations with catastrophic results. In this chapter we will consider the components of effective safety training in workplaces.

Sources: CBC, "Dying for a job: The Englishtown ferry accident" (April 25, 2006). Retrieved from http://www.cbc.ca/news/background/workplace-safety/ferry-accident.html, February 2, 2007; and CBC, "LeBlanc inquiry ends with recommendations" (October 25, 2006). Retrieved from http://www.cbc.ca/news/story/2006/10/25/leblanc-wrap.html, February 2, 2007.

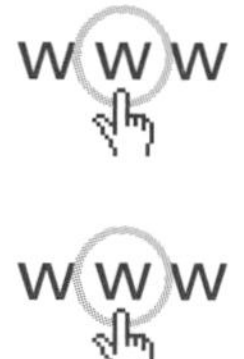

The tragedy of the Englishtown Ferry accident illustrates the disastrous events that can happen when the appropriate health and safety training is not delivered in workplaces. The dangers of the workplace are a reality for all workers. Workers of all ages, experience levels, and job types can and do experience accidents at work. Many workers in Canada have not received adequate safety training. A recent study of 60,000 Canadian workers reported that only 12 percent of women and 16 percent of men had received workplace safety training in the previous year.[1] Although employees who were new to their jobs were more likely to receive training, the proportion who did remains disappointingly low, at only 20 percent.[2] Even though young workers and those in physically demanding jobs are at higher risk for injury, neither were more likely to receive training. In this chapter we explore the topic of health and safety training. We apply a basic model of training in organizations to the specific concerns of training workers in the area of occupational health and safety. In particular we consider the processes of designing, implementing, and evaluating a health and safety training program in an organization.

The Role of Occupational Health and Safety Training

All workers have several rights pertaining to their health and safety while at work. Three basic rights apply to all Canadian employees:

1. *The right to know*. Workers have a right to be informed about dangerous or unsafe materials and machinery in the workplace.

2. *The right to participate*. Workers have a right to take part actively in the protection of their own health and safety. This participation generally involves reporting unsafe work practices and conditions.
3. *The right to refuse unsafe work*. Workers have a right to withhold their services if they are asked to perform a task that they deem to be unsafe or are asked to use equipment that is not in good repair.

Occupational Health and Safety Today 9.1

The LifeQuilt

The Canadian LifeQuilt is a memorial that honours the lives of young Canadian workers who have been injured or killed on the job. *Shawna Michele Vezina*, 19, was hit and killed by an oncoming vehicle while working as a traffic controller at a road construction site. *David Ellis* was only 18 years old when he was pulled into an industrial mixer on the second day of his temporary job at a bakery. Nineteen-year-old *Sean Kells* died in 1994 in an explosion that occurred while he was pouring a highly flammable chemical. This event occurred on Sean's third day on the job. He had not been advised that the activity was dangerous. *Kelly Newton*, 22, was crushed by logs moving on a skidder. Kelly had been on the job less than three weeks when this tragedy occurred. At the time of his death, he was working without supervision and had not received training.

The Canadian LifeQuilt represents a sad reality. Estimates suggest that one in seven young workers is injured on the job. Programs like the LifeQuilt raise awareness among parents, youth, and employers about young workers' safety. As part of the awareness campaign, the Young Worker Zone on the CCOHS website includes resources and recommendations for young workers, their parents, and their employers. A major recommendation for employers is for the provision of health and safety training for new employees, particularly young workers. Young workers are encouraged to know their rights and ask questions about safety at work. Many youth who are injured at work report they were not aware of the life-threatening hazards in the workplace. In fact, reports from many accidents involving young workers indicate that injuries could easily have been avoided if basic safety rules had been followed. Trusting young workers, eager to please their new employers, often believe that someone is looking out for their safety while at work. However, many companies do not provide adequate safety training regarding the hazards in the workplace.

Sources: "Young workers memorial LifeQuilt." Retrieved from http://www.youngworkerquilt.ca, February 13, 2007; Canadian Centre for Occupational Health and Safety, "Young Workers Zone." Retrieved from http://www.ccohs.ca/youngworkers, February 13, 2007; Chapeskie, K. K., & Breslin, C. F. (2003). "Securing a safe and healthy future: The road to injury prevention of Ontario's young workers." *In Focus, 34a.* Retrieved from The Institute for Work and Health, http://www.iwh.on.ca, February 13, 2007.

RPC 9.1

RPC 9.2

RPC 9.3

WWW

It is easy to see the vital role of training in the fulfillment of these basic rights. First, employees—especially new employees—must be advised of these rights. The communication of these basic rights might take place in a safety orientation when a person starts a new job.

Once employees are aware of their basic rights regarding health and safety at work, safety-related training is needed to help individuals ensure that these rights are being upheld. For instance, with respect to the right to know, employees must receive training on the potential dangers in their workplaces. Similarly, regarding the right to refuse unsafe work, effective health and safety training will help individuals evaluate accurately what tasks are indeed unsafe. As such, health and safety training plays a vital role in the protection of an employee's basic rights, and its provision is mandated in occupational health and safety acts across the country. The importance of health and safety training is recognized internationally as well. For example, in the United States, training is prominently placed as one of five essential elements of occupational health and safety programs, along with employer commitment, hazard surveillance, hazard control and prevention, and program evaluation.[3]

Given the importance of the effective communication of health and safety information in today's workplaces, the question of how to develop and implement effective health and safety training programs is vital. In the remainder of this chapter, we will consider the process of implementing a health and safety training program. As our starting point we take a basic model of training in organizations and discuss its application to health and safety–related concerns.

Occupational Health and Safety Today 9.2

The Vital Role of Health and Safety Training Following the "Westray" Legislation

Many Canadians report they have not received health and safety training in their workplaces. Organizations failing to provide safety training are in fact failing to meet legal requirements. All employees have the right to be fully aware of the hazards associated with their work and receive training that allows them to operate in a safe manner while working. Because employers are responsible for the health and safety of workers, organizations that fail to provide health and safety training or provide inadequate training can be held responsible for any accidents or other safety-related incidents that occur.

Bill C-45, commonly referred to as the "Westray Bill," became law on March 31, 2004. This law means that the ramifications for employers failing to provide appropriate health and safety training have become more severe in Canada. This bill amends the Criminal Code of Canada to hold corporations and their stakeholders accountable for work-related acts that are deemed criminally negligent. Employers bear a large responsibility to ensure Canadian workers know about hazards in the workplace and are able to refuse work deemed unsafe. This new legislation means that failure to provide appropriate health and safety training can be labelled a criminal offence and can ultimately result in criminal charges against organizations.

Health and Safety Training Programs

As our starting point we take the **instructional systems design (ISD) model of training.**[4] The ISD model of training incorporates a three-part process: (1) needs analysis, (2) training design and delivery, and (3) training evaluation. The model is depicted in Figure 9.1. Each stage of the model, with its applicability to health and safety training, is detailed in the sections that follow.

instructional systems design (ISD) model of training
a general model of the training process that incorporates needs analysis, training design and delivery, and training evaluation, and notes the interdependencies among the three major components of the training process

Needs Analysis

The training and development process begins when some form of need or concern arises. With respect to health and safety training, that concern might be the occurrence of a number of accidents or injuries in the workplace. Following such incidents, company officials may be concerned about the safety of their workers and want to develop a training program to improve workplace safety. A large number of workplace accidents in a particular company may also draw attention from various occupational health and safety governing bodies. These groups may determine that safety training is required and mandate training within a particular organization. Alternatively, the move toward safety training could be prompted by new legislation requiring that a particular type of health and safety training be offered in all workplaces within a certain industry or to deal with identified hazards. Whatever the case, a health and safety training development process begins with a **needs analysis.**

RPC 9.4

RPC 9.5

needs analysis
the initial stage of the training development process, intended to identify employee and organizational deficiencies that can be addressed with training and to recognize potential obstacles to the success of a training program

Needs analysis is the recommended starting point in many models of organizational training.[5] A needs analysis helps determine the nature of the problem at hand. Needs analysis is a way to determine the "gap between the way things are and the way things should be."[6] Needs analysis can also be used to identify potential obstacles to the effectiveness of a training program so that they can be dealt with early in the training and development process. Such an analysis ideally includes an assessment of the organization, the task

FIGURE 9.1

The Instructional Systems Design Model of Training

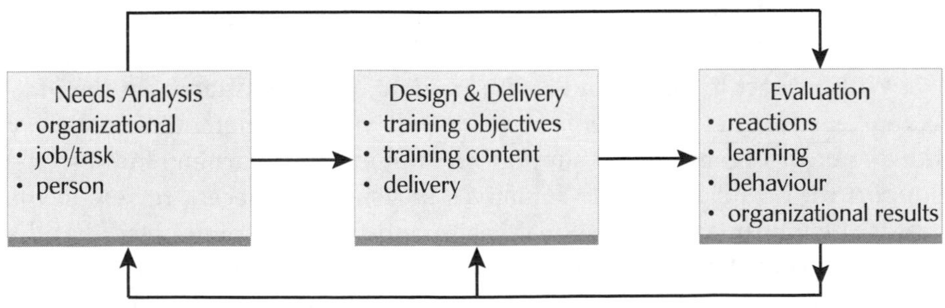

Source: Adapted from Saks, A. M., & Haccoun, R. R. (2004). *Managing performance through training and development* (3rd ed.). Toronto: Nelson Canada. Reprinted with permission of Nelson, a division of Thomson Learning: www.thomsonrights.com Fax 800 730-2215.

or job at hand, and the employee(s) in question. The inclusion of all three levels in the initial analysis will help answer questions about what groundwork must be done before training begins, what the content of the training program should be, who should receive training, and how the program should be delivered. Let's consider the pertinent issues when assessing the needs of the organization, the task or job, and the employee.

RPC 9.6

Organizational Analysis

organizational analysis
an analysis of the entire organization designed to examine its resources, strategy, and environment in order to assess the organization's support for training

A needs analysis at the organizational level should be the starting point in any training intervention.[7] The **organizational analysis** should involve a study of the whole organization, considering such areas as the resources and strategy of the organization and the industry in which it operates. The organizational analysis can identify the health and safety areas that need improvement and may be targets for a training program. This analysis should also highlight any constraints that may limit the success of a training program before the design and delivery of the training.

Successful training initiatives tend to be those that are in line with the organization's overall strategy. Similarly, it is important to consider the resources that the organization can dedicate to the training process. The extent of the available resources can influence the nature of the training program. For example, if the organization has training facilities on-site, this may influence decisions about the delivery of the training. The budget available for training should also be considered, as financial constraints will influence decisions later in the training development process. Similarly, it is important to consider the industry and environmental factors that may affect the training program. For instance, if the organization is unionized, one must consider the role of the union in training program development.

Another major goal of the organizational analysis should be to establish the degree of organizational support for a training intervention. This can be done by developing a relationship with management. Support from the organization is vital to the success of any training program. If an organization truly values training, it will provide the necessary resources to make the training program a success. For instance, an organization that supports a training intervention is more likely to encourage its employees to take part actively in the program than is an organization that is merely going through the motions of implementing some form of training.

With respect to health and safety training, it is important that the individual conducting the organizational needs analysis determine not only the degree of organizational support for training and learning, but also the support for health and safety initiatives in general. A recent review of the research literature on occupational health and safety training noted that the effectiveness of health and safety efforts "will be a function of the organization's overall commitment to providing a safe work environment and the employee's perception and recognition of that commitment."[8] Certainly, studies show that organizational support plays a vital role in the success of health and safety training initiatives. In one examination of the effectiveness of health and safety training among employees at toxic waste sites, trainees reported that attempts to act on what they had learned in training were far more likely to succeed and had a better chance of success when their managers were supportive of the program.[9] In general, investigations of the impact of management attitudes toward health and safety training illustrate the importance of managerial support for sustaining the positive outcomes associated with such training.

One way for the individual(s) conducting the needs analysis to determine the extent of organizational support for a health and safety training program is to examine the **safety climate** of the organization. An organization's safety climate relates to the perceptions regarding safety-related policies, procedures, and practices that are shared by all the stakeholders in the organization.[10] An organization that has explicitly enacted policies on safety, encourages safety-related training, and promotes safety might be said to have a strong safety climate. A company that has a strong safety climate is likely to support and enable initiatives relating to health and safety training. These organizations will invest the necessary money and time to make the training program a success, and employees are likely to be responsive to the effort.

safety climate
shared perceptions of the importance of safety in the workplace

However, consider an organization that does not place a high value on safety; that is, a company that does not have a strong safety climate. This type of operation may be hesitant to provide the type of support necessary to make health and safety training a successful endeavour. Similarly, employees of such an organization may be suspicious of the training program—wondering why the company suddenly appears to be concerned about their health and well-being. If the organizational analysis reveals that the safety climate of the organization is not currently conducive to safety training, the next logical step may be to emphasize to organizational management the need for increased organizational attention to safety and the necessity of communicating to employees the intended move toward a health and safety focus. These efforts, if launched early in the overall training development process, will lay important groundwork for a health and safety training effort and ultimately contribute to the success of the training program.

One situation that might arise when conducting an organizational analysis regarding health and safety training needs is finding an organization that does not generally focus on employee health and safety and does not have a strong safety climate, but that is mandated to offer safety training because of legislation. There is no easy answer for how to deal with such a situation. However, we suggest that individuals involved in a training needs analysis with such an organization should emphasize the importance of a supportive organizational environment in successful training. Managers in this type of organization may respond to a bottom-line approach—an argument based on the return on investment of training dollars. If management can be convinced that their support will result in increased training effectiveness and ultimately tangible organizational benefits, they will be more likely to make an effort to provide a supportive training environment.

Job/Task Analysis

job/task analysis
a component of the training needs analysis process during which the jobs and specific job tasks that are in need of training are identified and studied

Following the organizational analysis, the second step in the training needs analysis is to conduct a **job/task analysis.** The first critical step is to identify the jobs that are targeted for training. With respect to health and safety training, the scope of the jobs involved in a training program will depend on the nature of the training programs. Some forms of training, like a basic safety orientation or a seminar on the role of a health and safety committee, will apply to employees in many positions within the organization. Other types of training will be far more specific in its target jobs. For example, training on the safe operation of a particular piece of machinery will apply only to those individuals whose jobs bring them into contact with the equipment in question.

Once the target job has been identified, one should obtain a detailed job description that outlines the tasks, duties, and responsibilities for individuals who hold that position. By working with a group of job incumbents and subject matter experts, one can rate the required tasks on their importance and frequency in the job. With respect to health and safety–related training, incumbents and subject matter experts should also be surveyed on the health and safety risks involved in each task and their perceived competence to perform the task in a safe manner. The person developing the training program might also want to observe several people performing the tasks in question to identify potential health and safety concerns that were not mentioned by the subject matter experts. From here, the information can be analyzed and interpreted.

The evaluation of the job in question and the inclusion of people with experience performing the job can greatly inform the training program that will ultimately be offered. The task analysis can help determine the exact nature and scope of the problem to be solved. To consider a health and safety example, the survey component of the task analysis might reveal that although employees are vigilant about wearing their protective equipment, they tend to use it incorrectly. In that case, the training program should focus more on instruction in the proper use of the equipment rather than on convincing people to wear the equipment. This point might have been missed if it were not for the completion of a task analysis.

Person Analysis

person analysis
a component of the training needs analysis process during which individual employees' behaviour is studied to identify gaps in performance

The final assessment to be carried out in the training needs analysis is to investigate the training needs of individual employees. Individual employees' behaviour is considered to see if performance meets desired standards. The ultimate goal in the **person analysis** is to determine who needs training. Such a decision can be made by comparing a person's current performance with a desired standard or level of performance. Which individuals will be included at this stage of the analysis will be largely determined by the needs of the organization. In some cases the consultant or training director may be asked to assess those individuals who have demonstrated poor or unsafe performance in the past. In other organizations, employees included in the person analysis may be chosen randomly.

The next step in the individual assessment is to identify the method of assessment. Common needs assessment techniques include observation, work samples, and tests.[11] From here the relationship between the desired standard for performance and the actual performance can be measured and the potential reason for performance gaps can be determined. The data gathered during this stage of the process inform the next steps in developing a training program. In some cases the person analysis may reveal that training will not be able to address the barriers to effective performance. For instance, one might discover that certain safety concerns are the result of worn equipment that is continually in a state of ill repair. In this case, the maintenance or replacement of equipment, rather than a training program, would be the next logical step. In other situations, training will be a viable option to address the problems uncovered in the needs analysis.

The type of training offered will depend on the nature of the problem. For example, if the person analysis reveals that safety concerns stem from the fact that individuals are not well versed in the operation of dangerous equipment, the training program to follow should focus on delivering knowledge about the proper operation of the machinery. Again, consider a case in which the person analysis revealed that although individuals are aware of safety regulations in the operation of equipment and are capable of complying with these protocols, they choose to ignore them. In this situation, the training would best focus on safety-related attitudes in the workplace.

Training Design and Delivery

Following the needs analysis process, an informed decision about the potential effectiveness of training as an option to address health and safety concerns can be made. If training has a role to play in the solution to a health and safety problem, several decisions must now be made. These decisions involve translating what was learned from the needs assessment into the actual training initiative. Some of the pertinent decisions include the following:

1. What are the objectives for training?
2. Will the training program be designed or purchased?
3. What is the appropriate content for the training?
4. Who will receive the training?
5. Who will deliver the training?
6. Where will the training take place?

Let's consider some of these questions as they apply to the case of occupational health and safety training.

The first pressing question involves the objectives for training. In other words, what do you hope the trainees will take away from the training program? In general the **training objectives** will involve the knowledge, skill, and behavioural changes that will be acquired through training. Objectives serve a number of important functions, including setting the groundwork for the needed training content and providing a starting point for tools to evaluate the effectiveness of the training program.

training objectives
statements regarding the knowledge, skill, and behavioural changes that trainees should acquire in the training program

Occupational Health and Safety Notebook 9.1

An Example of Training Objectives for a Health and Safety Course

The Workers' Compensation Board of British Columbia offers several WorkSafe health and safety training courses on such vital topics as hazard recognition; control, prevention, and investigation of musculoskeletal injury (MSI); and joint health and safety committees. As an example of training objectives in an occupational health and safety course, consider the objectives laid out for the course in preventing and investigating MSI. According to the WorkSafe website, the course aims to provide both employers and employees with the knowledge and skill to prevent and investigate MSI incidents. The course contains four modules: ergonomic requirements and the prevention process, risk identification and assessment, risk control and early treatment, and investigation of MSI incidents. The course objectives as listed in the course description are as follows:

Successful completion of this course will enable participants to

1. Identify key components of the ergonomics (MSI) requirements
2. Explain the seven-step musculoskeletal injury prevention (MSIP) process
3. Explain five categories of risk factors associated with MSI
4. Explain three main types of risk control of the risk factors
5. Use a checklist to identify and address risk factors
6. Determine ways to control identified risk factors
7. Apply early treatment and intervention principles
8. Investigate MSI incidents to prevent recurrence

The value of these objectives in designing the content of the training program and deciding appropriate ways to assess what the trainees learned during training is obvious. Every health and safety training program should have a set of clearly stated objectives that provide specific information about what trainees will know and be able to do upon completion of the program.

Source: BC Workers' Compensation Board WorkSafe course descriptions are available online at http://www.worksafebc.com/news_room/courses/default.asp.

RPC 9.7

RPC 9.8

A second question in the development of a training program is whether an existing training package can be purchased or an original program needs to be designed. In many cases the purchase of an existing prepackaged program is more economical and fully meets the needs of the organization. With the case of health and safety concerns, many existing training programs are readily available for purchase. For instance, institutions such as St. John Ambulance specialize in first-aid and CPR training. In fact, St. John Ambulance offers readily available generic and custom first-aid and CPR programs. In the case of an organization wanting to institute a first-aid training program for individuals involved in particular high-risk jobs, it would make sense to choose a proven, prepackaged program from a reputable provider. The time and cost of developing a first-aid course, paying a qualified trainer, and purchasing the necessary tools would be both unnecessary and prohibitive given the quality and accessibility of existing programs.

In other cases the final decision reached by an organization will be to design a custom health and safety training program from scratch, either in-house or via the services of a consultant. In what situations might an organization decide that a customized program is needed? We suggest that in cases in which the content of the program is highly specific to the organization in question, the custom design of a program may be necessary. For instance, a company wanting to offer a health and safety orientation for their new hires would need to incorporate information that is unique to their company; such a program would be difficult to purchase in a prepackaged form. Additionally, training in the safe use of particular equipment or the performance of particular tasks may require a training program that is not readily available for purchase, and as such a customized program may be the only option.

With respect to training content, it is important that the content of the training program matches the needs identified in the needs analysis and allows trainees to achieve the training objectives. Even if the training program is purchased, there is likely some flexibility in the material that will be presented. One way to ensure that the training content is appropriate is to consult subject matter experts in the area in question. For instance, in a training program on the safe handling of hazardous materials, individuals who have expertise in industrial hygiene may be consulted and asked for their input on the needed components of the training program.

Who will receive the training is also an important question at this phase of the curriculum development. In some cases, the answer will be obvious. If law mandates that all operators of a particular type of machinery must have training in the operation of that equipment, then all operators must be trained. In this situation, the job of selecting who receives training is as simple as identifying the operators. Similarly, if the training program is a health and safety orientation for all new employees, each employee will complete the program on joining the organization. In other cases, the decision of who receives training will not be as obvious. For instance, provincial and territorial legislation requires that organizations have a certain number of trained first-aid providers on site. Only a small number of employees will need to complete this training. The decision of who enters the program is one that will have to be dealt with case by case.

A related issue to who will receive training is that of how many people will be trained at the same time. The accumulated research on training in general and that pertaining to health and safety training in particular shows that smaller groups make for more effective learning environments.[12] Individuals within the training groups should also have similar jobs characterized by common risk exposure.[13] This combination of people will contribute to the maximal success of health and safety training initiatives.

Another issue to consider when designing training programs is who will deliver the training. An effective trainer is a vital aspect of a successful training program. Of course, the trainer should be both knowledgeable about the material and an effective communicator. In some cases the trainer will require certification in a particular area—for instance, the person who delivers first-aid training will need certification as an instructor.

Another approach to finding effective trainers who are both subject matter experts and effective educators is to use a **train the trainer** program. In train the trainer initiatives, a subject matter expert with the appropriate content skills is given coaching in such areas as program delivery and

train the trainer
programs designed to offer subject matter experts in various content areas skills in program delivery and communication

Occupational Health and Safety Notebook 9.2

How to Select a Good Training Provider

Once a decision that health and safety training is an appropriate intervention has been made, organizations are in the position to decide who will deliver that training program. If skilled trainers are not available in-house, the organization will turn to an external, professional trainer. What steps can the organization take to ensure it hires a good training provider?

The following are some qualities that organizations will want to ensure their training provider possesses:

- Knowledge of training models
- Experience in training
- Occupational health and safety expertise and experience
- Industry experience
- Willingness to customize the training to meet organizational needs
- Good references

Source: Broadbent, B. (2007). "Training providers: How to pick a winner." *OHS Canada.* Retrieved from http://www.ohscanada.com/Training/training.asp, February 2, 2007.

communication. An effective train the trainer program can provide organizations with the ability to use in-house individuals to deliver training programs. For example, an individual who is a member of an organization's health and safety committee may be trained to deliver the health and safety orientation for new employees.

The research literature has examined the effectiveness of subject matter experts who have undergone train the trainer programs in the delivery of occupational health and safety training. Generally, it appears that trainees respond well to subject matter experts as trainers and that such an approach to training delivery can result in improved safety performance in the workplace.[14]

RPC 9.9

The final training delivery question that we will consider in the current discussion is where the training will take place. Traditionally, this has been a question of on-the-job or off-the-job training. On-the-job training takes place while individuals are at work performing their regular job tasks. In other words, the training is incorporated while the task is being conducted. For example, on-the-job training in the safe operation of a particular tool may have subject matter experts demonstrate the safe use of the tool while a new hire observes the process. The new hire may then have the opportunity to use the tool under the guidance of the subject matter expert.

Off-the-job training is training that takes place away from the area where the work is conducted. It may be in a room on-site or in a different facility. The nature of the room will depend on the nature of the training. Some forms of training may require little more than a boardroom and PowerPoint slides. Other forms of training may require simulators or particular equipment.

More recently, a third dimension has been added to the question of where health and safety training will occur. Some health and safety training programs are now being offered via the World Wide Web. For example, courses in the

Occupational Health and Safety Notebook 9.3

Learning Theory and Training Delivery

How information is presented is a vital decision in the design of any training effort, including occupational health and safety training. The ultimate goal is that the knowledge and skills gained in the training environment are transferred to the workplace. Principles determined from extensive psychological research on learning can help create such a training environment. Two major approaches to the study of learning are the behaviourist perspective and the cognitive perspective. How might these learning theories from the behaviourist and cognitive approaches influence the design of health and safety training programs?

Behaviourist Theory

The behaviourist approach characterizes learning in terms of observable stimuli and responses, without reference to any activity that occurs inside the individual.[a] Behaviourists state that a person's behaviour is a product of the person's past experience in an environment. Certainly, this notion applies to the training context; the experience gained during training should influence later job performance.

Several behaviourist principles have been used to inform the design of training programs. A substantial concern for training designers is transfer of training. Transfer of training refers to the degree to which the knowledge, skills, and abilities gained in the training environment are then applied in the job environment. Four basic learning principles have been used extensively in an attempt to maximize transfer of training.[b] These are reviewed below.

1. *Identical elements.* According to this principle, transfer of training is maximized to the extent that the stimuli in the training environment are identical to those in the transfer environment. Therefore, the training environment should be as similar as possible to the job environment. For instance, in a safety training program on the proper use of protective equipment, the very same brand and type of safety gear that is used on the job site should also be used in the training program.
2. *General principles.* Learning theory suggests that transfer of training is improved when trainees are taught not only applicable skills, but also general rules that underlie the training content. For example, a training program on the safe operation of a piece of heavy equipment should also stress underlying principles regarding the widespread importance of safe behaviour in the workplace and the basic workings of the machinery itself.
3. *Stimulus variability.* Multiple examples of a concept should be provided for trainees. Having access to multiple examples allows trainees to see the applicability of the training content in their job environment and thus enhances transfer of training. To apply this notion to safety training, consider an emergency preparedness training program. The trainers should be sure to provide examples from several types of emergency scenarios.
4. *Conditions of practice.* Conditions of practice refers to the manner in which the trainee is exposed to the content of the training program.
   a. *Whole versus part learning* addresses whether the knowledge, skills, and abilities being covered in the training program should be introduced to trainees as the whole task or as separate task elements. Whole learning involves practising an entire duty, whereas part learning asks participants to practise pieces of a larger task separately. The general finding is that for tasks that have highly interdependent parts, whole learning is preferred. However, tasks that have largely independent elements should be trained using part learning.
   b. *Spaced versus massed practice* concerns the dispersion of practice sessions. With spaced trials, a rest period is allowed between practice sessions, whereas with massed practice the trainee practises the task continually until mastery. It is generally accepted that spaced trials are preferable. This conclusion is generally applicable in safety training as well.[c] However, massed practice may be used in a case in which errors are critical and learning from errors is important.

(continued)

Occupational Health and Safety Notebook 9.3

Learning Theory and Training Delivery (continued)

c. *Overlearning* implies that a task should be practised until it can be performed with few attentional resources (i.e., automatically). Overlearning is invaluable in health and safety–related training programs, specifically those involving safety procedures in an emergency situation, when actions must be performed under pressure and quickly.

Cognitive Learning Theories

The increasingly complex nature of many jobs requires that workers have complex cognitive skills.[d] One popular cognitive approach to learning is social learning theory, which posits that people observe others to learn. Observing others can help us learn various motor skills or styles of behaving. For instance, observing more experienced people can help a new employee learn how to properly use safety equipment at work. The people we observe during social learning are called models. The psychologist most often associated with social learning theory is Canadian Albert Bandura. Bandura proposed that four mental processes facilitate social learning:[e]

1. *Attention.* The learner must notice the behavioural models and find them interesting. For instance, new employees who are looking for models will likely look to experienced employees who attract their attention and seem willing to help.
2. *Memory.* The learner must be able to remember the information obtained by observation to use at a later time. New employees who are observing senior employees operate a particular piece of machinery must remember all the actions taken by the senior employees as they complete the task.
3. *Motor control.* Learners must be able to use the information obtained from observation to guide their own actions. With respect to safe behaviour in the workplace, new employees who have been observing others must be able to reproduce their behaviour. If a particular work task involves heavy lifting, the new employees must be capable of lifting that weight.
4. *Motivation.* The learner must have some reason to perform the modelled actions. In the case of occupational health and safety, the learner must be motivated to perform the job in a safe manner.

It is clear that the four components of Bandura's social learning theory can be useful in the training environment. The trainer assumes the role of the model. The trainer must capture the attention of the trainee and appear interesting. Thus, the trainer should be perceived as an expert in the relevant field and be credible and appealing to the trainees. The information should be presented in such a manner that the trainees store it in memory and draw on this information to guide their performance in the future (i.e., when they are back on the job). Social learning theory also stresses the importance of motivation in training, an issue we will consider extensively in Chapter 10.

References:

a. Gazzaniga, M. S., & Heatherton, T. F. (2006). *Psychological science: Mind, brain, and behavior* (2nd ed.). New York: Norton.

b. Baldwin, T. T., & Ford, J. K. (1988). "Transfer of training: A review and directions for future research." *Personnel Psychology, 41,* 63–105.

c. Colligan, M. J., & Cohen, A. (2004). "The role of training in promoting workplace safety and health." In J. Barling & M. Frone (Eds.), *Handbook of workplace safety* (pp. 223–248). Washington, DC: American Psychological Association.

d. Goldstein, I. L. (1993). *Training in organizations: Needs assessments, development and evaluation* (3rd ed.). Pacific Grove, CA: Brooks/Cole Publishing.

e. Bandura, A. (1986). *Social functions of thought and action: A social cognitive theory.* Englewood Cliffs, NJ: Prentice Hall.

Workplace Hazardous Materials Information System (WHMIS), a legislated program in the safe handling of hazardous materials, are now being offered online. For more information on this program, see Occupational Health and Safety Today 9.3. Web-based training in programs such as WHMIS may prove useful to a company that frequently has new hires who are computer savvy. However, it may not be as appealing or effective when the individuals who require training do not have access to or a high degree of comfort using computers and the Internet. Ultimately, the program delivery choice will depend on the unique needs of the organization and employees.

WHMIS

Workplace Hazardous Materials Information System; a legislated training program in the handling of potentially hazardous chemicals in the workplace that ensures Canadian workers recognize hazardous materials and are knowledgeable in emergency procedures following a chemical spill

Regardless of the chosen location for training, research on the effectiveness of various health and safety training initiatives emphasizes the importance of active approaches to learning.[15] Training efforts predominantly relying on posters or videos result in initial improvements in safety behaviour, but the results may be short lived. Alternatively, more active forms of training such as hands-on or interactive electronic techniques appear to have a stronger, more durable effect on behaviour.

Even when safety training programs have demonstrated a positive impact on safety-related actions in the workplace, continued upgrading of skills may be important if employees are to maintain the knowledge and skills they gained in training. Consider the case of employees who are designated first-aid providers in their workplaces. It is conceivable that these individuals

Occupational Health and Safety Today 9.3

Online WHMIS Courses

A quick Internet search will reveal any number of providers offering online training programs in WHMIS. Most of these websites note the speed, ease, and convenience of using Internet-based training for this often-required health and safety training program. One such provider, WHMIS-in-Minutes, provides training programs in both English and French and promotes its online course as suitable for individuals who are interested in a refresher course and for those who are learning about hazardous materials for the first time. This program features a certificate of completion and does not require the organization to pay startup fees. Rather, the fee is on a per-user basis, at a cost of about $10 per user. WHMIS-in-Minutes notes a number of well-known clients, including Human Resources and Social Development Canada, Xerox, and several provincial governments. An administrative feature enables the system to track for organizations which of their employees have completed the training program. Another basis on which the online service is promoted is the possibility of customization. Additional questions, customized to the organization's needs, can be added to the standard WHMIS program.

Source: WHMIS-in-Minutes. Retrieved from http://www.whmis.net, February 6, 2007.

could experience long periods when they are not called on to use their first-aid skills. However, in the event of an emergency, it is imperative that they correctly recall what they learned in training. Periodic refresher courses that reinforce what employees learned in their initial training program will go a long way in ensuring that first-aid providers correctly and quickly recall their treatment skills when called on to do so.[16] In fact, retraining, upgrading, and refresher courses are valuable in all areas of safety training. The more often employees are reminded of safety-related issues in the workplace, the more likely they are to properly enact safety behaviour.

Training Evaluation

training evaluation
a component of the ISD training model designed to assess the value added for individuals and organizations following the implementation of a training program

9.10

Evaluation efforts following training programs consider the extent to which the training program has added value to the organization and the individual employees. Information gathered during **training evaluation** may be useful for identifying strengths and weaknesses in the training program and thus guide further curriculum development. Evaluation results may also be used to estimate the economic value of a training program. In a safety training endeavour, an economic factor that may be evaluated is the number of accidents or injuries. If a training program designed to improve safety in the workplace actually reduces injury rates, it will save the company money in days lost and compensation claims.

What type of information should be considered in the evaluation of a health and safety training program? Kirkpatrick's hierarchical model, a frequently used training evaluation model, suggests that there are four important levels of training outcomes that provide insight into the effectiveness of a training program.[17] Kirkpatrick suggests that a training evaluation effort should ask the following four questions:

1. Did the trainees have positive *reactions* to the training?
2. Did the trainees *learn* the material covered in the training?
3. Did the trainees apply what they learned in training and realize a change in their work *behaviour*?
4. Did the organization see positive *organizational results* following training?

According to Kirkpatrick, these levels of evaluation outcomes form a hierarchy—with succeeding levels providing increasingly important information regarding the value of the training program. Training programs in which trainees report positive reactions, successfully learn the material, apply that learning to their workplace behaviour, and contribute to positive organizational outcomes (e.g., increased productivity, fewer lost-time injuries) are considered effective.

How might a training evaluator go about gathering information on these four levels of training outcomes? The HR manager or training consultant has several measurement options open to him or her. Individual reactions to the training program might be assessed using such tools as surveys, interviews, or focus groups. Questions should be designed to assess all aspects of the program—including overall reactions and attitudes toward particular aspects of the training schedule. For instance, a training evaluation questionnaire for a workplace safety orientation might ask trainees to share their perceptions of the presentation by the health and safety committee chairperson, to indicate whether they thought the safety walkabout—where the trainees tour various parts of the building to discuss the safety issues at each site—was informative, to report their degree of satisfaction with the overall curriculum, and to rate the effectiveness of the orientation facilitator. From these examples, you can see that both affective reactions and utility-based reactions can be garnered at this stage of the evaluation. Affective reactions involve whether the trainees enjoyed the program, and utility reactions incorporate the trainees' perceptions of the usefulness of the program.[18] Positive affective and utility reactions are important in training programs. If employees do not enjoy the training program or do not feel it is useful, they may be less likely to give it their full attention. As such they are unlikely to take away the important messages delivered in the program.

Efforts to measure learning must assess trainee mastery of the information presented in the training session. Evaluators are generally interested in how well the trainees recall that information and the extent to which they are able to incorporate the information into actions. For instance, in a health and safety training program designed to teach the safe operating procedures for heavy machinery, the evaluator would be interested in the trainee's ability to recall the points on the safety inspection checklist for a particular piece of equipment. There are a number of ways to assess this knowledge. An evaluation may measure a trainee's ability to recognize the material covered in training using multiple-choice tests. The mastery of skills introduced in the training program can also be assessed using longer, written test formats. To continue the example given above, a trainee may be asked to list all the steps included in the safety inspection for a particular piece of equipment. Obviously, a successful training program is one that results in considerable knowledge and skill acquisition on the part of trainees.

Behavioural outcomes following training are assessed in the workplace. On-the-job behaviour may be assessed using self-report inventories in which trainees rate their own behaviour or by having supervisors complete a report on trainees' actions when performing the task in question. Similarly, the training evaluator may observe the employees' on-the-job performance. For example, following the training program on the safe operation of heavy machinery introduced above, a supervisor may observe an employee performing a safety inspection on the piece of equipment in question and rate his or her performance. The evaluator may also be able to use objective indexes of performance to assess behavioural change. For instance, after a training program on the importance and use of safety equipment such as earplugs for loud environments, a behavioural assessment may include observing employees at work to see whether they have a high rate of compliance in using their earplugs and other safety equipment.

Organizational results following training initiatives can also be assessed. Usually, the assessment of organizational outcomes involves the analysis of organizational records. With respect to health and safety training initiatives, a number of organizational outcomes may be particularly relevant:

close call

a series of events that could have led to an accident but did not

lost-time injuries

injuries in which the injured employee misses some work time because of the injury in the days following the incident

1. *Accident, injury, and fatality rates.* Safety training programs designed to increase safe behaviour should contribute to reduced accident rates and ultimately reduced injury and death rates.
2. *Incidence of* **close calls.** Close calls or near misses occur when accidents or injuries are narrowly avoided. Effective safety training programs should reduce the number of near misses.
3. *Incidence of* **lost-time injuries.** Lost-time injuries are those in which the employee involved misses some work time because of the injury in the days following the incident. Safety training programs that are successful should see a reduction in lost-time injuries.
4. *Absenteeism.* This objective factor may be of particular importance in evaluating health-related training programs designed to reduce stress.
5. *Workers' Compensation claims and costs.* Ultimately, health and safety training programs should see decreased usage of Workers' Compensation programs, as successful training programs should decrease accident and injury rates.
6. *Employee benefit costs.* Effective safety training can contribute to reduced usage of programs such as physiotherapy and occupational therapy.
7. *Safety inspection reports.* If an organization is subject to internal or external safety inspections, improved performance on these inspections should be seen in areas that have been the subject of health and safety training.

The training evaluator will want to compare the organization's performance on factors such as those noted above after the training program is complete with its performance before training. Having both pretraining and posttraining information will allow the evaluator to reach a conclusion about any improvements in organizational outcomes that are a result of training.

However, training evaluators will want to take great care to ensure that their measures of pretraining and posttraining variables are accurate. The training evaluator must consider a number of factors when assessing organizational indexes of health and safety. We note above that accident, injury, and fatality rates are indicators of safe or unsafe behaviour in the workplace. Most discussions about occupational safety, whether in the academic literature or in workplaces themselves, focus on accidents or fatalities. As a result, the focus is often on the number of accidents, the amount of lost time, whether the accident resulted in a claim for Workers' Compensation, and occasionally the number of workplace fatalities. Concentrating on such variables is understandable given their visibility and the social and economic interest they attract.

Several factors, however, limit the reliability and utility of accident and fatality measures for organizational research and practice. First, major accidents with injuries and especially fatalities occur relatively infrequently. As such, the distribution of major accidents and fatalities is positively skewed, rather than normally distributed, thus introducing challenges into the statistical analysis of such data. Second, there are invariably distinct definitional differences as to what constitutes an occupational injury across different jurisdictions. For example, what one province or territory accepts as evidence of a back injury requiring time off work, another might refuse, which renders any comparisons of injury rates across jurisdictions limited at best. Third, there is considerable concern that organizations' databases on accidents and fatalities may misrepresent the actual prevalence of the problem.

A recent report shows that logs of lost-time injuries maintained by government agencies actually underrepresent the magnitude of these incidents.[19] This report suggests that records of initial episodes of lost-time injury may be accurately reported, but that lost time due to reinjury or the persistence of problems following return to work are underreported. The in-house record-keeping processes that organizations use may contribute to this problem.[20] Occupational Health and Safety Notebook 9.4 outlines some of the problematic record-keeping practices that lead to the underreporting of accident statistics. Because of concerns relating to the underreporting of accidents and injuries, both researchers and practitioners have increasingly turned away from the use of accident reports as a primary source of information.

To offset the statistical imbalance, researchers have begun to ask how accident reports can be improved. For example, the inclusion of close calls may provide a useful supplement to accident reports, because they occur with greater frequency than do accidents. Also, the difference between a close call

Occupational Health and Safety Notebook 9.4

Underreporting of Injury and Illness: A Question of Record Keeping?

Estimates suggest that 40 to 50 percent of work-related injuries in Canada are unreported. From a health and safety management perspective this is problematic on a number of levels, not the least of which are that it underestimates the cost of occupational injuries and illness and it may deter some organizations from engaging in preventive health and safety programs like safety training.

Several organizational practices contribute to the underreporting of occupational injury and illness:

1. *Neglect of the record-keeping process.* Some organizations undervalue the importance of record keeping by assigning the task a low priority level and employing record keepers who do not have adequate training.
2. *Lack of internal communication.* It is difficult to maintain accurate company-wide records if communication among departments is poor.
3. *Reward systems that focus on reducing lost-time injuries.* In some organizations managers and employees are given bonuses or promotion opportunities if there are no lost-time injuries. As such, there may be little motivation to report injuries that do occur.

Sources: Shannon, H., & Lowe, G. S. (2002). "How many injured workers do not file claims for workers' compensation benefits?" *American Journal of Industrial Medicine, 42,* 467–473; Thompson, A. (2007). "The consequences of underreporting workers' compensation claims." *Canadian Medical Association Journal, 76,* 343–344; and adapted from Conway, H., & Svenson, J. (1998). "Occupational injury and illness rates, 1992–1996: Why they fell." *Monthly Labor Review, 121(11),* 36–58.

and an accident may be no more than a little luck. Therefore, including close calls in incident reporting is important for a more complete picture of safety-related events.

Self-reported measures of occupational events and injuries may provide a more valid indication than compulsory reports by the organization to government agencies, as there appears to be little incentive for "workers to deliberately misreport their accidents and injury experiences to independent researchers."[21] Although there could be legitimate errors as a result of memory lapses, these would occur randomly across people and organizations and therefore would not bias the reporting of injuries or accidents in any way. A potential solution is to use multiple sources or records in identifying the "real" rates of incidents, accidents, and injuries.[22]

Occupational Health and Safety Today 9.4

Safety Training Receiving Increased Attention in Accident Prevention and Investigation

If you read recent articles about organizations aiming to reduce their accident rate or increase worker safety, or reports from accident investigations, you'll see an increased focus on safety training. For example, The Farm Safety Association of Ontario offers a series of safety training seminars free of charge to its member firms. Trainers will provide training on such topics as Health and Safety Management, Worksite Inspections, and Accident Investigation at the member firm's location. They also offer online training on things like tractor safety, dangerous gases, and safe lifting.

With respect to accident investigations, Dial Oilfield Services, an Alberta oilfield company, was recently found guilty of failing to protect the health and safety of two workers who were badly burned in an explosion because the company had not provided proper safety training. Several safety violations were detected at the scene of the accident. Michael Richardson and Jason Chamberlain, the injured workers, testified that when they joined the company their only safety training comprised receiving copies of safety and hazards manuals, which they were asked to read over by themselves; they were to check their names off a list once they had completed this task. No one in the company reviewed the material with them to ensure they understood the information.

Similarly, a contractor in Ontario was sentenced to a month of jail time and faced fines in excess of $65,000 for violations of the health and safety act related to a fall sustained by a young worker. This worker fell from a roof on his first day on the job, sustaining minor injuries. He had not been given a safety harness prior to the ascent. An investigation by the Ministry of Labour revealed that a supervisor placed a harness on the employee, asking him to tell investigators he had been wearing it when he fell. The constructor was found guilty of failing to ensure the worker was protected and failing to ensure the worker was adequately trained.

Sources: Farm Safety Association. Retrieved from http://www.farmsafety.ca/pages/about_fsa.html, February 13, 2007; Canadian Press, "Alberta oilfield company guilty for not protecting workers caught in explosion" (January 19, 2007). Retrieved from http://www.ohscanada.com/issues/, January 26, 2007; Ontario Government Newswire, "Seeley's Bay contractor jailed 30 days for health and safety violation." Retrieved from http://ogov.newswire.ca/ontario/GPOE/2006/10/25/c4613.html?lmatch=&lang=_e.html, January 31, 2007.

Common Safety Training Initiatives

The health and safety training needs of any particular organization will be largely determined by factors unique to that company—its size and the industry in question being two factors that largely contribute to safety training needs. However, several common safety training initiatives are applicable to organizations of all sizes and sectors. We review three of these, safety orientations, first-aid training, and WHMIS, next.

RPC 9.11

RPC 9.12

Safety Orientation

Organizations with successful safety programs and safety records frequently begin to emphasize health and safety via an orientation program from the time employees join the organization. Integrating health and safety into the employee orientation program ensures that all employees are provided with a base level of health and safety training and reinforces the development of a safety climate in the workplace.

Although the details will vary with the needs of specific workplaces, a general orientation to health and safety should include a review and introduction to

- fire and emergency safety procedures
- accident policies (e.g., reporting, procedures for obtaining first aid)
- hazards unique to the workplace (e.g., material hazards, chemical hazards, physical hazards)
- protective personal equipment (e.g., how to obtain, how to use)
- WHMIS training
- the role of the joint health and safety committee
- the roles and responsibilities of individual employees
- job-specific safety procedures (e.g., proper lifting technique, decontamination, lockout procedures)
- housekeeping and safety awareness

First Aid

Many Canadian employers are required under occupational health and safety acts to provide first-aid training to employees. The number of employees requiring certification in first aid in any given organization depends on several factors. Provincial or territorial health and safety legislation determines first-aid requirements based on such factors as the number of workers per shift, the distance away from fixed medical services, and the hazard level of the workplace. Larger, isolated, higher-hazard worksites require more trained first-aid providers. The exact number of first-aid certificates and the level of certification required differ among the provinces and territories. For example, in Prince Edward Island work shifts of 5 to 15 people must have an attendant with an emergency first-aid certificate, and shifts of 16 to 100 must have an attendant with certification in standard first aid. In Alberta, for a low-hazard worksite with 2 to 9 workers that is close to hospital services there is no requirement for a first-aid attendant. However, if the worksite is isolated, an attendant with standard first aid is required.

Organizations such as St. John Ambulance provide first-aid training programs that help employers meet or exceed the requirements set forth in provincial and territorial occupational health and safety acts. In fact, St. John Ambulance provides full services in the provision and management of workplace first-aid training programs. For instance, via its key account program, St. John Ambulance tracks the training and certificates of employees within an organization and notifies the organization when recertification is required.

WHMIS Training

The Workplace Hazardous Materials Information System (WHMIS) has been discussed throughout this book. It is the standard for the communication of information about hazards in Canada. Under WHMIS, hazardous or controlled products are labelled in a standardized manner and information regarding the safe handling of these products is provided via material safety data sheets and worker training programs. The federal, provincial, and territorial health and safety jurisdictions incorporate WHMIS. Employers are required to properly store and dispose of hazardous materials and ensure that workers receive training in handling and using controlled products. Occupational Health and Safety Today 9.3 considers Web-based WHMIS training.

Summary

Even though Canadian employees have the right to be informed about the hazards they may encounter in the workplace and occupational health and safety acts mandate the provision of health and safety training, many Canadians report that they have never received any safety training at work. Recent legislation means that employers who fail to comply in the provision of a safe workplace may face charges of criminal negligence.

Occupational health and safety training can be described under a general training model. The ISD model, applied to the issue of health and safety, emphasizes the importance of a complete needs analysis before training is designed and offered. Needs analysis includes a consideration of the organization, the job, and the person. One very important issue in health and safety training is ensuring that the organization is supportive of the initiative. If a company is not supportive of health and safety issues in general, the training effort is likely to encounter roadblocks.

Several factors must be considered in the design and delivery of occupational health and safety training, including the content of the training, who will receive training, and who will act as the trainer. Organizations must be careful that the training programs they offer comply with the standards set out in their jurisdictional occupational health and safety act.

Health and safety training efforts should be subject to evaluations that consider whether the trainees had positive reactions to the training and learned the material covered in the program. Evaluation should also consider the extent to which employee behaviour and organizational outcomes are influenced by the training. Health and safety training programs should be evaluated for their impact on safety-related outcomes in the workplace, such as accident, injury, and fatality rates and the incidence of close calls. Safety training programs designed to increase safe behaviour should reduce accident rates and ultimately reduce injury and death rates, as well as reducing the number of near misses and lost-time injuries.

Key Terms

close call 256
instructional systems design (ISD) model of training 243
job/task analysis 246
lost-time injuries 256
needs analysis 243
organizational analysis 244
person analysis 246
safety climate 245
train the trainer 249
training evaluation 254
training objectives 247
WHMIS 253

Weblinks

CBC Indepth, "Workplace Safety"

http://www.cbc.ca/news/background/workplace-safety (p. 240)

Institute for Work and Health

http://www.iwh.on.ca (p. 240)

Young Workers Memorial Life Quilt

http://www.youngworkerquilt.ca (p. 241)

Canadian Centre for Occupational Health and Safety, "Young Workers Zone"

http://www.ccohs.ca/youngworkers/ (p. 241)

Canadian Centre for Occupational Health and Safety

http://www.ccohs.ca (p. 242)

Canada's National Occupational Health and Safety Web Site

http://www.canoshweb.org (p. 242)

WorkSafeBC

http://www.worksafebc.com (p. 248)

St. John Ambulance

http://www.sja.ca (p. 248)

OHS Canada

http://www.ohscanada.com (p. 250)

WHMIS-in-Minutes

http://whmis.net (p. 253)

Farm Safety Association

http://www.farmsafety.ca (p. 258)

RPC Icons

RPC 9.1 Ensures legislated training obligations are met within the organization.

- training requirements due to employment legislation
- common and statutory law (e.g., employment standard: labour relations
- roles of the federal and provincial governments in providing training and development
- roles of municipal governments, unions, and professional associations in training and development

RPC 9.2 Ensures due diligence and strict liability requirements are met, e.g. records are kept and formal procedures established.

- relevant legislation and common law
- company policies and procedures
- industry best practices
- program and policy development
- training and development techniques
- risk analysis
- common and statutory law (e.g., employment standard: labour relations)
- Worker Protection (including health and safety and Workers' Compensation)
- theories and practices for protection of individuals and groups

Task & Knowledge Requirements

- Occupational health and safety legislation (e.g., Occupational Health and Safety Act of Ontario, Workplace Safety & Insurance Act—Bill 99, Workplace Hazardous Materials Information System, Transportation of Dangerous Goods legislation, environmental legislation, smoking in the workplace legislation, civil rights legislation)
- management techniques for OH&S programs

RPC 9.3 Responds to any refusals to perform work believed to be unsafe.

- relevant Occupational Health and Safety legislation
- procedure for dealing with work refusals
- policy and program development
- conflict resolution procedures
- emergency procedures

- government inspection agencies such as the Ministry of Labour
- common and statutory law (e.g., employment standard: labour relations
- Worker Protection (including health and safety and Workers' Compensation)
- communication theories and techniques
- concepts and processes of politics and conflict
- hazard identification and control
- Occupational health and safety legislation (e.g., Occupational Health and Safety Act of Ontario, Workplace Safety & Insurance Act—Bill 99, Workplace Hazardous Materials Information System, Transportation of Dangerous Goods legislation, environmental legislation, smoking in the workplace legislation, civil rights legislation)

RPC 9.4 Conducts training need assessments by identifying individual and corporate learning requirements.

- needs analysis methods and techniques
- organizational development principles
- instructional design
- training and development needs analysis techniques (i.e., skill assessment strategies and levels of training needs analysis)

RPC 9.5 Ensures that mechanisms are in place for responding to crises in the workplace, including critical incident stress management.

- oral and written communication
- training and development techniques
- industry best practices
- the workplace environment including the availability of emergency equipment
- policy and program development and evaluation
- intervention strategies
- relevant legislation (e.g., fire code, Workers' Compensation)
- investigation techniques
- stress management techniques
- types of employee assistance programs
- hazard identification and control
- accident investigation procedures
- emergency preparedness procedures
- management techniques for OH&S Programs
- conceptual definition and implications of occupational stressors (e.g., potential stressors, methods of identifying potential stressors and strain outcomes, response to organizational stressors, and management of employee strain outcomes)
- Occupational health and safety legislation (e.g., Occupational Health and Safety Act of Ontario, Workplace Safety & Insurance Act—Bill 99, Workplace Hazardous Materials Information System, Transportation of Dangerous Goods legislation, environmental legislation, smoking in the workplace legislation, civil rights legislation)

RPC 9.6 Analyses risk to the health and safety of employees and determines appropriate preventative measures, including training, provision of required safety equipment, and administrative practices.

- relevant legislation
- nature of the business and physical work environment
- hazard recognition
- workplace inspection techniques
- safety programs, equipment, and emergency procedures
- ergonomics
- functions of the JHSC
- training and development/presentation techniques
- industry best practices
- relevant technical terminology
- the collective agreement
- services and equipment available in the community
- Worker Protection (including health and safety and Workers' Compensation)
- training and development program design and administration

Task & Knowledge Requirements

- Occupational health and safety legislation (e.g., Occupational Health and Safety Act of Ontario, Workplace Safety & Insurance Act—Bill 99, Workplace Hazardous Materials Information System, Transportation of Dangerous Goods legislation, environmental legislation, smoking in the workplace legislation, civil rights legislation)
- hazard identification and control
- emergency preparedness procedures
- management techniques for OH&S Programs
- types of employee assistance and wellness programs

RPC 9.7 Links training to development programs, organizational goals, objectives, strategies, culture and other HR activities.

- organizational development principles
- instructional design
- techniques to analyse and interpret training results
- stakeholders in training & development
- the identification, assessment, development, implementation, maintenance, and monitoring processes of effective systems of managing HR information
- the measurement, analysis, and conditioning of the workforce to achieve organizational objectives

RPC 9.8 Recommends the most appropriate way to meet identified learning needs, (e.g., courses, secondments, and on-the-job activities).

- needs analysis methods and techniques
- organizational development principles
- instructional design
- training and development program design and administration
- methods of training and development (games and simulations, case method, lecturing, on-the-job training, distance learning, role-play, video-conferencing, group discussion)
- domains and levels of learning
- effective learning objectives
- training programs delivery techniques

RPC 9.9 Establishes effective programs for accident prevention, incident investigation, inspections, fire and emergency response, and required training.

- relevant legislation
- workplace inspection and accident investigation techniques
- nature of the business and physical work environment
- potential risks and hazards in the workplace
- emergency response planning
- community emergency response services
- training and development
- industry best practices
- Worker Protection (including health and safety and Workers' Compensation)
- training and development program design and administration
- hazard identification and control
- accident investigation procedures
- emergency preparedness procedures
- management techniques for OH&S Programs

RPC 9.10 Ensures participant and organizational feedback is documented and evaluated.

- evaluation techniques
- interpretation of results

TASK & KNOWLEDGE REQUIREMENTS

- survey and basic statistical techniques
- procedures for information collection, manipulation, and analysis
- research methods and designs (including measurement of HR)

- validity and reliability (conceptual definitions and assessment techniques)
- measurement tools and their limitations
- statistical analyses and evaluation
- importance, criteria, and techniques of program evaluation
- evaluation issues (including behaviourally anchored rating scales and staffing tables)

RPC 9.11 Implements and evaluates practices in the areas of health, safety, security, and Workers' Compensation.

- investigative techniques
- hazard recognition
- disaster recovery techniques
- relevant legislation
- resource information
- common health and safety practices
- company policies and procedures
- Worker Protection (including health and safety and Workers' Compensation)
- theories and practices for protection of individuals and groups
- Occupational health and safety legislation (e.g., Occupational Health and Safety Act of Ontario, Workplace Safety & Insurance Act—Bill 99, Workplace Hazardous Materials Information System, Transportation of Dangerous Goods legislation, environmental legislation, smoking in the workplace legislation, civil rights legislation)
- hazard identification and control
- management techniques for OH&S Programs

RPC 9.12 Provides information to employees and managers on available programs.

- elements of EAP program
- promotional and marketing tools and techniques
- communication tools and techniques
- training and development techniques
- management techniques for OH&S Programs
- types of employee assistance and wellness programs
- trends in occupational health and safety

Task & Knowledge Requirements

- importance, criteria, and techniques of program evaluation

Discussion Questions

1. Canadian statistics suggest that many Canadians are not receiving appropriate safety training in the workplace. What are some of the reasons organizational managers might give for not providing safety training for their employees? Imagine that you are a health and safety consultant trying to convince top management of a negligent organization to provide a health and safety orientation to new employees. What are some arguments you might use to convince the organization to support the training program?
2. Why is organizational support for a health and safety training initiative so important for the success of the training program?
3. What are some important organizational outcomes that can be used to evaluate the value that a training program has added to an organization?
4. What are some of the advantages and disadvantages associated with the use of Web-based health and safety training programs for individual employees? for organizations?

Using the Internet

1. The provincial and territorial governments have their own health and safety legislation. Each one refers to the importance and role of health and safety training. Using the Internet, look up the health and safety legislation in your province or territory. Note the ways in which training can help organizations and employees adhere to the law.
2. Using various Web resources, find out more about young worker safety. Along with your classmates, brainstorm ways to build health and safety knowledge among young Canadians entering the workforce. How might we educate parents and employers about the health and safety risks associated with young workers?
3. Visit the websites of some large organizations in various industries, and look for information about their health and safety policies. What portion of the sites you visited contained information about health and safety training? Did the attention given to training or the type of training described vary by industry or organizational size?
4. Search your school's website to investigate the health and safety training programs offered in your institution.

Exercises

1. Young workers are at considerable risk for accidents and injury in the workplace. Perform a person analysis by interviewing a young person who has recently entered the workforce. Based on what you have learned about occupational health and safety in this course, try to get an idea of that individual's awareness of health and safety in the workplace and the extent to which he or she is worried about his or her own safety at work. If you are unable to interview a new worker, have a classmate think back to his or her very first job and try to recall his or her health and safety–related attitudes upon entering the workforce. You will want to find out some information about the tasks this person performed at work and identify some of the potential hazards that were associated with the job.
2. Think back to various jobs that you have held—what types of health and safety training did you receive? Were the training programs effective? Compare your experiences with those of your classmates.
3. To find out more about health and safety training, contact a human resource professional and ask about health and safety training programs in his or her organization. You might use some of the following questions to guide your discussion.

    a. Does your organization have a health and safety orientation program? If so, what types of information does it cover?
    b. How many trained first-aid providers are required per shift in your organization?
    c. What are some of the safety hazards and concerns employees in your organization encounter? Do you thinking that training is a useful option to help employees manage their exposure to these risks? Why or why not?
    d. Under what conditions does your organization rely on purchased, preexisting health and safety programs? When might the company opt for custom-designed health and safety training programs? What factors influence this decision?
    e. What is the general attitude toward occupational health and safety training among employees in your organization? among management?

4. Bill C-45, the "Westray Bill," went into effect March 31, 2004. Research this legislation. How many charges could you find? How many convictions? What impact do you think this legislation will have on Canadian employees' access to health and safety training? Do you think it will influence Canadian employers' attitudes about health and safety training? Debate these issues with your classmates.

Case 1

The New HR Manager at A1 Manufacturing

Sabine is the new HR manager at A1 Manufacturing. When she began her new position, she quickly realized that A1 did not pay much attention to issues of occupational health and safety. In fact, she determined that this company was in violation of a number of legislated health and safety requirements. She approached members of upper management with her concerns. At first they seemed unruffled by her warnings about health and safety violations throughout the company. Only when she reminded the upper management that the organization could face fines and some executive-level individuals could face criminal charges if there was a safety-related incident did they sit up and listen. Sabine was given the job of fixing the problem.

She has determined that the organization needs to provide more health and safety training programs. She has contacted you, a training consultant, to help her design and implement new programs. What steps do you take in helping Sabine determine her training needs and implement training programs? Is there anything about the organization or Sabine's conclusion that training is the answer that concerns you? What are some potential obstacles to a potential training effort?

Case 2

A Young Worker's Quandary

Eighteen-year-old Gurjit has just started his very first job, working at a lumber yard. On his first day, Gurjit was given a hardhat and told he should purchase steel-toed boots. A more senior employee gave him some basic instruction about how to operate the forklift and told him to be careful. After his first shift, Gurjit has a feeling he can't shake. His new job feels dangerous, yet the company managers and his fellow employees do not appear particularly concerned about training him on safe work procedures. He doesn't want to let down the boss, who has given him his first job, by complaining. He doesn't want to disappoint his family, who are proud that he is working, by quitting—and besides, he needs the money. What options does Gurjit have? Whom can he contact about his health and safety concerns?

Endnotes

1. Smith, P., & Mustard, C. (2007, March). *How many Canadian employees receive safety training during their first year of a new job?* Plenary talk to be given at the Institute for Work and Health, Toronto. Abstract retrieved from http://www.iwh.on.ca/about/plen_030607.php, February 13, 2007.

2. Smith, P., & Mustard, C. (2007, March). *How many Canadian employees receive safety training during their first year of a new job?* Plenary talk to be given at the Institute for Work and Health, Toronto. Abstract retrieved from http://www.iwh.on.ca/about/plen_030607.php, February 13, 2007.
3. Colligan, M. J., & Cohen, A. (2004). The role of training in promoting workplace safety and health. In J. Barling & M. Frone (Eds.), *Handbook of workplace safety* (pp. 223–248). Washington, DC: American Psychological Association.
4. Saks, A. M., & Haccoun, R. R. (2004). *Managing performance through training and development* (3rd ed.). Toronto: Nelson Canada.
5. Goldstein, I. L. (1993). *Training in organizations: Needs assessments, development and evaluation* (3rd ed.). Pacific Grove, CA: Brooks/Cole Publishing; and Saks, A. M., & Haccoun, R. R. (2004). *Managing performance through training and development* (3rd ed.). Toronto: Nelson Canada.
6. Saks, A. M., & Haccoun, R. R. (2004). *Managing performance through training and development* (3rd ed.). Toronto: Nelson Canada.
7. Goldstein, I. L. (1993). *Training in organizations: Needs assessments, development and evaluation* (3rd ed.). Pacific Grove, CA: Brooks/Cole Publishing; and Saks, A. M., & Haccoun, R. R. (2004). *Managing performance through training and development* (3rd ed.). Toronto: Nelson Canada.
8. Colligan, M. J., & Cohen, A. (2004). The role of training in promoting workplace safety and health. In J. Barling & M. Frone (Eds.), *Handbook of workplace safety* (pp. 223–248). Washington, DC: American Psychological Association.
9. Cole, B. L., & Brown, M. P. (1996). Action on worksite health and safety problems: A follow-up survey of workers participating in a hazardous waste worker training program. *American Journal of Industrial Medicine, 30,* 730–743.
10. Zohar, D. (1980). Safety climate in industrial organizations: Theoretical and applied implications. *Journal of Applied Psychology, 65,* 96–102; and Zohar, D. (2002). The effects of leadership dimensions, safety climate, and assigned priorities on minor injuries in work groups. *Journal of Organizational Behavior, 23,* 75–92.
11. Goldstein, I. L. (1993). *Training in organizations: Needs assessments, development and evaluation* (3rd ed.). Pacific Grove, CA: Brooks/Cole Publishing.
12. Colligan, M. J., & Cohen, A. (2004). The role of training in promoting workplace safety and health. In J. Barling & M. Frone (Eds.), *Handbook of workplace safety* (pp. 223–248). Washington, DC: American Psychological Association; and Saarela, K. L. (1990). An intervention program utilizing small groups: A comparative study. *Journal of Safety Research, 21,* 149–156.
13. Colligan, M. J., & Cohen, A. (2004). The role of training in promoting workplace safety and health. In J. Barling & M. Frone (Eds.), *Handbook of workplace safety* (pp. 223–248). Washington, DC: American Psychological Association.
14. Colligan, M. J., & Cohen, A. (2004). The role of training in promoting workplace safety and health. In J. Barling & M. Frone (Eds.), *Handbook of workplace safety* (pp. 223–248). Washington, DC: American Psychological Association.
15. Colligan, M. J., & Cohen, A. (2004). The role of training in promoting workplace safety and health. In J. Barling & M. Frone (Eds.), *Handbook of workplace safety* (pp. 223–248). Washington, DC: American Psychological Association.
16. Arnold, D. (2003). A matter of life and death. *Occupational Health, 55,* 21–23.
17. Kirkpatrick, D. L. (1976). Evaluation of training. In R. L. Craig (Ed.), *Training and development handbook: A guide to human resource development* (2nd ed.). New York: McGraw-Hill; and Saks, A. M., & Haccoun, R. R. (2004). *Managing performance through training and development* (3rd ed.). Toronto: Nelson Canada.
18. Saks, A. M., & Haccoun, R. R. (2004). *Managing performance through training and development* (3rd ed.). Toronto: Nelson Canada.

19. Evanoff, B., Abedin, S., Grayson, D., Dale, A. M., Wolfe, L., & Bohr, P. (2002). Is disability under-reported following work injury? *Journal of Occupational Rehabilitation, 12,* 139–150.
20. Conway, H., & Svenson, J. (1998). Occupational injury and illness rates, 1992–1996: Why they fell. *Monthly Labor Review, 121*(11), 36–58.
21. Grunberg, L., Moore, S., & Greenberg, E. (1996). The relationship of employee ownership and participation to workplace safety. *Economic and Industrial Democracy, 17,* 221–241.
22. Conway, H., & Svenson, J. (1998). Occupational injury and illness rates, 1992–1996: Why they fell. *Monthly Labor Review, 121*(11), 36–58.

Chapter 10

Motivating Safety Behaviour at Work

Chapter Learning Objectives

After reading this chapter, you should be able to:

- discuss the importance of safety behaviour in the workplace
- identify the categories of safety behaviour
- explain the importance of individual motivation in safety behaviour
- describe behaviour modification approaches to motivating safety
- recognize the importance of goal setting and feedback in safety behaviour in the workplace
- evaluate the role of organizational support for safety in contributing to safety behaviour
- discuss the role of the safety climate in the performance of safety behaviours
- understand the role that safety leadership plays in creating a safe work environment
- outline how to implement an effective occupational health and safety program

Ontario Power Generation

Ontario Power Generation (OPG) is an Ontario-based corporation that both generates and sells electricity. Aiming to be the premier producer of electricity in North America, OPG is working toward this goal by focusing on safety and environmental sustainability. Its efforts have been acknowledged. In 2005, OPG was inaugural winner of the Electrical and Utilities Safety Association (E&USA) Gold Award. This award recognized OPG's effective safety management programs and positive company-wide safety culture.

This corporation has several systems in place to support its focus on safety behaviour at work. With the slogan "Zero injuries: Believe it. Achieve it," OPG has a multifaceted safety management system that includes organizational resources, organizational culture, and the structure of work. A visit to the OPG website illustrates the focus on continuous improvement to achieve the goal of zero injuries. OPG also recognizes the risks to young workers and has made an explicit commitment to young worker safety.

The OPG employee health and safety policy is available to download and is an excellent example of corporate responsibility for safety. OPG believes that "healthy employees working safely in an injury-free and healthy workplace is good business." The policy notes how continual improvement will contribute to the physical, psychological, and social health of its employees. Importantly, the safety policy clearly lays out the safety-related responsibilities of employees and management. The policy outlines that employees are accountable for taking positive steps to be healthy and working safely. They are also responsible for identifying and communicating workplace hazards. Similarly, management is accountable for such things as "ensuring the work environment is designed to protect the health and safety of workers" and "providing employees with the information, training, tools, procedures and support required to do their job safely and without harming other [workers'] health."

This policy is a good example of corporate responsibility in the area of health and safety. It illustrates the importance of employees' involvement in their own safety at work and the vital role of organizational support for health and safety initiatives. The policy also states that health and safety performance will be assessed and recognized in the workplace. The OPG policy statement highlights several topics that we will cover in this chapter—most notably safety behaviour and the roles of individual and organizational responsibility in achieving a safe workplace.

Source: Ontario Power Generation, "Safety at OPG." Retrieved from http://www.opg.com/safety/safety.asp, February 13, 2007.

In the previous chapter we considered the importance of health and safety training in the workplace. In this chapter we consider the equally important issues of (1) how to ensure employees utilize the knowledge and skills gained during training and consistently perform their work duties in a safe manner, and (2) the role of the organization in supporting employee safety efforts. Because of their focus on performing in a safe manner, the issues we consider in this chapter concentrate on preventing accidents and injuries at work rather than simply responding to workplace accidents.

Several psychological variables provide the basis for a discussion of accident and injury prevention. Psychological research in the area of motivation provides a useful starting point for considering how to motivate the safe performance of work tasks. Other psychological factors, including an assessment of organizational safety culture and safety leadership, are useful in establishing the value that an organization places on safety. Before we turn our attention to these psychological variables, we first consider the issue of safety behaviour to illustrate the value of behaviour-based efforts in accident and injury prevention in the workplace.

Safety Behaviour

There are several ways of categorizing health and safety programs. One categorization system breaks these programs into engineering interventions, administrative interventions, and behavioural interventions.[1] *Engineering interventions* typically focus on changing the physical environment to reduce exposure to hazards either by providing personal protective equipment or redesigning the physical workplace. *Administrative interventions* are those that modify procedures and exposure in the work environment. Techniques such as job rotation, the scheduling of work breaks, the use of safety officers, and the use of standard operating procedures all count as administrative interventions. Finally, *behavioural interventions* focus on changing employee attitudes, knowledge, or behaviour about occupational health and safety. Information campaigns, risk awareness, skills training, or the implementation of behaviour-modification techniques are all behavioural interventions. Each of the three types of intervention is at least somewhat successful in improving health and safety at work. A recent review of the empirical research on comprehensive occupational health and safety management systems—those encompassing multiple categories of interventions—reports mostly favourable results for these programs on such outcomes as safety climate, injury rates, and economic factors like insurance rates.[2] However, the authors of that review warn that the number of available studies is small and that many that do exist have methodological limitations such as small samples and lack of comparison groups.

All things being equal, it is preferable to remove or eliminate the hazard via an engineering solution than it is to rely on other types of health and safety programming. However, such engineering controls are not always possible.[3] Therefore, much psychological research in the area of occupational safety has focused on behavioural interventions, in particular those designed

safety behaviours behaviours leading to safe performance of a particular job

to increase safety-related behaviours. There is a relationship between **safety behaviours** and injury rates.[4] Reviews of the research illustrate that targeting employee behaviour is an effective injury prevention strategy.[5] Generally, as behaviourally based safety programs are introduced, the number of safety-related events, including accidents and injuries, is decreased.

At least eight general categories of behaviour contribute to safe working performance:[6]

1. Proper use of hazard control systems in the workplace
2. Development of safe work habits
3. Increased awareness and recognition of workplace hazards
4. Acceptance and use of personal protective equipment
5. Maintenance of housekeeping and maintenance standards
6. Maintenance of accepted hygiene practices
7. Proper responses to emergency situations
8. Self-monitoring and recognition of symptoms of hazardous exposure

Health and safety programs have been largely targeted toward encouraging one or more of these general classes of behaviour. Some of these categories will be familiar to you as the targets of the health and safety training efforts that we described in Chapter 9. For example, training programs might teach proper lifting techniques (i.e., develop safe work habits), and Workplace Hazardous Materials Information System (WHMIS) training is designed to enhance the worker's ability to recognize chemical hazards in the workplace. However, the equation for promoting safety in the workplace goes beyond ability-based training.

Generally, for individuals to work safely at least three conditions are necessary. First, workers must have the ability to work safely—that is, workers must have the knowledge, skills, and abilities necessary to perform their jobs in a safe manner. This requirement is generally addressed via the provision of

Occupational Health and Safety Notebook 10.1

Elements of a Behaviour-based Safety Program

The content of a behaviour-based safety initiative will vary depending on the context in which it is offered (e.g., organization, type of job), but several basic elements are common across behaviour-based safety programs:

1. Identifying observable behaviours that have an effect on safety-related outcomes
2. Outlining precise measurement of the identified behaviours
3. Providing feedback on how to perform the behaviour more safely
4. Highlighting the consequences of the behaviour to motivate employees
5. Rewarding safe performance of the targeted behaviour

Sources: Adapted from Geller, E. S. (2001). "Behavior-based safety in industry: Realizing the large-scale potential of psychology to promote human welfare." *Applied and Preventive Psychology, 10,* 87–105; and adapted from Sulzer-Azaroff, B., & Austin, J. (2000, July). "Does BBS work? Behavior-based safety & injury reduction: A survey of the evidence." *Professional Safety,* 19–24.

occupational health and safety training. Second, workers must be motivated to work safely—that is, workers must intend to use their knowledge and skills to enhance safe working performance. Finally, workers must have the opportunity to work safely—that is, the environment or organization must support and encourage safe work.

These three factors combine in a multiplicative rather than an additive fashion (see Figure 10.1). Thus,

Safety performance = Ability × Motivation × Opportunity

An important implication of this multiplicative equation is that the model of safety performance is noncompensatory. Having a high level of motivation and numerous opportunities does not compensate for a lack of ability. Similarly, a high level of ability and motivation cannot make up for a work environment that does not provide the opportunity and support for safe working. Safety performance relies on ability, motivation, and opportunity. If any one of these components is missing, safety performance in the workplace will not be realized. The question for health and safety programs is, How do we use this model to increase safe work behaviours?

The basic premise of the multiplicative model of safety performance is that safety can be enhanced by increasing an employee's ability, motivation, and opportunity to work safely. Having said this, it is important to note that all three components of the model must be implemented for safety performance to be enhanced. For example, training (i.e., increasing ability) alone is insufficient to change safety behaviours over the long term.[7] However, safety training coupled with motivational programs appears to be an effective combination in changing safety behaviours. Given the great deal of attention paid to increasing employees' ability to perform safety behaviours in Chapter 9, this chapter focuses on issues of motivation and opportunity. We will consider these facets of safety performance in turn.

FIGURE 10.1

Ability, Motivation, Opportunity

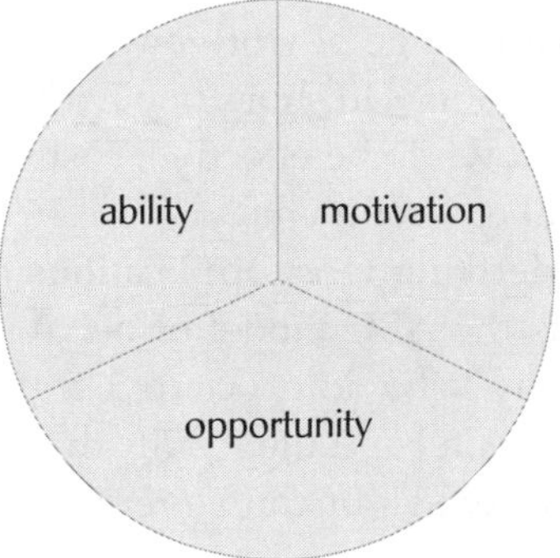

Safety performance relies on ability, motivation, and opportunity. This figure presents safety behaviour as a full circle. You can see that if any one of these important components is missing the full circle of safety behaviour is not achieved and thus safety performance in the workplace will not be realized.

Motivating Safety Behaviour

motivation
the process that initiates, directs, and sustains behaviour

The word *motivation* comes from the Latin *movere,* "to move." Generally, **motivation** is considered the process that initiates, directs, and sustains behaviour.[8] Some psychological researchers consider the motivation process as it applies to very basic biological functions such as eating and sleeping. Others focus their attention on motivation as it applies to goal-directed behaviour. In this section we will consider the role of motivation in safety behaviour at work. Our analysis will focus on two major theoretical explanations of motivation: reinforcement theory (or behaviour modification) and goal-setting theory.

Reinforcement Theory

Reinforcement theory focuses on the power of external rewards and punishments in the motivation of behaviour. Reinforcement theory, forwarded by learning theorists who adhere to the school of psychology called behaviourism, states that the likelihood of an action being performed in the future is determined by its current consequences. Generally, the chances of a behaviour being performed again increase when a current performance of that behaviour is followed by reinforcement (i.e., a reward) and decrease when it is followed by punishment. Rewards can be things such as a prize, money, or praise. Reinforcement theory has been used in organizations in the form of incentive systems. Employees are promised a reward if they meet some behavioural expectation—for example improved sales, increased productivity, or, of particular importance for the current discussion, improved safety behaviour. The application of reinforcement theory in this way is sometimes called behaviour modification.

The use of behaviour modification principles to increase safety behaviours in the workplace has been largely successful.[9] Ample evidence suggests that behavioural programs are effective in promoting safe working behaviours and are associated with substantial reductions in accident rates. For example, a survey of behavioural safety studies found that more than 95 percent of studies that reported incidence rates of accidents and injuries saw a reduction in injury rates as a result of applying behavioural principles to safety in the workplace.[10]

Moreover, behavioural interventions appear to be effective in promoting safety behaviours in a wide range of work environments including mining,[11] bus driving,[12] and construction.[13] In short, behavioural approaches to occupational safety have been shown to be effective, cost efficient, and adaptable to a wide range of industrial environments.

The basic model underlying most applications of behavioural programming in the workplace is the ABC model of behaviour.[14] Simply stated, the ABC model holds that any behaviour occurs because of events that trigger the behaviour (the antecedents) and the results that follow the behaviour (the consequences). Thus, any behaviour can be represented as

Antecedent → Behaviour → Consequence

To change a specific behaviour, we have to change either the antecedent or the consequence of the behaviour. Most applications of behavioural programming focus on changing the consequences of behaviour. If we want to understand why workers perform unsafe acts or fail to engage in safe practices, a good place to begin is by considering the consequences of both safe and unsafe behaviours.[15] Such consequences can be characterized along three dimensions: consequences can be positive or negative, immediate or delayed, and contingent or noncontingent. Generally, behaviour that is followed by immediate, positive, and contingent consequences is more likely to occur again. Conversely, consequences that are delayed, negative, or noncontingent have either a minimal or an adverse effect on safety behaviour.

Even a brief consideration of most safety behaviours suggests that the consequences of safe behaviour are typically delayed, negative, or noncontingent. It is rare for coworkers to praise or even recognize an individual for proper lifting techniques or for wearing safety goggles. Indeed the most likely consequence of engaging in such practices is the lack of notice from either supervisors or coworkers. Some safe actions such as mopping up spills or putting on safety goggles require extra time, thereby slowing down the work. This may be a negative consequence, especially if working slower is associated with disciplinary warnings. Some forms of personal protective equipment may also be uncomfortable, again a negative consequence. Even when there are positive consequences associated with behaviour, these consequences are often delayed or noncontingent. For example, a worker safety award may be given to an individual based on behaviours that occurred a year or more ago, irrespective of what behaviours the worker engaged in that day.

In contrast, there are often positive, immediate, and contingent rewards associated with unsafe behaviours. For example, the result of not wearing protective equipment may be increased comfort and speed of work. Negative consequences such as disciplinary warnings or injuries are typically rare and often delayed. Individuals may go months and even years not wearing safety goggles and never experience an injury as the result. Even this simplistic consideration suggests that wearing the protective clothing is unlikely based on the consequences associated with not wearing the clothing.

Given these observations, the goal of behavioural safety programs is to change the consequences associated with specific behaviours. Specifically, behavioural programs attempt to institute positive, immediate, and contingent consequences for safe working procedures. By far the most popular form of consequence is simple feedback; individuals are typically observed as they perform their job and given immediate feedback on the safety of their work practices. Second in popularity is the use of incentive-based programs in which employees are offered incentives such as free lunches or lottery tickets for their safe behaviour. Generally, the organizational behaviour-modification literature suggests that feedback alone, without the use of material rewards and incentives, is an effective means of behavioural change. For example, one experimental study in an industrial setting illustrated that increased feedback from supervisors regarding safety incidents and the use of personal protective equipment increased hearing protection use, reduced injury, and improved perceptions of safety climate.[16]

Occupational Health and Safety Notebook 10.2

A Risky Side of Behaviour-based Safety Programs?

Behaviour-based safety programs appear successful in reducing workplace incidents. However, some stakeholders are wary of this approach, even questioning whether it revives the notion of "accident proneness" as an explanation for why some workers get injured. Some workers' groups note the downsides of safety programs that focus exclusively on behavioural interventions.

Some point out that the use of safety incentives can be intimidating for employees. No one wants to be the person who costs coworkers a reward for achieving a reduction in injury rates. As such, some workers feel peer pressure not to report an actual injury and may even rely on their leave days rather than file a Workers' Compensation claim.

Other workers fear discipline if they are injured; thus, an employee who sustains an injury may fear reprisal from the organization and decide not to report the incident. Of course, the result in these cases is the underreporting of workplace injury and illness.

Others have pointed out that far too often the actions rewarded under behaviour-based programs are the avoidance of negatives that may be out of the control of the individual (e.g., the reduction in lost-time injuries) rather than the achievement of positives that are under an individual's control (e.g., consistently wearing protective equipment, refusing unsafe work). Critics also note that a focus on employee behaviour as an avenue for injury reduction sometimes leaves real hazards unabated in the workplace, diverting attention away from the core concern of making the workplace safer. Additionally, they question whether such an approach is effective in the reduction of occupational illnesses.

How might an HR manager address these concerns about behaviour-based safety programs? Certainly, the use of engineering interventions whenever possible will reduce the burden placed on individual employees. Additionally, comprehensive safety programs also incorporate administrative interventions in the health and safety management program. The organization should have a progressive health and safety policy, strive for a positive safety culture, and truly support employee safety initiatives. Employees need to have the opportunity to work as safely as possible. If value is truly placed on the well-being of every worker, rather than on the interpretation of injury or accident statistics alone, employees may feel less threatened by behavioural interventions at work.

When the decision is made to include incentives as part of a behaviour-based safety program, keep the following in mind:

a. feedback alone may be a sufficient incentive
b. incentives should be tied to behaviours under individual control (e.g., the proper use of a personal protective device) rather than to outcomes such as incidents or injuries that may be beyond control
c. incentive programs do not attempt to compensate for a lack of training, shoddy equipment, poor maintenance, or, more generally, other failures in the safety systems
d. all employees are eligible to receive incentives
e. incentives are meaningful

Sources: Workers' Health and Safety Centre. Retrieved from http://www.whsc.on.ca/pubs/res_lines2.cfm?resID=49, February 13, 2007; and Canadian Auto Workers. Retrieved from http://www.caw.ca/whatwedo/health&safety/factsheet/hsfsissueno14.asp, February 13, 2007.

Goal Setting

Theories of motivation based on the notion of goal setting point out that behaviour is in fact motivated by our own internal intentions. These intentions might be described as the goals we want to achieve.[17] A large number of studies illustrate that setting goals can have desirable behavioural effects.[18] Goal setting has been extensively applied in organizations, and its effectiveness in influencing a wide array of behaviours is well documented in the research literature. Like behaviour modification, goal setting is a method for changing behaviour. However, unlike behaviour modification, goal setting does not focus on changing the consequences of behaviour; rather, it concerns itself with the antecedents of behaviour—that is, the "A" of the ABC model described above. One interesting study examined how changing the antecedents of a behaviour can influence attendance at a health and safety training program for university staff members. In this study researchers manipulated the type of mailing that the staff members received about the training program. Some received messages that stressed the importance of the content of the training program and invited them to take part in a session. Alternatively, others received a mailing that asked them to commit to attending a particular session. Those who signed up for a session in advance had a higher rate of actual attendance at the training program than did those who received the message encouraging them to attend.[19]

Setting a specific goal (e.g., wearing personal protective equipment 95 percent of the time) provides an antecedent for the behaviour by reminding the individual of what he or she is expected to do. Goals serve as antecedents to behaviour in four main ways:

1. Goals direct attention and action to the desired behaviour.
2. Goals mobilize effort toward actions to achieve the goal.
3. Goals increase persistence.
4. Goals motivate the search for effective strategies to help obtain them.

Several investigators have demonstrated that goal-setting techniques provide a valuable adjunct to feedback systems in motivating desired behaviours. It appears that five factors augment the effectiveness of goal setting:[20]

1. Goals must be *difficult and challenging* to result in improved performance. If we set our goals too low, we often stop thinking about them. Goals should be a stretch for the individual, and those that are have more of an impact on performance than easy goals or the absence of goals.
2. Goals must be *achievable* to lead to better performance. Goals that are too hard can quickly become demotivating.
3. Goals must be *specific*. Goals have a more positive impact on behaviour when they are specific rather than vague. The goal must identify specific behaviours, specify how many times they must be performed, and specify the performance standard. Nonspecific goals that are too broad are more like wishes or desires—not goals.

4. Individuals must be *committed* to the goals. The person must accept the goal as being reasonable and achievable. Goals that aren't accepted aren't acted on. People tend to accept goals when they see the importance of the goal, when they participate in setting the goal, when they trust the coach, and when they see the behaviour as something they can control.
5. *Feedback* regarding the degree to which the goal is being met is also helpful in goal achievement.

Behavioural modification, feedback, and goal setting have all proven their worth as components of effective health and safety programming. Reviews of the research literature consistently make a strong case for behavioural approaches to enhancing health and safety.[21]

Increasing Opportunity for Safety Behaviour

Even when workers are well trained and highly motivated, they may not perform safely on the job. The final component that must be in place to promote safety behaviour is the provision of resources and organizational support. The need for workers to have an opportunity to perform safely is evident in the following list of the factors that contribute to the use of personal protective equipment:[22]

- Workers must be aware of the hazard that surrounds them.
- The protective equipment must be easily and conveniently available and properly fitted.
- Workers must understand how the equipment works and how to use it properly.
- There must be no other factors present that would interfere with the workers' use of the equipment.

Even in this brief description, the role of management in promoting health and safety is apparent. Management must make equipment and training available. Perhaps more important, management must demonstrate a commitment to health and safety that is communicated and transmitted throughout the organization.

Management commitment to health and safety has emerged as a key requirement for the improvement of workplace health and safety in numerous studies. For instance, a review of the empirical literature on health and safety training initiatives shows that a high level of management support for safety increases the impact of health and safety–related training in workplaces.[23] Certainly, managers who are committed to health and safety can help create opportunities for employees to engage in safety behaviours. For instance, managers can encourage safety behaviours by not placing productivity-related goals before employee safety.[24] Knowing that their safety comes first will allow employees the freedom to take the time to work safely, properly use protective equipment, and halt work operations if there is a risk to safety.

Although top management has an important role to play in the promotion of workplace health and safety, it is also apparent that management initiatives are delivered through frontline supervisors, and supervisory attitudes play an important role in shaping risk perceptions. Coworker attitudes help shape individual perceptions of workplace hazards and encourage or inhibit self-protective behaviour. A study of manufacturing employees illustrates the impact of other employees' safety commitment on individual safety attitudes. The study found that workers' perceptions of risk were primarily influenced by their perceptions of management, supervisory, and coworker commitment to health and safety. Moreover, perceptions of others' commitment to health and safety had a much larger effect (approximately three times as large) on perceptions of risk as did workers' own experiences with accidents in the workplace.[25]

In short, management has a central role to play in improving safety performance. By sending a strong message about the importance of health and safety in the organization, by holding individuals responsible for their own and their subordinates' safety performance, and by taking safety concerns seriously, managers establish an orientation toward health and safety that allows individuals to perform their jobs safely. We suggest that there are two important vehicles by which management communicates the value placed on safety in their organization: via the safety climate and through safety leadership. We will consider each of these in turn.

Safety Climate

safety climate
shared perceptions of the importance of safety in the workplace

RPC 10.1

You will recall from the previous chapter that an organization's **safety climate** reflects the shared perceptions among all employees and organizational stakeholders regarding the importance of safety in the workplace.[26] If employees are to have positive perceptions regarding the safety climate in their workplace, the organization itself must be committed to workplace safety. An organization can promote a positive safety climate in several ways. One approach is to have explicit and enacted policies on safety. If employees are aware of the organizational safety policy and believe that the organization stands behind that policy, they should feel secure in making safety a priority in their own actions. As such, the policy will contribute to safe conduct.

A second approach that organizations can take to promoting a healthy awareness of safety in the workplace, and as such promote a positive safety climate, is to include safety-related information in the communication of production-related goals. A managerial focus on achieving high productivity may inadvertently deter employee safety. To the extent that employees want to reach or exceed the organizational production expectations, they may become so focused on working quickly that they ignore safety protocols. Certainly, such a course of events is most likely in cases in which following safety procedures slows the pace of work. Therefore, managers should be careful to stress that the achievement of production goals does not come before employee safety at work.

As we noted in Chapter 9, an organization can also foster a positive safety climate by ensuring that employees have the appropriate safety training and encouraging the utilization on the worksite of knowledge gained in such training. The provision of training ensures that employees have the needed ability to engage in safety behaviour at work.

Some organizations choose to promote safety, and influence the safety climate, by rewarding safe behaviour. In these organizations, individuals or groups who have good safety records will benefit from various bonuses or even job promotions. Other companies opt to withhold rewards from those who have a safety violation on their record. Still others promote their reputation as a safe organization by making their safety records—such as number of days without a lost-time injury—available to the public.

Perceived safety climate is indeed a substantial predictor of employees' safety performance.[27] One study of restaurant employees nicely illustrates the impact of an organization's safety climate on safety-related outcomes. The study reported that positive safety climate perceptions were related to a reduction in safety-related events common in restaurants (e.g., knife slips, grease spatters, trips). This decrease in safety events in turn contributed to a reduction in occupational injuries (e.g., cuts, burns, fractured bones).[28]

safety compliance
the extent to which employees follow safety rules and procedures

safety initiative
the extent to which employees go beyond compliance and work to actively improve safety

Thus, it seems that a positive safety climate encourages employees to engage in **safety compliance**. Safety compliance is achieved when employees follow safety-related rules and generally work in a safe manner. Certainly safety compliance helps reduce injuries and safety incidents.[29] However, it is also possible that a positive safety climate can contribute to the safety initiative of employees. **Safety initiative** refers to employee behaviours that go beyond simply working within safety standards and safety compliance. Rather, it involves employees behaving proactively to improve safety levels in the working environment. For example, proactive employees engage in such behaviours as volunteering to participate in safety audits and encouraging their supervisor to take action to improve safety. Both safety compliance and safety initiative are components of overall safety performance.

Safety Leadership

safety leadership
organizational leadership that is actively focused on and promotes occupational health and safety

One effective way for organizations to promote a positive safety climate is to have **safety leadership**; that is, an organizational leader who is focused on and promotes safety. Substantial accumulated evidence suggests that when leaders actively promote safety, employees and organizations alike experience better safety records and more positive safety outcomes.[30] For instance, employees' perceptions of managers' and supervisors' commitments to safety are strongly related to safety-related outcomes including perceived risk on the part of employees.[31] Similarly, employees' perceptions of managerial receptiveness to safety issues predict individual willingness to raise work-related safety concerns.[32] Additionally, employees' perceptions of supervisors' safety-related leadership are positively associated with safety consciousness, perceptions of the safety climate, and, through these intervening variables, safety events and actual injuries.[33]

The accumulated research illustrates the importance of active leader behaviour in the realization of positive safety-related attitudes and safety behaviour in the workplace. It is vital for organizational leaders to be champions of safety. One way that leaders can actively promote safety is to apply **transformational leadership** skills to issues of safety.

transformational leadership
highly effective approach to leadership that emphasizes employee well-being and is characterized by idealized influence, inspirational motivation, intellectual stimulation, and individualized consideration

Transformational leaders are highly effective leaders who also show a substantial degree of concern for the well-being of their employees.[34] Transformational leaders exhibit four characteristics in their interactions with their employees: idealized influence, inspirational motivation, intellectual stimulation, and individualized consideration.[35] Transformational leaders provide idealized influence in that they are admired and trusted role models. Via inspirational motivation, transformational leaders communicate high expectations to their subordinates and provide a sense of meaning and challenge for followers. Transformational leaders intellectually stimulate their followers in that they encourage creativity and questioning of the status quo. Finally, transformational leaders provide individualized consideration in that they pay attention to each employee as an individual and act as a mentor or coach.

When these characteristics are directed toward safety-related concerns, improved safety behaviours tend to follow.[36] For instance, a leader who communicates high expectations regarding the safe performance of work tasks, motivates employees to behave safely and report safety concerns, encourages employees to question the assumption that working safely is working slowly, and individually discusses safety concerns with employees is engaging in safety-specific transformational leadership. Such a leader is likely to realize a highly safe work environment.

Occupational Health and Safety Today 10.1

Safety Leadership at Canadian Pacific Railway: "Fundamental Social Responsibility"

Canadian Pacific Railway (CPR) was founded in 1881 to link Eastern Canada to the West. Almost 125 years later, CPR continues to thrive with a commitment to its clients, the communities it services, and its employees. Reflecting this commitment, CPR makes safety a priority.

CP Rail recognizes that organizational support is a vital component of a safe work environment and pledges to provide the leadership, training, and resources needed to maintain a healthy and safe workplace. Management asks employees to make a commitment to safety, and follow this up by prioritizing safety and making it an integral part of the organization's identity. The corporate health and safety policy clearly states, "No job on our railway will ever be so important that we can't take the time to do it safely." In particular, CP Rail notes the role of safety leadership by the health and safety management committee in efforts to continually improve the safety of operations, employees, and communities. CPR's dedication to safety is paying off—it leads North America in train accident performance, and its injury rates are on a steady and continual decline.

Source: Adapted from CP Rail, "Safety." Retrieved from http://www8.cpr.ca/cms/English/General+Public/CSR/Safety.htm, February 15, 2007.

For an organization looking to improve its safety climate and provide an environment in which employees feel able to engage in safety behaviours, an increased focus on transformational leadership may be one option. Studies suggest that transformational leadership can be effectively trained.[37]

Academic research provides further support for the importance of the active championing of safety among organizational leaders. In a recent study, the tendency for leaders to take a passive approach to safety rather than actively promoting safe behaviour among employees was associated with negative health and safety–related outcomes.[38] Leaders who ignore safety concerns and "turn a blind eye" to safety-related issues may think that they are not doing any harm. However, it appears that such leaders are sending a message to their employees that safety issues are not important and thus are discouraging safe performance of work-related tasks.

Bringing It All Together: Organizational Health and Safety Programs

Throughout this chapter and the previous chapter on training, we have considered the issue of how to promote safe behaviour in the workplace. We have concluded that the utilization of safety behaviour requires that employees have the needed skills, are motivated to act in a safe manner, and have the opportunity to engage in safe behaviour while at work. We now briefly turn our attention to the aspects of workplace health and safety programs that might contribute to the realization of these three requirements in workplaces. Workplace health and safety plans aimed at injury and accident prevention tend to have the following elements, designed to ensure an efficient implementation: (1) identified program objectives, (2) written policy, (3) accountability, and (4) an auditing process.

Program Objectives

Health and safety programs should have clearly stated goals or objectives. The program objectives may be developed from input by joint health and safety committees; environmental committees; representatives from senior management, middle management, operations, maintenance, purchasing, and engineering; and other employee representatives. The objectives should include the following criteria, which must be clearly communicated to all levels:

- Obtain and maintain support for the program at all levels of the organization, including employee groups and parties to collective agreements.
- Motivate, educate, and train all levels of management and employee groups in the recognition, reporting, and correction of hazards in the workplace, which will improve the level of understanding of all staff regarding the connection among safety, productivity, quality, mutual respect, and work satisfaction.

- Provide controls for worker exposure to potential hazards through the use of work practices, engineering controls, and personal protective equipment, and plan for a program of inspection and preventive maintenance for machinery, equipment, tools, and facilities.

The objective of compliance with all environmental and OH&S legislation, as well as with applicable codes and standards, is to reduce the liability faced by all employers in the event of a catastrophic accident.

Policy

The second component of the plan is the creation and adoption of a formal policy. The policy should be written and signed by the chief executive officer or president of the organization and then made available to all employees. The corporate health and safety policy is the most visible sign of management commitment to health and safety. As a result, this commitment should be expressed clearly and unambiguously.

Policy statements can range from simple, strong statements of the organization's commitment to occupational health and safety to long, detailed documents outlining the purpose of the program and defining the involvement and responsibilities of all employees. For example, the following is an

Occupational Health and Safety Notebook 10.3

The 5*22 Program

The New Brunswick Workplace Health, Safety and Compensation Commission (WHSCC) developed the 5*22 Program as a resource for organizations working to improve occupational health and safety. This initiative uses 5 fundamentals of health and safety to group 22 specific topics. The fundamentals, with examples of subtopics, are:

1. Health and Safety Responsibility
   a. Health and safety policies
   b. Health and safety practices
   c. Legal obligations
2. Management Commitment
   a. Communication
   b. Support
3. Employee Involvement
   a. Participation
   b. Safe work practices
4. Hazard and Risk Management
   a. Hazard identification and control
   b. Accident reporting and investigation
5. Health and Safety Education
   a. Assessment of education needs
   b. Delivery and evaluation of OHS training

This model provides a good example of the interconnectedness of occupational health and safety fundamentals. Effectively managing workplace hazards and risks involves the full participation and commitment of informed employees and managers who are working in an organization that has articulated its health and safety policies, procedures, and goals.

Source: New Brunswick Workplace Health, Safety and Compensation Commission, "5*22 Program." Retrieved from http://www.whscc.nb.ca/522_e.asp#, February 13, 2007.

Occupational Health and Safety Today 10.2

Setting a Goal for Safety: "Nobody Gets Hurt" at Imperial Oil

Imperial Oil is committed to a safe and productive workplace with the goal "Nobody gets hurt." The company is working toward this goal via a comprehensive health and safety management system that values trust, communication, and fair treatment. Imperial Oil believes its health and safety focus contributes to organizational performance and increases its competitive advantage.

Imperial Oil's commitment to health and safety is showing results. Health and safety incidents are reduced by 33 percent from 2004 and 68 percent from 2001. The company has also seen improvements in contractor safety. What programs are contributing to these impressive results? The Imperial Oil health and safety program comprises a number of components that focus on both health and safety. Components of the comprehensive program include safety leadership training, ergonomic training, contractor communication efforts, and health surveillance and preventive programs. Imperial Oil also involves employees at all major sites and its contractors in discussions about health and safety priorities via its "Fresh Start for Safety" meetings.

Source: Imperial Oil. Retrieved from http://www.imperialoil.ca/Canada-English/Corporate_Citizenship/CC_Workperf05.asp, February 13, 2007.

excerpt from the University of Toronto's policy statement of March 29, 2004. This section illustrates the University's commitment to the health and safety of all its constituents.

> The University of Toronto is committed to the promotion of the health, safety and wellbeing of all members of the University community, to the provision of a safe and healthy work and study environment, and to the prevention of occupational injuries and illnesses.
>
> The Governing Council, the President and all levels of management will work in consultation and cooperation with University employees, joint health and safety committees, students, contractors and visitors to ensure that the requirements of the Occupational Health and Safety Act and its regulations, other applicable legislation, and the University's Occupational Health and Safety Management System are fully implemented and integrated into all University work and study activities.
>
> Where reasonable, the University will strive to exceed the legislated requirements by adopting the best practices available to protect the University community and to promote a positive health and safety culture. The University will work towards continuous improvement in its health and safety program.[39]

RPC 10.3

RPC 10.4

The policy should be developed in consultation with employee groups. Once adopted, it should be widely publicized by means of meetings, newsletters, pamphlets, and so forth. The policy should be posted in management offices to serve as a constant reminder of the commitment and responsibility of the executive branch. For more information, see the tips for writing a health and safety policy outlined in Occupational Health and Safety Notebook 10.4.

Accountability

A policy that is not enforced, or a policy "without teeth," is virtually useless. Individuals must understand their role in enacting the health and safety policy. After the policy statement has been inaugurated, administrative regulations should be developed outlining the responsibility for the program at various levels. The regulations should include accountability for program

Occupational Health and Safety Notebook 10.4

Health and Safety Policy Checklist

An organizational health and safety policy must be comprehensive and effective. The Canadian Centre for Occupational Health and Safety provides useful information regarding policy development and evaluation on its website. Below is a list of example questions that a health and safety committee might ask when evaluating its own policy. Responses to checklist questions of this type will help guide further development and refining of the policy.

- Is a clear commitment to health and safety evident in the policy statement?
- Is the senior officer responsible for implementation and review of the policy identified?
- Is the policy signed by the president or CEO?
- Have the views of all stakeholders (e.g., employees, managers, supervisors, safety representatives, and safety committees) been incorporated?
- Was the safe performance of work tasks discussed with employees? Is there a clear statement of how their performance will be assessed?
- Is the role of employees in health and safety matters stated (e.g., the position on inspection teams and safety committees)?
- Are individual responsibilities for health and safety duties clearly allocated?
- Are the people responsible for such functions as accident reports, safety inspections, and first aid identified?
- Is health and safety given as great a priority as economic and marketing matters?
- Is the employer's duty to provide health and safety training to all employees stated in the policy?
- Does the policy ensure that health and safety issues will be considered when planning new methods or processes?
- Is the financing of health and safety programs detailed and ensured?
- Are all employees aware of the policy? Are copies of the policy available to all employees?
- Are there periodic revisions and updates of the safety policy? Are the procedures for and timing of such reviews clarified?
- Does the policy make clear that the ultimate responsibility for safety rests with senior management?
- Is safety and health performance included in employee performance reviews?
- Does the policy list arrangements for liaison with contractors?
- Does the policy help to make individuals aware of their legal responsibilities?

For additional information on how to implement occupational health and safety programs, visit the WorkSafeBC website. The Workers' Compensation Board of B.C. has a useful publication on program development that can be downloaded (see the Weblinks section).

Source: Canadian Centre for Occupational Health and Safety, "Guide to writing an OHS policy statement." Retrieved from http://www.ccohs.ca/oshanswers/hsprograms/osh_policy.html, February 13, 2007.

elements assigned to senior management and responsibility for occupational health and safety in performance evaluations at all levels of supervision. Employees should be held responsible for safe work practices, including the reporting of all observed unsafe practices, procedures, and hazards to the appropriate supervisor. All employees should be required to participate in OH&S training and development programs.

A timetable for the review and evaluation of the policy and regulations by the chief executive officer, president, or board should be outlined in the program, along with a procedure for budget development, monitoring, and control. The assignment of appropriate resources with responsibility and authority for the administration of the program should also be included. Finally, the administrative regulation should contain a mechanism for addressing and responding to recommendations from the joint health and safety committees within a specific length of time. Written responses to recommendations are legislated in many jurisdictions.

Auditing the Program

Occupational health and safety programs should undergo periodic reviews or audits to ensure that all aspects of the program are being correctly implemented. Auditing for the sake of regulatory compliance and for continual improvement are the most cost-effective types of audits in the present environment of regulatory standards and enforcement. However, packaged audits that do little but create volumes of paper will not reveal how a program is functioning unless some direction is established. Besides ensuring that the audit has a purpose, management should decide whether the results will be shared with the employees, the joint committee, or the public.

The audit should be designed with a set of standards against which it will be measured. The scope of the audit should also be determined; does it encompass, for example, occupational health and safety, fire protection, emergency plans, and environmental controls? Selection of the audit team is also important. Are there knowledgeable, trained, and experienced staff in-house, or is outside expertise required?

An audit protocol must be designed to provide a step-by-step procedure to assist the team in conducting a systematic review. Such a protocol may involve the creation of a checklist that highlights each aspect of the program—including the objectives, state of the written policy, and systems of accountability. It must lead the auditors to ask the right questions not only about the quality of compliance but also about the strength of the management systems to maintain the appropriate level of compliance. The audit may include a review of previous audits, a physical survey of the location, examination of administrative records, and interviews with management staff, workers, and the health and safety committee. All these elements should be accurately documented and communicated to the appropriate levels in the organization. There must also be a comprehensive action plan in place to follow up on the documented findings of the audit. Responsible personnel and completion dates should accompany each action item.

A common misconception exists that written procedures and audits raise the liability of the corporation in terms of regulatory compliance or in the event of an accident. In fact, many courts are basing the severity of civil and criminal penalties in part on the employer's ability to prove that it was duly diligent in auditing and correcting deficiencies in its own operation. If the corporation does not have written procedures and documented audits, how will it prove beyond a reasonable doubt that it has taken every reasonable precaution to ensure the health and safety of the workers and the environment?

In Canada, what was once the maximum fine for OH&S violations—$25,000—is now routine. Corporations in some jurisdictions can be fined up to $500,000 for each offence. Individuals can be fined up to $25,000 and sentenced to one year in jail. As of March 31, 2004, Bill C-45, the Westray Bill, became an enforceable law in Canada. Under this law, employers whose occupational health and safety violations are deemed negligent can be criminally charged and face substantial jail time. As such, conducting appropriate audits of health and safety programs is increasingly important for Canadian employers.

Summary

A comprehensive approach to increasing health and safety in the workplace should emphasize employees' ability to act in a safe manner, their motivation to do so, and the provision of opportunities to perform their tasks safely. A number of efforts can be made to increase employees' safety motivation, including the use of behaviour modification and goal setting. The organizational context in which the employee is asked to perform his or her work should also emphasize safety. We stressed the importance of a positive safety climate and transformational safety leadership in setting the stage for safety behaviours. No matter what the program, management commitment to safety appears to be a critical variable in health and safety initiatives; management's expressed and actual commitment to the program will be a key determinant of program success.

Key Terms

motivation 278
safety behaviours 276
safety climate 283
safety compliance 284
safety initiative 284
safety leadership 284
transformational leadership 285

Weblinks

Ontario Power Generation

http://www.opg.com (p. 275)

Workers Health and Safety Centre

http://www.whsc.on.ca (p. 281)

Transport Canada, "Score Your Safety Culture (TP 13844)"

http://www.tc.gc.ca/civilaviation/systemsafety/Brochures/tp13844/menu.htm (p. 283)

CP Rail

http://www8.cpr.ca (p. 286)

New Brunswick Workplace Health, Safety and Compensation Commission (WHSCC)

http://www.whscc.nb.ca/ (p. 287)

Imperial Oil

http://www.imperialoil.ca (p. 288)

Canadian Centre for Occupational Health and Safety, "OSH Answers"

http://www.ccohs.ca/oshanswers (p. 289)

WorkSafeBC, "How to Implement a Formal Occupational Health and Safety Program"

http://www.worksafebc.com/publications/default.asp (p. 289)

Workplace Safety and Insurance Board of Ontario

http://www.wsib.on.ca (p. 290)

RPC Icons

RPC 10.1 Develops or provides for wellness and employee assistance programs to support organizational effectiveness.

- policy/procedure development
- collective agreements
- industry best practices
- outside service providers
- the organization's culture
- conflict resolution techniques
- problem solving techniques
- report writing and record keeping
- the relationship between employee wellness and productivity
- performance goals of the organization and how these are affected by employee wellness
- key components of an EAP such as intake, assessments, counseling, traumatic incident debriefing, and cap on service
- cost/benefit analysis

- types of employee assistance programs
- types of employee assistance and wellness programs
- conceptual definition and implications of occupational stressors (e.g., potential stressors, methods of identifying potential stressors and strain outcomes, response to organizational stressors, and management of employee strain outcomes)
- trends in occupational health and safety

RPC 10.2 Ensures that mechanisms are in place for responding to crises in the workplace, including critical incident stress management.

- oral and written communication
- training and development techniques
- industry best practices
- the workplace environment including the availability of emergency equipment
- policy and program development and evaluation
- intervention strategies
- relevant legislation (e.g., fire code, Workers' Compensation)
- investigation techniques
- stress management techniques
- types of employee assistance programs
- Occupational health and safety legislation (e.g., Occupational Health and Safety Act of Ontario, Workplace Safety & Insurance Act—Bill 99, Workplace Hazardous Materials Information System, Transportation of Dangerous Goods legislation, environmental legislation, smoking in the workplace legislation, civil rights legislation)
- hazard identification and control
- accident investigation procedures
- emergency preparedness procedures
- management techniques for OH&S Programs
- conceptual definition and implications of occupational stressors (e.g., potential stressors, methods of identifying potential stressors and strain outcomes, response to organizational stressors, and management of employee strain outcomes)

RPC 10.3 Implements and evaluates practices in the areas of health, safety, security, and Workers' Compensation.

- investigative techniques
- hazard recognition
- disaster recovery techniques
- relevant legislation
- resource information
- common health and safety practices
- company policies and procedures
- Worker Protection (including health and safety and Workers' Compensation)
- theories and practices for protection of individuals and groups

- Occupational health and safety legislation (e.g., Occupational Health and Safety Act of Ontario, Workplace Safety & Insurance Act—Bill 99, Workplace Hazardous Materials Information System, Transportation of Dangerous Goods legislation, environmental legislation, smoking in the workplace legislation, civil rights legislation)
- hazard identification and control
- management techniques for OH&S Programs

RPC 10.4 Ensures due diligence and strict liability requirements are met, e.g. records are kept and formal procedures established.

- relevant legislation and common law
- company policies and procedures
- industry best practices
- program and policy development
- training and development techniques
- risk analysis
- common and statutory law (e.g., employment standard: labour relations)
- Worker Protection (including health and safety and Workers' Compensation)
- theories and practices for protection of individuals and groups

Task & Knowledge Requirements

- Occupational health and safety legislation (e.g., Occupational Health and Safety Act of Ontario, Workplace Safety & Insurance Act—Bill 99, Workplace Hazardous Materials Information System, Transportation of Dangerous Goods legislation, environmental legislation, smoking in the workplace legislation, civil rights legislation)
- management techniques for OH&S Programs

RPC 10.5 Analyses risk to the health and safety of employees and determines appropriate preventative measures, including training, provision of required safety equipment, and administrative practices.

- relevant legislation
- nature of the business and physical work environment
- hazard recognition
- workplace inspection techniques
- safety programs, equipment, and emergency procedures
- ergonomics
- functions of the JHSC
- training and development/presentation techniques
- industry best practices
- relevant technical terminology
- the collective agreement
- services and equipment available in the community
- Worker Protection (including health and safety and Workers' Compensation)
- training and development program design and administration

TASK & KNOWLEDGE REQUIREMENTS

- Occupational health and safety legislation (e.g., Occupational Health and Safety Act of Ontario, Workplace Safety & Insurance Act—Bill 99, Workplace Hazardous Materials Information System, Transportation of Dangerous Goods legislation, environmental legislation, smoking in the workplace legislation, civil rights legislation)
- hazard identification and control
- emergency preparedness procedures
- management techniques for OH&S Programs
- types of employee assistance and wellness programs

Discussion Questions

1. Although considerable empirical data support their effectiveness, debate also exists about the use of behaviourally based safety programs in industry. Employees and unions have frequently rejected such programs. Why do you think this is so? What can be done to enhance the acceptance of such programs?
2. Explain how focusing on behaviours rather than on accidents might be a better approach to improving occupational health and safety.
3. Why do you think setting goals can influence an employee's safety-related actions in the workplace?
4. Describe the role of an organization's safety climate in the promotion of safety behaviours at work.
5. What role do organizational leaders have to play in creating a safety-focused workforce?
6. What are the characteristics of successful occupational safety programs?

Using the Internet

1. Many organizations have their health and safety policies posted on their websites. With a group of classmates, examine these policies. Each of you should choose a different organization in a different market sector. How long are the policies? What information do they cover? Do they establish the unique responsibilities of management and employees? Do they make reference to the organization's safety leadership? Compare your findings with those of your classmates.
2. Various health and safety organizations provide online resources to help human resource personnel create health and safety programs. Search the Web to find guidelines for creating an occupational health and safety program, including writing the policy, communicating accountability, and performing safety audits. Discuss the information you find with your classmates and instructor. Do you think these resources would help you develop a comprehensive health and safety program?

3. Assess the safety climate of your school or workplace. The following Weblink may give you some ideas about questions that assess factors related to safety climate: http://www.tc.gc.ca/civilaviation/system-safety/Brochures/tp13844/menu.htm.

Exercises

1. In discussing health and safety programs, we have emphasized the responsibilities and role of management in establishing and enforcing safety standards. What is the role of employees in these programs? To what extent should employees be responsible for taking initiative to enhance health and safety in the workplace?
2. Imagine you are on a newly formed national committee that will be awarding safety awards to Canadian organizations. The mandate of this committee is to recognize excellence in the promotion of safety at work. What criteria do you think should be used to assess organizations' performance in this area? Create a draft of a rating form that the committee might use to evaluate nominated organizations.
3. Throughout this chapter we emphasized the importance of managerial support for health and safety initiatives. In particular, we noted the importance of a positive safety climate in the realization of safety-related goals. Imagine you are the newly hired human resources director in a manufacturing organization that currently does not place a high degree of value on health and safety—in other words, an organization with a negative safety climate. Top executives have indicated that they would like this situation to change, and they tell you that part of your job is to improve safety performance in the organization. What are the first three initiatives that you would launch to improve the safety climate of this organization?
4. With a small group of classmates, create a proposal for developing an effective occupational health and safety program for an organization that one of the team members has worked in (or is knowledgeable about). You will need to identify the health and safety concerns in that organization, suggest ways that these concerns could be addressed, and describe how you (as an HRM consulting team) would go about solving these problems. Here are some questions you will need to consider:

    a. What do you think the critical issues and real problems are and why?
    b. What occupational health and safety knowledge that you have gained in this course can be applied to the problems you have identified?
    c. What solutions do you propose and why?
    d. How would you implement your plan? Why?

Prepare a written proposal (8 to 10 doubled-spaced pages) detailing the proposed program. Your proposal must include an executive summary of no more than one page. Then, develop an audiovisual presentation based on that proposal and deliver it to the class. (Based on an exercise by Catherine Fitzgerald)

Case 1

Noncompliance with Safety Standards

Pat Singh is confused. As plant manager at a manufacturing plant, he has tried to comply with all applicable legislation. Based on his experiences as a line employee, Pat is particularly keen on health and safety initiatives and has spent a considerable sum of money to purchase the best protective gear (i.e., hearing protectors, safety glasses, hardhats) on the market. Yet today when he walked through the plant, he saw many employees with the hearing protectors draped around their necks, the safety glasses tucked into their shirt pockets, and the hardhats hung on convenient pegs. Pat does not understand why workers won't wear the equipment bought for their protection. Pat has turned to you as a recognized expert in health and safety programming to improve conditions at the plant. What should Pat do?

Case 2

Safety in the Bakery

Su Mei Lawrence is manager of the bakery department of a large grocery store. She oversees 20 employees working 3 shifts (the store is open 24 hours/day). Most employees are part-time, working 20 hours/week or less—many are high-school and university students working to help pay their way through school. In the last three weeks, Su Mei has noticed a marked increase in the number of safety-related incidents in the department. Several employees have injured their backs lifting racks of bread into position, and product has been crushed by the careless use of a forklift in the rear storage area. Today, one employee was knocked to the floor when a stack of 15 trays of bread fell on him. Su Mei is convinced that it is time to take action to improve the safety of working conditions in the department, but she needs your help in deciding exactly what to do.

Case 3

Working to Change Safety

Ali Al-Farsi has recently purchased a medium-sized sawmill. He recognizes that health and safety has been a problem at the mill in the past—just last year, one worker lost a limb in an accident. However, Ali and his new management team are serious about safety and want to improve the mill's safety performance. You are the health and safety consultant who has been contracted to help Ali and his team engineer a safety turnaround at the mill. Your primary task is to help design and implement a health and safety management program. What are the vital components of a successful health and safety program? What steps would you work through with the team? How might Ali convince skeptical employees that a safer workplace is truly a priority?

Endnotes

1. Goldenhar, L. M., & Schulte, P. A. (1994). Intervention research in occupational health and safety. *Journal of Occupational Medicine, 36,* 763–775.
2. Robson, L. S., Clarke, J. A., Cullen., K., Bielecky, A., Severin, C., Bigelow, P. L., Irvin, E., Culyer, A., & Mahood, Q. (2007). The effectiveness of occupational health and safety management system interventions: A systematic review. *Safety Science, 45,* 329–353.
3. Colligan, M. J., & Cohen, A. (2004). The role of training in promoting workplace safety and health. In J. Barling & M. Frone (Eds.), *Handbook of workplace safety* (pp. 223–248). Washington, DC: American Psychological Association.
4. Johnson, S. E. (2003, October). Behavioral safety theory: Understanding the theoretical foundation. *Professional Safety,* 39–44; and Sulzer-Azaroff, B., & Austin, J. (2000, July). Does BBS work? Behavior-based safety and injury reduction: A survey of the evidence. *Professional Safety,* 19–24.
5. Geller, E. S. (2001). Behavior-based safety in industry: Realizing the large-scale potential of psychology to promote human welfare. *Applied and Preventive Psychology, 10,* 87–105; and Sulzer-Azaroff, B., & Austin, J. (2000, July). Does BBS work? Behavior-based safety and injury reduction: A survey of the evidence. *Professional Safety,* 19–24.
6. Cohen, A., & Colligan, M. J. (1997). Accepting occupational health and safety regimens. In D. S. Gochman (Ed.), *Handbook of health behaviour research II: Provider determinants* (pp. 379–394). New York: Plenum Press.
7. Sulzer-Azaroff, B., Harris, T. C., & McCann, K. B. (1994). Beyond training: Organizational performance management techniques. In M. J. Colligan (Ed.), *Occupational safety and health training* (pp. 321–340). Philadelphia: Hanley and Befus.
8. Gazzaniga, M. S., & Heatherton, T. F. (2006). *Psychological science*. New York: W. W. Norton.
9. Geller, E. S. (2001). Behavior-based safety in industry: Realizing the large-scale potential of psychology to promote human welfare. *Applied and Preventive Psychology, 10,* 87–105; and Saari, J. (1994). When does behaviour modification prevent accidents? *Leadership and Organizational Development Journal, 15,* 11–15.
10. Sulzer-Azaroff, B., & Austin, J. (2000, July). Does BBS work? Behavior-based safety and injury reduction: A survey of the evidence. *Professional Safety,* 19–24.
11. Hickman, J. S., & Geller, E. S. (2003). A safety self-management intervention for mining operations. *Journal of Safety Research, 34,* 299–308.
12. Hutton, K. A., Sibley, C. G., Harper, D. N., & Hunt, M. (2001). Modifying driver behaviour with passenger feedback. *Transportation Research Part F: Traffic Psychology and Behaviour, 4,* 257–269.
13. Cooper, M. D., Phillips, R. A., & Robertson, I. T. (1993). Improving safety on construction sites by psychologically based techniques: Alternative approaches to the measurement of safety behaviour. *European Review of Applied Psychology, 43,* 33–37.

14. Frederiksen, L. W. (Ed.). (1982). *Handbook of organizational behaviour management*. New York: John Wiley & Sons; and Geller, E. S. (2001). Behavior-based safety in industry: Realizing the large-scale potential of psychology to promote human welfare. *Applied and Preventive Psychology, 10,* 87–105.
15. Komaki, J. (1986). Promoting job safety and accident prevention. In M. F. Cataldo & J. Coates (Eds.), *Health and industry: A behavioural medicine perspective* (pp. 301–319). New York: John Wiley & Sons.
16. Zohar, D. (2002a). Modifying supervisory practices to improve subunit safety: A leadership-based intervention model. *Journal of Applied Psychology, 87,* 156–163.
17. Ambrose, M. L., & Kulik, C. T. (1999). Old friends, new faces: Motivation research in the 1990s. *Journal of Management, 25,* 231–292; and Locke, E. A., & Latham, G. P. (2002). Building a practically useful theory of goal setting and task motivation: A 35-year odyssey. *American Psychologist, 57,* 705–717.
18. Locke, E. A., & Latham, G. P. (2002). Building a practically useful theory of goal setting and task motivation: A 35-year odyssey. *American Psychologist, 57,* 705–717.
19. Sheeran, P., & Silverman, M. (2003). Evaluation of three interventions to promote workplace health and safety: Evidence for the utility of implementation intentions. *Social Science & Medicine, 56(10),* 2153–2163.
20. Locke, E. A., & Latham, G. P. (2002). Building a practically useful theory of goal setting and task motivation: A 35-year odyssey. *American Psychologist, 57,* 705–717.
21. Johnson, S. E. (2003, October). Behavioral safety theory: Understanding the theoretical foundation. *Professional Safety,* 39–44; Sulzer-Azaroff, B., & Austin, J. (2000, July). Does BBS work? Behavior-based safety and injury reduction: A survey of the evidence. *Professional Safety,* 19–24; and Sulzer-Azaroff, B., Harris, T. C., & McCann, K. B. (1994). Beyond training: organizational performance management techniques. In M. J. Colligan (Ed.), *Occupational Safety and Health Training* (pp. 321–340). Philadelphia: Hanley and Befus.
22. Feeney, R. J. (1986). Why is there resistance to wearing protective equipment at work? Possible strategies for overcoming this. *Journal of Occupational Accidents, 8,* 207–213.
23. Colligan, M. J., & Cohen, A. (2004). The role of training in promoting workplace safety and health. In J. Barling & M. Frone (Eds.), *Handbook of workplace safety* (pp. 223–248). Washington, DC: American Psychological Association.
24. Smith, M. J., Karsh, B. T., Carayon, P., & Conway. F. T. (2003). Controlling occupational safety and health hazards. In J. C. Quick & L. E. Tetrick (Eds.), *Handbook of occupational health psychology* (pp. 35–68). Washington, DC: American Psychological Association.
25. Cree, T., & Kelloway, E. K. (1997). Responses to occupational hazards: Exit and participation. *Journal of Occupational Health Psychology, 2,* 304–311.
26. Zohar, D. (1980). Safety climate in industrial organizations: Theoretical and applied implications. *Journal of Applied Psychology, 65,* 96–102; and Zohar, D. (2002). The effects of leadership dimensions, safety climate, and assigned priorities on minor injuries in work groups. *Journal of Organizational Behavior, 23,* 75–92.
27. Hemingway, M., & Smith, C. S. (1999). Organizational climate and occupational stressors as predictors of withdrawal behaviours and injuries in nurses. *Journal of Occupational and Organizational Psychology, 72,* 285–299; and Hofmann, D. A., & Stetzer, A. (1996). A cross-level investigation of factors influencing unsafe behaviours and accidents. *Personnel Psychology, 49,* 307–339.
28. Barling, J., Loughlin, C., & Kelloway, E. K. (2002). Development and test of a model linking safety-specific transformational leadership and occupational safety. *Journal of Applied Psychology, 87,* 488–496.
29. Griffin, M. A., & Neal, A. (2000). Perception of safety at work: A framework for linking safety climate to safety performance, knowledge, and motivation. *Journal of Occupational Health Psychology, 17,* 347–358.

30. Barling, J., Loughlin, C., & Kelloway, E. K. (2002). Development and test of a model linking safety-specific transformational leadership and occupational safety. *Journal of Applied Psychology, 87,* 488–496; Hofmann, D. A., Jacobs, R., & Landy, F. (1995). High reliability process industries: Individual, micro, and macro organizational influences on safety performance. *Journal of Safety Research, 26,* 131–149; Mullen, J. (2005). Testing a model of employee willingness to raise safety issues. *Canadian Journal of Behavioural Science, 37(4),* 273–282; and Shannon, H. S., Mayr, J., & Haines, T. (1997). Overview of the relationship between organizational and workplace factors and injury rates. *Safety Science, 26,* 201–217.
31. Cree, T., & Kelloway, E. K. (1997). Responses to occupational hazards: Exit and participation. *Journal of Occupational Health Psychology, 2,* 304–311.
32. Kelloway, E. K., Mullen, J., & Francis, L. (2006). The divergent effects of transformational and passive leadership on employee safety. *Journal of Occupational Health Psychology, 11,* 76–86.
33. Barling, J., Loughlin, C., & Kelloway, E. K. (2002). Development and test of a model linking safety-specific transformational leadership and occupational safety. *Journal of Applied Psychology, 87,* 488–496.
34. Bass, B. M. (1985). *Leadership and performance beyond expectations*. New York: Free Press; and Judge, T. A., & Bono, J. E. (2000). Five-factor model of personality and transformational leadership. *Journal of Applied Psychology, 85,* 751–765.
35. Bass, B. M. (1990). From transactional to transformational leadership: Learning to share the vision. *Organizational Dynamics, 18(3),* 19–31.
36. Barling, J., Loughlin, C., & Kelloway, E. K. (2002). Development and test of a model linking safety-specific transformational leadership and occupational safety. *Journal of Applied Psychology, 87,* 488–496.
37. Barling, J., Weber, T., & Kelloway, E. K. (1996). Effects of transformational leadership training on attitudinal and financial outcomes: A field experiment. *Journal of Applied Psychology, 81,* 827–832; and Kelloway, E. K., Barling, J., & Helluer, J. (2000). Enhancing transformational leadership: The roles of training and feedback. *Leadership and Organizational Development Journal, 21,* 145–149.
38. Kelloway, E. K., Mullen, J., & Francis, L. (2006). The divergent effects of transformational and passive leadership on employee safety. *Journal of Occupational Health Psychology, 11,* 76–86.
39. University of Toronto, Health and Safety Policy. (2004, March 29). Retrieved from http://www.utoronto.ca/govcncl/pap/policies/healthsa.html, February 15, 2007.

Chapter 11

Emergency Response and Emergency Preparedness

Chapter Learning Objectives

After reading this chapter, you should be able to:

- define an emergency
- list the key elements in emergency preparedness
- describe the concept of an emergency plan
- explain the necessity of having emergency and evacuation plans
- describe the principles of fire prevention and suppression

WIND STORM IN BRITISH COLUMBIA

The spokesperson for BC Hydro called it a "multi-day" event. In the fall of 2006 a series of powerful wind and torrential rain storms pounded British Columbia. The storms are credited with causing multiple deaths in the U.S., flooding, massive power outages, and millions of dollars in property damage—including the devastation of Vancouver's famous Stanley Park. Highway closures and disruption of rail service made commuting almost impossible. Experts predict that severe weather events such as this will become more frequent as a result of climate change.

Source: CBC, "Tens of thousands still in dark after massive B.C. storm." Retrieved from http://www.cbc.ca/canada/british-columbia/story/2006/12/15/wind-storm.html, February 8, 2007.

Introduction

The widespread impact of the 1998 ice storm in Ontario and Quebec, the events of September 11, 2001, the subsequent rash of anthrax-related scares, the outbreak of Severe Acute Respiratory Syndrome (SARS) in Canadian cities, and the devastation of Hurricane Juan in Nova Scotia in 2003 are all recent examples of emergencies. Some, such as the events of 9/11 or the SARS outbreak, happened within workplaces. The others were not specific to workplaces but required a response from both employers and employees.

In Canada, emergency response is largely up to individuals and each individual is responsible for knowing what to do in an emergency. As events overwhelm an individual's capacity to respond, governments respond in a progressive manner.

First, local emergency organizations (e.g., municipal emergency services, emergency measures organizations) respond. At the next level, each province and territory has an emergency measures organization (EMO) that is tasked with managing large-scale emergencies and supporting local organizations as required. Finally, the federal government and its agencies may become involved in emergency response efforts, depending on the nature of the disaster. For example, during Hurricane Juan in Nova Scotia, the Canadian Forces were deployed to assist in the cleanup efforts.

Organizations must consider the possibility of a disaster, in which the potential for loss is very high. No safety program is complete without a planned response to the threat of a disaster.

In this chapter we consider two central aspects of emergency planning in organizations. First, we consider issues related to emergency preparedness. Second, we address the organization's response to emergency. Because of the commonality of such procedures, we finish the chapter with a specific consideration of fire and evacuation plans.

Occupational Health and Safety Notebook 11.1

Emergency Measures Organizations

Each province and territory has its own emergency measures organization (EMO). EMOs specialize in emergency preparedness and emergency response and are often the best source of information on emergency-related topics. A contact list is provided below.

Alberta

Emergency Management Alberta
Phone: (780) 422-9000
Toll-free in Alberta: 310-0000
Fax: (780) 422-1549
Website: http://www.municipalaffairs.gov.ab.ca/ema_index.htm

British Columbia

Provincial Emergency Program (PEP)
Phone: (250) 952-4913
Fax: (250) 952-4888
Website: http://www.pep.bc.ca

Manitoba

Emergency Measures Organization
Phone: (204) 945-4772
Toll-free: 1 (888) 267-8298
Fax: (204) 945-4620
Website: http://www.manitobaemo.ca

New Brunswick

Emergency Measures Organization
Phone: (506) 453-2133
Toll-free: 1 (800) 561-4034
Fax: (506) 453-5513
Website: http://www.gnb.ca/cnb/emo-omu/index-e.asp

Newfoundland and Labrador

Emergency Measures Division
Phone: (709) 729-3703
Fax: (709) 729-3857
Website: http://www.gov.nf.ca/mpa/emo.html

Northwest Territories

Emergency Measures Organization
Phone: (867) 873-7083
Website: http://www.maca.gov.nt.ca/safety/emergency_measures/

Nova Scotia

Emergency Measures Organization
Phone: (902) 424-5620
Fax: (902) 424-5376
Website: http://www.gov.ns.ca/emo/

Nunavut

Nunavut Emergency Management
Phone: (867) 975-5319
Fax: (867) 979-4221

Ontario

Ontario Emergency Management
Phone: (416) 314-3723
Fax: (416) 314-3758
Website: http://www.mpss.jus.gov.on.ca/english/pub_security/emo/about_emo.html

Prince Edward Island

Emergency Measures Organization
Phone: (902) 368-6361
Fax: (902) 368-6362
Website: http://www.gov.pe.ca/cca/index.php3?number=1002515

Quebec

Sécurité Publique Quebec
Phone: (418) 644-6826
Fax: (418) 643-3194
Or one of the regional offices:
Gatineau: (819) 772-3737
Montreal: (514) 873-1300
Rimouski: (418) 727-3589
Sillery (Quebec): (418) 643-3244
Trois-Rivières: (819) 371-6703 or your municipality
Website: http://www.msp.gouv.qc.ca/secivile/secivile_en.asp?txtSection=oscq

Saskatchewan

Emergency Management Organization
Phone: (306) 787-9563
Fax: (306) 787-1694
Website: http://www.cps.gov.sk.ca/Safety/emergency/default.shtml

(continued)

Occupational Health and Safety Notebook 11.1

Emergency Measures Organizations (continued)

Yukon

Emergency Measures Organization
Phone: (867) 667-5220
Toll-free (in Yukon): 1-800-661-0408
Fax: (867) 393-6266
Website: http://www.community.gov.yk.ca/emo/index.html

In addition, a federal department, Public Safety and Emergency Preparedness, was formed in December 2003 to secure public safety in Canada. The department has several functions, of which emergency preparedness and response is one. The department of Public Safety and Emergency Preparedness can be found on the Web at http://www.psepc.gc.ca/index_e.asp.

Emergency Preparedness

emergency
a sudden, generally unexpected occurrence or set of circumstances demanding immediate action

An **emergency** is any sudden set of circumstances demanding immediate action. For the most part, we are concerned with emergencies that either cause or threaten to cause the loss of, or damage to, property or life. Being a victim of a computer virus or having your computer crash is also an emergency (and one that business needs to be concerned with), but we will limit our consideration to health and safety–related emergencies.

Emergencies can be either naturally occurring or caused by humans. Naturally occurring emergencies include disease epidemics (animal, human, and plant) and weather conditions (e.g., blizzards, hail, hurricanes, earthquakes, storm surges, torrential rain). Such emergencies may be deceptive, as the severity of the emergency might not be immediately apparent. For example, at the beginning of the SARS outbreak, nobody recognized the seriousness of the impending crisis—indeed, the initial diagnosis was atypical pneumonia. It was only a month after the initial reports from China that the World Health Organization issued a health alert.

Other emergencies are caused by humans. They can include explosions, accidents, fires, and chemical spills. They can also include riots, civil disorder, terrorism, and acts of workplace violence. Although riots and civil disorder have always been traditional concerns of health and safety professionals, we now also recognize the need to anticipate and respond to terrorism and acts of violence.

Although the general probability of any of these emergencies actually happening may be low, they *can* happen and a company (or the home) is remiss if it does not institute an emergency plan. The results of a disaster may be prevented or mitigated by the effectiveness of the emergency plan.

Although many organizations focus on how they responded during an emergency, true emergency planning begins long before the onset of any emergency and continues long afterward. Emergency planning involves anticipating and planning for emergencies, putting those plans into action as needed, and then both (1) getting back to work and (2) refining plans in light of new learning.

Occupational Health and Safety Today 11.1

Norwalk Outbreak at Mount Allison

Mount Allison University, a small undergraduate university in Sackville, New Brunswick, reported an outbreak of the Norwalk virus on October 12, 2006. The outbreak had apparently begun five days earlier, and more than 300 students were thought to be affected. The university cancelled classes on Friday, October 13, and suspended all campus activities for the weekend; hand-washing stations were established throughout the university and all public areas of the university underwent decontamination procedures. These strategies were effective, and classes resumed on the Monday without further incident. However, students who were still recuperating from the illness were encouraged to not attend classes. On the advice of Public Health officials, the university resumed extracurricular activities and events on Wednesday, October 18.

Norwalk is actually a family of viruses that are spread primarily through fecal–oral contact. Contamination of food, water, or other vehicles as well as person-to-person transmission is possible. As such, Norwalk is highly contagious, and the Norwalk virus is the likely culprit behind many outbreaks of "stomach flu." Outbreaks are fairly frequent, especially in institutional settings (e.g., nursing homes, hospitals) and in close quarters (e.g., cruise ships). The virus results in a variety of gastro-intestinal symptoms and "is characterized by acute onset of nausea, vomiting, abdominal cramps, and diarrhea" (CDC, 2001, p. 3). The symptoms typically last one or two days.

Sources: CBC, "Norwalk virus identified as culprit in NB university outbreak." Retrieved from http://www.cbc.ca/cp/national/061018/n101854.html, February 8, 2007; and Centers for Disease Control. (2001). *"Norwalk-like viruses": Public health consequences and outbreak management*. Atlanta, GA: Author.

A recent study describes a five-stage crisis-management process that generates specific strategies at each stage.[1] The first step, signal detection, is targeted at prevention and begins with the recognition that an emergency is possible or imminent. The next step, preparation, involves senior management in the adoption of a crisis-management mindset, the creation of a response plan, and the introduction of response training. The third stage, damage containment, constitutes the majority of an organization's crisis-management resources. The literature on organizational communication, organizational support, employee assistance programs (EAPs), and stress interventions largely focuses on activities in this stage. The fourth stage, recovery, involves the development of short-term and long-term plans to resume normal business.[2] The final stage is learning, in which the focus is on assessing and reflecting on the incident with a view to improving operations and procedures.[3]

Although the benefits of a proactive response to emergencies are well known,[4] many organizations resist this view and, in fact, do not implement any systematic preparation for emergencies.[5] Management commitment to emergency preparedness seems to be a critical determinant of how organizations prepare for emergencies. Response strategies typically begin with organizational leaders.[6] Moreover, organizational leaders are responsible for both minimizing risk and responding to events in an effort to aid recovery and readjustment after the events have occurred.[7]

With respect to workplace violence, organizations make a huge mistake when they "focus on systems, operations, infrastructures and public relations and ignore the people . . . [employees] need to be assured of their safety and have their trust in leadership reinforced."[8] The importance of "people" issues was shown by a recent study in the aftermath of the Mount Allison University Norwalk outbreak (see Occupational Health and Safety Today 11.1).[9] Student perceptions of how well the university administration handled the crisis were a better predictor of their fear of future contamination and resulting stress than students' own experiences with the virus. Clearly, given the importance of these issues, HR has a major role to play in developing and implementing emergency plans.[10]

Just as was the case for other forms of hazard control (see Chapter 8), an emergency plan needs to consider issues at the precontact, contact, and postcontact stages of any emergency. Issues at the precontact stage include assessing hazards and planning potential responses. Issues at the contact stage include evacuation, caring for the injured, and ensuring emergency response. Issues at the postcontact stage include dealing with the emotional trauma of an emergency and issues regarding the orderly return to work.

Precontact

The necessary elements in the management of emergencies include an emergency plan, an emergency manager, a fire plan, an evacuation plan, and a medical attention plan.

An Emergency Plan

The first thing that is required is a formal, rapid-response, workable, well-controlled emergency plan. Low levels of loss depend on this plan. The joint health and safety committees as well as the local government should be involved in developing the plan.

An organization requires hazard evaluation, an emergency response plan, an evacuation plan, notification of authorities, supplies, and drills.

Hazard Evaluation HR and safety professionals (and managers) must evaluate the hazards that could cause an emergency (e.g., storage of flammable solvents near static electricity or ignition sources) as well as the hazards with the greatest risk and loss potential. They must also understand how the emergency plans could be aborted or sidetracked if an emergency were to occur; the extent of possible damage and injuries or fatalities; and the possibility of the financial loss of the total plant, its individual departments, and critical equipment or processes.

An emergency is a rare occurrence; knowledge of these hazards can be augmented by consulting Emergency Planning Canada, the Fire Commissioner of Canada, and Environment Canada, as well as fire departments and insurance companies. The likelihood of natural disasters varies according to region, but the federal government provides a Natural Hazards Map of Canada (see the Weblinks at the end of this chapter) that can assist in determining the risk for various disasters in your area based on historical precedent.

Occupational Health and Safety Notebook 11.2

Futureproofing

Writing for the Canadian Centre for Emergency Preparedness, Geary Sikich uses the term "futureproofing" to denote an integrated approach to emergency preparedness. Futureproofing is based on the notion that organizations have to anticipate and assess the potential risk and consequences of a wide range of emergencies in order to be protected from unexpected events. This approach is based on "graceful degradation" and "agile restoration"—that is, the ability of the organization to identify an event, determine its consequences, establish a minimal functionality, and begin to direct efforts toward restoration in a timely fashion.

Source: Sikich, G., "Futureproofing—The process of active analysis." Retrieved from http://www.ccep.ca/sikich.html, February 7, 2007.

Emergency Response Plan A response plan for different types of emergencies must be created. These plans should be written, published, and posted. There must be good alarm facilities with emergency communication devices, and everyone in the plant must be familiar with their locations and use.

A list should be published of the people in charge of every aspect of any emergency activity. Accompanying the list should be information on the actual event, security and protection for the workers, protection of what is left, documentation of damage and injuries, and liaison with bureaucrats, insurance, and media.

Evacuation Plan Plans for evacuating employees and clients in the event of a major emergency or disaster are a key element in emergency preparedness. Every worker in the plant must know exactly where to congregate when the

Occupational Health and Safety Today 11.2

Pandemic Planning

Health experts generally agree that there is a real risk of a pandemic flu outbreak in the near future. Unlike the annual flu outbreaks we all are used to, pandemic influenza is highly infectious and the World Health Organization suggests we are closer to an outbreak now than we have been since 1968 (the last major pandemic). Any such outbreak is going to present substantial challenges to businesses. Imagine, for example, how businesses will cope with absenteeism rates in the neighbourhood of 35 to 50 percent, disruptions in key supplies, and the loss of key customers—conditions that may last for six weeks or more. Health care organizations will be particularly hard hit, as they are expected to experience the same staff and material shortages while at the same time being overwhelmed by the sudden increase in demand for their services. Staff will experience exceptionally high levels of stress from workload—and the predicted mounting death rate will also extract a toll on health care workers. To begin preparing for the potential outbreak, the federal government has launched a coordinating website (http://www.influenza.gc.ca/index_e.html), as have provincial agencies (e.g., http://www.wsib.on.ca/wsib/wsibsite.nsf/public/flu_resources; http://www.healthservices.gov.bc.ca/pandemic/planning.html) and larger municipalities (http://www.toronto.ca/health/pandemicflu/pandemicflu_plan.htm). As is the case for emergency planning in general, these plans attempt to forecast the likely effects of a pandemic and outline the necessary responses of various organizations.

need arises and be aware of at least two evacuation routes. There should be well-marked, unobstructed evacuation paths with well-lit exits. Notices about exit procedures should be posted, along with instructions about notifying appropriate personnel of the emergency. Designated assembly areas and assigned assistance should be part of the plan.

A roll call (head count) should be done at the assembly site, and a list of missing employees should be given to the command centre. No one should be allowed to reenter a building until all personnel are accounted for and debriefed.

The following are some basic requirements of evacuation plans.

1. The site must be divided into small, related areas. The workers in each area must be identified and trained to recognize and remember workers who are not part of their section. This probably happens routinely during working hours, but the noted presence of these "outsiders" must become second nature. In case of a major emergency, all workers must be accounted for.
2. Outside the building and away from any roadways there should be assembly points that allow for the movement of emergency vehicles. The personnel from each work area noted above must be trained to quickly move to their respective assembly points and remain there until a head count is complete and missing workers are accounted for.
3. Once every employee has been accounted for and the extent of the emergency has been determined, employees can be instructed to return to work or to go home and report when called.
4. Any critical equipment or process that may increase the overall risk of the emergency should be addressed. For example, the supply sources of flammable materials such as gas must be shut off. These tasks should be undertaken only by maintenance personnel who are highly trained in emergency procedures.
5. The end of the emergency can be called only by the senior person responsible for the operation's emergency procedures.
6. A postevacuation assessment must be done to identify problems in the evacuation plan. Remedial measures can then be taken.

Occupational Health and Safety Notebook 11.3

Evacuation Plans

Public agencies such as universities typically have well-developed evacuation plans that are made widely available. Most plans specify the authority structure (e.g., fire wardens, fire marshals) and means of evacuation. Although not complete, a representative sampling of university evacuation plans can be found on the Web.

University	Link to Evacuation Plan
Dalhousie University	http://pharmacy.dal.ca/Files/safeplan2002.pdf
Queen's University	http://www.queensu.ca/quic/intledu/files/evacuationtemplate.pdf
University of Saskatchewan	http://www.cls.usask.ca/machine/pdf/0.12.37.1.Rev0.pdf

The Canadian Standards Association has developed a standard for emergency response plans (ERP) that provides further information on evacuation requirements (CAN/CSA-Z731-03).

Notification of Authorities Companies should be aware of any legislative requirements, such as the requirement to notify the Ministry of Labour, police, and so on, of an emergency. In locations with the 911 emergency system, an industrial call for medical assistance will automatically bring police, ministry, and other associated specialists, along with medical assistance.

Supplies Emergency first-line equipment such as fire extinguishers must be in well-defined, easily accessible locations. Designated workers must be trained in their use.

Drills Regular emergency drills, with the occasional unannounced drill to keep everyone current and knowledgeable, are a standard part of most plans. Rehearsals are an important part of training. Simulating disasters will help employees deal effectively with real emergencies. Fire drills are rehearsals that require employees to be aware of reporting requirements and the location of exits and fire extinguishers. Drills test the response capability of the organization. The results (evacuation times, etc.) are monitored and reported to management. A full-scale dress rehearsal involves simulated injuries and provides a measure of an organization's ability to respond.

Emergency Manager

In addition to the foregoing requirements, any emergency plan must have a senior person—generally the plant manager—who will be in charge of all the emergency activities. This individual should speak for the organization and must be committed to the plan. If the emergency manager works a regular day shift and the plant is on multiple shifts, then there must be assistants on each of the other shifts with the authority and training to handle emergencies. The command centre, with a designated chain of command, is a critical component of the plan.

Contact

Fire Plan

The fire plan will have the same characteristics as the main emergency plan, although some of the requirements dealing with major damage and fatalities may not be followed if the fire gets out of control and a full-blown emergency results. A group of workers must be trained in firefighting techniques and be part of the plant fire brigade. In small to mid-sized businesses in which an in-house fire brigade is not economically feasible, workers should receive fire-extinguisher training and participate in ongoing practice sessions.

The local fire department is a good source of training for any in-house firefighting team that may be required. The fire department can also assist in fire hazard evaluations and regular inspections. Fire prevention and suppression is discussed next.

Occupational Health and Safety Notebook 11.4

Emergency Operations Centres (EOCs)

Also called the command post or the command centre, an EOC is a geographic space dedicated to the strategic management of an emergency. An EOC is typically geographically separate from the actual emergency site. The role of the EOC is to designate the individual in charge of the emergency site, facilitate communications with the public, disseminate emergency public information, and initiate the recovery process.

The requirements for an EOC vary with circumstances, but in general should include communications capabilities sufficient to allow coordination of efforts and space for briefings and decision making. Basic supplies (e.g., office supplies) should also be available along with connectivity through networks, radios, and so on.

Source: Canadian Centre for Emergency Preparedness, "CCEP newsletter for August 2003." Retrieved from http://www.ccep.ca/news0308.html#item1, February 7, 2007.

Fire Prevention and Suppression

fire
a chemical process in which fuel, oxygen, and heat are combined

A **fire** is a chemical process in which fuel, oxygen, and heat are combined to create a disastrous condition. The products of fire are gases, flame, heat, and smoke.

The fire process can be graphically represented by means of the fire triangle (see Figure 11.1). The new model is the fire tetrahedron (see Figure 11.2). The triangular model shows that the three elements—fuel, oxygen, and heat—must come together for a fire to be sustained. The second model adds a fourth element: the chain reaction. Once a fire starts, it is perpetuated by the ongoing (or chain) reaction of the other three elements.

FIGURE 11.1

Fire Triangle

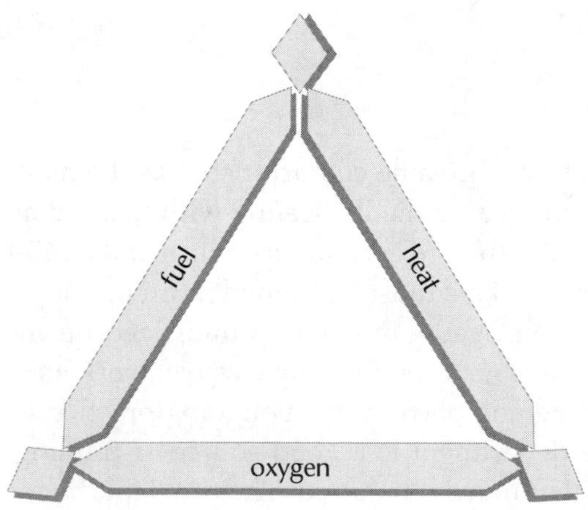

FIGURE 11.2

Fire Tetrahedron

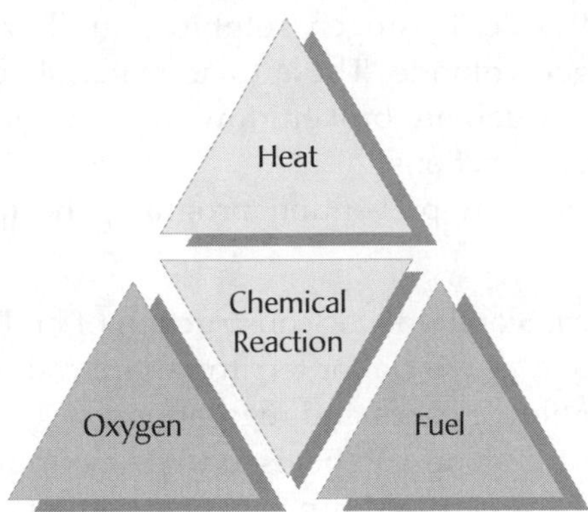

Fire has four stages:

1. The **incipient stage.** At this stage, a source of ignition (a cigarette butt or a hot electrical wire connection) and fuel (papers or wood) come together. This stage can continue for hours until the resultant heat from the initial reaction becomes great enough to cause combustion. The air is filled with molecule-sized products of combustion. The airborne particulate can be detected with an ionizing (smoke) detector. In the case of an explosion, this stage (and the next) is very short.

incipient stage
a source of ignition and fuel come together

2. The **smouldering stage.** The three elements are present and are causing the heat to rise through limited chain reaction. The area begins to fill with smoke, which increases in amount as the process continues. With visible airborne particulate (smoke) now present, a photoelectric detector is effective. This stage is short and can be measured in minutes.

smouldering stage
fuel, oxygen, and heat are present and are causing the heat to rise through limited chain reaction

3. The **free-burning stage.** This is the stage at which flames first appear. The rate of energy release (heat) is increasing very rapidly and the surrounding combustible materials are beginning to burn. The free-burning stage is very short and can be measured in minutes or less. A rate-of-rise detector can be effective at this stage because it senses the rapid temperature increase. This detector works well in conjunction with a sprinkler system.

free-burning stage
the stage at which flames first appear

4. The **uncontrolled fire stage.** The fire is out of control and major property damage is under way. All personnel must be evacuated. This stage can be measured in seconds. The rate of reaction doubles every 10 °C. No heat is lost during this reaction; rather, it becomes cumulative.

uncontrolled fire stage
fire is out of control and major property damage is under way

The fire triangle or tetrahedron (refer to Figures 11.1 and 11.2) can serve to illustrate the requirements for extinguishment. By removing any one of the parts of these models, the fire cannot be sustained and will be put out. For instance, a carbon dioxide fire extinguisher will blanket the fire with a gas that will displace the oxygen, thereby smothering the fire. Similarly, water sprayed on the fire will cool the conditions or reduce the heat, also resulting in extinguishment (see Table 11.1).

Hazardous by-products of fires besides heat and smoke include carbon monoxide, carbon dioxide, hydrogen sulphide, sulphur dioxide, hydrogen cyanide, and hydrogen chloride. These toxic materials are produced when the burning materials (fuel) are broken down into original chemicals under extreme heat and chain reactions.

When developing a fire-prevention program, the following should be considered:

1. *Structural design*. Standards for construction of buildings are detailed in the federal and provincial or territorial fire codes, as well as fire marshal and building codes and regulations.
2. *Barriers*. Walls and floors can be used to delay or prevent the spread of fire. Specially constructed fire barriers should be maintained.
3. *Detection and suppression*. Most buildings have a detection system, which senses heat and smoke. When triggered, sprinklers are activated to suppress the fire.
4. *Storage*. Combustible materials should be rated and stored in separate or isolated areas. They should *not* be stored near exits, and **reactive materials** should not be stored near flammable materials.

reactive material
causes a violent, explosive reaction when it comes in contact with another material, such as acetylene with water, or bleach with chlorinated cleaner

Many fires are triggered by unsafe acts (e.g., a person tries to weld a container containing flammable liquid residue without cleaning it) and unsafe conditions (e.g., faulty or improper equipment is installed near a potentially flammable material).

TABLE 11.1

Classes of Fire

CLASS	GROUP	MATERIAL	SYMBOL	COLOUR	EXTINGUISHER
A	Combustible	Paper, wood	Triangle	Green	Water
B	Flammable liquid	Oil, grease, gas	Square	Red	CO_2, dry chemical
C	Electrical	Wiring	Circle	Blue	CO_2, halon
D	Metals	Flammable metals such as magnesium or titanium	Star	Yellow	Powder
K	Grease	Cooking oil, fat	Frying pan or K	Black	Wet grease chemical

Notes: Although comparatively rare, Class D fires require metal/sand extinguishers that work by smothering the fire. The most common extinguishing agent in this class is sodium chloride, but powdered copper metal (for lithium fires) and other materials are used. Class K is a more recent designation of fires. Extinguishers of this class are specially designed to supplement the fire suppression systems found in commercial kitchens. They use a wet chemical agent such as potassium acetate.

Occupational Health and Safety Notebook 11.5

Rescues

As a result of some emergency conditions, individuals may be trapped in buildings that have been damaged. Rescue work is highly specialized, requiring both specialized training and equipment. During the 1985 earthquake in Mexico City, some 130 untrained or ill-equipped volunteer rescuers died attempting to save others. A rescue proceeds in five stages:

1. Reconnaissance and dealing with surface casualties
2. Location and removal of lightly trapped casualties
3. Exploration of likely survival points
4. Further exploration and debris removal
5. Systematic debris removal

Source: Adapted from *Keeping Canadians Safe: Basic Rescue Skills*, published by Public Safety Canada. http://www.ps-sp.gc.ca/prg/em/gds/brs-en.asp Reproduced with the Permission of the Minister of Public Works and Government Services Canada, 2007.

First Aid and Medical Attention

The various provincial and territorial regulations spell out in detail the requirements for first-aid and medical-aid facilities. Medical services run the gamut from a first-aid kit in a small firm to a fully equipped hospital with doctors in very large firms. Degree of risk can be an additional factor in determining the extent of medical services. An insurance office with a staff of 4,000 would not likely need the same facilities as an automobile manufacturer with the same number of workers.

RPC 11.2

Beyond conforming to legal requirements, every company should arrange to have at least one trained first-aid attendant present at each shift. All employees should be given the opportunity to take a cardiopulmonary resuscitation (CPR) course. A cost–benefit analysis may show the advantages of

Occupational Health and Safety Notebook 11.6

Chemical Spills

A chemical spill is an uncontrolled release of gas, liquid, or solid chemical. Chemicals can, of course, be highly toxic and emergency procedures must be oriented on avoiding exposure to the chemical. Good procedures for a chemical spill include the following:

- Avoid coming into contact with the chemical and warn others in the area.
- Isolate the area around the spill.
- Assist those who are injured but do not risk exposing yourself to the chemical.
- Determine the level of response. If the spill is minor and trained personnel are available with the necessary protective gear and materials, then the material should be cleaned up. Otherwise, the authorities should be contacted.

Source: University of Alberta, Environmental Health and Safety, "Chemical spills." Retrieved from http://www.ehs.ualberta.ca/index.aspx?Pg=52#Spill, February 7, 2007.

Occupational Health and Safety Notebook 11.7

Legislated First-Aid Requirements

First-aid training and supplies are mandated in occupational health and safety legislation. The exact requirements vary by (1) jurisdiction, (2) the number of workers in the workplace, (3) the nature (and danger) of the work, and (4) the distance to the nearest medical facility. Regulations typically specify the number of trained first-aiders, the level of training required, and the amount and type of first-aid equipment that must be present. In cases of remote workplaces, employers may also be required to provide emergency medical transportation.

Source: Saskatchewan Department of Labour, "First aid in Saskatchewan workplaces." Retrieved from http://www.labour.gov.sk.ca/safety/firstaid/index.htm, February 7, 2007.

contracting with a local occupational health clinic for medical-aid services. These services can include pre-employment and post-employment medicals, exposure medical testing, and potential occupational illness identification. Complete first-aid records must be kept and maintained.

Postcontact

Postcontact efforts are really focused in two areas: helping individuals deal with the stresses associated with experiencing or witnessing an emergency situation, and getting back to "normal" operations.

Stress

An emergency is an acute or catastrophic stressor (Chapter 6), and individuals may experience long-lasting consequences as a result. Acute stressors can be more psychologically devastating, and their effects more enduring, than chronic stressors, suggesting the need to understand their effects. For example, individuals exposed to hurricanes and other traumatic stressors have reported ongoing impairments of psychological well-being, including symptoms of posttraumatic stress that endure for much longer than the actual precipitating event.[11] Studies of a wide variety of traumatic stressors suggest several dimensions that may be important to understanding the impact of stressors on individuals.

Studies have highlighted the role of control perceptions when individuals are exposed to stressful situations, including acute stressors.[12] Natural disasters such as hurricanes or blizzards may involve an almost total lack of control, suggesting that their effects may be pronounced.[13]

The multivariate risk/resilience model was developed to explain individual reactions to disasters.[14] The model incorporates situational factors such as the extent to which the individual receives social support on an ongoing basis, targeted social support, or social support received in direct response to the disaster, as well as the individual's exposure to the disaster.[15]

One approach to crisis response has been referred to as **critical incident stress debriefing (CISD).** Although the characteristics of CISDs may vary, they generally involve the provision of help and assistance (by psychologists or other trained personnel) immediately following a traumatic event in order to prevent the development of serious or lasting negative consequences. CISDs consist of elements such as ensuring confidentiality; providing individuals with the opportunity to talk about their perspective on, thoughts about, and emotional reactions to the incident; assessing psychological and physical symptoms; and providing information about stress responses and coping strategies.[16] CISD interventions are very popular among individuals regularly exposed to traumatic stressors. For example, almost every police, fire, and ambulance service in the country has some form of CISD intervention for their employees. The Canadian Forces uses CISD to debrief returning peacekeepers.

critical incident stress debriefing (CISD)
a posttrauma intervention focused on providing victims with an opportunity to discuss their experiences and reactions to a traumatic event

One study of the effectiveness of CISD compared the coping strategies and levels of anger of two groups of police officers that had experienced a traumatic event.[17] One group of officers received CISD and the other did not. The results suggested that the CISD group exhibited more adaptive coping strategies and lower levels of anger than did those in the non-CISD group. The lack of random assignment to conditions cast some doubt on the validity of these findings, although they do provide preliminary evidence of the efficacy of CISD following exposure to traumatic work-related events. If these results were replicable, it would be unethical to withhold such debriefings from employees who experience traumatic events.

Unfortunately, despite these promising results, the research literature also provides a basis on which to question the effectiveness of CISD. First, a review of 67 studies concluded that debriefing does not mitigate the effects of traumatic stress.[18] Second, based on a meta-analytic review, other authors found that single-session debriefing was less effective than other forms of intervention and less effective than no intervention in reducing the effects of traumatic stress.[19] Finally, growing lists of studies suggest that individuals receiving CISD interventions may experience exacerbated traumatic reactions and more adverse outcomes.[20] These findings violate the widely accepted maxim that psychological interventions should in the first instance do no harm. The inconsistent findings as to the effectiveness of CISDs suggest the need for more research in this area, to identify whether some elements of CISDs are helpful and should be retained and which are harmful and should be removed from such programs.

Getting Back to Normal

Getting back to normal after an emergency is not as straightforward as a simple return to work. Depending on circumstances, individuals may continue to experience stress reactions. They may also continue to live with the effects of the emergency (e.g., damaged housing, loss of income, transportation) long after the acute phase of the emergency has passed. For example, Hurricane Juan in Nova Scotia passed in one night, but some individuals were without electricity for up to 14 days after the hurricane.

Occupational Health and Safety Notebook 11.8

Business Continuity Planning

Even during an emergency, critical services must be continued. Some employers may have to continue operations during an emergency, and all employers will eventually have to return to "normal" operations. Business continuity planning is a proactive approach to ensuring that critical services and products continue during an emergency. Developing a business continuity plan will help to ensure that employers recover data, assets, and facilities and have the necessary resources (including human resources) to continue business.

Source: Adapted from *Keeping Canadians Safe: A Guide to Business Continuity Planning*. Published by Public Safety Canada. http://www.ps-sp.gc.ca/prg/em/gds/bcp-en.asp#4 Reproduced with the permission of the Minister of Public Works and Government Services Canada, 2007.

Given these potential reactions and experiences, it is unlikely that individuals will return to the workplace focused on the task at hand. Recognizing the need to get back to work, employers should display some tolerance for distractions and the need for employees to share their experiences. Adjusting to normal work may take some time.

WWW

Employers may inadvertently increase employee stress by the way they handle personnel decisions around the emergency. In Halifax following Hurricane Juan, employers had to make several decisions that affected their employees. For instance, employers had to make decisions about compensation for lost workdays following the storm and employee attendance during the state of emergency. Similar decisions were made after the February Blizzard (White Juan) and elicited considerable anger from some employees (for an example, see the Weblinks section).

Summary

The goals of an emergency plan are to reduce injuries and property damage, and to restore the organization to its normal operations. Emergency preparedness consists of preparing an emergency response plan, designating and training those responsible for its implementation, and communicating it to employees. Developing an evacuation plan, establishing a fire-prevention and suppression program, and controlling fire hazards are other elements of emergency preparedness.

Key Terms

critical incident stress debriefing (CISD) 315
emergency 304
fire 310
free-burning stage 311
incipient stage 311
reactive material 312
smouldering stage 311
uncontrolled fire stage 311

Weblinks

Canadian Centre for Emergency Preparedness

http://www.ccep.ca/ (p. 302)

Hurricane Juan Photos

http://www.vektor.ca/juan/ (p. 302)

CBC News, Indepth: SARS—Severe Acute Respiratory Syndrome

http://www.cbc.ca/news/background/sars/ (p. 304)

Government of Canada, "Safety and Security for Canadians"

http://canada.gc.ca/SSC/SSC_e.html (p. 304)

Office of Critical Infrastructure Protection and Emergency Preparedness, "Natural Hazards of Canada"

http://www.psepc.gc.ca/res/em/nh/index-en.asp (p. 306)

University of Guelph, "Emergency Response Plan"

http://www.uoguelph.ca/security/Police/ERP.html (p. 307)

Simon Fraser University, "SFU Emergency Plan (GP 34)"

http://www2.sfu.ca/policies/general/gp34.htm (p. 307)

Canadian Standards Association

http://www.csa.ca (p. 309)

Government of Nova Scotia, "911: Nova Scotia's Emergency Telephone Reporting System"

http://www.gov.ns.ca/emo/AbsPage.aspx?id51116&siteid51&lang51 (p. 309)

Canadian Red Cross

http://www.redcross.ca (p. 313)

St. John Ambulance

http://www.sja.ca (p. 314)

Nova Scotia Power

http://www.nspower.ca (p. 315)

Environment Canada, "White Juan"

http://www.atl.ec.gc.ca/weather/severe/2003-2004/whitejuan_e.html (p. 316)

RPC Icons

RPC 11.1 Ensures that mechanisms are in place for responding to crises in the workplace, including critical incident stress management.

- oral and written communication
- training and development techniques
- industry best practices
- the workplace environment including the availability of emergency equipment
- policy and program development and evaluation
- intervention strategies
- relevant legislation (e.g., fire code, Workers' Compensation)
- investigation techniques
- stress management techniques
- types of employee assistance programs
- Occupational health and safety legislation (e.g., Occupational Health and Safety Act of Ontario, Workplace Safety & Insurance Act—Bill 99, Workplace Hazardous Materials Information System, Transportation of Dangerous Goods legislation, environmental legislation, smoking in the workplace legislation, civil rights legislation)
- hazard identification and control
- accident investigation procedures
- emergency preparedness procedures
- management techniques for OH&S Programs
- conceptual definition and implications of occupational stressors (e.g., potential stressors, methods of identifying potential stressors and strain outcomes, response to organizational stressors, and management of employee strain outcomes)

RPC 11.2 Establishes effective programs for accident prevention, incident investigation, inspections, fire and emergency response, and required training.

- relevant legislation
- workplace inspection and accident investigation techniques
- nature of the business and physical work environment
- potential risks and hazards in the workplace
- emergency response planning
- community emergency response services
- training and development
- industry best practices
- Worker Protection (including health and safety and Workers' Compensation)
- training and development program design and administration
- hazard identification and control
- accident investigation procedures
- emergency preparedness procedures
- management techniques for OH&S Programs

RPC 11.3 Responds to serious injury or fatality in the workplace.

- program and policy development
- investigation procedures

TASK & KNOWLEDGE REQUIREMENTS

- relevant legislative requirements
- first aid training and emergency response equipment
- relevant legislative bodies
- pension and insurance benefits/policies
- common and statutory law (e.g., employment standard: labour relations
- Worker Protection (including health and safety and Workers' Compensation)
- Occupational health and safety legislation (e.g., Occupational Health and Safety Act of Ontario, Workplace Safety & Insurance Act—Bill 99, Workplace Hazardous Materials Information System, Transportation of Dangerous Goods legislation, environmental legislation, smoking in the workplace legislation, civil rights legislation)
- hazard identification and control
- accident investigation procedures
- emergency preparedness procedures

Discussion Questions

1. Who should be involved in developing emergency response plans?
2. What types of emergencies should organizations in your area be prepared for?
3. Decide what type of fire extinguisher would be most effective in the following fire situations:
    a. a hair dryer engulfed in smoke
    b. grease burning in a frying pan
    c. rags smoking in the garage
    d. a log that has rolled from the fireplace onto the living-room floor
    e. a coffee machine whose wires are shooting flames
4. Although this chapter has focused on health and safety implications, there are also public relations issues in an emergency. What principles would be appropriate for an organization to adopt in dealing with the media and public during an emergency?

Using the Internet

1. What emergencies have occurred in your local area in the past five years? How effective was the emergency response? (*Hint:* Local EMO sites often have debriefing reports on past emergency responses.)

2. What plans are being made for the predicted flu pandemic in your area? (*Hint:* What information is available from government agencies; what firms are publishing pandemic plans)?

Exercises

1. Determine whether your workplace or school has an emergency response plan. Compare this plan with the one outlined in this chapter.
2. Prepare a fire-prevention and suppression plan for your own home or apartment.

Case

Biological Terrorism

In recent weeks, there have been heightened concerns about biological terrorism. Specifically, there is concern that it is possible to spread toxic organisms (e.g., anthrax) by mailing them. In the last three months there have been at least four incidents in which a firm or office building has been the target of such an attack (i.e., a suspicious envelope or parcel arrives in the mailroom with some indication that it contains a highly contagious toxin). Senior management in your firm is concerned. They have asked you to develop an emergency plan for dealing with such an occurrence. What do you need to consider and do to develop such a plan? Identify the elements of emergency preparedness and how each should be implemented.

Endnotes

1. Pearson, C. M., Clair, J. A., Misra, S. K., & Mitroff, I. I. (1997). Managing the unthinkable. *Organizational Dynamics, 26,* 51–64.
2. Blythe, B. T. (2002). *Blindsided: A manager's guide to catastrophic incidents in the workplace.* New York: Portfolio.
3. Pearson, C. M., Clair, J. A., Misra, S. K., & Mitroff, I. I. (1997). Managing the unthinkable. *Organizational Dynamics, 26,* 51–64.
4. Pearson, C. M., & Clair, J. A. (1998). Reframing crisis management. *Academy of Management Review, 23*(1), 59–76.
5. Mitroff, I. I., Pearson, C. M., & Harrigan, L. K. (1996). *The essential guide to managing corporate crises.* New York: Oxford University.
6. Blythe, B. T. (2002). *Blindsided: A manager's guide to catastrophic incidents in the workplace.* New York: Portfolio.
7. Pearson, C. M., & Clair, J. A. (1998). Reframing crisis management. *Academy of Management Review, 23*(1), 59–76.
8. Braverman, M. (2003). Managing the human impact of crisis. *Risk Management, 50*(5), 10–14.
9. Kelloway, E. K., & Mullen, J. (2007). *The stress (of an) epidemic.* Manuscript submitted for publication.
10. Lockwood, N. R. (2005). Crisis management in today's business environment: HR's strategic role. *HR Magazine, 50,* 1–9.

11. Norris, F. H., Byrne, C. M., Diaz, E., & Kaniasty, K. (2001). *50,000 disaster victims speak: An empirical review of the empirical literature, 1981–2001*. Retrieved from http:// obssr.od.nih.gov/ activities/911/attack.htm, October 12, 2004.
12. Schat, A. C. H., & Kelloway, E. K. (2003). Reducing the adverse consequences of work-place aggression and violence: The buffering effects of organizational support. *Journal of Occupational Health Psychology, 8,* 110–122.
13. Baum, A., Fleming, R., & Davidson, L. M. (1983). Natural and technological catastrophe. *Environment and Behavior, 15,* 333–354.
14. Freedy, J. R., Saladin, M. E., Kilpatrick, D. G., & Resnick, H. S. (1994). Understanding acute psychological distress following natural disaster. *Journal of Traumatic Stress, 7*(2), 257–273.
15. Byron, K., & Peterson, S. (2002). The impact of a large-scale traumatic event on individual and organizational outcomes: Exploring employee and company reactions to September 11. *Journal of Organizational Behavior, 23*(8), 895–910.
16. Mitchell, J., & Bray, G. (1990). *Emergency services stress*. Englewood Cliffs, NJ: Prentice-Hall.
17. Leonard, R., & Alison, L. (1999). Critical incident stress debriefing and its effects on coping strategies and anger in a sample of Australian police officers involved in shooting incidents. *Work and Stress, 13,* 144–161.
18. Arendt, M., & Elklit, A. (2001). Effectiveness of psychological debriefing. *Acta Psychiatry Scandanavia, 104,* 423–437.
19. Van Emmerik, A. A. P., Kamphuis, J. H., Hulsbosch, A. M., & Emmelkamp, P. M. G. (2002). Single session debriefing after psychological trauma: A meta-analysis. *The Lancet, 340,* 768–771.
20. Carlier, I. V. E., Lamberts, R. D., Van Uchelin, A. J., & Gersons, B. P. R. (1998). Disaster-related posttraumatic stress in police officers: A field study of the impact of debriefing. *Stress Medicine, 14,* 143–148; Mayou, R. A., Ehler, A., & Hobbs, M. (2000). Psychological debriefing for road accident victims: Three-year follow up of randomized control trial. *British Journal of Psychiatry, 176,* 589–593; and Small, R., Lumley, J., Donohue, L., Potter, A., & Waldenstroem, U. (2001). Randomized controlled trial of midwife led debriefing to reduce maternal depression after operative childbirth. *British Medical Journal, 321,* 1043–1047.

Chapter 12

Accident Investigation

Chapter Learning Objectives

After reading this chapter, you should be able to:

- describe the intent and steps of an accident investigation
- gather information to analyze the human, situational, and environmental factors contributing to accidents
- outline the legal requirements of accident investigation results
- explain the concept of a walkthrough survey
- list the steps to conducting interviews concerning an accident
- conduct a reenactment
- complete the various types of incident, accident, and injury reports

The CAIB Report

Perhaps the most intensive accident investigation in recent history was the investigation conducted by the *Columbia* Accident Investigation Board (CAIB). The *Columbia* space shuttle broke up on February 1, 2003, killing the seven astronauts on board. The resulting investigation took 7 months and employed a staff of 120, in addition to the 400 NASA engineers. The Board reviewed 30,000 documents, conducted 200 formal interviews, and heard testimony from dozens of experts in addition to 3,000 members of the public.

The Board determined that the immediate physical cause of the loss of the *Columbia* was a breach in the thermal protection system on the left wing. However, the Board extended its investigation to include the culture of NASA, the historical development of the space program, and the social and political environment. The Board concluded that cultural and organizational practices (including relying on past success rather than current engineering tests) had a role to play in the accident. The Board made sweeping recommendations regarding both physical and organizational or cultural factors.

Although none of the actions of the Board can redress the tragic loss of life, it is hoped that implementing the recommendations will prevent the occurrence of a similar tragedy.

Source: *Columbia* Accident Investigation Board, "The CAIB report—Volume 1, August 2003." Retrieved from http://www.caib.us/news/report/volume1/default.html, February 8, 2007.

RPC 12.1

RPC 12.2

RPC 12.3

The investigation of incidents and accidents is a critical component of an organization's health and safety program. This chapter describes the rationale for accident investigations, the critical factors in the investigative process, the types of information to be collected, and the investigative methods and tools used to conduct an investigation. The importance of reporting and keeping records is also discussed.

Rationale for Accident Investigation

RAC program
a hazard recognition, assessment, and control program; a key element in most health and safety programs

The investigation of accidents is an important component in a hazard recognition, assessment, and control **(RAC) program,** which in turn is an integral part of a health and safety program. One study identifies the benefits of accident investigation as follows:[1]

1. *Determines direct causes*. An investigation will uncover the direct causes of an accident, thereby allowing for the subsequent exploration of corrective measures.
2. *Identifies contributing causes*. Some accidents may be the result of many factors. For example, although the direct cause of an accident may be

the inadequate safeguards on the equipment, contributing factors may include loose clothing on the employee and a lack of instruction in the proper procedures for equipment use.

3. *Prevents similar accidents.* Once the direct and contributing causes are identified, corrective measures such as training programs or equipment design improvements can be implemented to prevent similar accidents.
4. *Creates a permanent record.* The reports generated by an investigation can be used by HR and safety specialists to identify trends (i.e., sites of frequent incidents, inefficient layouts and designs, unsafe acts, or improper operating procedures). Reports can also be valuable in the case of litigation or compensation claims. Actions taken to improve safety records can be cost efficient in the sense that money and time will be allocated to sites or equipment for which the most frequent or most severe accidents and injuries occur.
5. *Determines cost.* The delineation of the exact situation may help the organization determine the actual costs accruing from an accident. All factors, even a worker's lost time, count more than once if there were multiple activities by this worker directly related to the event.
6. *Promotes safety awareness among employees.* If a thorough investigation is conducted, employees will realize that management is serious about safety and interested in their well-being. This should motivate employees to show a greater concern for safe practices.

Critical Factors in the Investigative Process

Accident investigations are strongly influenced by timing, severity, and legal requirements.

Timing

Timing is a critical factor in the investigation of accidents. Time affects several types of information. Delays in an investigation may lead to partial or complete memory loss by the witnesses, changes at the accident site, and removal of important evidence. Furthermore, those directly involved in the accident, whether they are witnesses or late arrivals, tend to discuss the accident, and details may become distorted in the retelling.

Of course, the investigation should start only after any injured people receive medical attention and the accident site has been secured to prevent access, further injuries, and attempts by helpful observers to "fix" the hazard.

Severity

Given the time-consuming nature of investigation, companies tend to examine only those accidents that have the most serious consequences. However, incidents and accidents that result in minor injuries are often signals of a hazard that may one day have more serious consequences.

Occupational Health and Safety Today 12.1

What to Investigate

A wide variety of safety-related events may be subject to investigation. Occupational health and safety legislation may mandate post-accident investigations in some cases, depending on the severity and nature of the accident. For example, when a workplace death occurs, it is clear that external agencies such as the police will become involved and assume the primary investigative role. When injury-causing accidents are severe or continually recurring, provincial or territorial and federal health and safety agencies (such as the Labour Program of Human Resources and Social Development Canada) may appoint an investigator to inspect the workplace or may require the submission of a formal report. Employers may also mandate the scope of accident investigations based on local standards or specific concerns. The occupational health and safety policy at Dalhousie University, for example, mandates the investigation of the following types of accidents:

1. All serious-injury accidents that result in hospitalization or absences for two or more days
2. All fires or explosions
3. All major spills or releases of chemicals
4. Any accident or series of accidents that the environmental health and safety committee wants to have investigated

Sources: Dalhousie University, "Health and safety policy and procedures." Retrieved from http://www.dal.ca/~ehs/police2.htm, February 8, 2007; and Kelloway, E. K., Stinson, V., & MacLean, C. (2004). "Can eyewitness research improve occupational health and safety? Towards a research agenda." *Law and Human Behavior, 28,* 115.

One corporate director of health and safety recommends that the following types of accidents be investigated: those resulting in lost-time injuries beyond the day of the accident; accidents in which the injury was minor, but the employee was treated by a doctor and there was potential for a serious injury; close calls; accidents without injuries but property damage in excess of $1,000; and lost-time accidents resulting from aggravation of a previous injury.[2] Regardless of the system used to judge seriousness, organizations have a legal obligation to report injury-related accidents.

Legal Requirements

Depending on the seriousness of the accident, the presence of an injury, and the jurisdiction in which the accident happened, employers have to fulfill reporting requirements. Certain types of events—those in which an injury requires medical aid or results in lost time, for instance—must be reported to a Workers' Compensation Board, normally within three days. Forms are supplied by the Board.

Types of Information Collected

Most incidents and accidents are the result of many contributing factors. The Three Mile Island disaster (a nuclear plant disaster that occurred near Harrisburg, Pennsylvania, on March 28, 1979) was preceded by multiple contributing factors ranging from inadequate emergency training, through equipment failing to shut down, to fail-safe systems that failed to take into consideration the human equation. Although no lives were lost in the incident, public trust in the nuclear-power industry plummeted.

The area supervisor should conduct this investigation, assisted by the HR or safety specialist. When investigating an accident, the HR or safety specialist should concentrate on three factors: human, situational, and environmental. These factors, while similar in name, are not the same as the sources of hazards described in Chapter 7.

Human Factors

Studying the worker as a source of accidents does not mean the investigator is looking for a scapegoat. As highlighted throughout this text, the intent is to collect facts, not assign blame. The following are some questions that could be asked when investigating human factors:

- What was the worker doing at the time of the accident? Was he or she performing a regular task or a different task, doing maintenance work, or helping a coworker?
- Was the work being performed according to procedures? Were the tasks or procedures new?
- Was a supervisor present?
- What was the employment status of the worker—seasonal, part-time, or full-time?
- How much experience did the employee have with respect to this particular operation?
- What was the posture and location of the employee?
- Did some unsafe act contribute to the event?

Occupational Health and Safety Notebook **12.1**

The Eyewitness

Most accident investigations rely on eyewitness accounts and those of individuals involved in the incident. Yet there is good reason to suspect the accuracy of eyewitness statements. A review of the literature on eyewitness testimony showed that "what we know about eyewitness memory comes from hundreds of studies. . . . Overall, this body of research tells us that eyewitness testimony is not like a videotape recorder; memory is fragile, malleable, and susceptible to forgetting, even in optimal conditions." The authors cite an example of an airplane crash that killed nine people. Dozens of people witnessed the crash and at least one insisted at the inquest that the plane nose-dived into the ground. Photographic evidence proved that, in fact, the plane coasted down and skidded for nearly 300 metres.

Source: Kelloway, E. K., Stinson, V., & MacLean, C. (2004). "Can eyewitness research improve occupational health and safety? Towards a research agenda." *Law and Human Behavior, 28*, 115.

Situational Factors

An analysis of the unsafe conditions that led to the accident is a critical step in an accident investigation. The equipment and tools must be examined. The following questions could be asked when investigating situational factors:

- Was the machine operating in a satisfactory manner?
- Were all the control and display positions working and ergonomically sound?
- Were the safety measures satisfactory and functioning?
- Did the analysis of failed materials or equipment indicate how the accident happened? For instance, if a shaft broke, causing a machine part to fly off, an engineer can examine the break and determine the mode of failure. Failure of metal through shear or bending modes will leave definite patterns in the failed ends. Once the mode is known, the cause is usually easily determined.
- What was the site or location of the accident?
- What tools, equipment, or objects were involved in the accident?
- Was the correct equipment available and being used to do the job?
- What personal protective equipment (gloves, goggles, etc.) was being worn?
- Were guards in place?
- What time of day did the accident occur?
- What shift was being worked?

Environmental Factors

Sometimes environmental factors such as light and noise may increase the likelihood that an accident will occur. The setting sun may blind the driver of a delivery truck; the noise of a machine may mask the approach of a vehicle; the vibrations of a certain piece of equipment may dislodge another tool.

Who Investigates?

Numerous individuals may be involved in accident investigations, including the following:

- *The supervisor:* The supervisor possesses a detailed knowledge of the work and the working conditions and is therefore well positioned to conduct the investigation. In most companies, supervisors assume principal responsibility for the investigation.
- *Technical advisers and specialists:* It may be appropriate to bring in technical advisers or specialists when accidents are serious and involve highly technical processes. Bringing in outside expertise may also enhance the objectivity of the investigation.
- *Safety and health officer:* The department or company health and safety officer can also offer guidance in coordinating an accident investigation. The health and safety representative may be more aware of, and familiar with, health and safety issues than is the supervisor.

- *Safety and health committee or representative:* Where there is an established health and safety committee, the health and safety committee must take part in an investigation.
- *A safety team:* In the event of a serious accident and, specifically, when it is not easy to determine the cause of an accident, a team approach is highly recommended. The team would include the supervisor, health and safety officer, members of the health and safety committee, and, possibly, outside experts.

Investigative Methods

A variety of methods may be used in conducting the investigation.

Observations or Walkthroughs

At the beginning of an investigation, an overall picture of the total environment is achieved by means of a **walkthrough**. Observation of causal factors, physical conditions, and work habits will help the specialist to identify potential causes of the accident. Because the manager may not be totally familiar with the details of the operation, the specialist should turn to the supervisor for any necessary information.

walkthrough
inspection of the accident scene to get a picture of the total environment

Occupational Health and Safety Notebook 12.2

Analysis of an Accident

A carpenter is making some tool holders and needs to trim about 0.5 cm off the length of a piece of 4 × 4 wood. The 4 × 4 is 121 cm long. The carpenter spends 15 minutes adjusting the table saw to remove the correct width of material. In the process, the carpenter also removes the legally required saw guard because it tends to interfere with cutting. The supervisor had been after the company to purchase a new and proper guard for the saw. The usual answer was, "Why buy a new guard when one came with the machine?" The carpenter decides not to replace the guard for this cut because the last time this operation was performed, the wood snagged on the guard support and allowed the blade to burn the cut surface. This necessitated extra sanding to remove the stain. However, this time, even though the carpenter uses the proper hand pusher and guides, the saw hits a knot, and the work piece jumps up from the spinning blade. Luckily, the carpenter receives only minor lacerations.

The unsafe acts in this accident are (1) the carpenter removing the guard and leaving it off during the operation, (2) the supervisor allowing the saw to be used with the poor guard and not insisting on replacing the defective guard, (3) the carpenter continuing to use a piece of unsafe equipment, and (4) the company purchasing the saw without specifying the correct type of guard.

The unsafe conditions are (1) having the improper guard on the machine, (2) providing a machine without a proper guard, and perhaps (3) the supervisor being unaware of the use of the improper guard.

In most provinces and territories, a company official such as the plant manager could be found liable if an identified unsafe act or condition is ignored. The carpenter displayed voluntary risk in that the saw was used even though it was known to have a defective guard.

Can you identify the human, situational, and environmental factors that contributed to this accident?

Interviews

The following are some basic rules for conducting an interview:

1. Interview witnesses on the spot as soon as possible after the event while their memories are still fresh. Inform each witness of the purpose of the interview and what you hope to accomplish.
2. Interview witnesses separately and in a neutral location, such as the cafeteria. Do not use your office, since it could have an authority stigma associated with it. The witness should be permitted to have a worker representative present if he or she desires. Make sure that the representative listens and says little or nothing.
3. Put the witness at ease. If the person witnessed a serious injury, he or she may well be shaken or upset. If the person witnessed a death, counselling may be necessary before any discussion can take place. Reassure the witness that you are simply trying to gather information, not to lay blame.
4. Let the individual recall the event in his or her own way. Do not try to bias the account with questions that are pointed or directed. "Will you please tell me in your own words what you saw or heard?" is much better than, "Can you think what prompted John to do what he did?"
5. Ask necessary questions at appropriate times, without interrupting the speaker's train of thought. The questions should serve to clarify a point or fill in gaps, not to support conclusions you may be forming. "Can you explain again how you knew the machine was turned off?" is preferable to, "You commented that the table saw was not running—did you see the worker turn it off?"
6. Give the witness feedback. "Based on what you said, this is my understanding of what you saw. If there is something I missed or haven't got right, please add to or clarify it." When you are finished, both you and the witness should be able to agree that the statement is a factual representation of what was said.
7. Make sure that critical information—either from the witnesses or from your own observations—is recorded in a timely fashion. The longer the delay, the more bias will affect the results. Supplement your written record with visuals (e.g., sketches, photographs, videos).
8. End the interview on a positive note by thanking the witness for his or her valuable time and assistance. Encourage the witness to come to you with any further information that may emerge.

Reenactments

reenactment
a simulation designed to recreate the circumstances leading up to an incident

Reenactment is a powerful incident or accident recall method that requires very careful handling and planning. The most obvious problem is the danger that simulating an actual injury will produce another one.

Circumstances will dictate whether a reenactment is essential to complete a thorough investigation. In one documented case, the safety professional was on-site when a worker was impaled between the couplers of two boxcars in the rail yard of a company. The safety specialist filmed the car separation and the removal of the body. Then, while all the witnesses were present and all of the details were fresh—horribly so—in their minds, he had each witness walk through what he or she saw. The local coroner complimented the safety officer on the thoroughness of the evidence, and a reenactment was obviously unnecessary.

The following are some guidelines for conducting a reenactment:

1. *A qualified observer is necessary.* If none is available, then the in-house specialist will have to do the job. If it appears that evidence is being gathered for an inquest or court hearing, then every possible explanation, even suicide, must be considered.
2. *Do not show—tell.* Have all the witnesses relate in their own words what they observed. You as the analyst have to know precisely what took place during the event in question. Their stories will provide that information. You cannot afford any surprises that might lead to additional injury. Filming can be very helpful, but if, and only if, the witness agrees.
3. *Shut down every energy source and lock them out.* Follow the lockout procedures discussed in Chapter 8. Have the professional who is conducting the reenactment control the major key for the lockout.
4. *Carefully act out the events.* The witness will describe what happened at each step (just as he or she did when verbally describing the events), and then, with the specialist's approval, will act out that step. For obvious reasons, the reenactment will stop before the point of accident.

Occupational Health and Safety Notebook 12.3

Cognitive Interviewing

Cognitive interviewing is a technique that was developed for police officers conducting forensic investigations. A great deal of research suggests that cognitive interviews are effective in retrieving accurate eyewitness testimony. Cognitive interviews result in more information and a higher accuracy rate than do "regular" investigative interviews. Some preliminary evidence shows that the cognitive interview elicits more accurate statements from accident witnesses.* A typical cognitive interview follows the following sequence:

Introduction–Develop rapport, communicate needs, encourage active participation

Open-ended narration–Establish mental context, note mental images, develop plan for probing

Probing–Use richest images to probe, ask questions related to images

Review–Review information reported

Close–Finish official business and encourage future contact

*MacLeJan, C., Stinson, V., & Kelloway, E. K. (2004). *Cognitive interviewing of accident witnesses: An initial test.* Paper presented at the annual meeting of the Canadian Psychological Association, St John's, NL.

Sources: Fisher, R. P. (1995). "Interviewing victims and witnesses of crime." *Psychology, Public Policy, and Law, 1,* 732–764; Fisher, R. P., Geiselman, R. E., & Amador, M. (1989). "Field test of the cognitive interview: Enhancing the recollection of actual victims and witnesses of crime." *Journal of Applied Psychology, 74,* 722–727; and Fisher, R. P., McCauley, M. R., & Geiselman, R. E. (1994). "Improving eyewitness testimony with the cognitive interview." In D. F. Ross, J. D. Read, & M. P. Toglia (Eds.), *Adult eyewitness testimony: Current trends and developments* (pp. 245–272). New York: Cambridge University Press.

Investigative Tools

The walkthrough, the interview, and the reenactment can be supplemented by the following:

- *Photographs:* Accident photography is helpful and even necessary for efficient accident investigation. When pictures are being taken, make sure they show the whole area, as well as every angle and every nook and cranny. Colour is best, although black and white can be useful. One advantage of black-and-white photographs is that they can be scanned and included in the accident report. Investigators with limited photographic experience will find a Polaroid camera relatively easy to use. Photographs taken with this camera can be examined on the spot for focus and framing problems. Point and shoot cameras also require minimal operator skill. Digital video cameras are effective and preferred since the film can be viewed immediately and the data can be entered into the computer.
- *Drawings:* After the interview, prepare a series of sketches or drawings of the accident scene. These can be complemented by "instant" photographs or video. A good CAD program such as Cadkey or Cadkey Lite will facilitate the drawing process. If you do not have access to CAD software and the training to use it, then a scale pencil sketch is fine. Make sure all parts of the drawing are well labelled.
- *Computers:* Incident recall involves the gathering and recording of large amounts of information. A computer with a user-friendly database is a necessity. Portable laptops can be taken directly to the scene of an accident. Any computer will facilitate the structured entry of data and facts into the safety files.
- *Other tools:* Depending on the circumstances of the event, other tools such as tape measures, clipboards, water-resistant pens, and flashlights will be of assistance to the investigator.
- *Record check:* Training records and maintenance or production schedules can offer the investigator some valuable insights. A careful review of training records can provide the answers to some questions: Was the worker properly instructed in the accepted and safe methods of doing the job or task? Was he or she aware of the rules of operation and were they followed? Has the worker signed a training attendance sheet or examination form? Maintenance logs and records should provide information about potential hazards within the company and what, if anything, was done about them. Preventive maintenance data are particularly important, since they can be used to predict possible future failures in equipment.

RPC 12.4

Accident/Incident Reports

Once all the information from the investigation has been gathered, the accident/incident reports must be completed. These reports should provide some explanation of causal factors. Although the principal causes remain unsafe acts (e.g., not using a personal protective device) or unsafe conditions (e.g., a broken guard), other explanatory conditions may exist. The factor most closely associated with the cause of an accident is referred to as the *agency*. The following are some examples of agents:

- animals (insects, dogs, raccoons, etc.)
- pressure vessels (boilers, piping)
- chemicals (solvents, explosives)
- materials-handling systems (conveyers, forklift trucks)
- dust, fumes, smoke, mists (silica, wood)
- electrical equipment (motors, fuses, wiring)
- elevating devices (elevators, vertical stop belts)
- tools (hammers, wrenches)
- lifting devices (hoists, cranes)
- machine tools (lathe, drill press)
- motive power sources (engines, vehicles)
- radiation (X-ray, ultraviolet)

The *agency* refers to the subgroup of the factors listed above. For example, a dog bite would be the agency part of the animal group.

Another consideration in reports is the *accident type,* which attempts to categorize the nature of the accident. Some examples include the following:

- caught in or between (e.g., crushed between two moving machines)
- struck by (impact or blow to the body by an object)
- struck against (walking into a door)
- fall to the same level (tripping on a level walkway)
- fall to a lower level (falling off a ladder)
- fall to a higher level (tripping while walking up steps)
- abraded, scratched, or punctured (an injury such as hitting the face when falling)
- overexertion (sprains, strains, etc., caused by a greater-than-average effort)
- contact with an energy (mechanical, kinetic, electrical, chemical, thermal, gravity, or radiation)

Personal factors (e.g., lack of knowledge, fatigue, restricted vision) should also be included in the accident investigation form to assist in entry, record keeping, and analysis.

The actual report format will vary by company. (Samples of short and long reports are provided in Figures 12.1 and 12.2, respectively.) Organization and layout should be straightforward. Accuracy and thoroughness are also important. Where information is unknown or is not applicable, the respondent should indicate "information unknown" or "not applicable." Abbreviations such as "n/a" for "not applicable" should not be used (it can mean "not available" as well). Do not leave the space blank!

Reports that must be submitted to outside parties such as OH&S agencies or WCBs should include basic information about the company (i.e., type of industry, number of employees, etc.).

FIGURE 12.1a

Short Report

PE+E Supervisor's Accident/Incident Report

A. General Information

last name: *first name:* *gender: [ ] male [ ] female*

department: *job title:*

type: *[ ] full time* *[ ] part time* *[ ] casual*

date of injury: *time of injury:* *[ ] am [ ] pm*

date reported: *time reported:* *[ ] am [ ] pm*

incident category: *[ ] illness* *[ ] injury* *[ ] first aid* *[ ] medical aid*

B. Accident Investigation

Nature and extent of injury: [ ] left [ ] right

What job was the employee performing:

Was this part of regular duties: [ ] yes [ ] no

Length of time employee performing this type of work:

Exact location of accident:

Describe sequence of events leading to accident. Name tools, machines, materials used. Provide sketch on reverse if necessary.

Describe any unsafe mechanical or physical condition involved in accident:

Describe any unsafe act involved in accident:

Name and address of hospital or clinic: [ ] company doctor:

Doctor's name: Doctor's estimate of lost time:

Measures taken to prevent similar accidents:

FIGURE 12.1b

Short Report

C. Diagrams

Diagrams or photographs may be placed here:

Witness name:	Witness name:
Address:	Address:
Phone: Res:	Phone: Res:
Bus:	Bus:
Supervisor's signature:	Date:
Employee's signature:	Date:

Please have this document processed and forwarded to *Original to:* *Manager, Safety and Environment*
Copies to: *Vice President, Manufacturing,*
Manager, Human Resources
Department

The information you provide on this document will enable PE+E to effectively manage claims. Thank you for taking as much time as possible.

FIGURE 12.2a

Long Report

Supervisor's Accident/Incident Report

To be completed by the supervisor with the employee immediately after an accident/incident

Please Print

last name *first name* *gender*

street *apt* *city* *prov*

postal code *telephone* *date of birth* *marital status*

date of employment *department* *job title*

[ ] full time *[ ] part time* *[ ] casual* *hrs/week*

years' experience *social insurance number*

accident/incident occurred: *yyyy mm dd (* *)* *hhmm (* *) am/pm*

reported to employer: *yyyy mm dd (* *)* *hhmm (* *) am/pm*

who was accident reported to

location of accident (dept, machine, location of machine)

supervisor's name

witness name(s)

Has this employee ever had a similar work-related injury or non-work-related injury? [ ] yes [ ] no

If yes, explain:

List the employee's job description/task analysis at the time of the injury

(Include job title, duties, weights, sizes of equipment, tools, etc.)

What physical effort was involved? (List job function plus weights and sizes of materials used.)

FIGURE 12.2b

Long Report

Investigation of accident/incident (*who, what, why, where, how*)

Who was involved? ____________________

____

Where did the accident/incident occur? ____________________

____

What happened to cause the accident/incident? (explain—facts only) ____________________

____

____

____

____

Why did the accident/incident occur? (be objective, do not lay blame) ____________________

____

____

How did the accident/incident occur? (based on facts only) ____________________

____

____

Injury

[ ] lost time [ ] medical aid [ ] first aid [ ] information only or [ ] hazardous condition, no injury

treatment memorandum sent [ ] yes [ ] no modified work form sent [ ] yes [ ] no

Causes

[ ] unsafe act [ ] unsafe condition [ ] information only or [ ] poor/damaged equipment

[ ] no/poor training [ ] no/poor procedures [ ] other

Explain

____

____

____

____

____

____

____

(continued)

FIGURE 12.2c

Long Report

Accident type

[ ] overexertion/strain [ ] caught in/between [ ] slip/fall [ ] struck by/against [ ] exposed to

[ ] motor vehicle [ ] contact with/by [ ] other

Explain:

Injury type

[ ] bruise [ ] burn (heat) [ ] burn (chemical) [ ] cut [ ] crush [ ] strain

[ ] twist [ ] lift [ ] electric shock [ ] inhalation [ ] occupational illness

[ ] rash [ ] other

Explain:

Part of body injured ***[ ] left*** ***[ ] right***

[ ] head [ ] face [ ] eye [ ] ear [ ] neck [ ] chest

[ ] lungs [ ] abdomen [ ] groin [ ] back-upper [ ] back-middle [ ] back-lower

[ ] buttock [ ] shoulder [ ] arm [ ] wrist [ ] hand [ ] finger: th 2 3 4 5

[ ] leg [ ] knee [ ] ankle [ ] foot [ ] toe: big 2 3 4 5 [ ] other

Explain:

Suggested corrective action

[ ] review procedures [ ] protective equipment [ ] repair equipment [ ] develop procedure

[ ] re-instruction of staff

Explain:

FIGURE 12.2d

Long Report

name & address of hospital or clinic

name of attending doctor estimated time off work

name of family physician

address

date & hour last worked Work hours: from to

shift information: [ ] Day [ ] Afternoon [ ] Midnight

hours worked: from: to: days/week:

provide average gross earnings [ ] hourly [ ] daily

Additional information

Diagram of accident

Employee's signature Date

Supervisor's signature Date

MAKE COPIES AND SEND TO:

[ ] Manager, Loss Control (original) *[ ] Human Resources* *[ ] Department*

A description of any injury that was sustained should be included. A separate physician's report (see Figure 12.3) should also be provided, along with a witness report (see Figure 12.4).

FIGURE 12.3a

Physician's Report

INJURY/ILLNESS ASSESSMENT FORM

to accompany employee to physician

For use in on-duty instances of sickness or injury to determine the rehabilitation duties to which an employee can return in the workplace as presented in Bill 162 of the Workers' Compensation Act.

To be completed by an Employee's Supervisor (please print)

A. Personal Data Date:____________________

Employee's Name: *Signature:*

Job Title: *SIN:*

Date of illness or injury on duty: *Date of birth:*

Date absence commenced: *Health No.:*

Nature of injury:

Supervisor's Name: *Department:* *Telephone:*

To be completed by Physician (please print)

B. Assessment of fitness to work

1. [ ] Employee is fit to return to regular work.

2. [ ] Employee is fit to return to modified work—with restrictions as indicated in C & D (reverse).

Indicate number of hours to be worked and on what basis?

[____________] hours [ ] daily [ ] weekly

Estimate date of return to modified work:____________________

3. [ ] Not fit for work at this time.

Employee to return for medical reassessment on (yyyy mm dd) ____________________

See reverse side for Physical Evaluation to be completed by the Physician

Please return this completed form to the Manager, Loss Control via the Employee

FIGURE 12.3b

Physician's Report

To be completed by the treating Physician

C. Physical Evaluation

Step 1 *Location of problem*

a) head: include vision, hearing, speech
b) neck
c) upper back, chest or upper abdomen
d) lower back, lower abdomen or genitalia
e) shoulder or upper arm
f) elbow or lower arm
g) wrist or hand
h) hip or upper leg
i) knee or lower leg
j) ankle or foot
k) systemic or internal organ

A
B
E E
C
F F
G D G
H H
Right I I Left
J J

Step 2 *Please indicate restrictions for modified work*

1. Walking:	[ ] only short distances		[ ] other	
2. Standing, not more than:	[ ] 15 minutes	[ ] 30 minutes	[ ] other	
3. Sitting, no more than:	[ ] 30 minutes	[ ] 60 minutes	[ ] 2 hours	[ ] other
4. Bending and twisting, explain:				
5. Lifting, floor to waist, not more than:	[ ] 7 kg	[ ] 14 kg	[ ] 25 kg	[ ] other
6. Lifting, waist to head, not more than:	[ ] 7 kg	[ ] 14 kg	[ ] 25 kg	[ ] other
7. Carrying, not more than:	[ ] 7 kg	[ ] 14 kg	[ ] 25 kg	[ ] other
8. Climbing stairs:	[ ] no stair climbing	[ ] 2 or 3 steps only	[ ] only short flight	
9. Climbing ladder:	[ ] no climbing	[ ] 2 or 3 steps only	[ ] 4 or 6 steps only	
10. Manual dexterity, not able to:		[ ] type	[ ] sort	[ ] other
11. Pushing and pulling trolley, not more than:		[ ] 16 kg	[ ] 25 kg	[ ] other
12. Can operate motorized equipment:		[ ] any vehicle	[ ] forklifts	[ ] not recommended
13. Vision, potential safety hazard		[ ] yes	[ ] no	[ ] other
14. Other comments (explain)				

D. Treatment

1. Is the employee's prescribed treatment likely to impair performance or safety? [ ] yes [ ] no
2. Is the employee referred to: [ ] physiotherapy Date commenced:__________
   [ ] occupational therapy Duration:__________

Physician's Name: Telephone:

Address:

Date: Signature:

FIGURE 12.4

Witness Report

Accident/Incident Witness Statement

Injured employee: ______ Date of injury: ______

Witness name: ______

Does the witness have knowledge of the accident or injury? [ ] yes [ ] no

Did the witness see the injury happen? [ ] yes [ ] no

If yes to either of the above, please explain below:

Knowledge of injury: Explain what you know about the injury/accident (e.g., what type of work was being done at the time of the injury/accident, what happened to cause the injury/accident, how seriously was the injured employee hurt).

What witness actually saw: Please identify what you saw before the injury/accident, during the injury/accident, and immediately after the injury/accident.

Give your **opinion** as to how this injury/accident could have been prevented.

Witness signature: ______ Date: ______

Completed reports are submitted to the senior managers, the joint health and safety committee, others directly involved, and possibly the Ministry of Labour if the accident involved serious injuries. It is then up to the senior manager directly responsible for the operation in question to implement the recommendations contained in the report.

Accident Analysis

Once the data are collected, the next task is to analyze the information to identify the cause of the accident. A variety of analytic models and techniques are available for use in assessing the cause of an accident.

Domino Theory

Every event—accident or disaster—comprises a series of happenings that result in some negative condition. The **domino theory**, developed by H. W. Heinrich, is based on a set of five dominos labelled as follows:[3]

domino theory
the theory that every accident results from a series of events

1. *Background:* a lack of control over the management function (planning, organizing, leading, and controlling)
2. *Personal defects:* personal factors such as physical or mental problems, and job factors such as normal wear and tear of equipment
3. *Unsafe acts and conditions:* (described earlier)
4. *Accident:* a series of undesired events with release of energies that can cause harm
5. *Injury:* the most undesired result (e.g., trauma or property damage)

Although there are other models, such as those dealing with the release of energy[4] and with the theory of multiple factors,[5] the domino model is the easiest to illustrate. The domino theory asserts that if any one of the domino categories does not happen, then the injury probably will not occur (see Figure 12.5). For example, if a worker trying to make a production quota (background) was wearing loose clothing (personal defects or unsafe conditions) and operated a machine at unsafe speeds (unsafe act), then an accident or injury would be more likely to occur. However, if the worker were to wear well-fitting clothes or operate the machine at the proper speed (removal of domino number 2 or 3), then the risk of an accident occurring would be greatly reduced.

Occupational Health and Safety Today 12.2

Hazardous Occurrence Investigation in the Canadian Forces

The Canadian Forces through the Director General Safety advocates the analysis of hazardous occurrences as a means of preventing their recurrence. Their focus is on the identification of the root causes of accidents by assembling, categorizing, and analyzing all relevant data. In their view, the fact that an incident has occurred is evidence of a failure in one or more of five major categories: Materials, Task, Management, Personnel, or The Environment.

Source: Ministry of National Defence, "A DND/CF hazardous occurrences investigator's guide." Retrieved from http://www.vcds.forces.gc.ca/dsafeg/pubs/HOIGuide/j-HOIGuide_e.asp, February 8, 2007.

FIGURE 12.5

Heinrich's Domino Model

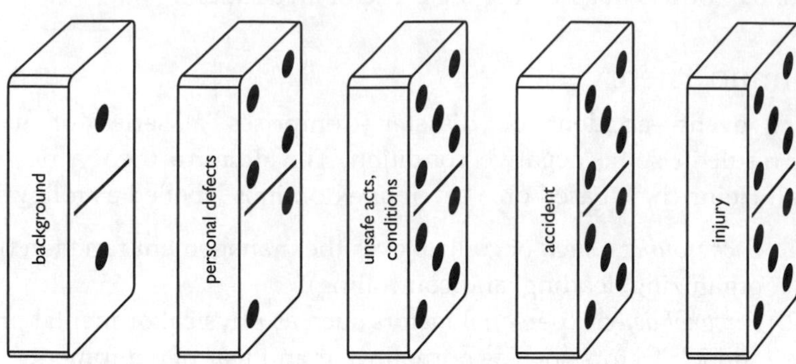

a) five factors in accident sequence

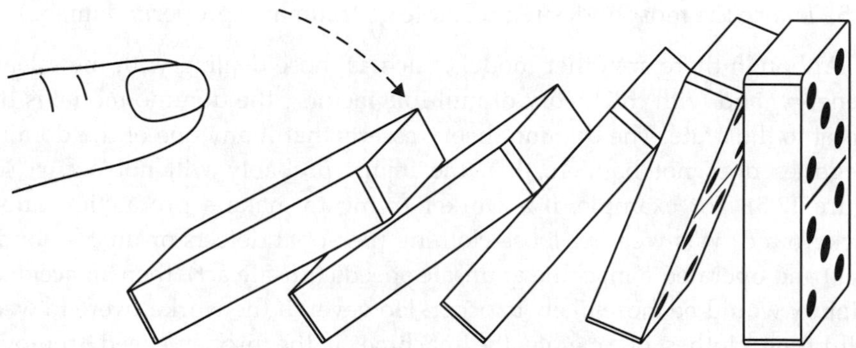

b) injury caused by action of preceding factors

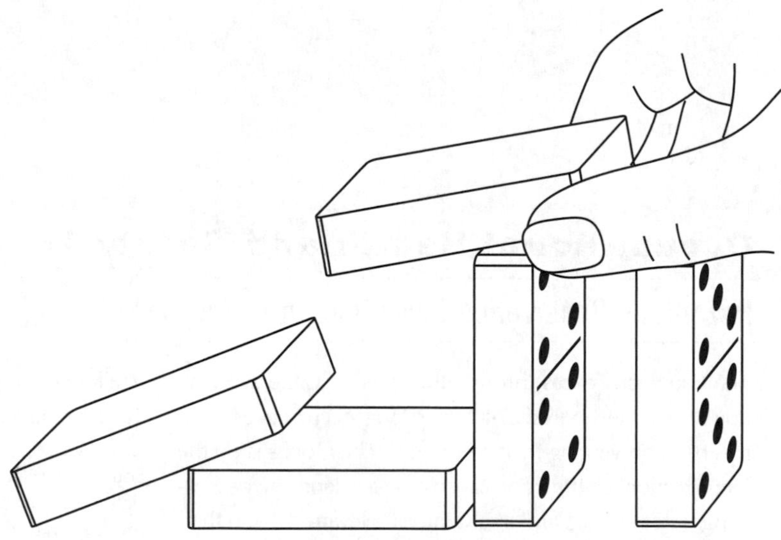

c) removal of a factor may prevent the accident from occurring

The Swiss Cheese Model

J. Reason presented an updated version of the domino model that is often depicted as series of dominoes with holes in them.[6] In this view (often called the "Swiss cheese model"), an accident results when the holes line up (i.e., there are failures at multiple levels). Reason's model focuses on the series of events that must occur for an accident to occur. His model emphasizes that unsafe acts cannot be viewed in isolation; they are a product of the organizational culture, the level of supervision, and a variety of other contextual factors. It follows that accident analysis then focuses on identifying these factors to "plug the holes" in the Swiss cheese.

Reason's accident causation model specifies four levels of defence:

1. Organizational influences
2. Local working conditions
3. Unsafe acts
4. Defences, barriers, and safeguards

For example, an organization with a poor safety culture may not have a high accident rate if it has well-developed safe working procedures or safety-conscious supervisors. Similarly, committing an unsafe act may not result in an accident if appropriate safeguards are in place. It is only when organizational influences and local working conditions allow for an unsafe act and there are no safeguards against such an act that an accident results.

Normal Accidents

The theory of **normal accidents**,[7] particularly in **high-reliability organizations** (e.g., chemical plants, nuclear plants),[8] suggests that accidents result from the interactive complexities in the technological system. That is, no single event causes an accident, and the search for a single discrete cause, analogous to a single perpetrator, might well be fruitless in such an environment. The futility of the endeavour may be difficult to recognize, given the common tendency to make sense out of organizational events. As one researcher notes, "people who know the outcome of a complex prior history of tangled, indeterminate events remember that history as being much more determinant, leading 'inevitably' to the outcome they already knew."[9]

normal accidents
the theory that accidents are expected outcomes of interactive complexities

high-reliability organizations
organizations in hazardous industries that maintain a high safety record over time

The Psychology of Accidents: Cognitive Failures

In many accident investigations focus is placed on the notion of human error. As a result, we often end up concluding that highly trained and experienced workers simply "made a mistake" in the routine performance of their duties. Psychologists refer to these slips or lapses as a "cognitive failure."[10] There seem to be at least three forms of cognitive failure; these relate to memory, focus, and physical skills. Forgetfulness is when you forget (even momentarily) things you ordinarily know (e.g., the name of your spouse or partner). Distractability is a failure in focus—finishing reading a page of text and realizing you have no idea what you just read is a common example of distractability. Finally, physical blunders include actions such as tripping over your own feet or bumping into things. Although much more research is required, we know that **cognitive failures** are often a sign of individuals under stress and that cognitive failures are related to the occurrence of both motor vehicle and work-related accidents.[11]

cognitive failure

a mistake or failure in the performance of an action that an individual is normally capable of performing

Summary

Accident investigation is a very important part of an OH&S program. The reasons for conducting an investigation are primarily to identify direct and contributing causes and to ensure that the accident does not recur. Timing and severity are the important variables in investigations. The types of information collected can be grouped under human factors, situational factors, and environmental factors. The investigative methods include observations or walkthroughs, interviews, and reenactments, all of which are complemented by investigative tools such as cameras and computers. Records also supply information that might be important in determining causes. The reporting and analysis of information collected is the last step in accident investigation.

Key Terms

cognitive failure 346
domino theory 343
high-reliability organizations 345
normal accidents 345
RAC program 324
reenactment 330
walkthrough 329

Weblinks

Canadian Centre for Occupational Health and Safety, "What Is an Accident and Why Should It Be Investigated?"

http://www.ccohs.ca/oshanswers/hsprograms/investig.html (p. 324)

WorkSafe Saskatchewan, "Accident Investigations"

http://www.worksafesask.ca/topics/essentials/accident_inv.html?noframe (p. 325)

RPC Icons

RPC 12.1 Responds to serious injury or fatality in the workplace.

- program and policy development
- investigation procedures

TASK & KNOWLEDGE REQUIREMENTS

- relevant legislative requirements

- first aid training and emergency response equipment
- relevant legislative bodies
- pension and insurance benefits/policies
- common and statutory law (e.g., employment standard: labour relations
- Worker Protection (including health and safety and Workers' Compensation)
- Occupational health and safety legislation (e.g., Occupational Health and Safety Act of Ontario, Workplace Safety & Insurance Act—Bill 99, Workplace Hazardous Materials Information System, Transportation of Dangerous Goods legislation, environmental legislation, smoking in the workplace legislation, civil rights legislation)
- hazard identification and control
- accident investigation procedures
- emergency preparedness procedures

RPC 12.2 Analyses risk to the health and safety of employees and determines appropriate preventative measures, including training, provision of required safety equipment, and administrative practices.

- relevant legislation
- nature of the business and physical work environment
- hazard recognition
- workplace inspection techniques
- safety programs, equipment, and emergency procedures
- ergonomics
- functions of the JHSC
- training and development/presentation techniques
- industry best practices
- relevant technical terminology
- the collective agreement
- services and equipment available in the community
- Worker Protection (including health and safety and Workers' Compensation)
- training and development program design and administration

Task & Knowledge Requirements

- Occupational health and safety legislation (e.g., Occupational Health and Safety Act of Ontario, Workplace Safety & Insurance Act—Bill 99, Workplace Hazardous Materials Information System, Transportation of Dangerous Goods legislation, environmental legislation, smoking in the workplace legislation, civil rights legislation)
- hazard identification and control
- emergency preparedness procedures

- management techniques for OH&S Programs
- types of employee assistance and wellness programs

RPC 12.3 Establishes effective programs for accident prevention, incident investigation, inspections, fire and emergency response, and required training.

- relevant legislation
- workplace inspection and accident investigation techniques
- nature of the business and physical work environment
- potential risks and hazards in the workplace
- emergency response planning
- community emergency response services
- training and development
- industry best practices
- Worker Protection (including health and safety and Workers' Compensation)
- training and development program design and administration
- hazard identification and control
- accident investigation procedures
- emergency preparedness procedures
- management techniques for OH&S Programs

RPC 12.4 Ensures due diligence and strict liability requirements are met, e.g. records are kept and formal procedures established.

- relevant legislation and common law
- company policies and procedures
- industry best practices
- program and policy development
- training and development techniques
- risk analysis
- common and statutory law (e.g., employment standard: labour relations)
- Worker Protection (including health and safety and Workers' Compensation)
- theories and practices for protection of individuals and groups

TASK & KNOWLEDGE REQUIREMENTS

- Occupational health and safety legislation (e.g., Occupational Health and Safety Act of Ontario, Workplace Safety & Insurance Act—Bill 99, Workplace Hazardous Materials Information System, Transportation of Dangerous Goods legislation, environmental legislation, smoking in the workplace legislation, civil rights legislation)
- management techniques for OH&S Programs

Discussion Questions

1. What are the three factors that should be considered as potential contributors to any accident?
2. Describe the methods that can be used in accident investigation.
3. What tools can assist the accident investigator?
4. What steps should be taken to properly reenact an accident?
5. Give an example of how human, environmental, and situational factors can combine to result in an accident.
6. Given our focus on analyzing and understanding accident causation, it is worth noting that some safety professionals now refuse to use the term "accident." They claim that doing so implies accidents are random, unforeseeable events, whereas we know that most accidents result from a foreseeable series of events. What are the merits (pros and cons) of this position? Do "accidents happen," or are all accidents preventable?
7. Some safety professionals now talk about the notion of "system risk." In essence, they suggest that accidents or incidents do not result from single causes. Rather, they suggest that accidents are the result of multiple events working together. How might the factors identified in this chapter interact to result in an accident?

Using the Internet

1. Search news media and online reports to find accounts of workplace accidents. For at least one such report, try to identify the human, situational, and environmental factors contributing to the accident.

Exercise

1. Many accident investigations, such as traffic and airline accident investigations, conclude that "human error" was the principal cause. We know that situational and environmental factors also play a role. Why do we emphasize the role of humans in accident causation? Does this result in an underemphasis of these other factors?

Case 1

Accident Investigation

You are the president and largest shareholder of an original equipment manufacturer (OEM) that employs 300 workers. You do not have a safety specialist, but you do take a personal interest in accident prevention. Recently, you assigned general responsibility for safety to the day-shift superintendents as a minor part of their regular duties.

The plant has never been thoroughly analyzed for hazards, and you are aware that the operation is not as safe as it could be. Many of the operations require considerable ongoing maintenance by the workers to prevent accidents. Since for several years the business has only been breaking even, you have delayed making any improvements to the plant and equipment. You and the superintendents have concentrated your efforts on preventing unsafe acts by the employees. An elaborate system of worker reminders, such as posters and instruction by supervisors, has been used to make the workforce safety conscious.

For the last few years, your performance with respect to medical aid and lost-time injuries has been average for your WCB rate group. Your company has escaped any lost-time injuries for the last two years, including the current year to date. The continuation of that record has become an important goal. Signs in the plant indicate the number of days that have passed without a lost-time injury. Today, at 15:30 hours, a container of nearly red-hot, upper-control-arm forgings was overturned. The hot forgings fell on a worker who was helping the drop forge machine operator. The worker suffered third-degree burns over 20 percent of his body. Although he is expected to recover, the worker will lose most of his right arm, right ear, and sight in his right eye. Describe the investigative methods and tools you would use to investigate this accident.

Case 2

Office Accident

Cathy Calvin is the newly appointed coordinator of health and safety for the local school board. She has just been told of an accident experienced by an employee in the administrative office. It seems that two employees were trying to move a full filing cabinet from one corner of the office to another. The cabinet tipped, crushing the foot of one of the employees. The office staff applied first aid and rushed the injured employee to the hospital. The employee will be off work for at least two weeks. Board policy requires a full investigation of any lost-time injury. As a relative newcomer to the health and safety role, Cathy has never conducted an accident investigation before. Can you help Cathy design an appropriate strategy for approaching the investigation?

Endnotes

1. Laing, P. (Ed.). (1992). *Accident prevention manual for business and industry: Administration and programs* (10th ed.). Washington, D.C.: National Safety Council.
2. Ryan, T. (1991). Accident investigations: II group investigations. In F. Briggs (Ed.), *Guide to health and safety management*. Don Mills, ON: Southam Business Publications.
3. Heinrich, H. W. (1936). *Industrial accident prevention*. New York: McGraw-Hill.
4. Haddon, W., Jr. (1968). The changing approach to epidemiology, prevention and amelioration of trauma: The transition to approaches etiological rather than descriptively based. *American Journal of Public Health, 58,* 8.

5. Gross, V. L. (1972, August). System safety in rapid rail transit. *ASSE Journal*.
6. Reason, J. (1990). *Human error*. Cambridge, UK: University of Cambridge Press.
7. Perrow, C. (1984). *Normal accidents: Living with high-risk technologies*. NY: Basic Books; and Perrow, C. (1994). Accidents in high risk systems. *Technological Studies, 1,* 1–20.
8. Roberts, K. (1989). Some characteristics of high reliability organizations. *Organization Science, 2,* 160–176; and Weick, K. E., Sutcliffe, K. M., & Obstfeld, D. (1999). Organizing for high reliability: Processes of collective mindfulness. *Research in Organizational Behavior, 21,* 81–123.
9. Weick, K. (1995). *Sensemaking in organizations*. Thousand Oaks, CA: Sage Publications.
10. Wallace, J. C., & Vodanovich, S. J. (2003). Can accidents and industrial mishaps be predicted? Further investigation into the relationships between cognitive failure and reports of accidents. *Journal of Business and Psychology, 17,* 503–514.
11. Wallace, J. C., & Vodanovich, S. J. (2003). Can accidents and industrial mishaps be predicted? Further investigation into the relationships between cognitive failure and reports of accidents. *Journal of Business and Psychology, 17,* 503–514.

Chapter 13

Workplace Wellness: Work–Family and Worksite Health-Promotion Programs

Chapter Learning Objectives

After reading this chapter, you should be able to:

- discuss the concept of healthy workplaces
- describe the goals of worksite health-promotion and family-friendly programs
- discuss the various types of worksite health-promotion and family-friendly programs
- comment on the effectiveness of various types of worksite health-promotion and family-friendly programs
- identify variables critical to the success of worksite health-promotion and family-friendly programs
- discuss the importance of systematic evaluation of worksite health-promotion and family-friendly policies

Snoozing on the Job: Not Such a Bad Idea After All?

You snooze, you lose. Not that long ago, suggesting someone was asleep on the job was a severe criticism. It implied a person was lazy or not respectful of company time. Recent research on sleep deprivation suggests a nap at work might be just what the doctor—and HR manager—orders.

Today's busy workplaces and lifestyles are prompting many people to sacrifice their sleep hours to meet all their work and family demands. This strategy is detrimental to one's health. Not getting enough sleep is associated with a number of health problems including hypertension, heart disease, and depression. A 2007 study in the *Archives of Internal Medicine* demonstrated that afternoon naps are associated with a decreased risk for coronary morality. From a business perspective, estimates suggest that sleep deprivation is costing American employers $150 billion annually in reduced performance and accidents. A power nap might be the solution.

A new book by Sara Mednick called *Take a Nap! Change Your Life* advocates naps at work. It prescribes a nap during a work shift as a potential remedy for the productivity and health and safety costs associated with a sleep-deprived workforce. Some employers are taking notice, providing nap rooms for sleep-starved employees. The afternoon power snooze might just be the coffee break of the future when it comes to revitalizing employees.

Intuit Canada is one company that sees the value in allowing employees the freedom to nap. Intuit offers nap rooms at its Edmonton offices. The nap rooms are one aspect of a health and wellness program that includes on-site fitness facilities, a games room, and extensive health and leave benefits. Programs like these help Intuit Canada live up to its corporate operating values of attracting the best employees and focusing on its people.

The "nap room" is a novel idea for employee health promotion. It can benefit both the employee and the employer in many ways. In this chapter we will explore a variety of workplace wellness programs designed to improve employee health, well-being, and productivity.

Sources: CBC, "Siestas have heart-healthy effects, study suggests," February 12, 2007. Retrieved from http://www.cbc.ca/health/story/2007/02/12/siesta-heart.html, February 16, 2007; CTV News, "A nap a day keeps lost productivity at bay," January 15, 2007. Retrieved from http://www.ctv.ca/servlet/ArticleNews/story/CTVNews/20070115/takeanap_070115/20070115/February 14, 2007; Intuit Canada Career: Why Intuit. Retrieved from http://www.intuit.ca/en/intuit/careers_who.jsp, February 16, 2007; Mednick, S., & Ehrman, M. (2006). *Take a Nap! Change your Life.* Workman Publishing Company, Inc.; and Naska, A., Oikonomou, E., Trichopoulou, A, Psaltopoulou, T., & Trichopoulos, D. (2007). "Siesta in healthy adults and coronary mortality in the general population," *Archives of Internal Medicine, 167*, 296–301.

Given that people spend a substantial portion of their time at work, most would agree active attempts should be made to ensure the work environment is healthy and safe. Throughout the 1990s, the concept of wellness at work emerged as an occupational health concern, adding to the more traditional organizational health concern of employee safety. This interest in workplace wellness continues to grow. Some estimate that health-related programs are evident in as many as 90 percent of mid-sized companies in the United States.[1] A recent survey of more than 1,000 U.S. employers found that more than 90 percent of responding organizations offered their employees eight or more programs or policies to help support work and life balance.[2] The major motivators of this trend include a desire to reduce rising health care costs, improve productivity, and build a supportive organizational culture.

Workplace wellness initiatives are also present in Canadian companies. Recent estimates indicate that 64 percent of Canadian companies offer some form of wellness program.[3] Health-promotion programs may have been slower to develop in Canadian companies because of our public health care system. Because Canadian companies assume less of the cost for illness, traditionally there has been less of a financial impetus for them to develop employee health initiatives. However, the focus on health at work is now rapidly growing in Canada. For instance, Health Canada, in partnership with the National Quality Institute, has created the well-publicized healthy

FIGURE 13.1

A Flow Chart of Workplace Well-Being Initiatives

workplace awards, the healthy workplace week, and other programs to help organizations address psychosocial and environmental factors that affect employee health.

Many experts believe that health is more than just the absence of illness and that an active attempt to improve health will result in individuals "feeling good" as opposed to "not feeling bad"; this notion is sometimes referred to as "positive health." Indeed, the World Health Organization defines health not simply as the absence of illness or disease, but rather as an overall state of mental, physical, and social well-being.

RPC 13.1

RPC 13.2

RPC 13.3

RPC 13.4

RPC 13.5

It makes sense to focus on health at work. Employed adults spend a great deal of time in the workplace, so the worksite provides a convenient means of reaching many adults. Additionally, the health of employees affects their performance at work; therefore, companies should be interested in promoting worker health. In this chapter we will consider two broad categories of initiatives that companies can use to promote well-being at work, namely family-friendly policies and health-promotion programs (see Figure 13.1).

Work–Family Conflict: Family-Friendly Policies in the Workplace

Work and family are two of the most central elements of many people's lives. Recent demographic shifts, such as those outlined in Occupational Health and Safety Today 13.1, have increased the extent to which responsibilities to work and to family interfere with each other. For instance, the increased proportion of the workforce who also have childcare demands and the prevalence of dual-income families means that working parents will sometimes be torn between work demands and childcare responsibilities. For example, a child who is home sick from school may prompt a working parent to miss work to care for the child. Studies suggest that work–family conflict is prevalent among Canadian workers.[4] For example, in one recent study of the Nova

Scotia workforce, half of the respondents reported high work–family conflict.[5] Researchers are interested in the factors that contribute to **work–family conflict**, the outcomes of this type of conflict, and how organizations can help employees meet their multiple work and family roles.

work–family conflict
a type of interrole conflict in which the role pressures experienced in the work and family domains are incompatible

Organizational experts define work–family conflict as a form of interrole conflict. That is, it is a type of conflict in which the responsibilities of two separate roles are incompatible in some respect. In other words,

Occupational Health and Safety Today 13.1

Work-Life Balance: Some Canadian Statistics

Balancing multiple commitments, including work and family, is a reality for Canadians. Here are some recently compiled Canadian statistics on family, work, and well-being.

In a recent study of more than 30,000 Canadian employees from 100 organizations:[a]

- 58 percent reported high levels of role overload. This represents an increase of 11 percent in a single decade. Women report more role overload than men.
- 25 percent of respondents indicated that their work seriously interferes with their family responsibilities. Another 40 percent reported a moderate degree of work to family interference. However, only 1 in 10 indicated they allow family demands to interfere with their work responsibilities.
- Women spent more time per week in non-work activities such as child care and household tasks than did men.
- About 25 percent experienced high levels of strain due to caring for an elderly or disabled person.
- One-third reported a high degree of job stress, and one-quarter of respondents are thinking of leaving their organization; almost half met the criteria for high absenteeism. Job stress and absenteeism appears to be on the rise in Canada. Almost three times as many respondents in this survey reported high stress than did so in a comparable study a decade prior.

Other important work–family facts include:[b]

- The number of women in the workforce has increased. Women currently account for 46 percent of the workforce, compared with 37 percent in 1976. In fact, in 1999, 61 percent of Canadian women with a child under the age of three worked (relative to only 28 percent in 1976).
- Both men and women in the Canadian labour force have childcare demands. Statistics from the mid-1990s suggest that nearly half of working Canadians have children living in the home. Furthermore, 15 percent of these individuals also care for elderly family members.
- Almost half of all Canadian children between the ages of one and five were in nonparental care.
- Family-friendly workplace policies are on the rise in Canadian organizations. A recent survey of Canadian employers found that 88 percent offered flextime, 50 percent made provisions for telework, and 63 percent offered family-responsibility leave. However, other data suggest that there is limited access to flexible work arrangements even in organizations that offer this benefit and that the provision of childcare benefits in Canadian workplaces is low, with only 15 percent of companies indicating they provided on-site or near-site daycares.

References

a. Duxbury, L., & Higgins, C. (2003). *Work–life conflict in Canada in the new millennium: A status report* (Final Report). Retrieved from http://www.phac-aspc.gc.ca/publicat/work-travail/index.html, February 16, 2007.

b. Johnson, K. L., Lero, D. S., & Rooney, J. A. (2001). *Work-life compendium 2001:150 Canadian statistics on work, family and well-being*. Guelph, ON: Centre for Families, Work, and Well-Being.

pressures experienced in the work and family domains are in opposition.[6] Participation in one role is made more difficult by virtue of participation in the other role.

Some experts in this area further distinguish between two categories of work–family conflict.[7] They note that work–family conflict is bi-directional: work might interfere with a person's ability to meet family demands and family responsibilities can interfere with an individual's ability to keep pace with work demands. These two categories have been labelled **work to family conflict** and **family to work conflict,** respectively. Work to family conflict is a real problem for Canadian families. As indicated in Occupational Health and Safety Today 13.1, one in four respondents to a recent national survey reported that their work seriously interferes with their family responsibilities. Another 40 percent reported that work interferes with their family roles to a moderate degree.[8]

work to family conflict
a form of work–family conflict in which work demands interfere with the fulfillment of family responsibilities

family to work conflict
a form of work–family conflict in which family demands interfere with the fulfillment of work responsibilities

Causes of Work–Family Conflict

Several elements of work and family roles contribute to work–family conflict. One such element is the amount of time a person spends in each role, or their **behavioural involvement** in the role. Generally, the more time dedicated to one role means the less time available to spend in the other role. Certainly, increased time devoted to work is associated with increased incidence of work to family conflict. Similarly, the more time a person spends on family pursuits and responsibilities in the home, the more likely that individual is to experience family to work conflict.[9]

behavioural involvement
the amount of time a person spends in a particular role

A person's **psychological involvement** in their work and family roles has also been implicated as a predictor of work–family conflict. Psychological involvement reflects the degree to which a person identifies with a particular role and sees the role as a central component of his or her self-concept. For example, a woman who considers her status as a mother to be the defining feature in her life has a high degree of psychological involvement in her mother role. A high degree of involvement in one role can cause it to conflict with other responsibilities.

psychological involvement
the degree to which a person identifies with a particular role and sees the role as a central component of his or her self-concept

Stress in either the work or the family role is also associated with work–family conflict. In particular, the experience of family-related stress, such as many family demands or dissatisfaction with family life, is associated with family to work conflict. Similarly, the experience of work-related stress, such as many work demands or job dissatisfaction, is associated with work to family conflict.[10]

Outcomes of Work–Family Conflict

Both work to family and family to work conflict are associated with negative consequences. Interestingly, the outcomes tend to be in the opposite domain as the cause of the conflict. That is, work to family conflict tends to affect family-related outcomes and family to work conflict affects work-related outcomes. For instance, family to work conflict is linked with decreased work performance and absenteeism from work. Conversely, work to family conflict is associated with reduced performance in the family role and absences from family events.[11]

Work–family conflict is expensive for organizations. A recent Canadian report finds that high work–family conflict is associated with reduced work performance and higher rates of absenteeism. This report estimates the direct organizational costs of work–life conflict to be in the range of $3 billion to $5 billion annually.[12] Of course, factoring in the indirect costs, this is considerably higher—an estimated $6 billion to $10 billion per year.[13]

Work–family conflict is also associated with substantial health and well-being costs for individuals. A high degree of work–family conflict, be it work to family or family to work, contributes to perceived stress, lowered physical health, decreased family functioning, increased mental health concerns (depression, anxiety, psychological distress), and increased alcohol use.[14] Thus, it is important that individuals and organizations aim to reduce the extent to which they or their employees experience this type of interrole conflict.[15] In the following sections we will consider some of the family-friendly policies that organizations have implemented in an effort to reduce the experience of work–family conflict and in turn avoid the resulting negative outcomes. Such policies are assuming greater importance as companies recognize that a growing number of employees have both childcare and eldercare (i.e., caring for elderly relatives) responsibilities in addition to their work responsibilities. As such, the existence of these policies helps organizations in recruiting and retaining employees. For the most part, family-friendly policies attempt to help employees balance their work and family responsibilities. Given that the focus of this chapter is workplace policies and programs, we emphasize organizational, rather than individual, efforts to reduce work–family conflict. We will consider three broad categories of family-friendly programs: flexible work arrangements, work-leave systems, and family-friendly employee benefits.

Family-Friendly Policies

Flexible Work Arrangements

Flexible work arrangements (FWAs) are modifications to the traditional work schedule. There are two basic versions of FWAs. First, some programs are designed to help mitigate work–family conflict by reducing the amount of *time* spent in the workplace. An example of this type of FWA is the **compressed workweek.** Under this option, employees can choose to work full-time hours in fewer days, for instance 40 hours in four days rather than five.

The compressed work schedule can help employees reduce work–family conflict by allowing longer stretches of time at home and saving time spent in commuting to and from the workplace. Job sharing and job splitting programs also fall under this category of FWA. In **job sharing** programs two employees share the responsibilities of a single position. In this case,

flexible work arrangements (FWAs)
family-friendly policies that involve modifications to the traditional work schedule

compressed workweek
flexible work arrangement in which employees work full-time hours in fewer days per week

job sharing
flexible work arrangement in which two employees share the responsibilities of a single position

the two employees have overlapping duties and must be sure to communicate with each other about all aspects of the work. In **job splitting**, two employees may split job responsibilities such that they each take sole responsibility for various components of the job. Job sharing and job splitting arrangements typically benefit employees who want to work part-time hours. Job sharing and splitting options reduce the amount of time an employee must spend on work-related tasks and likely lead to a reduction in work-role overload. As such, these types of arrangements may reduce the incidence of work–family conflict.

job splitting
flexible work arrangement in which two employees divide the responsibilities of a single position

The second large category consists of FWA programs designed to increase the amount of *control* individuals have over their work schedule. A common example of this type of arrangement is **flextime.** In flextime schedules employees are permitted to have variable start and finish times to their workday. For instance, one employee at a company offering flextime may choose to work from 7 a.m. to 3 p.m. Another employee may opt to start work at 10 a.m. and work until 6 p.m. In this case, during several hours of the day all employees are at work and group or team-related matters can be dealt with. However, the degree of control over start and finish times can help employees better manage their work and family demands. For instance, Edward, a working father who worries about his children being home alone after school, prefers to start early and finish at 3 p.m. so that he can supervise his children after school or help them get to and from after-school activities.

flextime
flexible work arrangement that permits employees to have variable start and finish times to their workday

Telecommuting is a second exemplar of this category of FWA. Telecommuting (also known as telework or work at home) programs allow employees to complete their work assignments away from the office. The employee uses telecommunications technology such as the Internet and phone to keep in touch with the worksite. Such an option can help some employees better blend their work and family responsibilities. For instance, a person who works from home can delay the start of the workday until children leave for school and then immediately start working without losing time to things like commuting to and from work. Telework may also be helpful for individuals who have elders living in their homes, as they are able to be at home in case there is an emergency.

telecommuting
flexible work arrangement in which an employee regularly makes use of telecommunications technology to complete work assignments away from the office, usually at home

Personal Leave Systems

Another broad category of family-friendly policies involves the provision of leave time to employees. Some examples include maternity leave, parental leave, personal days, family leave, and sick leave. These leave programs are designed to help employees meet their family demands, thereby reducing the occurrence of family to work conflict. Consider an employee who has a chronically ill child. This individual may use family leave and personal days to accompany the child on doctor's visits and to care for the child. The existence of such a leave program should reduce the incidence of unexcused absenteeism and tardiness. Maternity leave programs allow new mothers to take paid time away from work shortly before and for some time after the birth of a child. Parental leave programs permit new mothers and fathers to take a leave from work responsibilities when a child is born or placed with them through an adoption. In Canada, the federal government provides a one-year maternity and parental leave program that permits an individual to collect a portion of his or her regular earnings via the Employment Insurance program. Some companies have chosen to provide additional parental benefits that top up the amount the parent earns while on leave. For instance, a company may continue to pay employees a top up amount so that their total earnings while on leave equals 95 percent of their regular earnings. Employment Insurance pays an employee 55 percent of insurable earnings (up to a limit of $423 per week).

Leave-related benefits aim to reduce the amount of work–family conflict experienced by employees. Consider the case of a new parent: Having to return to work shortly after the birth of a child likely contributes to a high degree of work–family conflict. The new parent is adjusting to newly increased family demands, and these demands can often interfere with work performance. The availability of company-sponsored financial benefits for parental leave also reduces the considerable financial strain that might otherwise prompt an individual to return to work earlier than initially planned.

Family-Care Benefits

The final category of family-friendly policies that we will discuss in this chapter is family-care benefit programs. The provision of daycare or eldercare benefits is an initiative that falls under this category. Employers can help their employees who have children reduce their experience of work–family conflict by supporting daycare programs. This might involve an on-site daycare, which reduces the stress associated with dropping children off at various locations before getting in to work. Additionally, on-site daycares may reduce some of the stress associated with having children in non-parental care. If the daycare is at the work location, the working parent knows that he or she is nearby in case of an emergency. Additionally, the parent can drop in to see the child while at work. They may also have increased trust in the daycare provider, as it is a division of their own workplace. In some cases, employers who cannot provide an on-site daycare can arrange to have daycare facilities near the worksite.

Another option under this category of family-friendly programs is the provision of subsidized dependant care. In this case, organizations might provide employees with money to help cover the cost of eldercare or childcare or to enroll elders or children in various programs. For instance, an employee who cares for an elderly parent might use this budget to enroll the parent in a seniors' program. As another example, consider the organization that sponsors summer camps for children of employees. In each case, we can see how these programs could reduce worries about dependant-care responsibilities.

Family-Friendly Policies: An Evaluation

Data from the United States suggest that family-friendly options are increasingly available to employees. The prevalence of telework increased throughout the 1990s, with estimates now suggesting that anywhere from 16 to 28 million American workers are currently engaged in this work arrangement.[16]

It also appears that family-friendly policies are increasingly common on the Canadian organizational landscape. However, the available data are somewhat mixed regarding the availability of family-friendly work programs in Canadian organizations. A Conference Board of Canada survey suggests that as of 1999, 88 percent of Canadian employers offered flextime, 48 percent offered compressed workweeks, 52 percent provided job sharing options, 50 percent made provisions for telework, and 63 percent offered family-responsibility leave. However, a 2003 analysis of Statistics Canada's Workplace Employee Survey of more than 20,000 employees from more than 6,000 employers differs in its conclusion. This report supported the claim that flextime is the most prevalent family-friendly work option, but indicated that only about one-third of employees had access to it. Rates of telework and access to childcare services were even lower, at about 5 percent. The report identified organizational factors that appear to moderate the availability of family-friendly programs. Flextime and telework were more commonly reported by employees who worked in small organizations, whereas child and eldercare benefits seemed more prevalent in larger workplaces.[17]

Despite their growing availability, little systematic research has been conducted on the effectiveness of the family-friendly policies described in this chapter. As such, the extent to which these programs actually reduce work–family conflict and their impact on organizational functioning are unknown. Certainly, anecdotal evidence attesting to their effectiveness in reducing work–family conflict is readily available. However, the available research provides mixed results as to their actual impact on work–family conflict.[18] Some studies suggest that family-friendly policies do indeed reduce the existence of work–family conflict.[19] Flextime has been associated with an increase in the extent to which people feel they are in control of their work and family lives.[20] Other studies report that family-friendly policies such as flextime and telework do not affect the occurrence of work–family conflict, and may even increase one's experience of work–life conflict.[21] One interesting study found that the availability of family-friendly policies reduced the extent to which work interfered with family responsibilities but had no impact on family to work conflict.[22] However, other studies illustrate that telework in particular may reduce work interference with family, but increase family to work conflict.[23] A recent study on the issue of telework found that several contextual factors play a role in the success of this strategy. People who spent more of their working hours engaged in telework reported reduced work to family interference, but more family to work interference. Further, those who had higher degrees of autonomy and flexibility in their jobs reported a greater positive effect of telework on their experiences of work–family conflict.[24] This study implies that the effectiveness of family-friendly work programs is influenced by a number of factors.

Researchers have also considered the impact of family-friendly policies on organizational outcomes. Again, there are mixed results for the effectiveness of family-friendly initiatives. One recent study found that telework was associated with increased commitment to the organization and reduced intentions to quit.[25] It appears that flexible work options, such as flextime and

Occupational Health and Safety Notebook 13.1

Reducing Work–Life Conflict: Strategies for Organizations

A recent Health Canada–sponsored report on work–family conflict suggests employers aiming to help employees create work–life balance should *reduce demands* placed on employees and *increase the control* that employees have over their work. Some of the specific recommendations include the following:

- Reduce employee workloads
- Recognize when work demands are unrealistic and acknowledge that such loads are not sustainable
- Track the costs of understaffing and unrealistic work demands
- Avoid reliance on overtime work; hire more people if the need arises
- Track the direct and indirect costs of role overload and work–life conflict (absenteeism, overtime, employee assistance programs, and turnover)
- Have policies about the use of office technology (e.g., change expectations about after-hours email)
- Offer "cafeteria-style" benefits programs so that employees can choose the services that benefit them
- Support child- and dependant-care needs (paid leave, care options)

Source: Duxbury, L., & Higgins, C. (2003). *Work-life conflict in Canada in the new millennium: A status report (Final Report).* Retrieved from http://www.phac-aspc.gc.ca/publicat/work-travail/index.html, February 16, 2007.

telecommuting, have a positive impact on job satisfaction and decrease absenteeism.[26] However, the impact of these policies on productivity is uncertain. Some studies report that flexible arrangements contribute to improved productivity, and others report no significant effects.[27]

Additional research on the organizational and individual impact of work–family policies is certainly warranted. This research should specifically consider the type of work–family policy and the nature of the conflict (i.e., work to family versus family to work).[28] It should also ask questions about why companies choose to implement the policies they do.[29] At present little research is available on the extent to which employers consider work–family policies to be strategic human resource initiatives, even though the existence of these programs may be important in the recruitment and retention of high-quality employees.[30]

Future studies should make a distinction between the availability of family-friendly policies and the extent to which employees actually use them. Employer and employee surveys paint a different picture regarding the availability of flexible work arrangements.[31] In some cases, employers who do have family-friendly options make those programs available to a select group of employees—for instance, people in a particular job classification. Other data suggest that in some organizations, employees choose not to use family-friendly policies such as flextime because they fear it will negatively affect their career progress. As such, the formal existence of a policy does not guarantee its use. In reality, the culture of the organization shapes the extent to which employees are willing to use work–family policies.

RPC 13.1
RPC 13.2
RPC 13.3
RPC 13.4
RPC 13.5
RPC 13.6
RPC 13.7
RPC 13.8

One report indicated that the characteristics of work groups affected whether employees opted to use FWAs.[32] Individuals who worked in groups that were more supportive made greater use of these options. This study stresses the importance of organizational support for family-friendly initiatives. If employees fear that they will be looked down on or sustain damage to their careers, they may choose not to take advantage of the family-friendly programs that do exist.

Health-Promotion Programs

Wellness or health-promotion programming is the active attempt to improve employee well-being through worksite intervention. The rationale for such programming is that many health-related concerns can be prevented through lifestyle changes such as diet, exercise, and smoking cessation. Given that employed adults spend many hours in the workplace and that the health of employees affects organizational and individual functioning, the workplace provides a convenient and appropriate means of reaching many adults. As a result of these observations, an increasing number of workplaces have launched various types of health-promotion programs.

health promotion
a combination of diagnostic, educational, and behavioural modification activities designed to support the attainment and maintenance of positive health

Efforts toward **health promotion** combine diagnostic, educational, and behavioural change initiatives with the goal of helping people attain and maintain positive health. An emerging concept in the realm of health promotion that is of particular interest for worksites is that of health and productivity management. Health and productivity management programs integrate health-promotion activities in a way that simultaneously increases employee well-being and decreases the health-related costs of the organization, such as absence from work and reduced work performance.[33] The history of such work-related health-promotion programs is found in early employee assistance plans (EAPs), and it is useful to review the emergence and structure of EAPs before addressing health-promotion programs (HPPs).

Employee Assistance Plans

employee assistance plans (EAPs)
programs designed to help employees with problems that may interfere with worker productivity, including alcohol and other drug abuse, emotional or behavioural problems among family members, and financial or legal problems

Employee assistance plans (EAPs) provide counselling and assistance to members of an organization, generally helping individual employees control personal concerns, such as alcoholism, drug use, and stress, which may affect their performance at work.[34] The roots of EAPs date back to the nineteenth century and the social betterment movement. Initiatives included inexpensive housing, company-sponsored unions, sanitary working conditions, insurance, pension plans, banking, recreation, medical care, and education facilities. After the social betterment movement subsided in the 1920s and 1930s, personal counselling emerged. Management trained some shop workers to listen to workers' problems to reduce their interference with productivity. For example, in 1917, Macy's Department Store established a program to assist employees who were dealing with personal problems. By 1920, one-third of the 431 largest companies in the United States had a full-time welfare secretary whose major role was as a counsellor.[35]

Occupational Health and Safety Notebook 13.2

Building a Business Case for Wellness

Canadian organizations have endorsed the use of employee assistance programs (EAPs), but have been somewhat slower to adopt broader-based wellness or health-promotion programming. When suggesting the need for more comprehensive programming, HR professionals will have to develop the business case for health-promotion planning. Potential benefits from such programs include the following:

- reduced absenteeism and associated costs
- reduced turnover and associated costs
- reduced insurance rates (e.g., from better disability management, reduced smoking)
- added inducement when recruiting new employees
- improved morale, job satisfaction, and reduced stress
- increased employee health while at work

Ill health while working has been associated with decreased productivity. For instance, conditions such as hypertension, migraines, and respiratory infections have been associated with three to four unproductive hours in an eight-hour shift.

Source: Adapted from Hummer, J., Sherman, B., & Quinn, N. (2002). "Present and unaccounted for." *Occupational Health & Safety, 71*(4), 40–44.

In the 1940s the Occupational Alcohol Movement, which is generally acknowledged as the direct predecessor of the EAP, arose.[36] Alcoholism was recognized as a serious impediment to productivity, and these programs sought to assist workers troubled by this problem by offering alcohol-related and personal-problem counselling. The 1970s were a period of rapid growth for EAPs. In the 1980s they expanded to include stress management. Today, EAP programs address all types of problems that may interfere with worker productivity, including alcohol and other drug abuse, emotional or behavioural problems among family members, and financial or legal problems.[37]

Currently, it is difficult to distinguish between EAPs and health-promotion programs, and health-promotion programs are now viewed as subsuming the earlier EAPs. The primary objectives of EAPs are to help employees address personal concerns and assist organizations in the identification and betterment of productivity concerns among employees.[38] Typically, health-promotion programs will include interventions aimed at stress management and lifestyle changes (e.g., diet, smoking cessation, and physical fitness). We will now turn our attention to each of these two classes of health-promotion initiatives.

Stress Management Programs

The goal of stress management programs is to educate workers about the causes and consequences of stress, and to teach relaxation and coping skills for managing physiological and psychological symptoms. The most common types of stress management programs are cognitive-behavioural skills training, progressive muscle relaxation and meditation, and programs designed to increase social support.[39]

Cognitive-Behavioural Skills Training

Cognitive-behavioural programs are developed under the framework of the cognitive model of stress, which posits that emotional responses to situations are largely determined by the way they are thought about and interpreted. The training helps people to think about events in new ways and to be aware of how they are viewing stressful events, and provides skills in learning to cope with stress. The goal is to alter both cognition of stressful events and behaviour toward them. For example, participants in stress-inoculation training might be given coping skills such as self-instruction training, cognitive restructuring, problem-solving training, and relaxation training. The training program itself makes use of such techniques as role-playing and classroom instruction.

Relaxation Training and Meditation

Relaxation training involves teaching individuals such things as progressive muscle relaxation and breathing exercises. If you have ever taken a class in yoga, martial arts, or even aerobics, you have probably experienced something similar to this. Someone may ask you to lie down on the floor, close your eyes, and focus your mind on your body and your muscles. Then, they may ask you to relax every muscle in your body, slowly working from the bottom up or top down. The purpose of this type of training is to provide people with skills to physically relax the body. Over time, individuals will learn to recognize the physical feelings associated with stress and to counteract these feelings by calling on the relaxation response. In doing so, they prevent stress leading to the type of strain reactions discussed earlier.

Just as relaxation training is focused on relaxing the physical body, the focus of meditation is on quieting the mind. There are numerous approaches to meditation and you are probably familiar with at least some of them. Meditation helps individuals withdraw from a stressful situation and reenergize through mental exercise. The most widely used form of meditation in the workplace involves sitting quietly for 20 minutes, repeating a single word on each exhalation.[40] Meditation practice appears to lead to positive physical and psychological outcomes in the workplace.[41]

Increasing Social Support

A different strategy to help reduce work-related stress is to provide a more supportive environment. One way of doing this is by training workers on how to seek social support and how to create a more supportive workplace. For example, caregiver-support programs are designed to assist people in dealing with the stresses of providing care for others. The goal of such programs is typically to increase social support and participation in work-related decisions. Caregiver-support programs are designed to teach employees the benefits of support systems, enhance their skills in mobilizing support, educate them about participatory problem-solving approaches, and show them how to build skills to implement these approaches in team meetings.

Effectiveness of Stress Management Training

Results are mixed on the effectiveness of stress management training programs. The lack of comprehensive, well designed studies on workplace stress management interventions makes it difficult to assess the effectiveness of such programs.[42] Some programs appear to be effective at reducing the experience of job-related stress, whereas others are not. For example, in one study on stress management training participants were exposed to a variety of stress management techniques, including cognitive restructuring, positive self-talk, deep muscle relaxation, autogenic instructions, and imagery exercises.[43] The training program included nine hours of instruction over six sessions. The researchers found that those receiving training did not show a significant increase in learning or job satisfaction, or a significant decrease in blood pressure, somatic data, or anxiety in comparison with a control group. However, when a self-management module was included as part of the training significant differences were found for all measures except job satisfaction. The self-management module included three hours of training in self-monitoring, specifying goals, evaluating behaviour against goals, and self-reinforcing. This study suggests that simply providing training is not sufficient to make a difference; participants must be provided with strategies to assist them in applying what they have learned. Interestingly, this is the same conclusion reached for safety programs in general—training alone is often insufficient to effect change.

Conversely, another study showed that stress management training was effective in reducing the interpersonal aspects of stress (anger inventory, use of emergency restraint, client abuse).[44] However, this program was custom designed with the needs of the users in mind and may be more effective than the typical "out of the can" stress management programs. Social support programs are also effective. Typically, such programs increase the amount of supportive feedback on the job, enhance perceptions about the ability to handle disagreements and work overload, and improve work team climate. Another study found that a high degree of participation in a program that targeted psychosocial stressors reduced the negative effects of a large personnel cutback in a health care setting.[45]

Worksite Health Promotion: A Focus on Lifestyle Changes

Worksite health-promotion programming can be classified into three categories: screening, education, and behavioural change. Many types of programs are being delivered in each of these various categories. The most common are those designed to affect an employee's health practices or physical lifestyle (e.g., exercise, eating habits, sleep patterns, weight control, alcohol use, smoking cessation, substance abuse). These efforts are often called lifestyle programming. It is generally thought that a healthy lifestyle will help to promote physical and mental health on the job. Some programs include activities designed to improve psychological aspects of an individual's lifestyle (e.g., social relations, intellectual activity, occupational conditions), but these programs are still the exception rather than the rule.

These types of programs may offer such things as on-site fitness facilities, or subsidies for private clubs, nutritional assessment and counselling, weight-control groups, and smoking-cessation programs. Typically, these opportunities are available on a voluntary basis and may be offered only to individuals at a certain level in the organization (e.g., membership in a health club for management employees). Although the organization may provide incentives for taking advantage of the program, it would have difficulty mandating that employees alter their lifestyle. Although it is possible to make safety training, or even stress-reduction training, mandatory, it would be difficult to insist that all employees quit smoking or have a perfect body mass index. Indeed, to the extent that addiction or obesity is considered a disability, doing so might violate human rights legislation. Rather than attempting to mandate such programs, organizations involved in worksite health promotion should develop cultures and environments that are highly supportive of healthful lifestyle practices.

Although health-promotion programs are diverse, many are secondary-level interventions designed to help individuals who are feeling stress and are at risk for illness. The typical components of a worksite health-promotion (WHP) program include three steps:

Step 1: physical or psychological assessment
Step 2: counselling concerning findings and recommendations about personal health promotion
Step 3: referral to in-house or community-based resources

If we focus on WHP programs that are more tertiary in nature—that is, those designed to help people who are currently experiencing symptoms or illness, such as alcohol and other substance abuse, hypertension, and psychological stress—the key components in such programs should include the following:

- The identification of currently symptomatic as well as high-risk individuals
- The appropriate referral or treatment of individuals
- Treatment directed at the symptom, delivered by the appropriate professionals
- Follow-up with the client to ensure the treatment was effective
- Evaluation of health improvement and cost efficacy

Components of an effective employer-sponsored health-promotion effort include employee education for health promotion or disease prevention, management training to raise awareness of occupational health issues and identification, EAP services, redesigned benefit programs to provide easy access to interventions, a comprehensive data-collection plan for use in program decision making, the integration of corporate health-related services, and a greater attention to organizational health. We will now turn our attention to some specific categories of WHP programs. In particular, we will look at efforts that are focused on changing some aspect of an employee's lifestyle (i.e., lifestyle programming).

Smoking Cessation

One of the most popular worksite health-promotion interventions in recent years has been the implementation of smoking cessation programs. As worksites have increasingly banned smoking, either voluntarily or because of legislation, more and more employers saw the wisdom of offering employees assistance in quitting smoking. Moreover, research has consistently documented that smokers are absent more than nonsmokers, providing employers with an economic incentive to provide assistance with smoking cessation.[46] Some estimate the costs associated with smoking (i.e., those attributable to absenteeism, lost productivity, and increased insurance premiums) to be in the neighbourhood of $2,500 per year per employee.

Smoking cessation programs typically involve a combination of education, group support, counselling, and behavioural change techniques. Traditionally, the success rates of such programs have varied between 25 and 60 percent. Several studies support the effectiveness of various targeted worksite interventions for the reduction of smoking.[47] More recently, pharmaceutical aids such as nicotine gum, the nicotine patch, and other medications have enhanced success rates. It is important to note that these aids do not replace traditional approaches. Rather, the greatest success seems to come from a combination of psychoeducational and pharmaceutical approaches to smoking cessation. The need for a comprehensive approach to smoking cessation within organizations is highlighted by the observation that organizations providing subsidized cessation programs for employees may, at the same time, have cigarette machines in the workplace.

Hypertension Screening

Hypertension, or high blood pressure, has been called the "silent killer." Individuals can have hypertension for a long time without knowing it or without experiencing symptoms. Although it may seem relatively innocuous, hypertension is considered one of the major (and most easily controlled) risk factors in heart-related diseases. Workplace programs aimed at affecting hypertension vary widely but typically consist of four interrelated steps:

hypertension
elevated blood pressure

1. *Education:* Employees are alerted to the dangers of hypertension and the benefits associated with treatment.
2. *Screening:* Employees are screened using blood-pressure clinics in which participants have their blood pressure read by a medical professional.
3. *Referral:* Employees with elevated readings are referred to medical treatment.
4. *Follow-up:* Referred employees are followed up to verify the outcome of treatment and to monitor progress.

Worksite hypertension programs typically result in approximately 25 percent of participants being identified as hypertensive—about the same prevalence as in the general population. Outcome studies suggest that programs are very effective in bringing hypertension under control through diet and medication. Moreover, some evidence shows programs with more elements (e.g., those that include frequent monitoring and follow-up) are more effective than are simple screening or educational programs.

Nutrition and Weight Control

Nutrition programs in the workplace typically take one of two forms. First, educational programs are aimed at providing instruction or information on the selection of foods, the basics of meal planning, and so on. Posters in the cafeteria promoting *Canada's Food Guide* are an example of educational programming. The second type of activity is to actually change the food available in the workplace. Providing healthy, low-fat alternatives in the cafeteria and changing the contents of vending machines in the workplace assist employees to maintain a healthy diet. There is empirical evidence for the effectiveness of some nutrition-focused worksite health-promotion programs.[48]

WWW

Weight-control programs are becoming increasingly popular and are often offered in conjunction with established weight-loss programs (e.g., Weight Watchers, Tops). Again, such programs rely on education, counselling, and group support. Several studies indicate that worksite weight-loss programs can be effective; however, attrition rates tend to be high. Thus, those who stay with the program may lose weight, but there is a high dropout rate and, hence, a large number of people for whom the programs are not effective.

Physical Fitness Programs

Fitness programs can be implemented in three levels.[49] The most basic efforts, Level I programs, focus on awareness and typically comprise newsletters, health fairs, screening sessions (e.g., body mass index assessments), posters, and brochures. Level I programs are not aimed at change per se, but rather at making individuals aware of the need for change and the resources available to support change.

Level II programs are specific programs that last at least 8 to 12 weeks and attempt to obtain a long-term effect through the formation of specific health-related habits. Corporations that offer specific fitness courses (e.g., strength training or lower back training) are engaged in Level II programming. Level III programs attempt to support individual change by creating a work environment that promotes a healthful lifestyle. Ensuring that cafeterias offer healthful foods, providing bike racks or locker facilities in the workplace, having on-site fitness facilities, or removing cigarette or candy machines from the workplace are all examples of Level III programs. All three levels of programming have proved effective in enhancing individual physical fitness.

Occupational Health and Safety Today 13.2

Healthy Organizations: Wellness and Work-Family Programming at Canadian Companies

Many Canadian companies have excellent and well-deserved reputations for the high level of wellness programming they endorse. Consider Dofasco Inc. as an example. This Hamilton, Ontario–based company is one of the most profitable steelmakers in North America. Its slogan "Our product is steel. Our strength is people" is fitting for a company with a longstanding emphasis on employee engagement and well-being. As part of its Healthy Lifestyles programs, Dofasco provides numerous family-friendly and health-focused options including employee access to a multi-sport recreation and learning centre and several health-promotion initiatives such as on-site, subsidized Weight Watchers meetings, smoking-cessation programs, first-aid training, a comprehensive employee assistance program, and health assessments. Dofasco's high investment in employees has been a success. There is a high degree of program participation and attendance among employees. From a financial perspective there has been a marked reduction in lost-time injuries, Workers' Compensation premiums, and incidence of non–work-related injuries since the health programs were initiated.

Husky Injection Molding Systems is another good example of a company that has successfully incorporated employee health and wellness into a successful business strategy. Husky is committed to its employees, the larger community, and the environment. Husky employees can gain company shares as reward for taking part in environmentally friendly practices like car pooling. Their program includes rewards for sticking to a fitness program, on-site daycare facilities, a 24-hour company gym, sponsored sports leagues, and a corporate wellness centre that includes the services of doctors, naturopaths, massage therapists, chiropractors, and fitness personnel. Its onsite Parent Resource Centre, The Copper House, is one of the best in North America. It has extended hours to accommodate employees' needs and offers a variety of care options (e.g., full time, before or after school, emergency basis) and services that save parents time (e.g., onsite haircuts for kids). Husky Injection Molding Systems is also committed to monitoring and evaluating the success of its programs, tracking absenteeism, turnover, injuries, Workers' Compensation claims, and benefits costs. This company spends more than $4 million each year on wellness programming, but it estimates the return on that investment in reduced absenteeism, higher productivity, lowered injury rates, and lower Workplace Safety and Insurance Board premiums and better use of resources is $8 million.

Sources: Dofasco. Retrieved from http://www.dofasco.ca, October 12, 2004; Canadian Labour and Business Centre, "Dofasco Inc.'s healthy lifestyle activities: A case study." Retrieved from http://www.clbc.ca/files/casestudies/dofasco.pdf, February 18, 2007; Husky Injection Molding Systems. Retrieved from http://www.husky.ca/, February 18, 2007; and Human Resources Development Canada Organizational Profiles: Husky Injection Molding. Retrieved from http://www.hrsdc.gc.ca/asp/gateway.asp?hr=/en/lp/spila/wlb/ell/08husky_injection_molding_systems.shtml&hs=, February 18, 2007.

Some studies report that workplace fitness programs are associated with decreased health care costs, decreased hospital admissions, and decreased absenteeism for those who take part in the programs.[50] Although little convincing evidence exists that such programs result in increased job performance, a substantial number of studies show increases in employee morale associated with the provision of fitness programming. Alternatively, other studies present a different view, suggesting that there is little research evidence supporting the effectiveness of workplace fitness interventions.[51]

However, research does show that individually tailored programs, those designed with a particular employee's needs in mind, appear to be more successful than generic fitness programming.[52]

Developing a Successful Worksite Health-Promotion Program

A program is worthwhile only if it is achieving its goals. A WHP program will be successful only if employees are making use of what it has to offer. Research on worksite health-promotion efforts has provided some key evidence-based insights on the factors that contribute to successfully implemented programs. The following list of essential elements for an EAP can easily be extended to WHP programs in general.[53]

1. *A clear, written policy regarding assistance*. The policy must balance worker privacy (e.g., if an employee voluntarily seeks help, it will be kept confidential) and the needs of the company (e.g., if a serious behaviour problem, such as the use of drugs on the job, is uncovered by a supervisor, disciplinary action will be taken). There is a need to avoid stigmatizing individuals and to ensure the confidentiality and safety of the service provided if an organization hopes that employees will take advantage of the program.
2. *Management support*. As with all important organizational initiatives, a lack of cooperation at any level can undermine the goals of the program.
3. *An on-site program coordinator*. This person coordinates and administrates the program, ensuring that those who seek help receive appropriate treatment. Thinking on whom this person should be varies. Some feel that anyone with a caring attitude can fill this position; others feel it should be someone with formal training (e.g., clinical psychologist, psychiatrist, social worker). This decision may depend on the extent to which problems will be handled in-house versus referred to outside agencies.
4. *Supervisory training*. Supervisors are frequently in a position where they must make referrals to the coordinator. It is these individuals who see the employees on a day-to-day basis and to whom the employees may go if they are experiencing problems. Supervisors must be trained in recognizing and acting on problems that arise.
5. *Employee education about the benefits of the program*. Promoting the program will help to ensure it is used and that employees are receiving assistance with work-related stress issues and health issues in general.
6. *Counselling*. Either in-house or external services may be available to employees. The advantage with external services is the reduced likelihood of conflicts of interest for the coordinator; the major drawback is that the referral agency may have little experience with work settings, so worker productivity is deemphasized in favour of counselling and more expensive treatments.

7. *Union support*. Businesses that want to institute an EAP program are wise to consult with the relevant unions and get them involved. This will help to build trust and cooperation and increase the likelihood that the program will be a success. EAP coordinators often have to walk a careful line between union and management. For example, management may view the EAP program with suspicion, particularly when it comes to cost; unions may feel that EAPs are the company's way of usurping union power.

Issues with EAPs and WHP Programs

The expanding definition of an EAP program, particularly now that it has been usurped by the broader worksite health-promotion (WHP) program, means that there may be some uncertainty concerning the policy's implementation. For example, how do you define "general mental health"? Where does an EAP coordinator draw the line in intervening? Successful EAPs must have clear guidelines that are understood by all levels of managers and employees.[54]

One of the shortcomings of EAPs is that they provide limited feedback to management about the sources and effects of stress in the organization. Because employees are approaching and using the intervention system on an individual basis, and are guaranteed confidentiality, there is no effective way for the program to inform the organization if there is a stress "hot zone." Another shortcoming is the same complaint expressed about secondary interventions: They focus on the characteristics of the employee and not on the working environment that may be the cause of the stress.[55]

The issue of confidentiality in EAPs is very important. If a person's privacy is not respected, people will be hesitant to seek help for fear that there will be job-related repercussions. As a result, all records should be kept confidential and separated from an employee's personnel file. Many programs with high compliance rates owe their success to the steps taken to ensure confidentiality and job security.

Unintended Consequences of WHP Programs

The goal of health promotion is to reduce costs to the organization in terms of health care, lost time, turnover, and so on. However, some unintended consequences of WHP programs need to be considered. First, the reduction of health care utilization by employees (offered through benefits plans) may lead to a higher unit cost for those employees who do use health and medical benefits. The individual cost of offering certain benefits decreases with a high enrollment rate because the risk to insurance companies of having to pay out on claims is reduced with a large subscription. Reduced enrollment in some aspects of a cafeteria-style benefits plan (in which employees have some options concerning the coverage they would like in areas such as medical, dental, life insurance, etc.) may make it prohibitive for those employees who need access to those benefits. A second potential consequence is that

participation in exercise or fitness programs may cause work-scheduling disruptions, increase fatigue, lower performance, and increase accidents among
those who are beginning such a program. Health promotion can also cause
friction among workers. For example, smoking restrictions may produce con-
RPC 13.2 flict between smokers and nonsmokers, produce negative attitudes about
smoking, and reduce productivity among smokers if they must leave the
RPC 13.4 workstation to smoke. Finally, the diagnosis of previously unknown risk factors may contribute to absenteeism (e.g., doctor's appointments). For example,
individuals who did not know they were hypertensive may exhibit increased
RPC 13.5 absenteeism as a result of being informed of their condition.

Overall Evaluation

How successful are worksite health-promotion programs? Once again, we find "success" to be a difficult thing to assess. Some studies show that these programs can be effective. A review of health-promotion studies that included organizational outcomes such as medical expenses and absenteeism showed that WHP programs returned $3.35 for every $1 spent.[56] One specific study evaluating a multi-faceted worksite health-promotion program that included multiple lifestyle features such as nutrition and exercise reported a reduction in absenteeism and its related costs.[57]

However, not all studies support the success of WHP programs. In fact, some authors argue that there is simply not enough systematic research on the various categories of WHP programs to reach a definitive conclusion about their efficacy.[58] Some point out that the available studies that do show positive effects are plagued with methodological weaknesses.[59] For instance, it is not uncommon for studies in this area to lack the necessary control groups, randomization of participants, and well-defined outcome measures that are needed to make strong conclusions about the program under investigation. Another problem common in this area of research is the use of cross-sectional rather than longitudinal designs. As such, researchers cannot assess the potential long-term benefits of WHP programs.

Overall, the jury is still out on the benefits of WHP programs. Some recent evidence suggests that comprehensive health programs are cost effective and yield positive cost and health-related benefits.[60] However, the links between health-promotion efforts and performance improvement, absenteeism and turnover, and morale and attitude improvement are spurious in the research literature making it difficult to reach firm conclusions on the success of such programs. The lack of evaluation studies relying on rigorous scientific methodology contributes to this problem. The available research does suggest that management support is vital if worksite health-promotion initiatives are to be a success.[61]

Beyond the lack of solid research to demonstrate their effectiveness indisputably, two additional factors have been noted as limitations to worksite health-promotion programs.[62] First, these initiatives have been criticized for focusing so heavily on individual attitudes and behaviour and often excluding organizational and management factors (e.g., job design) that also have a high degree of influence on employee health. Alternatively, a class of interventions called quality of work-life programs has objectives similar to worksite health promotion, but rather than presume the employee's lifestyle is responsible for health, well-being, and performance, they focus on what an employer can do to improve the employee's working conditions.

A second criticism of worksite health-promotion programs is that they are often carried out in isolation from other human resource practices. In this case, they have much in common with work–family policies that are often overlooked as strategic human resource functions.[63] The lack of integration with other human resources functions may be detrimental to the ultimate success of existing WHP programs. In reviewing key evidence-based elements for effective worksite health-promotion programs, one study noted that health-promotion programs are most likely to be effective when they are fully integrated into strategic human resource efforts.[64]

Occupational Health and Safety Notebook 13.3

Using Evaluation to Build a Business Case for Health-Promotion and Family-Friendly Programs

Given the large investment that organizations make in health-promotion and family-friendly workplace policies, it is important to investigate the effectiveness of such initiatives. In fact, one way that human resource managers might make a business case for continued or increased funding for workplace wellness and family-friendly programs is to demonstrate that they work. To that extent, the outcomes associated with such programs should be subject to systemic study. Organizations can conduct evaluation studies to assess the success of their health-related initiatives. Some characteristics of thorough evaluation studies include the following:

1. *Pre-intervention and post-intervention assessments of relevant variables.* This approach allows the evaluator to use the pre-intervention measure as a baseline to assess the extent of improvement experienced by the program participants and the organizations. Ideally, there should also be multiple post-intervention assessments to allow researchers to gain an understanding of the long-term effectiveness of the program.
2. *Consideration of the extent to which employees participate in the program.* Knowing whether employees take part will help the evaluator understand the outcomes associated with the program. If there does not appear to be improvement in important variables, it will be valuable to know whether the lack of change is associated with low participation or whether employees are participating in a program that is not working.
3. *Reliable and valid measures of relevant individual and organizational outcome variables.* Depending on the exact nature of the program, employees in a health-promotion program might fill out a questionnaire regarding their anxiety levels and degree of job satisfaction, or have their blood pressure monitored. The organization might monitor such factors as absenteeism rates, production rates, or incidence of lost-time injuries. If the program is effective, it is hoped that these variables would indicate the program is successful.
4. *Some type of control group, if possible.* Comparing the outcomes of those employees who took part in the program with a comparable group who did not participate provides valuable information regarding the effectiveness of the WHP initiative.

A recent report sponsored by Health Canada summarized the organizational factors that positively affect worker health.[65] The factors that contribute to a healthy work environment include leaders who value employees as key to organizational success, supervisors who support employees and wellness initiatives, communication throughout the organization, a high degree of employee participation and control, and an organization that values work–family balance and employee health. These ingredients contribute to a holistic approach to workplace wellness that involves individuals and organizations in the creation of healthier employees and workplaces.

Summary

A broad array of programs can be offered in organizations under the rubric of work–family and worksite health-promotion programming. For the most part, the jury is still out on whether these programs offer significant benefits to organizational outcomes. However, some evidence shows that work–family programs have some positive impact on the experience of work–family conflict. Similarly, health-promotion programming can be successful in changing individual behaviour to enhance health. One positive spinoff of the programs for organizations is the general increase in employee morale (e.g., satisfaction, commitment) that is associated with making health-promotion and family-friendly programs available in the workplace.

Key Terms

behavioural involvement 358
compressed workweek 359
employee assistance plans (EAPs) 364
family to work conflict 358
flexible work arrangements (FWAs) 359
flextime 360
health promotion 364
hypertension 369
job sharing 359
job splitting 360
psychological involvement 358
telecommuting 360
work to family conflict 358
work–family conflict 357

Weblinks

Intuit

http://www.intuit.ca (p. 355)

National Quality Institute

http://www.nqi.ca (p. 355)

Health Canada, "Workplace Health Strategies"

http://www.hc-sc.gc.ca/ewh-semt/occup-travail/work-travail/wh-mat-strategies_e.html (p. 355)

Canadian Centre for Occupational Health and Safety, "OSH Answers, Work–Life Balance"

http://www.ccohs.ca/oshanswers/psychosocial/worklife_balance.html (p. 358)

Centre for Families, Work, and Well-being, University of Guelph

http://www.uoguelph.ca/cfww/ (p. 359)

Canadian Centre for Occupational Health and Safety, "OSH Answers, Healthy Eating at Work"

www.ccohs.ca/oshanswers/psychosocial/healthyeating.html (p. 370)

Dofasco

http://www.dofasco.ca (p. 371)

Husky Injection Molding Systems

http://www.husky.ca/ (p. 371)

Public Health Agency of Canada, "Active Living At Work"

http://www.phac-aspc.gc.ca/pau-uap/fitness/work/index.html (p. 372)

Canadian Centre for Occupational Health and Safety, "OSH Answers, Active Living at Work"

http://www.ccohs.ca/oshanswers/psychosocial/active_living.html (p. 372)

RPC Icons

RPC 13.1 Develops or provides for wellness and employee assistance programs to support organizational effectiveness.

- policy/procedure development
- collective agreements
- industry best practices
- outside service providers
- the organization's culture
- conflict resolution techniques
- problem solving techniques
- report writing and record keeping
- the relationship between employee wellness and productivity
- performance goals of the organization and how these are affected by employee wellness
- key components of an EAP such as intake, assessments, counseling, traumatic incident debriefing, and cap on service
- cost/benefit analysis
- types of employee assistance programs
- types of employee assistance and wellness programs

- conceptual definition and implications of occupational stressors (e.g., potential stressors, methods of identifying potential stressors and strain outcomes, response to organizational stressors, and management of employee strain outcomes)
- trends in occupational health and safety

RPC 13.2 Implements and evaluates practices in the areas of health, safety, security, and Workers' Compensation.

- investigative technique
- hazard recognition
- disaster recovery techniques
- relevant legislation
- resource information
- common health and safety practices
- company policies and procedures
- Worker Protection (including health and safety and Workers' Compensation)
- theories and practices for protection of individuals and groups
- Occupational health and safety legislation (e.g., Occupational Health and Safety Act of Ontario, Workplace Safety & Insurance Act—Bill 99, Workplace Hazardous Materials Information System, Transportation of Dangerous Goods legislation, environmental legislation, smoking in the workplace legislation, civil rights legislation)
- hazard identification and control
- management techniques for OH&S Programs

RPC 13.3 Provides information to employees and managers on available programs.

- elements of EAP program
- promotional and marketing tools and techniques
- communication tools and techniques
- training and development techniques
- management techniques for OH&S Programs
- types of employee assistance and wellness programs
- trends in occupational health and safety

TASK & KNOWLEDGE REQUIREMENTS

- importance, criteria, and techniques of program evaluation

RPC 13.4 Analyzes rate grouping costs, early intervention and return to work programs, claims management programs, and claims appeals.

- capability of available resources such as rehabilitation centers, physiotherapists, ergonomists, and medical consultants
- relevant legislation including rate structures (e.g., Workers' Compensation, HR, occupational health)

- cost/benefit methods
- intervention processes
- Workers' Compensation billing and claims processes and guidelines
- industry best practices
- range of job functions within the organization's structure
- company benefit plans and policies
- Worker Protection (including health and safety and Workers' Compensation)
- objectives, processes, and conceptual foundations of financial and management accounting
- issues in identifying relevant costs (e.g., cost accuracy vs. relevance; costs & pricing; irrelevant costs; costing collective; bargaining proposals; cost-benefit analysis
- the economic, legal, technical, and moral impact of OHS
- types of employee assistance and wellness programs

Task & Knowledge Requirements

- conceptual definition and implications of occupational stressors (e.g., potential stressors, methods of identifying potential stressors and strain outcomes, response to organizational stressors, and management of employee strain outcomes)

RPC 13.5 Establishes and implements strategies to minimize compensation costs.

- relevant legislation
- cost/benefit techniques
- Workers' Compensation billing, rate structures, and claims adjudication processes
- industry best practices
- modified return to work program
- ergonomics and physical demands analysis
- training and development
- policy, procedure and program development
- Worker Protection (including health and safety and Workers' Compensation)
- measurement bases and underlying methodologies used in finance departments
- Occupational health and safety legislation (e.g., Occupational Health and Safety Act of Ontario, Workplace Safety & Insurance Act—Bill 99, Workplace Hazardous Materials Information System, Transportation of Dangerous Goods legislation, environmental legislation, smoking in the workplace legislation, civil rights legislation
- ergonomics
- management techniques for OH&S Programs
- types of employee assistance and wellness programs

RPC 13.6 Contributes to policy on the workplace environment (e.g., smoking, workplace violence, scent-free, communicable diseases, and addictions).

- relevant legislation
- program and policy development
- the culture of the organization
- conflict resolution
- record keeping and reporting
- technical terminology
- environmental hazards
- common and statutory law (e.g., employment standard: labour relations)
- Worker Protection (including health and safety and Workers' Compensation)
- theories and practices for protection of individuals and groups
- Occupational health and safety legislation (e.g., Occupational Health and Safety Act of Ontario, Workplace Safety & Insurance Act—Bill 99, Workplace Hazardous Materials Information System, Transportation of Dangerous Goods legislation, environmental legislation, smoking in the workplace legislation, civil rights legislation)
- management techniques for OH&S Programs
- trends in occupational health and safety

RPC 13.7 Ensures that mechanisms are in place for responding to crises in the workplace, including critical incident stress management.

- oral and written communication
- training and development techniques
- industry best practices
- the workplace environment including the availability of emergency equipment
- policy and program development and evaluation
- intervention strategies
- relevant legislation (e.g., fire code, Workers' Compensation)
- investigation techniques
- stress management techniques
- types of employee assistance programs
- Occupational health and safety legislation (e.g., Occupational Health and Safety Act of Ontario, Workplace Safety & Insurance Act—Bill 99, Workplace Hazardous Materials Information System, Transportation of Dangerous Goods legislation, environmental legislation, smoking in the workplace legislation, civil rights legislation)
- hazard identification and control
- accident investigation procedures
- emergency preparedness procedures
- management techniques for OH&S Programs

- conceptual definition and implications of occupational stressors (e.g., potential stressors, methods of identifying potential stressors and strain outcomes, response to organizational stressors, and management of employee strain outcomes)

RPC 13.8 Analyses risk to the health and safety of employees and determines appropriate preventative measures, including training, provision of required safety equipment, and administrative practices.

- relevant legislation
- nature of the business and physical work environment
- hazard recognition
- workplace inspection techniques
- safety programs, equipment, and emergency procedures
- ergonomics
- functions of the JHSC
- training and development/presentation techniques
- industry best practices
- relevant technical terminology
- the collective agreement
- services and equipment available in the community
- Worker Protection (including health and safety and Workers' Compensation)
- training and development program design and administration

Task & Knowledge Requirements

- Occupational health and safety legislation (e.g., Occupational Health and Safety Act of Ontario, Workplace Safety & Insurance Act—Bill 99, Workplace Hazardous Materials Information System, Transportation of Dangerous Goods legislation, environmental legislation, smoking in the workplace legislation, civil rights legislation)
- hazard identification and control
- emergency preparedness procedures
- management techniques for OH&S Programs
- types of employee assistance and wellness programs

Discussion Questions

1. EAPs often have two routes of entry. An individual can voluntarily contact the EAP for assistance with a problem, or a supervisor can refer the individual. In the latter case, a supervisor who notes a decline in performance can insist an individual seek assistance or be disciplined (including dismissal). Is this degree of coercion justified? Is it likely to facilitate a change in behaviour?

2. The logic of health-promotion programs in the workplace is based on the observation that the workplace provides a convenient way to reach large segments of the population. Yet many individuals are concerned about whether organizations have the right to get involved in employees' lifestyle choices. What do you think? Should organizations be involved in these programs?
3. What benefits would you expect to see from implementing a physical fitness program (e.g., paid memberships in the local health club) in your workplace?
4. Is stress management training an effective approach to dealing with workplace stress? Why or why not?
5. Generate some strategies that a dual-income couple might use to help them more effectively manage work and family demands. How might their employers help them enact some of these strategies?

Using the Internet

1. Visit the websites of a number of companies representing a variety of job sectors (e.g., manufacturing, high tech, communications, medical). Search the Web pages to find information on the types of health-promotion programs (e.g., smoking cessation, fitness) and family-friendly policies (e.g., flextime, telecommuting) they offer.

    a. Identify the proportion of the companies that offer health-promotion programs or family-friendly policies.
    b. Which health-promotion programs and family-friendly policies appear to be most commonly available?
    c. What are some of the company characteristics that appear to be related to the programs they offer? For instance, are companies in a particular sector or of a particular size more likely to offer health-promotion and family-friendly programs?
    d. Discuss with your classmates the extent to which the availability of health-promotion and family-friendly programs is important to them when they are looking for job. Which programs appear to be the most desirable to job seekers?

2. The "sandwiched generation" is particularly exposed to issues of work–family conflict. Using Internet resources, define the sandwiched generation. Why are they vulnerable to work–family conflict?
3. Health-promotion programs are more likely to be successful if based on a thorough needs assessment (i.e., assess the needs of the organizations and its employees). Design a needs assessment instrument for measuring the need for health-promotion programming in your current or a former workplace. If your work experience does not provide a suitable example for this Internet exercise, interview someone about his or her workplace and develop a needs assessment instrument for that work environment. The Internet will be very helpful in this task.

Search the Web using keywords such as "wellness," "health promotion," and so on. This search will result in the identification of many components of such a needs assessment instrument.

4. Search the Internet to find out details about the government-sponsored mandatory parental or maternal leave benefits in different countries (e.g., Canada, the United States, and the United Kingdom). Compare the policies in each country. Additionally, search the websites of various organizations that have operations in each of the countries you chose to determine whether they provide additional parental leave benefits to their employees. Afterward, discuss the following issues in class:
   a. What impact would the policies in each of these countries and companies have on a new parent's experience of work–family conflict? Would these policies help a working parent balance work and family roles?
   b. What are the advantages and disadvantages of these programs for the person taking the leave?
   c. What are the advantages and disadvantages of these programs for the organizations that have employees taking leave?

   What are the advantages and disadvantages of these programs for families?
5. Each year *Report On Business* magazine releases a ranking of the Top 50 Employers in Canada. Access a "50 Best Employers" list from a recent year, and search the websites of five of these top employers. Assess the extent to which they offer work–family friendly and worksite health-promotion programs. Describe some of the programs they offer.

Exercises

1. Issues of work–family conflict are highly prevalent for parents of young children. To find out more about the experience of work–family conflict, interview a working individual who also has responsibility for childcare. Some questions you might ask include the following:
   a. How many hours per week does the individual spend on paid work?
   b. How many hours per week does the individual spend on childcare activities?
   c. How many hours per week does the individual spend on nonpaid household chores and errands?
   d. If the individual has a spouse, in what ways does the spouse help him or her manage the multiple responsibilities of work and family commitments?

e. What are some of the special challenges the individual encounters in balancing work and family life?

f. What are some of the strategies the individual uses to meet all his or her work and family demands?

g. What efforts does the individual's employer make to help him or her manage work and family demands?

2. With a small group of classmates, discuss the following scenario: Imagine your current work hours are Monday to Friday, 9 to 5. At present, the start time of 9 a.m. is strictly enforced. However, the company is considering implementing a new flextime approach to work scheduling. Under this program employees will be able to start their eight-hour workday any time between 7 a.m. and 11 a.m. However, each employee must work a continuous shift (i.e., there is no flexibility midday).

   Each person in the group should reflect on how such a change would benefit or disadvantage him or her, given their current circumstances. Additionally, discuss how the move to flextime might affect the following individuals or groups:

   a. A working parent who has small school-aged children
   b. Someone who is not a morning person
   c. A person who commutes a long distance to work
   d. An individual who has substantial eldercare responsibilities
   e. Coworkers of individuals who opt to use the flextime arrangement
   f. The organization implementing the change

   What other types of flexible scheduling might help some of these people manage their multiple responsibilities to work and family?

3. In this chapter we discuss the importance of evaluating the success of health-promotion programs. For any program, a number of outcome variables might offer insight into the success or failure of the program. One way to categorize these categories is via the four types of strain introduced in Chapter 6 (organizational, psychological, physical, and behavioural). Along with your classmates, brainstorm some of the pertinent outcome variables from each of these broad categories to incorporate in each of the following types of health-promotion programs. The group should also consider how they might measure each of these variables.

   a. smoking cessation
   b. on-site physical fitness centre
   c. lunch-time Weight Watchers program
   d. off-site, call-in EAP
   e. subsidized yoga classes

Case 1

Mandatory Aerobics

As a new manager, Jean McDonald is eager to improve morale and productivity in the workgroup. Believing that you will work better if you feel better, Jean has scheduled a group aerobics class in which all group members must participate. Several group members object to enforced exercise and have approached you (as Jean's immediate supervisor) with their concerns. What do you tell the employees? What do you tell Jean?

Case 2

Evaluating the Benefits of WHPs

Quan Dar is the human resource manager of a mid-sized insurance firm. A faltering economy has resulted in the need to reexamine all current expenditures and to find areas in which to cut costs. Senior management is questioning the amount of money the firm spends on health-promotion programs. Currently, the firm offers weight-loss clinics, subsidized smoking-cessation products, an on-site fitness program, regular stress-prevention training programs, and an employee assistance program. Quan feels that these programs have value and add significant worth to the firm. However, senior management demands evidence. Quan has approached you for advice—how can he demonstrate the value of these programs to the firm?

Case 3

Job Sharing in a Telecommunications Firm

Sherry and Marco are both highly skilled marketing managers at a large telecommunications firm. In their time with the company, Marco and Sherry have worked very long hours. Indeed, they have worked well as a team to design several large-scale, successful advertising campaigns for new products and services. However, both are now parents of young children, and they are feeling the pressure of competing work and family demands. Of late both have expressed concerns about their ability to keep up with the fast pace of both their home and their work responsibilities and have mentioned the possibility of either cutting back their time at work or leaving their jobs altogether. As the director of human resources, you don't want to lose such valuable talent in the marketing department. You begin to think that Sherry and Marco might be ideal candidates for the company's new job-sharing program. How might you facilitate a job-sharing arrangement for Sherry and Marco? What types of working arrangement might you suggest to them?

Endnotes

1. Aldana, S. G. (2001). Financial impact of health promotion programs: A comprehensive review of the literature. *American Journal of Health Promotion, 15,* 281–288; and Riedel, J. E., Baase, C., Hymel, P., Lynch, W., McCabe, M., Mercer, W. R., & Peterson, K. (2001). The effect of disease prevention and health promotion on workplace productivity: A literature review. *American Journal of Health Promotion, 15,* 167–190.
2. Bond, J. T., Galinsky, E., Kim, S. S., & Brownfield, E. (2005). *2005 national survey of employers.* Families and Work Institute. Retrieved from http://familiesandwork.org/site/research/reports/2005nse.pdf, February 16, 2007.
3. Lowe, G. S. (2003). *Healthy workplaces and productivity: A discussion paper.* Ottawa: Minister of Public Works and Government Services.
4. Duxbury, L., & Higgins, C. (2003). *Work-life conflict in Canada in the new millennium: A status report* (*Final Report*). Public Health Agency of Canada. Retrieved from http://www.phac-aspc.gc.ca/publicat/work-travail/index.html, February 16, 2007.
5. Kelloway, E. K., & Francis, L. (2006, February). *Stress and strain in Nova Scotia organizations: Results of a recent province-wide study.* Paper presented at the Nova Scotia Psychologically Healthy Workplace Conference, Halifax.
6. Frone, M. R. (2003). Work-family balance. In J. C. Quick & L. E. Tetrick (Eds.), *Handbook of occupational health psychology* (pp. 143–162). Washington, DC: American Psychological Association.
7. Frone, M. R., Yardley, J. K., & Markel, K. (1997). Developing and testing an integrative model of work-family interface. *Journal of Vocational Behavior, 54,* 145–167.
8. Duxbury, L., & Higgins, C. (2003). *Work-life conflict in Canada in the new millennium: A status report* (*Final Report*). Public Health Agency of Canada. Retrieved from http://www.phac-aspc.gc.ca/publicat/work-travail/index.html, February 16, 2007.
9. Frone, M. R. (2003). Work-family balance. In J. C. Quick & L. E. Tetrick (Eds.), *Handbook of occupational health psychology* (pp. 143–162). Washington, DC: American Psychological Association.
10. Frone, M. R., Yardley, J. K., & Markel, K. (1997). Developing and testing an integrative model of work-family interface. *Journal of Vocational Behavior, 54,* 145–167.
11. Frone, M. R. (2003). Work-family balance. In J. C. Quick & L. E. Tetrick (Eds.), *Handbook of occupational health psychology* (pp. 143–162). Washington, DC: American Psychological Association.
12. Duxbury, L., & Higgins, C. (2003). *Work-life conflict in Canada in the new millennium: A status report* (*Final Report*). Public Health Agency of Canada. Retrieved from http://www.phac-aspc.gc.ca/publicat/work-travail/index.html, February 16, 2007.
13. Higgins, C., Duxbury, L., & Johnson, K. (2004). *Exploring the link between work-life conflict and demands on Canada's health care system.* Public Health Agency of Canada. Retrieved from http://www.phac-aspc.gc.ca/publicat/work-travail/report3/pdfs/fvwklfrprt_e.pdf, February 18, 2007.
14. Adams, G. A., King, L. A., & King, D. W. (1996). Relationships of job and family involvement, family social support, and work-family conflict with job and life satisfaction. *Journal of Applied Psychology, 81,* 411–420; Duxbury, L., & Higgins, C. (2003). *Work-life conflict in Canada in the new millennium: A status report* (*Final Report*). Public Health Agency of Canada. Retrieved from http://www.phac-aspc.gc.ca/publicat/work-travail/index.html, February 16, 2007; and Frone, M. R. (2003). Work-family balance. In J. C. Quick & L. E. Tetrick (Eds.), *Handbook of occupational health psychology* (pp. 143–162). Washington, DC: American Psychological Association.
15. Bachman, K. (2000). *Work-life balance: Are employers listening?* Ottawa: Conference Board of Canada.

16. Golden, T. D., Veiga, J., & Simsek, Z. (2006). Telecommuting's differential impact on work–family conflict: Is there no place like home? *Journal of Applied Psychology, 91,* 1340–1350; and NIOSH. (2002). *The changing organization of work and the safety and health of working people.* (DHHS [NIOSH]) Publication No. 2002–16.
17. Comfort, D., Johnson, K., & Wallace, D. (2003). *Part-time work and family-friendly practices in Canadian workplaces.* Statistics Canada, Human Resources Development Canada. Retrieved from http://www.statcan.ca/english/freepub/71-584-MIE/71-584-MIE2003006.pdf, February 18, 2007.
18. Frone, M. R. (2003). Work-family balance. In J. C. Quick & L. E. Tetrick (Eds.), *Handbook of occupational health psychology* (pp. 143–162). Washington, DC: American Psychological Association.
19. Thompson, C. A., Beauvais, L. L., & Lyness, K. S. (1999). When work-family benefits are not enough: The influence of work-family culture on benefit utilization, organizational attachment, and work family conflict. *Journal of Vocational Behavior, 54,* 392–415.
20. Thomas, L. T., & Ganster, D. C. (1995). Impact of family-supportive work variables on work-family conflict and strain: A control perspective. *Journal of Applied Psychology, 80,* 6–15.
21. Goff, S. J., Mount, M. K., & Jamieson, R. L. (1990). Employer supported childcare, work/family conflict and absenteeism: A field study. *Personnel Psychology, 43,* 793–809; and LaPierre, L. M., & Allen, T. D. (2006). Work-supportive family, family-supportive supervision, use of organizational benefits, and problem-focused coping: Implications for work–family conflict and employee well-being. *Journal of Occupational Health Psychology, 11,* 169–181.
22. Judge, T. A., Boudreau, J. W., & Retz, R. D. (1994). Job and life attitudes of male executives. *Journal of Applied Psychology, 79,* 767–782.
23. Golden, T. D., Veiga, J., & Simsek, Z. (2006). Telecommuting's differential impact on work–family conflict: Is there no place like home? *Journal of Applied Psychology, 91,* 1340–1350; and LaPierre, L. M., & Allen, T. D. (2006). Work-supportive family, family-supportive supervision, use of organizational benefits, and problem-focused coping: Implications for work–family conflict and employee well-being. *Journal of Occupational Health Psychology, 11,* 169–181.
24. Golden, T. D., Veiga, J., & Simsek, Z. (2006). Telecommuting's differential impact on work-family conflict: Is there no place like home? *Journal of Applied Psychology, 91,* 1340–1350.
25. Golden, T. D. (2006). Avoiding depletion in virtual work: Telework and the intervening impact of work exhaustion on commitment and turnover intentions. *Journal of Vocational Behavior, 69,* 176–187.
26. Baltes, B. B., Briggs, T. E., Huff, J. W., Wright, J. A., & Neiman, G. A. (1999). Flexible and compressed workweek schedules: A meta-analysis of their effects on work-related criteria. *Journal of Applied Psychology, 84,* 496–513; and Comfort, D., Johnson, K., & Wallace, D. (2003). *Part-time work and family-friendly practices in Canadian workplaces.* Statistics Canada, Human Resources Development Canada. Retrieved from http://www.statcan.ca/english/freepub/71-584-MIE/71-584-MIE2003006.pdf, February 18, 2007.
27. Baltes, B. B., Briggs, T. E., Huff, J. W., Wright, J. A., & Neiman, G. A. (1999). Flexible and compressed workweek schedules: A meta-analysis of their effects on work-related criteria. *Journal of Applied Psychology, 84,* 496–513; and Ralston, D. A. (1989). The benefits of flextime: Real or imagined? *Journal of Organizational Behavior, 10,* 369–373.
28. Frone, M. R. (2003). Work-family balance. In J. C. Quick & L. E. Tetrick (Eds.), *Handbook of occupational health psychology* (pp. 143–162). Washington, DC: American Psychological Association.
29. NIOSH. (2002). *The changing organization of work and the safety and health of working people.* (DHHS [NIOSH]) Publication No. 2002–16.
30. Kossek, E. E. (2003, June). Workplace policies and practices to support work and family: Gaps in implementation and linkages to individuals and organizational effectiveness. Paper presented at *Workforce/Workplace Mismatch: Work, Family, Health and Well-Being.* Washington, DC.

31. Johnson, K. L., Lero, D. S., & Rooney, J. A. (2001). *Work-life compendium 2001: 150 Canadian statistics on work, family and well-being*. Guelph, ON: Centre for Families, Work, and Well-Being.
32. Blair-Loy, M., & Wharton, A. S. (2002). Employees' use of work-family policies and the workplace social context. *Social Forces, 80*, 813–845.
33. Chapman, L. S., & Sullivan, S. (2003, July/August). Health and productivity management: An emerging paradigm for the workplace. *The Art of Health Promotion, 7*, 1–9.
34. Employee Assistance Professional Association. (1994). *Standards of practice and professional guidelines for employee assistance programs*. London: Author.
35. Popple, P. R. (1981). Social work in business and industry. *Social Services Review, 6*, 257–269.
36. Matteson, M. T., & Ivancevich, J. M. (1988). Health promotion at work. In C. L. Cooper & I. T. Robertson (Eds.), *International review of industrial and organizational psychology, 1988* (pp. 279–306). Chichester: John Wiley and Sons.
37. Cooper, C. L., Dewe, P., & O'Driscoll, M. (2003). Employee assistance programs. In J. C. Quick & L. E. Tetrick (Eds.), *Handbook of occupational health psychology* (pp. 289–304). Washington, DC: American Psychological Association.
38. Cooper, C. L., Dewe, P., & O'Driscoll, M. (2003). Employee assistance programs. In J. C. Quick & L. E. Tetrick (Eds.), *Handbook of occupational health psychology* (pp. 289–304). Washington, DC: American Psychological Association; and Employee Assistance Professional Association. (1994). *Standards of practice and professional guidelines for employee assistance programs*. London: Author.
39. Murphy, L. R., Hurrell, J. J., Jr., Sauter, S. L., & Keita, G. P. (1995). Introduction. In L. R. Murphy, J. J. Hurrell, Jr., S. L. Sauter, & G. P. Keita (Eds.), *Job stress interventions* (pp. xi–xiii). Washington, DC: American Psychological Association.
40. Quillian-Wolever, R. E., & Wolever, M. E. (2003). Stress management at work. In J. C. Quick & L. E. Tetrick (Eds.), *Handbook of occupational health psychology* (pp. 355–375). Washington, DC: American Psychological Association.
41. Murphy, L. R. (1996). Stress management in work settings: A critical review of the health effects. *American Journal of Health Promotion, 11*, 112–135.
42. Kenny, D. T., & Cooper, C. (2003). Introduction: Occupational stress and its management. *International Journal of Stress Management, 10*, 275–279.
43. Thomason, J. A., & Pond, S. B. (1995). Effects of instruction on stress management skills and self-management skills among blue-collar employees. In L. R. Murphy, J. J. Hurrell, Jr., S. L. Sauter, & G. P. Keita (Eds.), *Job stress interventions* (pp. 7–20). Washington, DC: American Psychological Association.
44. Keyes, J. B. (1995). Stress inoculation training for staff working with persons with mental retardation: A model program. In L. R. Murphy, J. J. Hurrell, Jr., S. L. Sauter, & G. P. Keita (Eds.), *Job stress interventions* (pp. 45–56). Washington, DC: American Psychological Association.
45. Petterson, I. L., & Arnetz, B. B. (1998). Psychosocial stressors and well-being in health care workers. The impact of an intervention program. *Social Science & Medicine, 47*, 1763–1772.
46. Henningfield, J. E., Ramstrom, L. M., Husten, C., Giovino, G., Barling, J., Weber, C., Kelloway, E. K., Strecher, V. J., & Jarvis, M. J. (1994). Smoking and the workplace: Realities and solutions. *Journal of Smoking-Related Diseases, 5*, 261–270.
47. Moshammer, H., & Neuberger, M. (in press). Long term success of short smoking cessation seminars supported by occupational health care. *Addictive Behaviors*; and Nerín, I., Crucelaegui, A., Más, A. Villalba, J.A., Guillén, D., & Gracia, A. (2005). Results of a comprehensive workplace program for the prevention and treatment of smoking addiction. *Archivos de Bronconeumologia, 41*, 197–201.
48. Beresford, S. A. A., Thompson, B., Feng, Z., Christianson, C., McLerran, D., & Patrick, D. L. (2001). Seattle 5 a day worksite program to increase fruit and vegetable consumption. *Preventive Medicine*, 32, 230–238; and Kramish Campbell, M., Tessaro, I., DeVellis, B., Benedict, S., Kelsey, K., Belton, L., & Sanhueza, A. (2002). Effects of a tailored health promotion program for female blue-collar workers: Health Works for women. *Preventive Medicine, 34*, 313–323.

49. Gebhardt, D. L., & Crump, C. E. (1990). Employee fitness and wellness programs in the workplace. *American Psychologist, 45,* 262–272.
50. Aldana, S. G., Merrill, R. M., Price, K., Hardy, A., & Hager, R. (2005). Financial impact of a comprehensive multisite workplace health promotion program. *Preventive Medicine, 40,* 131–137; and Gebhardt, D. L., & Crump, C. E. (1990). Employee fitness and wellness programs in the workplace. *American Psychologist, 45,* 262–272.
51. Dishman, R. K., Oldenburg, B., O'Neal, H., & Shephard, R. J. (1998). Worksite physical activity interventions. *American Journal of Preventive Medicine, 15,* 344–361; and Marshall, A. L. (2004). Challenges and opportunities for promoting physical activity in the workplace. *Journal of Science and Medicine in Sport, 7,* 60–66.
52. Dishman, R. K., Oldenburg, B., O'Neal, H., & Shephard, R. J. (1998). Worksite physical activity interventions. *American Journal of Preventive Medicine, 15,* 344–361; and Proper, K. I., Hildebrandt, V. H., Van der Beek, A. J., Twisk, J. W. R., & Van Mechelen, W. (2003). Effect of individual counseling on physical activity fitness and health: A randomized controlled trial in a workplace setting. *American Journal of Preventive Medicine, 24,* 218–226.
53. Mio, J. S., & Goishi, C. K. (1988). The employee assistance program: Raising productivity by lifting constraints. In P. Whitney & R. B. Ochsman (Eds.), *Psychology and productivity* (pp. 105–125). New York: Plenum Press.
54. Cooper, C. L., Dewe, P., & O'Driscoll, M. (2003). Employee assistance programs. In J. C. Quick & L. E. Tetrick (Eds.), *Handbook of occupational health psychology* (pp. 289–304). Washington, DC: American Psychological Association.
55. Murphy, L. R., Hurrell, J. J., Jr., Sauter, S. L., & Keita, G. P. (1995). Introduction. In L. R. Murphy, J. J. Hurrell, Jr., S. L. Sauter, & G. P. Keita (Eds.), *Job stress interventions* (pp. xi–xiii). Washington, DC: American Psychological Association.
56. Aldana, S. G. (1998, March/April). Financial impact of worksite health promotion and methodological quality of evidence. *The Art of Health Promotion, 2,* 1–8.
57. Aldana, S. G., Merrill, R. M., Price, K., Hardy, A., & Hager, R. (2005). Financial impact of a comprehensive multisite workplace health promotion program. *Preventive Medicine, 40,* 131–137.
58. DeRango, K., & Franzini, L. (2003). Economic evaluation of workplace health interventions: Theory and literature review. In J. C. Quick & L. E. Tetrick (Eds.), *Handbook of occupational health psychology* (pp. 417–430). Washington, DC: American Psychological Association.
59. DeRango, K., & Franzini, L. (2003). Economic evaluation of workplace health interventions: Theory and literature review. In J. C. Quick & L. E. Tetrick (Eds.), *Handbook of occupational health psychology* (pp. 417–430). Washington, DC: American Psychological Association.
60. Pelletier, K. R. (2005). A review and analysis of the clinical and cost-effectiveness studies of comprehensive health promotion and disease management programs at the worksite: Update VI 2000-2004. *Journal of Occupational & Environmental Medicine, 47,* 1051–1058.
61. Pelletier, K. R. (2001). A review and analysis of the clinical and cost-effectiveness studies of comprehensive health promotion and disease management programs at the worksite: 1998–2000 update. *American Journal of Health Promotion, 16,* 107–116.
62. Lowe, G. S. (2003). *Healthy workplaces and productivity: A discussion paper.* Ottawa: Minister of Public Works and Government Services.
63. Lowe, G. S. (2003). *Healthy workplaces and productivity: A discussion paper.* Ottawa: Minister of Public Works and Government Services.
64. Bennett, J. B., Cook, R. F., & Pelletier, K. (2003). Toward an integrated framework for comprehensive organizational wellness: Concepts, practices and research in workplace health promotion. In J. C. Quick & L. E. Tetrick (Eds.), *Handbook of occupational health psychology* (pp. 69–95). Washington, DC: American Psychological Association.
65. Lowe, G. S. (2003). *Healthy workplaces and productivity: A discussion paper.* Ottawa: Minister of Public Works and Government Services.

Index

ABC model of behaviour, 278–279
absenteeism, 256
accident, 171
accident/incident reports, 332–342, 334*f*, 336*f*, 340*f*, 342*f*
accident investigations
  accident analysis, 343
  accident/incident reports, 332–342, 334*f*, 340*f*, 342*f*
  analysis of an accident, 329
  benefits of, 324–325
  cognitive failures, 345–346
  cognitive interviewing, 331
  critical factors in investigative process, 325–326
  domino theory, 343, 344*f*
  environmental factors, 328
  eyewitness accounts, 327
  human factors, 327
  interviews, 330
  investigative methods, 329–331
  investigative tools, 332
  legal requirements, 326
  long report, 336
  normal accidents, 345
  observations or walkthroughs, 329
  psychology of accidents, 345–346
  rationale for, 324–325
  reenactments, 330–331
  severity, 325–326
  situational factors, 328
  Swiss cheese model, 345
  timing, 325
  training, 258
  types of information collected, 326–329
  what to investigate, 326
  who investigates, 328–329
accident prevention, 60
accident proneness, 8, 280
accident rates, 256
accountability, 289–290
acids, 121
act, 24
Act to Amend the Ontario Occupational Health and Safety Act, 33
action limit, 200–201
activity sampling, 184
acute stressors, 138
acute toxicity, 116
acute trauma, 171
administrative control
  awards, 212–213
  common examples, 211
  defined, 210
  described, 210–211
  housekeeping, 213–214
  importance of, 127
  incentives, 212–213
  preventive maintenance, 214–219
  safe work practices, 127
  safety awareness, 211
  struck-by-object injuries, 214
administrative interventions, 275
aerosols, 111
agents, 126
aggression. *See* workplace violence
AIDS, 121
alcoholism, 365
alkalines, 121
alveoli, 114
ambient, 82, 109
American Conference of Governmental Industrial Hygienists (ACGIH), 24–25, 87
American National Standards Institute (ANSI), 24
anesthetics, 117
anthrax, 108
anthropometry, 179
artistic occupations, 178
asbestos exposure, 115
asbestosis, 115
asphyxiants, 117
assessment of hazards. *See* hazard recognition and assessment
associated hazards, 109
assumption of risk, 7–8
asthma, occupational, 112
attention, 252
attenuation, 88
audiometer, 88
audit program, 231, 290–291
auditory system, 85*f*
audits, 185–186
auto-ignition temperature, 120
awards, 212–213
awareness events, 211, 212*t*
awkward working positions, 178

Bacillus anthracis, 108
bacterial biological agents, 123t
Bandura, Albert, 252
barrier guards, 228
barriers, 229, 312
bases, 121
Bata Industries Ltd., 43
BC Hydro, 302
behaviour-based safety initiative, 276, 280
behaviour modification principles, 278
behaviour sampling, 184
behavioural interventions, 275, 278
behavioural involvement, 358
behavioural strain, 144
behaviourist theory, 251–252
Berdahl, Jennifer, 151
Bethlehem Steel Company, 226
Bill C-45, 46, 242
biohazard, 108
  see also biological agents
biological agents
  ambient, 109
  classification, 125
  control of exposures, 124–127
  defined, 121
  described, 121
  personal hygiene practices, 127
  table of, 123
Biosafety Level 1 (BSL 1), 125
Biosafety Level 2 (BSL 2), 125
Biosafety Level 3 (BSL 3), 125
Biosafety Level 4 (BSL 4), 125
bioterrorism, 108
blank, 183
body as machine system, 92*f*
boiling point, 119
Bornstein, Stephen, 112
British Columbia (Public Service Employees Relations Commission) v. BCGSEU, 70
brown lung, 7

buffer, 141
buried fuel tanks, 43
business continuity planning, 316
byssinosis, 7

CAD-7, 66
Canada Labour Code, 213
Canada Labour (Safety) Code, 7
Canada Labour (Standards) Code, 7
Canadian Centre for Emergency Preparedness, 307
Canadian Centre for Occupational Health and Safety (CCOHS), 12, 149
Canadian Charter of Rights and Freedoms, 43
Canadian Community Health Survey, 177
Canadian Forces, 315, 343
Canadian Initiative on Workplace Violence, 136
Canadian LifeQuilt, 241
Canadian Pacific Railway (CPR), 285
Canadian registered safety professionals (CRSPs), 16
Canadian Standards Association (CSA), 24, 26, 227, 309
Canadian Superior, 210
cancer
  and asbestos, 115
  carcinogens, 118
  and fire fighters, 110
  lung cancer, 115
Capital District Health Authority (Nova Scotia), 136
carcinogens, 118
cardiopulmonary resuscitation (CPR) course, 313
career concerns, 139
cash allowance, 59
catastrophic consequences, 188
catastrophic stressors, 138
caught in, under, or between (CIUB) machinery, 170, 172–173
CCINFOWEB, 12
cell phones, 97
Certificate of Recognition (COR), 56
Chamberlain, Jason, 258
chemical agents
  aerosols, 111
  ambient, 109
  associated hazards, 109
  contaminants, 111
  control of exposures, 124–127
  defined, 108
  described, 109–111
  ingestion, 116
  liquid state, 111
  penetration, 119
  personal hygiene practices, 127
  presumptive legislation, 110
  respiration (inhalation), 112–114
  routes of entry, 111
  skin absorption, 114–115
  solvents, 119–121
  toxicity, 109–110
  toxicology, 111–119
  vapour or gas state, 111
chemical asphyxiants, 117
chemical pneumonitis, 116
chemical spills, 313
chlamydiae, 123*t*
chromic acid, 121
chronic toxicity, 116
chronic trauma, 171
cicumaural, 105*t*
close call, 256
Coalition Against Workplace Violence. *See* workplace violence
cognitive-behavioural skills training, 366
cognitive failures, 345–346
cognitive interviewing, 331
cognitive learning theories, 252
Coleman, Jon, 154
Columbia Accident Investigation Board (CAIB), 324
common-law duty, 25
compensation rates and methods, 59–62
compressed workweek, 359–360
computer use, 154–155
computer vision syndrome, 8
computers, 332
conduction, 92
conductive hearing loss, 84
Conference Board of Canada, 137, 362
confined space entry, 218–219, 219*f*
consequences, 188
Construction Safety Association of Ontario (CSAO), 184
constructors, 29
contact control
  fire plan, 309
  fire prevention and suppression, 310–312
  first aid and medical attention, 313–314
  hazard control, 210, 229–230
contact irritant, 117
contaminants, 111
contractors
  constructors, 29
  duties of, 27–29
control, 155
Controlled Products Regulations, 36
controls. *See* exposure controls; hazard control
controls (workspace design), 223
convection, 92
corporate homicide, 46
corporate liability, 45
costs
  direct costs, 9–10
  disability costs, 61
  economic costs, 9–10
  employee benefit costs, 256
  hazard identification program, 183
  iceberg model of health and safety costs, 172
  indirect costs, 9–10
  of unhealthy behaviour, 11
  workplace stress, 137
counselling, 371
crab asthma, 112
Criminal Code, 46
critical consequences, 188
critical incident stress debriefing (CISD), 315
crush injuries, 172–173
CSA Z1000-06 Occupational Health and Safety Management, 26
cumulative trauma disorder, 176

daily stressors, 138
Dalhousie University, 326

dangerous goods,
transportation, 45
daycare benefits, 361
decalcification, 90
defatting, 115
depression, 143
dermatitis, 115, 120
Dial Oilfield Services, 258
direct costs, 9–10
direct injury, 171
disability costs, 61
disability management
and human resources, 67–69
integrated disability
management, 67
return-to-work programs, 69–70
strategies for, 67–69
display panels, 223
distractibility, 345
distributive justice, 153
Dofasco inc., 371
domino theory, 343, 344*f*
dose, 116
dosimeter, 88
drawings, 332
drills, 309
due diligence, 10–11, 43
DuPont Canada, 213
dust, 111
duty to accommodate, 70

early warning change, 83
earplugs, 105*t*
economic costs, 9–10
eldercare benefits, 361
electromagnetic radiation, 96*f*
electronic mail, 154
Ellis, David, 229, 241
email, 154
emergency, 304, 306
emergency manager, 309
emergency measures organizations
(EMOs), 303–304
Emergency Operations Centres
(EOCs), 310
emergency plan
drills, 309
emergency response plan, 307
evacuation plan, 307–309
hazard evaluation, 306
notification of authorities, 309
supplies, 309
emergency planning. *See*
emergency preparedness and
response
Emergency Planning Canada, 306
emergency preparedness and
response
business continuity
planning, 316
contact, 309–314
described, 304–306
emergency plan, 306–309
emergency response in
Canada, 302
emergency response plan, 307
five-stage crisis-management
process, 305
getting back to normal, 315–316
pandemic planning, 307
postcontact, 314–315
precontact, 306–309
emergency response. *See*
emergency preparedness and
response
emergency response plan, 307
employee assistance plans (EAPs),
364–365, 373
employee benefit costs, 256
employees
duties of, 30
and perceived safety climate,
284
rights, 241–242
as stakeholders, 13
stress during emergencies, 316
employers
assessments (Workers'
Compensation), 64–65
common-law duty, 25
duties of, 25–26, 27–29
duty to accommodate, 70
during emergencies, 316
health-promotion efforts,
368–369
liability for discriminatory acts
of employees, 152
Meiorin decision, 70
responsibility of, 12
as stakeholders, 12–13
enclosure guards, 228
engineering control
defined, 220
exposure controls, 124*f*, 125
hand tool design, 220–221
isolation, 226
machine guarding, 227–228
process modification, 226
purchasing, 226–227
segregation, 226
substitution, 221
workstation design, 223–226
engineering interventions, 275
Englishtown Ferry, 240
Environment Canada, 306
environmental assessment, 43
environmental factors, 182, 328
environmental illness (EI), 114
environmental legislation, 42–44
Environmental Protection
Agency (B.C.), 147
equipment failures, 215
ergonomic design, 222
ergonomic factors, 179
evacuation plan, 307–309
event, 170
exchange rate, 86
experience rating, 65–67
exposure, 187
exposure controls
administrative controls, 127
engineering controls, 124*f*, 125
medical control measures, 124*f*
medical surveillance
programs, 128
personal protective equipment
(PPE), 127
work practices, 124*f*
ExxonMobil Canada, 210
eyewitness accounts, 327

fairness, 152–154
falls, 173, 214
family-care benefits, 361
family-friendly policies
see also work-family conflict
evaluation, 361–364, 375
family-care benefits, 361
flexible work arrangements
(FWAs), 359–360
personal leave systems, 360–361
family to work conflict, 358
farm safety, 32
Farm Safety Association of
Ontario, 258
fatality rates, 256

fault tree, 186
fault tree analysis, 195, 196–199, 196*f*, 197*f*, 198*f*, 199*f*, 200*f*
federal statutes, 43
feedback, 279–280
feeding tools, 228
Fiera Food Bakery, 229
fire, 310–312, 312*t*
Fire Commissioner of Canada, 306
fire fighters, 32, 87, 110
fire plan, 309
fire process, 310
fire tetrahedron, 311*f*
fire triangle, 310*f*
first aid, 259–260, 313–314
fitness programs, 370–372
5*22 Program, 287
flammability, 120
flash point, 120
flexible work arrangements (FWAs), 359–360
flextime, 360, 362
floor barriers, 228
fragmentation, 90
free-burning stage, 311
French, Glen, 136
frequency, 76
fume, 111
fungal, 123*t*
futureproofing, 307

gas, 111
gate arrangements, 197*f*
general adaptation syndrome, 140
goal setting, 281–282
Golyashov, Ivan, 229
government
  departments responsible for OH&S, 27
  occupational health and safety (OH&S) departments, 27
  as stakeholder, 11–12
gradual hearing loss, 84–85
guard design, 227–228
guarding by distance, 228
guidelines and policies, 24

Ham, James, 7
hammer configurations, 222*f*
hand-arm vibration syndrome (HAVS), 91
hand-removal devices, 228
hand tool design, 220–221
hazard, 170
hazard analysis, 186
hazard control
  administrative control, 210–219
  audit program, 231
  contact control, 210, 229–230
  defined, 210
  engineering control, 220–228
  monitoring, 231
  postcontact control, 210, 230
  precontact control, 210
  record keeping, 232
  source-path-human, 230, 230*f*
hazard evaluation, 306
hazard identification
  environmental factors, 182
  ergonomic factors, 179
  human factors, 179–181
  interaction of factors, 181
  situational factors, 182
  unsafe act, 180–181
hazard identification program
  audits, 185–186
  choosing, 183–184
  components of, 184–189
  cost, 183
  follow-up, 189
  geographical information, 184
  hazard analysis, 186
  job safety analysis, 186
  nature of hazards, 183
  plant analysis, 184
  reports, 185–186
  risk assessment, 186–189
  safety experts, 183–184
  safety sampling, 184
  source of request, 183
  task analysis, 185
  task and job inventory, 184
  walk-through survey, 184
hazard recognition and assessment
  accident, 171
  event, 170
  hazard identification, 179–182
  hazard identification program, 183–189
  incident, 171
  injury, 171
  repetitive-strain injury, 172
  terminology, 170–172
  types of injuries, 172–178
Hazardous Products Act, 36
health, 356
health and safety policy checklist, 289
health and safety professionals, 15, 16
health and safety programs. *See* organizational health and safety programs
health and safety training programs, 243–254
Health Canada, 355–356, 363, 376
health care workers, 32
health promotion
  case for wellness, 365
  defined, 364
  employee assistance plans (EAPs), 364–365, 373
  evaluation, 374–376
  issues, 373
  stress management programs, 365–367
  unintended consequences, 373–374
  worksite health promotion, 367–373
hearing loss
  see also noise
  auditory system, 85*f*
  conductive hearing loss, 84
  early warning change, 83
  gradual hearing loss, 84–85
  human hearing response, 83–84
  human hearing response curve, 83*f*
  permanent threshold shift (PTS), 84–85
  sensorineural hearing loss, 84
  temporary threshold shift (TTS), 84–85
  threshold of hearing, 83
  types of, 84–86
hearing protection types or classifications, 105, 105*t*
hearing protectors, 89
heat exposure, 93
heat of vaporization, 119
Heinrich's domino model, 344*f*
high-reliability organizations, 345

historical development
of modern occupational health and safety, 6–7
Workers' Compensation, 55
homeostasis, 92
hostile environment, 150
housekeeping, 213–214
human factors, 179–181, 327
human hearing response, 67–84
human hearing response curve, 83*f*
human resources
and disability management, 67–69
role of, 15–17
the three Es, 15–16
human rights statutes, 151
Hurricane Juan, 315, 316
Husky Injection Molding Systems, 371
hydrochloric acid, 121
hyperreflexia, 85
hypertension, 369
hypertension screening, 369–370

iceberg model of health and safety costs, 172
Imperial Oil, 288
incentives, 212–213
incident, 171
incident reports. *See* accident/incident reports
incipient stage, 311
indirect costs, 9–10
indirect injury, 171
Industrial Accident Prevention Association (IAPA), 14, 184
industrial hearing protection, 105, 105*t*
industrial presses, 172
Industrial Revolution, 7
industry assessment rates, 64–65
infrared radiation, 95
inhalation, 112–114
inhaled irritants, 117
injury
acute trauma, 171
awkward working positions, 178
"caught in, under, or between (CIUB) machinery," 170
chronic trauma, 171
crush injuries, 172–173
defined, 171
direct and indirect costs, 9
direct injury, 171
indirect injury, 171
injury frequency and severity rates, 76–77
lifting injuries, 174–176
needlestick injuries, 126
overexertion injuries, 172, 174–176
overt traumatic injuries, 172–173
repetitive-strain injury, 172, 176–178, 220, 222
second injury fund, 61
self-reported measures, 258
struck-by-object injuries, 214
types of injuries, 172–178
underreporting, 257
young workers, 173*t*
injury frequency and severity rates, 76–77
injury rates, 256, 276
injustice at work, 152–154
inorganic solvents, 120–121
instructional systems design (ISD) model of training
defined, 243
described, 243*f*
job/task analysis, 246
needs analysis, 243–244
organizational analysis, 244–245
person analysis, 246–247
train the trainer program, 249–250
training design and delivery, 247–254
integrated disability management, 67
interactional justice, 153
internal responsibility system (IRS), 30
International Labour Organization (ILO), 24
International Organization for Standardization (ISO), 24
Internet training, 250–253
interpersonal relations, 139
interpretability, 223
interviews, 330
Intuit Canada, 354
investigations. *See* accident investigations
investigative methods
cognitive interviewing, 331
interviews, 330
observations or walkthroughs, 329
reenactments, 330–331
investigative tools, 332
ionizing radiation, 94–95
irritants, 117
isolation, 155, 226, 230

job content and control, 139
job demands, 155
job description, 184
job design, 226
job inventory, 184
job safety analysis, 186
job sharing, 359–360
job specifications, 184
job splitting, 360
job/task analysis, 246
joint health and safety committees, 30–31

Kells, Sean, 14, 241
kickback, 228
kidney toxicants, 118

labels, 34–36, 38*f*
Labour Program of Human Resources and Social Development Canada, 326
latency period, 63
layout, 223
learning theory, 251–252
LeBlanc, Donald, 240
legal considerations
described, 10–11
due diligence, 10–11
legibility, 223
Legionnaires' disease, 121
legislative framework
accident investigations, 326
act, 24
Bill C-45 (Westray legislation), 46, 242
common-law duty, 25
corporate liability, 45

duties and responsibilities of major players, 27
duties of employers, owners and contractors, 27–29
duties of supervisors, 29–30
duties of workers, 30
environmental legislation, 42–44
first-aid requirements, 314
guidelines and policies, 24
joint health and safety committees, 30–31
jurisdictions and OH&S components, 28
noise level exposure limits, 86*t*
prescribed, 28
presumptive legislation, 110
provincial and territorial statutes, 44
regulations, 24
relevant federal statutes, 43
scope of OH&S legislation, 25–26
standards and codes, 24
stop-work provisions (Ontario), 33
transportation of dangerous goods, 45
work refusals, 32–33
Workplace Hazardous Materials Information System (WHMIS). *See* Workplace Hazardous Materials Information System (WHMIS)

liability
changing perspectives, 7–8
collective liability, 57
corporate liability, 45
for discriminatory acts of employees, 152

lifestyle changes, 367–373
lifting, 174, 175–176, 175*f*, 176*f*
lifting calculations (NIOSH method), 200–204
lighting, 225–226
limited right of refusal, 32
liquid, 111
liver toxicants, 118
local toxicity, 116
lockout procedures, 215–217
long report, 336*f*
loss of functional capacity, 60
lost-time injuries, 256
lost-time injuries province and territory, 6*t*
lower explosion limit (LEL), 120
lower flammability limit (LFL), 120
lung cancer, 115
lung toxicants, 118

machine guarding, 227–228
Macy's Department Store, 364
management
commitment to health and safety, 282–283
duties of, 29–30
role of, 282–283
support for worksite health promotion program, 372

marginal consequences, 188
material safety data sheets (MSDS), 36–42, 39*f*
materials handling, 174–176
maximum permissible limit, 200, 201
medical aid, 60, 313–314
medical surveillance programs, 128
meditation, 366
Mednick, Sara, 354
Meiorin decision, 70
memory, 252
Merit Adjusted Premium (MAP) Plan for Small Business, 66
mesothelioma, 115
microwave radiation, 95
mist, 111
moderators
classes of, 141
defined, 141
negative affectivity, 142
personality, 141–142
social context, 142
Type A behaviour, 141–142

modifications, 229
modified job assignment, 69
monitoring, 231
moral considerations, 11
motivation
defined, 278
goal setting, 281–282
reinforcement theory, 278–280
social learning theory, 252

motor control, 252
motor vehicle accidents, 173
Mount Allison University, 305
multiplicative model of safety performance, 277, 277*f*
multivariate risk/resilience model, 314
musculoskeletal injuries, 154–155, 176
mutagens, 118

naps, 354–355
narcotics, 117
National Institute for Occupational Safety and Health (NIOSH), 24–25, 140, 174–176
National Institute of Occupational Safety and Health (NIOSH), 137
National Quality Institute, 355–356
Natural Hazards Map of Canada, 306
necrosis, 90
needlestick injuries, 126
needs analysis, 243–244
negative affectivity, 142
negative publicity, 10
negligible consequences, 188
Neis, Barbara, 112
nerve deafness, 84
net earnings, 59
neurotoxins, 118
New Experimental Experience Rating (NEER), 10, 66
New Sun Cookies, 229
New Westminister Secondary School, 24
Newton, Kelly, 241
NIOSH lifting calculation method, 200–204
noise
see also hearing loss
attenuation, 88
audiometer, 88
calculation of noise levels, 102–104
defined, 83
dosimeter, 88
duration of sound, 84
early warning change, 83
effects of, 84–85
exchange rate, 86

extra-auditory effects, 85
hearing protection for fire fighters, 87
hearing protection types or classifications, 105, 105*t*
hearing protectors, 89
and human psychology, 85–86
hyperreflexia, 85
measurement of noise levels, 103*t*
noise control, 88
noise exposure standards, 86–88
noise exposure tests, 88
noise level exposure limits, 86*t*
octave band analyzer, 88
shift adjustment for noise exposure, 104
signs and levels, 87
sociological effects, 85
sound pressure level meter, 88
types of hearing loss, 84–86
vasoconstriction, 85
noise control, 88
noise exposure standards, 86–88
noise level exposure limits, 86*t*
nonionizing radiation, 95
nonlinear protectors, 105*t*
normal accidents, 345
Norwalk virus, 305
notification of authorities, 309
nutrition programs, 370

observable exposures, 184
observations, 329
Occidental chemical company, 10
Occupational Alcohol Movement, 365
occupational asthma, 112
occupational diseases, 63–64
Occupational Health and Safety Act of Ontario, 10, 32, 33
occupational health and safety legislation. *See* legislative framework
occupational health and safety (OH&S)
see also safety
barriers to implementation, 15
defined, 5
economic costs, 9–10
government departments, 27
historical development, 6–7
human resources, role of, 15–17
importance, 8–11
legal considerations, 10–11
moral considerations, 11
stakeholders, 11–15
occupational health and safety training. *See* training
occupational health psychology, 140
occupational illness, 6
occupational injury, 6
see also injury
occupational stress. *See* stress
Ocean Ranger, 181
octave band analyzer, 88
off-the-job training, 250
on-the-job training, 250
online training, 250–253
Ontario Hydro, 224–225
Ontario Power Generation, 274
organic solvents, 121, 122*t*
organizational analysis, 244–245
organizational health and safety programs
accountability, 289–290
auditing the program, 290–291
health and safety policy checklist, 289
health and safety training programs, 243–254
policy, 287–289
program objectives, 286–287
organizational strain, 144
organized labour
as stakeholders, 13–14
support for worksite health promotion program, 373
Ottawa-Carleton Transpo, 147
overexertion injuries, 172, 174–176
overt traumatic injuries, 172–173
overuse syndrome, 176
owners, duties of, 27–29

pandemic planning, 307
partnerships, 14–15
penetration, 119
permanent threshold shift (PTS), 84–85
person analysis, 246–247
personal hygiene practices, 127
personal leave systems, 360–361
personal protective equipment (PPE), 127
personality, 141–142
pesticides use or storage, 43
Pfizer Canada, 154
photoelectric eye, 228
photographs, 332
physical agents
acute, 82
ambient, 82
cell phones, 97
defined, 82
noise, 83–89
radiation, 94–95, 96*f*
thermal stress, 92–93
vibration, 90–91
in the workplace, 82
physical fitness programs, 370–372
physical rehabilitation, 62
physical strain, 144
physician's report, 340*f*
pinch points, 173
poisoning, 116
policy statements, 287–289
positive health, 356
positive tree, 186
postcontact control, 210, 230, 314–315
potassium hydroxide, 121
precontact control
emergency manager, 309
emergency plan, 306–309
hazard control, 210
predictable human factors, 179
prescribed, 28
presumptive legislation, 110
prevention, 56, 173
preventive maintenance
confined space entry, 218–219, 219*f*
defined, 214
equipment failures, 215
lockout procedures, 215–217
record keeping, 215
work permits, 215
preventive stress management, 145
primary interventions, 145
privacy, 155
probability, 187, 198–199
procedural justice, 153
process modification, 226

provincial and territorial
statutes, 44
provincial emergency measures
organizations (EMOs),
303–304
psychological involvement, 358
psychological strain, 143
psychology of accidents, 345–346
psychosocial hazards
depression, 143
injustice at work, 152–154
management of, 145–147
occupational health
psychology, 140
primary interventions, 145
secondary interventions,
145–146
sexual harassment, 150–152
strain, 142–144
stress. *See* stress
technology-related stressors,
154–155
tertiary interventions, 147
workplace violence, 136–137,
147–149
psychosocial model of health, 137
public health regulation, 43
purchasing, 226–227

*R. v. Bata Industries Ltd., Bata,
Marchant and Weston*, 43
R. v. Midland Transport Ltd., 45
RAC program, 324
radiation
defined, 93
electromagnetic radiation, 96*f*
infrared radiation, 95
ionizing radiation, 94–95
microwave radiation, 95
nonionizing radiation, 95
radio waves, 95
ultraviolet radiation, 95
radio waves, 95
random human factors, 179–180
Raynaud's phenomenon, 90
reactive materials, 312
Reason, J., 345
reasonable person test, 150
recognition of hazards. *See* hazard
recognition and assessment
record check, 332
record keeping, 215, 232, 257
reenactments, 330–331
regulations, 24
rehabilitation, 62
reinforcement theory, 278–280
relaxation training, 366
repetitive movements, 154–155
repetitive-strain injury, 172,
176–178, 220, 222
reports, 185–186
rescue work, 313
resonance, 90
respiration (inhalation), 112–114
respiratory system, 113*f*
return-to-work programs, 62,
69–70
Richardson, Michael, 258
rickettsia, 123*t*
right to know, 241
right to participate, 241
right to refuse unsafe work, 241
risk
accident proneness, 8
artistic occupations, 178
assessment, 186–189
assumption of risk, 7–8
behaviour-based safety
initiative, 280
changing perspectives, 7–8
defined, 187
evaluation of, 189*t*
risk factors, 141
Rogers, John, 170
role stressors, 139
roll call, 308
routes of entry
defined, 111
ingestion, 116
inhalation, 112–114
penetration, 119
skin absorption, 114–115
Rowan Gorilla V exploration
rig, 210
Royal Commission on the
Relations of Capital and
Labour in Canada, 7

safe work practices, 127
Safeguarding of Machinery
(Z432-94), 227
safety
see also occupational health and
safety (OH&S)
decrease in costs, 17
legislative compliance, 17
and other human resource
functions, 17
as people issue, 16
and workers' compensation, 54
safety and health committee or
representative, 329
safety and health officer, 328
safety awareness, 211
safety behaviours
ABC model of behaviour,
278–279
behaviour-based safety
initiative, 276
behaviour modification
principles, 278
categories of behaviour, 276
defined, 276
goal setting, 281–282
increasing opportunity for
safety behaviour, 282–286
and injury rates, 276
motivation, 278–282
multiplicative model of safety
performance, 277, 277*f*
noncompensatory model, 277
organizational health and safety
programs, 286–291
reinforcement theory, 278–280
safety climate, 283–284
safety leadership, 284–286
safety climate, 16, 245, 283–284
safety compliance, 284
safety experts, 183–184
safety initiative, 284
safety inspection reports, 256
safety leadership, 16, 284–286
safety orientation, 259–260
safety policies, 283
safety-related information, 283
safety sampling, 184
safety team, 329
SafetyNet, 112
scaffold use permit, 216*f*
scent-free policies, 114
screwdriver configurations, 221*f*
seating, 224–225
second injury fund, 61
secondary interventions, 145–146
segmental vibration, 90
segregation, 226

self-reported measures, 258
sensitizer, 118
sensorineural hearing loss, 84
severity, 77
sex discrimination, 151
sexual coercion, 150
sexual harassment, 150–152
shift adjustment for noise
    exposure, 104
short report, 334*f*
Sikich, Geary, 307
simple asphyxiants, 117
situational factors, 182, 328
slips, 214
smoke, 111
smoking cessation, 369
smouldering stage, 311
snow crab workers, 112
social learning theory, 252
social rehabilitation, 62
social support, 142, 366
sodium chloride, 121
sodium hydroxide, 121
solvents
  ability to dissolve fats, 120
  acids, 121
  bases, 121
  characteristics and properties,
      119–120
  and dermatitis, 120
  flammability, 120
  high vapour pressure, 119
  high volatility, 120
  inorganic solvents, 120–121
  low boiling point, 119
  low heat of vaporization, 119
  low surface tension, 119
  organic solvents, 121, 122*t*
sound pressure level meter, 88
source-path-human controls,
    230, 230*f*
St. John Ambulance, 248, 260
stakeholders
  duties and responsibilities of
      major players, 27
  employees, 13
  employers, 12–13
  government, 11–12
  organized labour, 13–14
  partnerships, 14–15
standards and codes, 24
stop-work provisions (Ontario), 33
storage, 312
strain
  behavioural strain, 144
  defined, 142
  organizational strain, 144
  physical strain, 144
  psychological strain, 143
stress
  see also stressors
  buffer, 141
  costs of, 137
  critical incident stress
      debriefing (CISD), 315
  defined, 139
  described, 63–64
  in emergencies, 314–315, 316
  general adaptation
      syndrome, 140
  individual differences, 141
  intervention strategies, 146*t*
  management of, 145–147
  moderators, 141–142
  multivariate risk / resilience
      model, 314
  preventive stress
      management, 145
  primary interventions, 145
  risk factors, 141
  secondary interventions,
      145–146
  strain, 142–144
  stress-related disabilities, 63
  tertiary interventions, 147
  thermal stress, 92–93, 94
  and work-family conflict, 358
  and workplace death, 137
stress management programs
  cognitive-behavioural skills
      training, 366
  effectiveness of, 367
  goal of, 365
  meditation, 366
  relaxation training, 366
  social support, 366
stressors
  see also stress
  acute stressors, 138
  catastrophic stressors, 138
  categories of, 138*t*
  daily stressors, 138
  defined, 138
  injustice at work, 152–154
  role stressors, 139
  sexual harassment, 150–152
  technology, 154–155
  in the workplace, 139
  workplace violence, 147–149
struck-by-object injuries, 214
structural design, 312
substandard practice, 181
substitution, 221, 229
sulphuric acid, 121
supervisors
  accident investigations, 328
  defined, 29
  duties of, 29–30
supplier label, 36, 37*f*
supplies, 309
suppression, 229
surface tension, 119
surfactant layer, 116
sweep away, 228
Swiss cheese model, 345
systemic poisons, 118
systemic toxicity, 116

target organs, 116
task analysis, 185
task and job inventory, 184
Taylor, Frederick, 226
teachers, 32
technical advisers and
    specialists, 328
technology, 154–155
telecommuting, 360, 361
temporary threshold shift
    (TTS), 84–85
teratogens, 118
tertiary interventions, 147
thermal stress, 92–93, 94
the three Es, 15–16
Three Mile Island, 326
threshold of hearing, 83
tinnitus, 84
top event, 196–197
toxicity, 109–110
toxicology
  acute toxicity, 116
  chronic toxicity, 116
  classification of toxic
      substances, 117–118
  dose, 116
  ingestion, 116

local toxicity, 116
overview, 111–119
penetration, 119
respiration (inhalation), 112–114
routes of entry, 111
systemic toxicity, 116
terminology, 116
train the trainer program, 249–250
training
accident prevention and investigation, 258
behavioural outcomes, 255
common safety training initiatives, 259–260
content, 249
delivery, 247–254
design, 247–254
first aid, 259–260
health and safety training programs, 243–254
instructional systems design (ISD) model of training, 243–254
Internet, 250–253
learning outcomes, 255
learning theory and training delivery, 251–252
off-the-job training, 250
on-the-job training, 250
organizational outcomes, 256
role of, 241–242
safety orientation, 259–260
train the trainer program, 249–250
training evaluation, 254–258
training objectives, 247, 248
Workplace Hazardous Materials Information System (WHMIS), 42, 260
training evaluation, 254–258
training objectives, 247, 248
transformational leadership, 285
transportation of dangerous goods, 45
turbinates, 112
Type A behaviour, 141–142

ultraviolet radiation, 95
uncontrolled fire stage, 311
underreporting, 257
unfairness, 152–154
unions. *See* organized labour
University of Toronto, 288
unsafe act, 180–181
unsafe conditions, 182
upper explosion limit (UEL), 120
user-friendliness, 223

vaporization, 120
vapour, 111
vapour pressure, 119
vasoconstriction, 85
Venture gas production rig, 210
Vezina, Shawna Michele, 241
vibration, 90–91
violence in the workplace. *See* workplace violence
viruses, 123*t*
visibility, 223
visible reminders of safety, 211
vocational rehabilitation, 62
volatility, 120

wage or earnings loss, 59
walk-through survey, 184
walkthroughs, 329
waste disposal legislation, 43
weight-control programs, 370
wellness. *See* workplace wellness
Westray, 13
Westray legislation, 46, 242
whole body vibration, 90–92
witness report, 342*f*
work-family conflict
see also family-friendly policies
behavioural involvement, 358
Canadian statistics, 357
causes of, 358
defined, 357
family to work conflict, 358
outcomes, 358–359
prevalence of, 356–357
psychological involvement, 358
strategies to reduce, 363
and stress, 358
work to family conflict, 358
work pace, 139
work permits, 215
work refusals, 32–33
work scheduling, 139
work seating, 224–225
work to family conflict, 358
workers. *See* employees
Workers' Compensation
see also Workers' Compensation Boards
accident prevention, 60
administration and responsibilities, 55–59
assessments, 64–65
in Canada, 55–59
cash allowance, 59
collective liability, 57
and common-law duty, 25
compensation rates and methods, 59–62
compulsory system, 57
coverage, 59
described, 54
experience rating, 65–67
forms of compensation, 59
historical roots, 55
industry assessment rates, 65
injury frequency and severity rates, 76–77
integrated disability management, 67
latency period, 63
loss of functional capacity, 60
medical aid, 60
net earnings, 59
occupational diseases, 63–64
premiums, 57
provision for second injuries, 61
rehabilitation, 62
return-to-work programs, 69–70
social goals, 61–62
underlying premises, 59
wage or earnings loss, 59
workplace stress, 63–64
Workers' Compensation Boards
accident statistics, 186
contact information, 58
described, 55
see also Workers' Compensation
experience-rating plans, 66
mandates, 56
regulations and responsibilities, 56
role of, 57–58
workload, 139

Workplace Hazardous Materials Information System (WHMIS)
  classes, 34–36, 35*f*
  defined, 253
  described, 33–34
  elements of legislation, 34
  establishment of, 7
  labels, 34–36, 38*f*
  material safety data sheets (MSDS), 36–42, 39*f*
  online training, 253
  subclasses, 34–36, 35*f*
  training, 42, 260
Workplace Health, Safety and Compensation Commission (WHSCC) (N.B.), 287
workplace labels, 34–36, 38*f*
workplace stress. *See* stress
workplace violence, 136–137, 147–149, 148*t*
workplace wellness
  at Canadian companies, 371
  family-friendly policies, 359–364
  flow chart of initiatives, 356*f*
  health-promotion programs, 364–373
  naps, 354–355
  wellness programs, 355–356
  work-family conflict, 356–359
  worksite health promotion, 367–373
worksite health promotion
  classification of, 367–368
  components of, 368
  criticisms, 374–375
  development of, 372–373
  evaluation, 374–376
  hypertension screening, 369–370
  issues, 373
  nutrition programs, 370
  physical fitness programs, 370–372
  smoking cessation, 369
  unintended consequences, 373–374
  weight control, 370
workspace design, 222
workstation design
  controls, 223
  display panels, 223
  layout, 223
  lighting, 225–226
  seating, 224–225
World Health Organization, 307, 356

X-radiation, 94

young worker awareness program, 212
young workers, 14, 173*t*